Spiritual Turning Points
of South American History

Spiritual Turning Points
of South American History

Luigi Morelli

2012
Lindisfarne Books

Lindisfarne Books
An imprint of SteinerBooks/Anthroposophic Press, Inc.
610 Main Street, Great Barrington, MA 01230

Cover Artwork Concept by Luigi R. Morelli
Graphics Kimberly Rose
Designed by Angi Shearstone

Copyright © 2012 Luigi R. Morelli

All rights reserved. No part of this book may be reproduced, stored in a retrieval system, or transmitted, in any form or by any means, electronic, mechanical, photocopying, recording, or otherwise, without the written prior permission of the publisher.

Library of Congress Cataloging-inPublication Data

Morelli, Luigi.
 Spiritual turning points of South American history / Luigi Morelli.
     p. cm.
 Includes bibliographical references.
 ISBN 978-1-58420-108-3
 1. Incas–Religion. 2. Inca mythology. 3. Indians of South America–Andes. 4. Indian mythology–Andes Region. I. Title.
 F3429.3.R3M67 2011
 980'.00498323– dc23
                                    2011040554

CONTENTS

Introduction   1

PART I
SOUTH AMERICAN PREHISTORY

1. From Mesoamerica to South America   8

2. First and Second Ages   13
   Andean Geography   13
   Andean Mythology and Chronology   19
   The Second Age and the Revolution of the Late Archaic   27
   Cult of the Andean Cross   35
   The Spiritua-Scientific Background   47

3. Third Age: Chavin   56
   Chavin: in Preparation of the Future   56
   Chavin's Decadence and Sechin   67
   Chankillo: First Solar Culture   74
   Spiritual-Scientific Considerations   75

4. Myths of the Collao: The Second Creation   78
   Creation Myth of the Collao   78
   A Comparative Look at the Myths   82

5. Fourth Age: The Time of Thunupa   86
   The North-Central Coast   87
   The Rise of Tiwanaku   89
   Andean Cosmology and the Mystery of the Nazca Lines   99
   Thunupa   110
   The Being of Thunupa: Esoteric Considerations   122

PART II
CULTURAL DECLINE AND THE INCA SPIRITUAL REVOLUTION

1. Age of the Warriors and Cultural Decline ... 131
   - Moche Culture ... 132
   - Middle Intermediate Horizon and the Emergence of Wari ... 145
   - Late Intermediate Horizon and the Chimú Kingdom ... 153
   - The Chancas ... 163
   - Conclusions ... 164

2. Inca Foundation Myths ... 167
   - The Myth ... 167
   - Myths and Inca Origin ... 174
   - The Incas and the Memory of Thunupa ... 181
   - Early Inca History ... 185

3. Inca Empire and the Fifth Age ... 188
   - Viracocha Inca and the Vision at Urcos ... 189
   - Pachacuti and the Legend of the Chancas ... 190
   - The Birth of Empire ... 197
   - Reform of the Calendar, Religion, and Political Power ... 199
   - Political Organization ... 218
   - Decimal Organization and the Economy ... 224

4. Inca Esoteric Knowledge ... 229
   - The Re-Writing of History by the Spaniards ... 230
   - Inca Historical Consciousness and Writing ... 236
   - The Order of the Heavens and the Ordering of Time ... 245
   - The Order of Earth and the Ordering of Space ... 252
   - Linking Heaven and Earth: the Ceques of Cuzco ... 259
   - An Appraisal of Pacacuti's Reforms ... 266

Conclusions: A Perspective on South and North American Spirituality	271
The Nature of the South American Mysteries	272
North and South America: Parallels and Contrasts	281

Notes and References	287
Bibliography	306
List of Illustrations	312

INTRODUCTION

This book addresses two major turning points of South American history. It comes in the wake of the previous studies about the main events of North American history (*Spiritual Turning Points of North American History*). In the first part of that study, the Popol Vuh formed the essential link to an understanding of North American history. Archaeology cannot prove or disprove the authenticity of the Popol Vuh. Nevertheless, it is possible to link its contents to a crucial turning point of Mesoamerican history that occurred two thousand years ago. In this manner history and myth mutually enrich each other.

Having stated this case and given a place and a time to a central event of American history provide us now with a basis to study the history of the southern continent. Here, unlike in Mesoamerica, legends cannot be traced to an exact point in time, for lack of known chronological records. No South American calendar is extant that provides us with unmistakable pointers to chronological events. Nevertheless, South American history is also tied to the central event depicted by the Popol Vuh and variously portrayed in myths of the southern continent and in Rudolf Steiner's key revelations about the so-called Mexican Mysteries.

South American myths are not as developed and detailed as the contents of the Popol Vuh and other Mesoamerican myths. Nevertheless there is a South American civilization that has preserved a wealth of mythological material, joined to a considerable historical record of monumental architecture and artistic artifacts. It developed in the region roughly corresponding to modern-day Peru and the Bolivian high plateaus, Ecuador, and northern Chili. Here we can also find a way to correlate historical research with the content of myths, continuing in this fashion the research inaugurated with *Spiritual Turning Points of North American History*.

The above statements may leave us under the impression that Andean culture is the poor parent of its Maya and Mesoamerican counterparts. This is hardly the case. In fact, as we will see from the first chapter, Andean civilization emerged earlier than any other significant Mesoamerican development. Moreover, at present evidence is surfacing—not always objectively scrutinized by the academic world—that throws a whole new light on the achievements of its culture, particularly on the complexity of its esoteric teachings, its refined knowledge of the solar calendar, and, surprisingly, even achievements such as writing.

Myths and legends will form the link between external history and the deeper cultural undercurrents that move under the surface of historical events. A first cycle of myths has been gathered in the region of Collao, situated around Lake Titicaca. They refer to two succeeding creations and focus more specifically on the so-called Second Creation. Looking at those myths will allow us to set the frame of reference for the first turning point of South American history.

The effects of the Second Creation, and the cultural renewal that followed, endured in time with alternate success and failure. Cyclically, decadence and warfare set in. Another spiritual message superseded the old one; then times of strife and instability set in. They formed an antithesis to the message of the Second Creation.

A second set of myths touches upon the rise of the Inca Empire. This is in effect the most widely acknowledged social and political transition into modern South American consciousness. It corresponds to the rise of a highly organized state, a change without equal in other parts of South America. Was there a reason for the Incas to link themselves and their legends to the first set of myths, and what was it? Did the Inca Empire bring a new spiritual impulse to the fore, and what was it?

Myths and legends form the collective memory of South America. Although often seemingly arbitrary, mythological language clothes in images exact spiritual-historical events. The myths will form the backdrop against which we will evolve an understanding of South American history.

This effort to outline the spiritual turning points of South American history rests on the foundation established with the studies of Central and North America. Fundamental to it are the work and discoveries of the anthropologist Rafael Girard. Additionally, until recently it would have been very difficult to penetrate the depth of Andean spirituality without the stream of new discoveries and revelations—particularly of the more esoteric foundations of Andean worldview—that has been made available since the beginning of the nineties. The author is particularly indebted to the ground-breaking work of F. E. and E. Elorrieta Salazar, J. A. Merejildo Chaski, M. O. Sanchez Macedo, Carlos Milla Villena, Laurencich Minelli, and others. The whole wealth of historical and esoteric information finds a final organizing thread in the ideas set forth in the spiritual-scientific work of Rudolf Steiner, which allows us to integrate the more classical scientific archaeological research with the revelations coming from within Andean esotericism.

The format of this book is slightly different from its North American counterpart. In order to render its reading accessible to all who may not have read the first volume, and avoid repetition to those who have read it, here the order of exploration will be reversed. In the first book an overview of evolutionary stages of humanity according to spiritual science was offered previous to the exploration of the historical and mythical accounts. In this book, we will first turn to the integration of history and myth, then later return to the conclusions we can reach through the perspective of spiritual science. Practically speaking, this means that these conclusions will be added at the end of the chapters. They will briefly point to what is developed more fully in the first volume. Nevertheless, we will start this exploration with the material of the Mexican Mysteries as they are narrated by the Maya and by Steiner. The reason for this is that there was only one prophet throughout the Americas and only one place in which he incarnated, which has proven to be the region of the Soconusco on the Pacific Coast at the border between Mexico and Guatemala.

A last word of caution about this work: although the author is confident about the reality, nature, and impact of the two turning points of South American history, this is only a first tentative step toward a systematic integration of South American myth, history, and the history of spiritual impulses. It is our hope that it will encourage other such efforts that would come in to complete and round off the picture. We invite the reader to undertake the study of South American history through the enduring legacy of its peoples' myths and legends.

PART I

SOUTH AMERICAN PREHISTORY

CHAPTER 1

From Mesoamerica to South America

Our previous explorations in *Spiritual Turning Points of North American History* highlighted a phenomenon of cultural continuity over fifteen or more centuries, from the time of Christ until the time of Mexico's conquest. Common mythological themes appear throughout Central and North America: the central theme of the virgin birth of an evolved individuality or initiate accompanies the mythical background of Maya, Aztec, and Iroquois mythology, as well as many other Native American groups. The following is a condensed summary of what has been explained in depth in the previous exploration of Central and North America.

Let us look at the essence of the life and deeds of the Twins, as they are commemorated in the Popol Vuh. Born from the encounter of a woman from the underworld, Ixquic, with the heavenly beings called Ahpus (Great Spirit), the Twins are the first human-divine beings to fully penetrate and comprehend the nature and spiritual function of the underworld. Standing against them are the Lords of the Xibalban underworld and their chiefs, the Camé.

The fate of the further evolution of the world lies in the hands of the Twins. Their confrontation with the Camé has at least two aims. The first is to restore the memory of their fathers, the Ahpus, who met their symbolic death at the hands of the Camé. In effect, in the first stages of their descent to the underworld, the Twins retrace the steps of their forerunners and spiritual fathers, the Ahpus. The Camé and the Xibalbans are those who have usurped the lawful authority of the Ahpus. These are the ones that Rudolf Steiner differentiates as the priesthood of the cults of Taotl and Quetzalcoatl. The first is a perverted form of the cult of the Great Spirit, which rested upon the practice of human sacrifice. The second esoteric cult, close in nature to the first, has the power to disseminate illness and death through black magic, as is also confirmed in the record of the Popol Vuh.

A further goal of the Twins, closely allied to the first, is the overcoming of the practice of human sacrifice. This is already announced through the deeds of Ixquic, the Twins' mother. At various places in the account of the fight against the powers of the underworld, the Twins oppose human sacrifice or forfeit their right to claim the life of the Xibalbans. Only at the end does the mystery of death play a central role in the outcome of the spiritual ordeal: the Camé die at the hands of the Twins. Let us see how Steiner describes the event. The most important part of Steiner's esoteric findings concerns the confrontation between the initiate and the high priest of the Taotl cult. This occurred at the same time as the ministry of the Christ in Palestine, i.e., between the years 30 and 33 AD. The initiate's struggle against the corrupt priesthood of Taotl culminated at the same time as the death on Golgotha. In America, however, it is the high priest who was crucified. This was the way to bring his power and esoteric knowledge to an end. Evolution recovered its normal course once the priest of Taotl was defeated—the threat to the human soul and to earth evolution that the sacrifices had set in motion is overcome by the deed of the initiate. Souls can therefore seek to continue to incarnate on earth. Previously this desire was threatened by human sacrifices. The danger of mechanization of the earth and estrangement of the soul from the purpose of earth evolution that Steiner refers to was overcome by the initiate's deed. The black magician was trying to bring to realization a world that would seduce human beings away from normal earth evolution. The souls would have sought to live in that world rather than hold the desire to incarnate on earth.

The overcoming of the Camé and Lords of Xibalba has a corollary of consequences, the first of them the curtailing of the powers of the underworld. Their evil was circumscribed and returns to play only a limited role within the area of influence of spiritual beings on earth. However, most puzzling of all is the event called "the Dawning" in the Popol Vuh. To the Native American, for whom the outer and inner worlds are intimately linked, the Dawning manifests outwardly with the appearance of the sun, moon, and stars in the heavens. What appeared previously as a dark world acquires a new luminosity and substance. Another way to present the phenomenon is to refer to the change of consciousness that allows the Maya and other tribes to perceive the world in a wholly different way. This transformation is described not only by the Maya but by many other ethnic groups throughout the Americas, the Hopis being a clear example among them. History and archaeology provide further proof that an important change of consciousness did in fact intervene at this crucial point in time. To outer history it is known that the Maya calendar was devised very close to the time of the events of Christ's ministry in Palestine.

History does not sufficiently underline the revolution of consciousness associated with the so-called Maya Long Count. Previous to that innovation, time was computed in fifty-two-year cycles through the so-called Calendar Wheel; this was accompanied by the fear of the "extinction of time" and the associated anguish over mortality and the fate of the soul. The Long Count is not a prosaically convenient tool. It corresponds to the gift that only one of the highest initiates could offer to the furthering of civilization. The Maya apprehended and brought an answer to the mystery of death that weighed heavily upon the consciousness of the previous epoch. The calendar enshrines a new understanding of the immortality of the soul and the notion of eternity, rather than cyclical time. The site of Izapa in Soconusco (Chiapas, Mexico), where the central events of the Popol Vuh appear for the first time, was also built close in time to the turn of our era. This explains the enigmatic but important role that history recognizes in the seemingly modest site, without being able to pinpoint the deeper causes of its influence.

Steiner's brief references to the so-called Mexican Mysteries confirms the images of the Popol Vuh and adds a historic dimension to its language. The main addition that he contributes to our understanding of the Popol Vuh is the world historical and spiritual context of the events. The life of the initiate—whom he calls Vitzliputzli—occurred in parallel with the life of Christ. Steiner refers to the tradition of the virgin birth of this individual, without confirming that this is indeed its nature. The fact that one individual appears in Western spiritual-scientific research and two appear in Maya tradition is only an apparent contradiction. The Popol Vuh is an imaginative document. A close analysis of the figures of the Twins shows that they really act as a unified entity. Whereas Ixbalamqué is the earthly-lunar principle, Hunahpu is the solar counterpart. In other words, Ixbalamqué is the initiate; Hunahpu the solar being who inspires him. Since Vitzliputzli is the name given to the initiate in the Aztec perverted version of spiritual history, we have preferred to return to the original name of the initiate, Ixbalamqué or Yax Balam, the "human twin."

Let us look at the finer details of the Popol Vuh odyssey, particularly the leadership of the Third Age, the period that in Mesoamerica precedes the events of Palestine. At that time, we are told, the Great Spirit has left the guidance of mankind to his sons Hun Batz and Hun Chouen. The brothers are the Maya counterparts of what Steiner calls the priesthood of Tezcatlipoca, which he describes as a Jehovah cult that had turned completely exoteric. It is in effect a cult relating to the seven Elohim, the Great Spirit, which had progressively lost its power. The Popol Vuh describes this evolution and decadence with the transformation of the brothers of the Third Age from guides, wise men, and artisans (*Batz*) into monkeys (*Chouen*). Maya esotericism defines the turning point of the Dawning as the emergence of a new consciousness of time. The question that the Third Age could not resolve was the matter of the immortality of the soul at the time of the American Twilight of the Gods. Outwardly this was reflected in the use of the Calendar Wheel and the dread of the extinction of time and world every fifty-two years, still known by the Aztecs and commemorated in their New Fire Ceremony. The Maya evolved the so-called Long Count and their elaborate astrology just at the time of the events that Steiner refers to in his two Mexican Mysteries lectures. The first historical stelae of the Maya date from the first century BC to the first century AD. Even more remarkable is the simultaneous appearance of the first graphic evidence of the images of the Popol Vuh in the site of Izapa. Dating of the ruins places them at between one to two centuries before the time of Christ to a little after. The remarkable Maya calendar, unique for Central and North America, is the concrete manifestation of the change of consciousness of the Fourth Age. This calendar goes beyond the earlier Calendar Wheel (Short Count) because it can move forward and backward in time, practically to infinity. Together with the image of the Twins' resurrection, immortality is reflected in this new astronomy that no longer dreads the end of time.

The above is just a brief overview of the facts that have been unearthed in relation to Mesoamerica in *Spiritual Turning Points*. Many more archaeological findings add to the importance of the interval of time running from the first century BC to the first century AD in American history

Another predictable phenomenon also appeared that runs parallel to European history. Whereas in Europe all historical referencing has revolved around the life and death of Christ, in America the same is true in relation to the initiate of the Americas, Ixbalamqué, the individual embodied by the Twins and elsewhere called Glooskap, Manabozho, Tacoma, etc. Eleven to fifteen centuries later, traits of this being appear in Huitchilopochtli of the Aztecs and Hiawatha of the Iroquois. The seeming spiritual continuity stands in contrast to diametrical spiritual practices between Aztecs and early Maya. The very same human sacrifice that the Popol Vuh and the Twins repudiate, constitutes the cornerstone of Aztec spirituality.

What is obvious in Europe appears in more subtle fashion in all of the Americas. All of European history refers in one way or another to the events of Palestine. Christianity has a central place in European affairs, for good or bad, our sympathies or antipathies notwithstanding. However, what goes under the name of Christianity is hardly a coherent whole. Let us place five streams over and against each other: the early Christianity of the catacombs, official Roman Christianity of Constantine, the Knights Templar, the Manicheans of Southern France, and the Holy Inquisition. It would be absurd to try to form an unequivocal and precise idea of Christianity from the sum of documents left behind by all of the above sources. In other words, under the name of Christianity, the most abominable deeds—such as those of the Inquisition—stand side by side with the pious zeal of the first Christians. What is obvious from Europe is not presently fully recognized by the majority of scholars in the Americas. Here ideas are formed by juxtaposing what Maya, Toltecs, Aztecs, and others have to tell us about one deity or concept. It should be obvious, however, that we cannot proceed thus in order to arrive at a conception of the Twins or of the Ahpus. What the Aztecs can contribute to this understanding will run counter to anything that the ancient Maya could have told us about them. For the Maya, the Twins are those who overcame human sacrifice; for the Aztecs, their counterpart—Huitzilopochtli—is the one who reinstates them at the very moment of his birth. Our analysis has abundantly illustrated all the minor or major modifications of the content of the Popol Vuh that allowed the Aztecs to claim spiritual continuity with a world outlook that stood at the opposite end from their truer aims.

We can now turn to South America, or more precisely to the Andean region of Peru and Bolivia. Here we will find some broad similarities with the general tendencies of Mesoamerica, together with what gives this region a wholly original spiritual impulse. Contrary to Mesoamerica, in South America we cannot resort to an unequivocal record of Ages or Suns as we have it from the record of the Popol Vuh. Our only brief sources are Guaman Poma and Blas Valera, who characterized four Ages and by inference a fifth, that of the Incas. According to this way of seeing, the Third Age corresponds to the time that we have defined as the Fourth Age in Mesoamerica. For reasons that will become clearer as we progress, we have maintained a definition of the Ages parallel to that of Mesoamerica. Thus in this book the First and Second Age correspond to the early civilizations; the Third Age is formed by the culture of Chavin, which archaeology sees as a close counterpart to Olmec civilization of the Mesoamerican Third Age. The Fourth Age corresponds to what we know as the epoch following the turning point of American history—called the Early Intermediate period in the Andes—and finally the Fifth Age will correspond to the historical emergence of Inca Empire. In passing we will refer to what Guaman Poma defines as the Fourth Age—or "Age of the Warriors." However, this epoch does not correspond to a novel spiritual impulse but rather to a stage of cultural decline of the previous age. Consequently, we have not kept it as a separate age.

CHAPTER 2

First and Second Ages

This work concerns itself with a particular portion of South America, one that is centrally defined by the presence of the Andes. Although the Andes spread from the Colombian Caribbean to southern Chile, the history that concerns us unfolded in the Central Andean territory, including a large part of Ecuador, most of Peru, western Bolivia, and a portion of northern Chile. If this territory gets narrowed down further, we essentially have to deal with Peru—Amazon excluded—and Bolivia.

Andean Geography

The whole territory under consideration (see Figure 2:1) is spread in a typically sub-tropical area, from the line of the equator to around the 18º south parallel. The temperatures decrease as one moves away from the equator. This spread of land represents 1 percent of the earth's landmass but presents a synthesis of all the climates of the earth. In this small portion of the earth are reflected climates and ecosystems similar to those of Europe, Asia, North America, and Africa. This diversity is created by two natural factors: the presence of the Andean Cordillera, and the complex oceanic-atmospheric phenomenon of the Pacific of which the cold Humboldt stream, flowing along the whole coast, is just one component.

The territory of the central Andes counts 28 of the earth's 32 climates (88 percent) and 84 of 103 ecosystems (82 percent) in only 1 percent of the surface of the earth.[1] In the space of twenty miles one can go from a desert to green valleys, from the cold of the high cordillera to a warm valley; go slightly farther and one moves from the small, temporary rivers of the coast to some of the largest and longest rivers in the Amazon. There is no other place on earth where such a contrast of extremes occurs. Add to this great variety the amount of apocalyptic scourges: volcanic eruptions, earthquakes and tsunamis, floods and droughts. In other words, all excesses are possible.

Figure 2:1: Main archaeological sites of this work

The Andean Cordillera

The Andean Cordillera is a recent geological formation dating back to the Tertiary epoch. The Andes stretch for 300 miles in the south, with high plateaus at heights of 13,000' and higher, snowy peaks of 20,000' and above.

In the north the cordillera narrows to 60 miles wide, making it possible for smoother climatic and environmental transitions between ecosystems. The summit of the cordillera is reached in the Cordillera Blanca with the Huascaran reaching almost 23,000'. The highest settlement, Cerro de Pasco, is situated at 14,250', almost as high as the European Alps.

The diversity of climates is multiplied due to the fact that the Andes form several parallel ranges of mountains. In Chile the cordillera forms only one range, north of Lima, while south of Trujillo the cordillera forms four parallel ranges, including Cordillera Blanca and Cordillera Negra. This means that the local geography presents valleys and plateaus at all imaginable heights. Moreover, these parallel mountain ranges form at places what are called "knots."

Three mountain ranges meet together in the knot of Loja in Ecuador first and then later in the center of the Central Andean territory at the gigantic Nudo de Pasco, on top of which is located a very high and cold meseta at more than 14,100'. A last knot is found in the south, at Vilcanota. Here three parallel ranges from the north converge and form two ranges that embrace the Titicaca (Collao) altiplano. This is the largest of high-altitude lakes at 12,500'.

Climate and Geography

The region comprises four main geographic zones:

- the Pacific coastal plains that form the deserts
- the cold, rugged area of the cordillera, including the Bolivian and Southern Peruvian altiplanos
- the warm and green eastern range of the cordillera
- the Amazon forest

The temperatures range from 14° F in the heights of the cordillera to 106° F in the Amazonian Selva. Precipitation ranges from virtually no rain in the coastal desert, to 27"–39" in the cordillera, 118"–157" in the eastern cordillera, and up to 314" in the Amazon.

The seasons present a marked contrast between the coast and the interior. On the coast, since there is no rain, seasonal differences are based on temperature. October to March is the warm season; April to September is the cold season with the eventual presence of a fine misty rain, called *garua*. In the interior, the rainy season extends from October to March, during which occurs 65 to 85 percent of the annual precipitation. The dry season extends from April to September. Notice the inversion between coast and sierra. When it is the summer on the coast, it is the rainy winter season in the sierras.

In the mountains and sierra, the temperatures vary little during the year; there is more difference between day and night temperatures, but only on the order of 18–22°F between early morning and noon. The temperature gradient is accentuated in the high mountains, particularly in the dry season. The highest difference of temperature appears in the *punas* landscapes of the high plateau with a gradient of 54°F and even 72°F. This is because these areas are further away from the equator.

Let us now look at the coast, which occupied an important role in the first stages of the Andean civilization. On the western cordillera, rains are short and infrequent during most of the year and long and intense in the rainy season (October to March). These and the melting of the snows provide water for forty short rivers that thread down to the Peruvian coast. During this period there often are the so-called *huaicos*, turbulent streams formed of mud and boulders. Rivers are progressively colder from the equator to southern Peru, and only seven of them carry water all year long. The Rio Santa presents a special condition, because it is the emissary of the waters of the Cordillera Blanca and Cordillera Negra, which run parallel to each other at very high altitudes.

Humboldt Stream and Ocean Atmospheric Phenomenon of the Southern Pacific

The earth's rotation and the direction of the trade winds gives rise to the phenomenon of the Humboldt Stream with the consequent uprising of deeper, colder waters to the surface. This means that the waters of the Pacific coast have temperatures of an average 21–23°F colder than corresponding tropical areas at the same latitudes. The lower temperatures limit water evaporation; they also favor the phenomenon of thermal inversion in the atmosphere by which temperatures are constant (64°F) from the surface up to about 3,300', where the reverse happens with temperatures becoming progressively warmer up to 79°F. The thermal inversion prevents the forming of cumulonimbus clouds, which generate rain.

The presence of cold water is the reason for the great abundance of fish: anchoveta (of the anchovy family), sardines, bonito, pejerrey, and others, and consequently for a great variety of birds that deposit their droppings, a rich source of fertilizer. This biodiversity was an important factor in the establishment of civilizations.

The Humboldt Stream is a capricious and variable ocean river. The exceptions to the norm of the Humboldt stream have been baptized El Niño, La Niña, Anti-Niño, No-Niño and more recently ENSO, standing for El Niño Southern Oscillation. In extreme circumstances one might hear mention of "Super-Niños" or "Super-ENSO" with durations ranging from decades to a century and a half, causing considerable climate change, particularly along the Ecuadorian and Peruvian coast.

The phenomena that create these El Niños and their variations go beyond the Humboldt Stream itself. They involve both the waters and atmosphere of the southern Pacific. The event of 1997 caused strong floods in northern Peru, southern Ecuador, the southeast of Brazil and Argentina, and the west of Canada and the United States. There was drought in Australia, Indonesia, and the Philippines as well as the Peruvian-Bolivian high plateau, the northeast of Brazil, and throughout Central America. El Niño irregularities vary in onset and duration. They can manifest up to one or two years after the onset and then disappear for a few years. They can be of low, average, or high intensity. They can start in February, May, or September and last up to six months.

The most notable symptom of the phenomenon is the abnormal warming of the surface of the waters of the Pacific along the Peruvian-Ecuadorian coastline between the 180° and 80° west meridians, a stretch almost 6,800 miles wide. The warming of the waters that causes torrential rains along the coast seems to be linked to droughts in the high plateau. Many other events accompany the rise of the temperature of the waters, particularly in the most dramatic instances:

- discontinuity of the phenomenon of thermal inversion of the air masses, the first cause for the abnormally low precipitation. A rise of 3.5°F in water temperature causes a mild phenomenon, 5.5°F defines a strong one; 7°F an exceptional one.
- rise of precipitation. An example: Piura, in Northern Peru, receives a normal average of almost 2"per year. During a mild phenomenon this amount is multiplied by 3. With a rise of 7°F, precipitation can reach 31.5" per month as was the case in 1983.
- rise in the volume of water in the rivers.
- rise of the water level of the ocean. In Callao (close to Lima) the

waters can rise to up to 1' 3/8"; in the south of Peru even up to 1' 5/8"![2] This can lead to the formation of temporary lakes and lagoons, especially in the northern Peruvian coast (Sechura Desert). Here up to nine separate lagunas can form. The desert is actually a depression whose bottom lies 111' below sea level. In 1983 and 1998, apart from the main depression itself, the other lagunas merged and formed a great lake 124 miles long and 15 miles wide—the second widest South American lake after the Titicaca![3]

– simultaneous presence of floods and droughts in different parts of the Peruvian territory. There are, however, no reliable statistical links between floods on the coast and droughts, except for the Puno region of the altiplano. With the 1983 event Puno experienced a precipitation reduction of 32 percent from average, the worst drought in fifty years. Other events were correlated in additional parts of the territory: the 1969 El Niño brought 48 percent less rain in the Cajamarca/Huanuco areas; the 1989–90 event affected Cajamarca and Huanuco once more but it caused 75 percent lower precipitations in Arequipa and Puno.[4]

El Niño events conditioned all of Peruvian history to a greater extent than any natural catastrophe would in the rest of the world. The following are some examples of natural catastrophes and of their frequency. In the years 562–594 BC the longest drought in history caused major changes all over Peru and particularly on the north coast. Other El Niño crises occurred in the years 511–12, 546, 576, 600, 610, 612, 650, and 681 AD.[5] The climatic fluctuations over the centuries have been such that they have affected Lake Titicaca in a dramatic fashion. Around 8000 BC it is estimated that the level of the waters lowered by 160–200'. In the years 5000–2500 BC the waters rose again. In 1000 BC they still were 16' higher than at present.[6]

In the glaciers of mountains surrounding the high plateau there is evidence of periods of drought and great periods of rain in the years from 650 to 800 AD. In conjunction with the collapse of the Wari Empire, there is evidence of prolonged droughts in the altiplano in the period 1200–1300 AD. The most severe manifestations are the ones that affect the coast further south. Some can affect it as far south as Nazca, 280 miles south of Lima.

Quinn reports 122 El Niño events in the last five hundred years, thus subdivided: 67 moderate ones (rise of 3.5°F); 45 strong (rise of 5.5°F); 10

exceptional (rise of 7°F or more) as can be ascertained from paleontological, archaeological and written sources.[7] The ten exceptional events in Peru were recorded in the years 1578–79, 1720, 1728, 1791, 1828, 1877–78, 1891, 1925–26, 1982–83, and 1997–98. Notice that the spread goes from a minimum of 8 years to as much as a 141 year interval! In 1891 along the Peruvian north coast, the rains in Piura lasted more than sixty days; the River Piura acquired a width of 490' and up to 23' deep, compared to 98' and 3' respectively, in normal times.[8]

In addition to El Niño we have mentioned its twin phenomenon of La Niña. In this instance the surface temperature of the ocean decreases. This is accompanied by the rising of the waters on the Western Pacific. From 1958 to the present there have been twelve such episodes, accompanied with abnormally low precipitations in Piura.[9] So La Niña is accompanied with extraordinary droughts, especially along the northern coast. Other phenomena accompany it, but they have not been as clearly elucidated as those of the more famous El Niño.

Andean Mythology and Chronology

Because of the uniqueness of Andean geography, cultural development occurred in relative isolation, until the period from 3000 to 2500 BC with the inauguration of more complex social organizations that exploited diverse ecosystems through interregional networks. It was a sudden cultural development.

In our earlier exploration of Mesoamerican history, we referred to the parallels between the Ages or "Suns" in Mesoamerica, South America, and even as far north as the Hopis and Pueblo Indians. In Peru one of the most complete understandings has been given to us by the native chronicler Guaman Poma. In addition we have the chronicles of Montesinos and Valera. Guaman Poma's Second and Third Ages do not coincide with the Second and Third Mesoamerican Ages of the Popol Vuh.

According to the chronicler, the First Age, Pakanmok Runa, corresponds to a primeval land inhabited by wild animals, giants, dwarves, and ghosts. The "People of the Dawn" that first inhabited the land were nomads dwelling in caves. They did not have organized religious ceremonies.

During the Second Age—or Age of the Wan Runa (indigenous people)—the god Alpamanta Rurac created the human being out of mud.

Human beings abandoned caves for the first dwellings called *pukullo*. The Second Age marked the beginning of sedentary life, of agricultural activity, and the invention of pottery. The people adored the lightning god Illapa, their symbol of life and death; the *kuntur* (condor), bird of the sun; and the *kuri poma*, the golden lion. The idea of the underworld was fully born. The Second Age ended with a flood, the rebellion of domestic animals, and the invention of utensils.

The Third Age is called the Age of the Purun Runa. The land was used more intensively. There were more cultivated plants, and llama and alpaca were domesticated. Cooperative work reached a climax. Among the inventions of the age were weaving, metal work, and the use of drums and flutes. Another typical introduction of this age was the ritual use of fermented drinks. The sovereigns, called Capac Apo, were carried in a litter, a characteristic of the Third Age that survives in many cultures.

The Fourth Age is the time of the Auka Runa, "people of the times of war." The internal struggles of the previous age reached a climax. This was the time of the fortified cities called *pukaras*. The farmers left the lowlands to take refuge in the high plateau. During this age the practices of cannibalism and human sacrifice, even with removal of the heart, reached a peak. The dead were buried with their food and goods, sometimes with their women. From our perspective we can see that even though this was called a Fourth Age, it was in reality only a stage of decadence of the Third Age. The three previous ages have similarities and correspondences with the ages of the Popol Vuh, although the Andean Second Age corresponds more closely to the Mesoamerican Third Age. In addition to the above four ages we add, from other chronicles and from the historical record, the Fifth Age of the Incas (Cristobal de Molina).

We can further deepen our appreciation for Andean mythical thinking with the dimension of its cycles of time, the millennial component. Blas Valera and Fernando Montesinos compiled a list of ninety-three pre-Inca kings, harkening back to the times of Pirua Manco, living millennia before Christ. Montesinos claims as his source an author who had consulted historians contemporary to the emperor Atahualpa. Valera, who was very close to these, may have been the primary source of both Montesinos and Guaman Poma. In his work Valera refers to the turning points of time as *pachacutis* or "Suns." That both larger and smaller cycles are called Suns is admittedly confusing, but we are dealing here with smaller cycles of time than what is involved with the five Ages. The way of defining the smaller ages is more explicitly stated in Montesinos's *Memorias Antiguas Historiales*. There were larger and smaller periods. The one-thousand-year interval was called *Capac-huata* or *Intip-huata*, "great year of the Sun." Each millennium was subdivided into two five-hundred-year periods known as *pachacuti*.

According to Montesinos, the first inhabitants of Peru would have arrived in 2957 BC, at the beginning of the Second Sun—remarkably close to the record of archaeology that places at this time the beginning of the Late Archaic with its momentous cultural changes. According to the chronicler, the Fourth Sun was completed forty-three years after Christ's birth in Bethlehem, and this corresponded to the second year of the reign of Manco Capac, the third Peruvian king to bear that name.

Archaeology differentiates the following periods of Andean history. Next to them we add the terminology of the ages that will be used throughout this work, a chronology that closely follows that of the Popol Vuh in many ways.

When we look at chronology in this way we see the First Age of civilization corresponding to pre-historical developments of the hunter-gatherer societies; the Third Age of the two parallel societies of the Olmecs and Chavin; the spectacular developments of the Maya culture reflected to the south by Tiwanaku, Nazca, and Gallinazo cultures, with their culmination following a period of accelerated decadence and arriving within a very clearly defined window of time. The same can be said of the correspondence between Inca and Aztec cultures, with their emphasis on the largest levels of social organizations. What stands out in contrast between the northern and southern continents is the particularly spectacular development of the Andean Second Age in the north-central coast of Peru.

Archaeological Periods	Dates	Ages
Early Archaic	8000–6000 BC	First Age: 8000–3000 BC
Middle Archaic	6000–3000 BC	
Late Archaic	3000–1500 BC	Second Age: 8000–1500 BC
Formative (Chavin)	1500–200 BC	Third Age: 1500 BC to year 0 See chapter 3.

Archaeological Periods	Dates	Ages
Early Intermediate Period (EIP): Tiwanaku, Gallinazo, Moche, Nazca, etc.	200 BC–AD 600	Fourth Age: year 0 to 1438 AD. See chapters 4 and 5.
Middle Intermediate Period (Middle Horizon): Wari	AD 600–1000	"Age of the Warriors" (Not a real age, but the second part of the Fourth Age). See chapter 6.
Late Intermediate Horizon: Chimu, Chancas.	AD 1000–1438	"Age of the Warriors" See chapter 6.
Late Horizon: Inca civilization	AD 1438–1533	Fifth Age: after 1438 AD. The date 1438 offered here is that of the estimated accession to the throne by Pachacuti Inca, ninth emperor and initiator of the Inca revolution. See chapters 7 to 9.

We can now turn to the earlier times of Andean civilization, to the period that is known to archaeology as the Archaic—which precedes the Formative Period, primarily characterized by the Chavin civilization to which we will turn in chapter 3. The First and Second Ages merely form a prelude to the Chavin and Early Intermediate Periods that capture the central interest of our study. Therefore, we will not analyze the First and Second Ages in the same depth as later epochs but will simply underline the importance of ceremonial life and its esoteric under-pinnings in light of their persistence in all the subsequent periods. Note in passing that we have chosen to date the EIP from 0 to 600 AD as some authors do, rather than from 200 BC. The reason will become apparent as we analyze the period in chapter 5.

The Archaic Period was not simultaneous throughout the Andes; it spread over various millennia according to location. The age can be roughly divided thus:

- Early Archaic: 8000–6000 BC
- Middle Archaic: 6000–3000 BC
- Late Archaic: 3000–1500 BC

According to most current research, the period from 3000 to 2500 BC ushered in the development of complex social organizations, including the formation of networks of interregional contacts. This was an important period of transition, one that will be central to our studies.

We will define the First Age as the societies of Early and Middle Archaic, and Second Age as the societies that followed the important changes of the Late Archaic. These changes were most keenly felt along the northern coast, which developed a wholly new monumental architecture.

First Age[10]

The earliest evidence of cultivation goes back to 8000 BC. The first plants to be domesticated were most likely roots and tubers: potato, oca (*Oxalis tuberosa*), camote (*Ipomaea batata*), achira (*Aracacia sp.*), olluco (*Ullucus tuberosus*), etc. Apart from these, legumes and fruits were introduced, such as pallar and canavalia (both leguminous), cucurbita, and mate (*cucurbitaceae*). Other species may have been wild-crafted: lucuma, guava, zapote (*Capparis angulata*), and ciruela del fraile (*Bunchosia armeniaca*).

The domestication of camelids in the puna goes back around 4000 to 3500 BC. Domestication of the guinea pig was reached in Ayacucho as early as the so-called Chihua period (4400–3100 BC). The domesticated species from the central sierra spread out to the other areas much later.

Early Archaic (8000–6000 BC)

We will characterize the developments of the Early Archaic through some examples taken from throughout the territory. The people of the "Paijan complex" of the north-central coast (9000–6000 BC) moved between the coastline and the piedmont. They mostly fished and hunted, and possibly gathered some vegetables. They used stone for blades, knives, spoons, picks, and scrapers. Groups of the south coast (8500–7000 BC) were likewise fishermen and hunters.

The populations of the sierra had recourse to a system of rotation between hunting and cultivation. The groups most studied are those of Guitarrero (Callejon de Huaylas) and Ayacucho, who exploited various ecological zones. The inhabitants of La Paloma (central coast) moved through ecosystems from the coast to the river and neighboring hills. A large part of the typical diet was supplied through fish, seafood, and birds; moreover, they gathered seeds, fruits, and tubers, and even had some cultivated plants such as cucurbitae, beans, and possibly guavas. In Ayacucho, groups of hunters moved between areas at 3,300' to 11,000' and up to the puna at 13,000' to 14,000'. Cavemen from the Puna of Junin (not far north of Lima) hunted deer and llama or other llama-related animals. They had main settlements and moved short distances from them. Other populations were more nomadic.

Middle Archaic (6000–3000 BC)

During this time there was a growth of population. However, there was no social stratification yet and no other distinctions than those of sex and age. The populations of the sierra exploited the resources of different ecosystems and developed cultivated species and domesticated animals such as the guinea pig. In the puna the natural animal abundance encouraged hunting, but there also was the first domestication of the animals of the llama family.

In the Zaña Valley of the north coast of Peru, 48 miles inland, there is evidence of about forty-nine settlements dating from this period. The inhabitants were hunter-gatherers, but vegetables had begun to play a larger part in their diet.

Second Age

Late Archaic (3000–1800 BC)

Around 3000 BC there were climatic changes leading to a progressive warming that continues to the present. This led to the extinction and reduction of fauna and flora species. The impact was probably felt in the decrease of hunting prey and may have provided the motivation for intensive agriculture. As in Mesoamerica, women were the initiators of the early agriculture, marking women's growing social role and the rise of matriarchy. The first steps toward cultivation were taken in the Andes. The begonia species played the role later played by maize as the main vegetable staple. Some cultivated plants originated from the Amazon, particularly yucca (manioc) and peanut. The coastal areas that could rely on abundant fishing had less of a pressing need and motivation for this innovative step. However, they depended on the cultivation of cotton for fishing nets. Cotton may have been cultivated as early as 2500 BC.

The societies of the north-central coast and those of the sierra next to them attained social organizations of a certain complexity. However, social differentiation was still minimal, based on the evidence of burials, such as those found in La Galgada (in the north-central sierra) and Aspero (Supe Valley, north coast). The settlements on the coast (La Paloma, Los Chinos I, Culebras, Rio Seco, Asia, Otuma, Chilca, etc.) started expanding especially after 2500 BC.

Plants and goods started circulating between the coast and the Amazon forest, building a web of relationships among societies who had long been isolated. This latter point is highlighted by the commonality of burial patterns, techniques and designs in weavings, and architectural elements. The societies of the coast were interdependent with those of the interior.

At this stage, ceremonialism acquired a growing importance and was accompanied by the building of monumental architecture. Almost all the ceremonial sites of this period introduced at some point the so-called sunken court. Most likely these were introduced by the societies of the coast, such as those from the Supe Valley. Together with the pyramids, they represent the three ritual levels of underworld (sunken courts), the surface of the earth (platforms), and heavens (truncated pyramids, platform-mounds).

The following conditions were instrumental to an increasingly sedentary life:

- technological innovations allowing the accumulation of surpluses. Along the coast that was the case with fishing technology. Perhaps already during the latter part of this period, the indigenous had boats, as is inferred from deep-sea fish as part of their diet. In the sierra, equivalent progress was achieved through irrigation or through the exploitation of different environments, all innovations of the Late Archaic

- interregional connection networks, useful to trade but also culturally stimulating

- a level of social management to coordinate the interregional activities and exchange.

Other conditions for sedentary life are still hotly debated:

- whether sedentary life was the consequence of agriculture; this was not the case along the Peruvian coast, due to the abundant marine resources
- whether pottery is automatically associated with sedentary life. Pottery in the Andes was manufactured only in the Formative Period, after 1500 BC. Even then some societies of the coast remained without pottery for some centuries despite trading with groups who used pottery.

Along the coast there were new developments in fishing technology and the cultivation of new plants along riverbanks. This allowed formation of agricultural surpluses, and the need for their management was another possible reason for social differentiation. More plants were cultivated, and basket weaving developed for the transportation and exchange of goods. Part of the agricultural surpluses were stored in silos dug in sand located in special nonresidential sectors of the city.

The diet was mostly composed of meats, legumes, and carbohydrates. In some places, such as Los Gavilanes (Valley of Huarmey), maize was also found. However, there is no evidence of the importance of maize in the societies of the coast until the Middle Formative of the Third Age (900 to 400 BC).[11]

In the north-central coast, there is evidence of a more harmonious integration between coast, sierra, and Amazon, with wider networks of exchange between those areas than in the far north or in southern areas. In the sierra, there was the innovation of irrigation through channels and small terraces; in the coast, the introduction of cotton nets.

The economy of a valley like Supe (north-central coast) was based on the accumulation of surpluses from fishing (e.g., Aspero) and the agricultural inland (e.g., Caral). The fishermen received cotton for their nets, gourds for floaters, etc. The farmers of Caral received dried fish. From Caral, trade exchange was carried further to the inland. This network was made possible through the establishment of strategic places for regional and interregional exchange. At that stage social stratification and trade coordination were based solely upon the role of religion; no military power was present, and all activities in the emerging ceremonial centers had religious overtones.

The Second Age and the Revolution of the Late Archaic

The Late Archaic was a meaningful time for the Americas as a whole. Starting around 3000 BC, the north-central coast of Peru saw the introduction of monumental architecture, the earliest appearing in the Americas. Archaeologists subdivide this cultural revolution into two stages, the Late Archaic going from 3000 to 1500 BC.

The Late Archaic Period was characterized by the development of large architectural sites. A whole new kind of architecture featuring mounds and truncated pyramids came to the fore from no known cultural precedent. In 2008, German and Peruvian archaeologists found evidence of the oldest known Peruvian monument. Carbon dating gives a reading of 3500–3000 BC, which could place the beginning of the monumental impulse even earlier than has so far been believed. The monument is a circular sunken plaza of stone and adobe, and is part of Sechin Bajo in Casma Valley in the Andes foothills, 206 miles north of Lima.[12]

One of the earliest sites is that of Aspero in the Supe Valley, covering about 32 acres and counting six truncated pyramids among its seventeen mounds. The largest is Waka de los Idolos, which measured 130' x 100' and 35' high and was topped with summit rooms and courts. Already we notice the presence of painted and modeled clay friezes. The outer platform walls are of large, angular basaltic rock set in mortar with a smooth outer surface.

The largest presence of early monumental architecture is found between the Chicama Valley to the north and the Rimac Valley to the south, concentrated close to the ocean, underscoring how the new development depended upon the exploitation of marine resources. In the next period, ceremonial centers moved further inland up the streams.

The rise of this kind of new architecture moves archaeologists to conclude that this was the beginning of a non-egalitarian society. However, there is little evidence of social differentiation such as intermediate forms of architecture or differentiation of residential quarters.

Late Archaic Architecture: U-shaped Mounds and Sunken Courts

There are at least thirty known sites belonging to this period, spreading from the north as far as the Lambayeque-La Leche drainage system, not far from the border with Ecuador, to Lurin Valley, not far from Lima in the south. The introduction of irrigated agriculture allowed the center of gravity of coastal occupation to shift inland, at some distance from the Pacific. This movement inland is observable for most if not all monumental centers of this epoch.

The architectural forms differentiated in two directions: U-shaped truncated pyramids and circular sunken courts. The U-shaped mounds seem to have originated from the south around the Chillon Valley and from there spread to the neighboring Lurin and Rimac valleys, and later further north. The mounds are formed by three neighboring truncated pyramids; the central, most massive, and highest one is accompanied by two longer and lower rectangular platforms that give the whole a U-shape (figure 2.2). None of the U-shape mounds have exactly the same shape but all of them enclose a plaza from three sides.

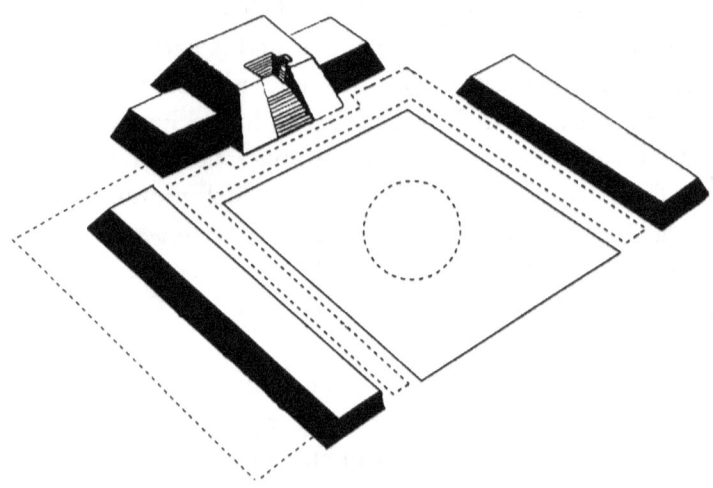

Figure 2.2: U-shaped mound

What the U-shaped mounds do share is a general orientation toward the north and east. Between Lurin and Chancay all of them are oriented between 13º and 64º east of north.[13] The open side of the U faces up the valley, either parallel to the axis of the valley or oriented to the mountain peak. The smaller sites in a valley often carry the same orientation of the larger pyramid. An example of this can be seen in the Chancay River Valley. The largest U-shaped complex of San Jacinto has a 1,650' x 2,000' wide plaza; the five U-shaped structures within a 1.5 mile radius of this center share similar plans and orientation.

In the U-shaped mounds we can recognize the cult of water and mountain deities, the attributes of the Tau God or Great Spirit of Atlantean memory. This is a first layer of Andean cosmology to which we will return at the end of the chapter—the worldview that relates the Great Spirit to the world of waters originating from mountains. A second important layer is that of the sunken courts. These acquired progressive importance in relation to the mounds, and their size went on increasing.

It appears that the circular sunken courts followed the U-shaped mounds. The earliest ones in the north-central coast are those of Salinas del Chao, Supe, and Salaverry. As their names indicate, they are circular in shape and sunken into the surrounding topography. The outer walls reach a height of about 10', partly dug in and partly supported by outer walls, and their diameter ranges from 60' to 160' and even 260'. The merging of the sunken courts with the U-shaped mounds occurred only in the later stages of the monumental complexes. The patterns of evolution of the U-shaped mounds, as described by Leon Carlos Williams, are indicative in this regard.[14] If we divide the coast from south to north in a central, north-central, and a northern sector, we find the following types and degrees of integration of the sunken courts with the U-shaped mounds.

Central Coast

Here the central pyramid is composed of a central nucleus and one or two asymmetrical arms of lesser width and elevation. The central platform has a front "atrium" in the form of a three-sided depression looking over the central plaza. A stairway joins the atrium and the plaza that is often of gigantic scale. The already-mentioned complex of San Jacinto measured 74 acres (30 ha) and could have hosted more than the entire population of the Central Andes.

North-Central Coast (north of the Chancay and Huaura Valleys)

The monuments in this region are characterized by sunken rectangular or circular courts in the platform. The atrium is missing.

North Coast

The pyramids are preceded by circular sunken courts. The earliest sunken courts are separated from the pyramids.

The courts are thus more intimately associated with the mounds in the north and north-central coast than in the central coast. The U-shaped pyramids had artwork painted in bright predominantly red and yellow colors, and in some cases high-relief polychrome friezes of modeled clay. In some places (e.g., Garagay) the motifs were painted with other colors as well, such as white, pink, and gray-blue. In the iconography appear the motifs of bird, felines, and spider anthropomorphs. It seems that the art was often placed in such a way as to be highly visible from the plazas. More and more of this evidence is surfacing at present.[15]

The sites of the Second Age lack the architectural differentiation normally associated with cities, the signs that indicate social differentiation, such as the specialization of productive activities. However, there is evidence from the structure of the monumental architecture of progressively restricted access, which most likely indicates the presence of a priestly class with a specialized function. That does not mean that there was formation of wealth consequent to that role.

Everything at this stage seems to point to a theocracy and no political class yet, and no presence of coercive structures, but rather a unified cultural consensus. This is what allowed the mobilization of concerted human labor on a grand scale, without apparent coercion. This last point deserves further scrutiny. Estimates for the man-hour labor for the Initial Period complexes built in the Lurin, Rimac, and Chillon valleys are 12 million person-days of work, or about 50 people working every day for 700 years! For the site of La Florida alone, Patterson estimates the necessary labor as 6.7 million person-days (about 50 people working every day for about 375 years), although the site was built and abandoned within 400 years.[16] Quite obviously early Andeans could avail themselves of the forces of their etheric bodies in ways similar to what people had been able to do in Atlantis. Consider the following: in reference to Sechin Alto, James Q. Jacobs indicates that the granite blocks there weighed over two tons.[17] Something similar occurred in Europe at around the same time with the Celtic culture. Stonehenge, built between 1800 and 1400 BC by the Celts who could avail themselves of the use of etheric forces and carry weights in a way that is not understandable to conventional science.

We will now look more closely at Caral, one of the oldest centers of the Initial Period that has been most exhaustively studied. This will offer us the opportunity for discerning other important facets of social organization and artistic expression of Andean society that were formed at this time and that endured over later centuries and millennia.

An Early Monumental Center: Caral

The Supe River Valley in the north-central coast, where Caral is located, contains thirty-six sunken courts at thirty sites. Caral is believed to be one of the oldest urban settings of the Americas, dating back to 2700 BC; its pyramids are contemporary with those of Egypt and Mesopotamia. The primordial city was probably abandoned around a millennium after its foundation.

At the time of Caral's foundation, the north-central area of the coast had probably developed a more harmonious integration between the coast, sierra, and Amazon, with wider networks of exchange between those areas than in the corresponding areas further north and south. There was also an exchange of goods and ideas between the societies of the north and central coasts, as is visible in the textile techniques and iconographic motifs that were shared between Huaca Prieta (north coast) and La Galgada (north-central sierra).[18]

Caral is located in the arid plain above the Supe River Valley over an alluvial terrace, 109 miles north of Lima, 14 miles from the ocean, at an altitude of 1,150'. The site covers 165 acres and is one of the largest in Peru, containing some thirty monumental structures. It is here and in similar sites that appears for the first time the division of the city in two halves; the upper town—Hanan—and the lower town—Hurin—a motif that accompanies Andean history to the present. Overall, monumental structures and enclosures are smaller in the Lower City. In Hanan are found the most important buildings, oriented toward a central open space. In Hurin we see the largest and most important of the two circular sunken courts and a structure that has been dubbed the "amphitheater."

Caral has two circular plazas, which Dr. Ruth Shady Solis speculates, on the basis of site discoveries, were used for performances. However, they probably served an astronomical purpose as well. It is very significant that the two sunken courts were associated with the two most significant structures of each half of the city.

Upper Half: Hanan

In the upper town is found the Templo Mayor, the largest and most extended building in Caral. It also has a circular sunken court and an imposing multitiered pyramid that reaches 65' high, resting on a base of 490' x 525'. The top of the pyramid measures 210' x 115'. The sunken court stretches to the north through a trapezoidal platform that ties it to the pyramid. It has a 69' to 72' internal diameter, and a 120' external diameter. The height of the internal walls reaches 10'.

There are three access stairs, one external facing SSW and almost rectangular, and two trapezoidal internal ones, opposite to each other and facing SSW and NNE. Interestingly, the two internal stairs face 25º east of north, but are at a slight angle of 1–2 degrees from the axis of the pyramid and its central staircase. The alignment of the sunken court was changed at a later stage, most likely indicating that it was originally aligned with the cosmology of the pyramid, and some astrological change occurred that called for the modifications. This is an important aspect to which we will return later when we will determine the function of the sunken courts.

The plaza was regularly cleaned and the floor of the court periodically changed, at least four times in minor ways. At the foot of the internal stairs there are three fallen monoliths. Two of them, 8' high to 2' wide, most likely stood to each side of the stairs at the bottom. The third one, wider and shorter, whose exact position could not be ascertained, most likely served as an altar on which the god's effigy stood. There is a central atrium in the pyramid in whose central space stands a so-called sacred hearth, essentially a hearth for the burning of sacred offerings. In a secondary enclosure to the west stands a square altar with another sacred hearth.

Lower Half: Hurin

The most developed pyramidal complex in the lower half of the city is the Temple of the Amphitheater and its sunken court. The court is larger than the one in Hanan. It has two access stairs in the upper half and is surrounded by two concentric platforms. The sunken court and the two platforms were added to the pyramid at a later time.

The pyramid defines three separate spaces; an atrium, a central enclosure, and another enclosure to the south. The atrium is formed of three U-shaped platforms, surrounding a central space in which is found the sacred hearth. It is in the central enclosure that the representation of the main deity was most likely found, and here that the most important ceremonies were held.[19]

The sacred hearth is worth a separate mention. This must have had a very restricted access and use—probably for just one person. In it there was a circular altar, reserved for very special and strictly ritual functions. The hearth was built in the middle of the circular altar and it had an oval form. On the ground level there are two aeration conduits that go respectively north and south under the platform.

Geoglyphs and Flutes

We will now turn to two aspects that mark a precedent in South American culture: the first is the appearance of a so-called geoglyph; the second, the discovery of flutes. On the desert floor just half a mile west of the site just described, at Chupacigarro, is an enormous geoglyph of a human face with long, streaming hair, closed eyes, and an open mouth. The geoglyph is built with angular stones of medium and large size (figure 2.3). The head, oriented to the east, is built over the north façade of a stabilized dune. This means that it can be seen whole only from the hills of the northwest—most likely the geoglyph had to be built with oversight from there. At that location we can find circular structures with architectural characteristics similar to those of the geoglyph. The site of Chupacigarro

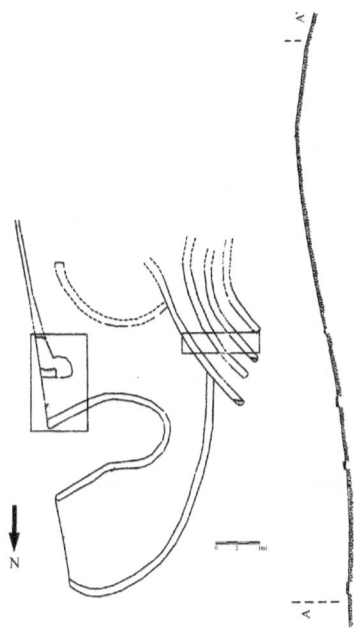

Figure 2.3: Geoglyph of Chupacigarro

itself was established in the Late Archaic. There are no elements in place pointing to later periods. The radiocarbon dating of the later construction phases of Chupacigarro yield dates of 2465–2125 and 2075–2055 BC. This geoglyph appears to be the earliest known of an enduring Andean tradition. The famous geoglyphs of the Nazca pampa appeared much later.

In the Hurin side of Caral, archaeologists have found thirty-two flutes just outside the sunken court to the southeast.[20] They are mostly carved from the midsection of the wing bones of pelicans and were buried according to a pattern. A few others were carved from condor bones. The flutes are decorated with various motifs of monkeys, human faces, birds, snakes with bird heads, and a double-head moti; and painted in black or red, or else just left plain. One of the motifs is a face that was spread out over two flutes, and that can be seen only when the two are set together. This is also the way in which the two were buried. In fact the flutes have grooves that indicate that they may have been tied together in a similar manner to pan flutes. All the instruments could be played at a higher octave by blowing harder. Here too is the first evidence of a tradition that continued uninterrupted in Andean culture.

Ceremonial Life

In Caral appear some of the earlier known funerary practices and also the practice of ritual burial of existing buildings. In the Hanan section of the city has been found what is believed to be a circular tomb.[21] It was built half-buried into a small natural elevation. Its diameter was 13.6' and the height of the existing walls around 1.5'. This is the only such form in the higher city, but there is a similar one in the lower city and both of them were found in marginal sections. It is possible that the two are tombs of important individuals of the two moieties. Both structures are clearly different from a sacred hearth, since no trace of burnt materials has been found in them. The only thing that suggests their use as tomb in Hanan is the recovery of a hairlock. However, a similar pattern has been discovered in La Galgada, also a center of the Late Archaic. There the hair of the corpse was cut and the head was covered with a bag or basket.

Another burial was done in Subsection C2 of the High Pyramid of Hanan Caral.[22] Here a child had been placed as an offering for the construction of a platform that was part of an enlargement of the structure. Subsection C2 was built in various stages, and the burial was done in relation to one of these enlargements. The funerary bundle was placed in the east-west orientation of the grave. The skull was found in the east side with the face looking toward the pyramid. The age has been established at twelve to fifteen. The corpse had been smoked, partially fragmented, and some organs and muscles removed. Evidence from the site of Sechin Bajo, quoted earlier, seems to indicate that there may have been practices of human sacrifice as early as 3000 BC. In that site is a six-foot-tall adobe frieze clearly depicting a "sacrificer" deity. The figure holds a ritual knife in one hand, and a severed human head in the other.[23] We will return to the theme of the sacrificer in more depth in relation to Chavin decadence in chapter 3.

The above information, still very fragmentary, forms the foundation upon which we can try to build an understanding of the elements of early Andean spirituality. However, there is a still more important clue that will lead us to this understanding.

Caral and the First Written Record

Ruth Shady Solis, who systematically explored the site of Caral, also unearthed a very significant artifact, a *khipu*—a system of knotted cords that can be spread out as a radiating circle. This *khipu* of brown cotton strings wrapped around thin sticks was found together with a series of offerings on a stairway of a public building. Solis said, "It was an offering placed on a stairway when they decided to bury this and put down a floor to build another structure on top."[24]

Anticipating what we will explore in the later chapters about the Incas, we can briefly mention that a *khipu* was a mnemonic device for counting. Growing evidence points to it being also a device for writing, an equivalent of the Celtic so-called Ogam consaine writing—a writing that uses only consonants, no vowels.

CULT OF THE ANDEAN CROSS

So far we have looked at what made the Second Age unique from the perspective of its monumental architecture, but have gleaned little in terms of what made its mysteries unique. The first element was offered by the language of the U-shaped mounds that indicate a cult of water and mountains, a continuation of the veneration of the Great Spirit, as it survived from Atlantean times in a similar way to what we find in North America. There is, however, another way to characterize Andean cosmology previous to the time of the Dawning and understand the nature of some of its ritual elements. It is found in the function of the sunken courts. We will turn to this in combining the information that astronomy offers to us in relation to architecture, through the new science of archaeoastronomy.

It is now well known that ancient and so-called primitive civilizations—particularly their initiate priesthood—had a far more advanced and subtle understanding and knowledge of the movements of the sun, planets, and stars than has been commonly assumed. We also know of a very common, and as yet little understood or explored, pervasive symbolism of the Andes: the so-called Andean Cross. The origin of the symbol is to be found in an important constellation of the southern hemisphere—the Southern Cross—a constellation that plays the equivalent role of Ursa Major in the northern hemisphere. It is this cross that is used as the pointer to the Southern Pole, that place that remains stationary in relation to all other circling stars. The line that goes from the upper (superior) star to the lower one (inferior) perpetually indicates the location of the southern pole in a similar way that Polaris indicates the northern pole. At its superior culmination, when the cross's major axis is oriented vertically at the zenith, the four stars almost point to the cardinal directions.

The Southern Cross—called *chakana* in the Andes—is still an important constellation for the indigenous people at the present time. This may be what is represented as "the eye of god" (built with sticks in the form of a cross and held together with interlaced cotton threads) that archaeologists have found in the site of Caral and elsewhere.[25]

In *Spiritual Turning Points of North American History*, we have pointed out that in Mesoamerica, Ursa Major (pointing to North Pole) played an important part in the symbolism of Vucub Caquix (7 Macaw) and everything that points to the First and Second Ages in the Popol Vuh. The reference to this mythological image finds at least strong supporting evidence in the realm of archaeology. As Popenoe Hatch elaborates, it would offer a plausible hypothesis about the central astronomical observations performed in the major Olmec centers.[26]

The strength of Popenoe Hatch's hypothesis lies in being able to explain the enigmatic abandonment of the ceremonial centers of the Olmecs, particularly La Venta. The researcher argues that at the time of the abandonment of the ceremonial centers, Ursa Major had significantly changed position in the heavens because of the precession of the equinoxes. This meant that a time came when it was no longer constantly observable on the horizon, at all times of the night and of the year, as it had been previously. This hypothesis finds confirmation in the images of the Popol Vuh in what is called the "Fall of 7 Macaw," who is identified with the constellation of Ursa Major in Maya spirituality. The sacred book describes in great imaginations the dethroning and demise of the god of a whole age.

It seems that the phenomenon of the building of structures that orient themselves to the heavens, and then lose their function once the heavenly geography changes, is also present in South America in the sunken courts. This may have led to their dismissal in the present era, although isolated examples remained even up to the fifth century AD and, in the case of Wari civilization, even later.

It lies beyond doubt that the Southern Cross played a central cosmological role in Andean culture. The old Andean agricultural calendars were tied to the superior culmination of the Southern Cross (May 3), which marked their beginning. Even today the date marks the beginning of the agricultural calendar and coincides with the Christian festival of the Holy Cross—a festival that was and is used to supersede a cult that had deep roots within Andean culture. In a manner typical of Native American history, the Spaniards' attempt to eradicate ancient tradition was only partially successful. It gave rise to a diffuse syncretism in which Christian names were used to cover the surviving use of ancient traditions, or blend them with the new worldview.

The Southern Cross is the celestial axis of the southern hemisphere. The constellation has four stars, whose arms are not exactly perpendicular. The relationship between the two arms is such that the minor arm is to the major as the side of a square is to its diagonal. This is the basis of the "sacred proportion," concludes Carlos Milla Villena, after analyzing an astrophoto and measuring the rapport between major and minor axes of the constellation.[27] The reasoning behind this thought finds strong supporting evidence in the layout of the observatory of Salinas del Chao that we will look at in full detail shortly.

The Southern Cross is located in the Milky Way, close to the Coal Sack, one of the so-called dark cloud constellations of the Milky Way. By *dark cloud constellations* are meant the dark outlines formed by the surrounding thick clusters of stars of the Milky Way (figure 2.4).

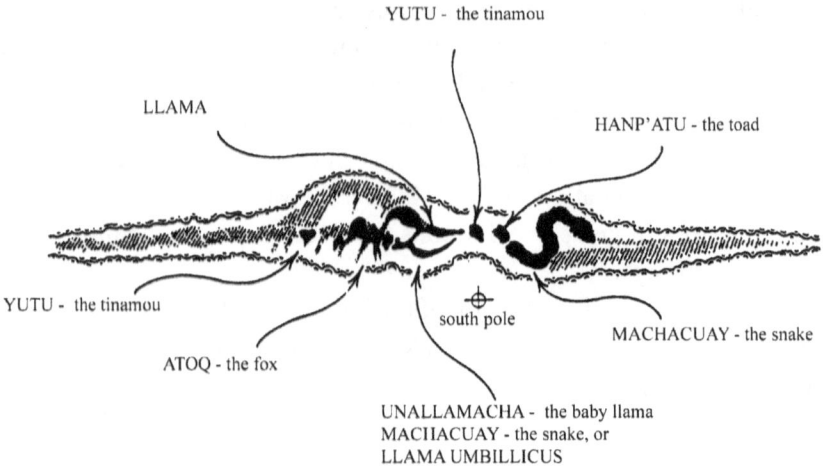

Figure 2.4: Dark cloud constellations

The Southern Cross also lies in immediate proximity to another central constellation of South America, the dark cloud constellation of the Sacred Llama. Two of the stars of the Llama—Alpha and Beta Centauri (*Llama ñawi*, the "eyes of the llama")—are some of the most brilliant stars of the firmament. Their heliacal rise and setting can be used to calculate the exact location of the geographic Southern Pole. To the immediate south of the cross is also found the constellation of the Fly, and further off, the constellation of the Chameleon.

In order to approach the evidence of the use of the Andean Cross in the Andes ever since the second millennium BC, let us look at a technique that has accompanied South American astronomical observations for millennia, the "astronomical water mirrors" that may have originated at this point in time. These look like large mortars carved in the rock. Their form and depth hardly fits their use as mortars, however. When filled with water, the mortars will reflect the light of a star by forming a silvery halo on the border of the circle, when the star is at the zenith. This is due to the fact that the surface of the mirror is concave and so is the surface of the water when it is filled. A result of the use of this technique is the mirror effect. The position of the mortars in space forms a mirror image to their counterparts in the heavens. This technique was resurrected at the time of the Incas.

Salinas del Chao

The water mirror technique is what was most likely used in the "Andean Cross geoglyph" of Salinas del Chao, situated in the Peruvian north coast, north of the Santa Valley and south of Virú Valley, next to the waters of the Pacific. Milla Villena attributes the geoglyph of Chao to the Late Archaic at around 2000 BC. The geoglyph itself is part of an extended site that had temples and ceremonial centers. Among the temples are also two sunken courts. The geoglyph complex is divided in two main parts (figure 2.5):

- a main quadrangle formed by low walls in which is inscribed the geoglyph of the Andean Cross. The markings (mortars) of the cross are inscribed in the center of this area. To the south (close to alpha of the cross) are found the markings of Alpha and Beta Centauri.
- a roughly square area enclosed by walls to the southeast of the first quadrangle. In the middle of it are two geoglyphic carvings that seem to correspond to the stars Alpha and Beta Musca (of the constellation of the Fly).

The Southern Cross is portrayed in the position it assumes at the Winter Solstice, an orientation of 31° 30' right of north; it is reproduced in a reflected position in the geoglyph.

Milla Villena has examined the measurements of the Southern Cross stars, as obtained from an astrophoto, and the measurements obtained on the site of Salinas del Chao for the marks corresponding to the stars; and compared the following proportions between the two sets of measurements: major axis/minor axis; northern section (between two contiguous stars)/southern section; western section/eastern section. There is an extremely high, statistically significant correspondence between each of the sets of two.[28] The cross is not oriented to the cardinal directions. However, the roughly northeast to southwest diagonal of the large quadrangle goes exactly through the middle of the cross. The major axis of the cross forms an angle of 31° 30' with true north. What is remarkable in this construction is the fact that the angle between the east-west axis and the minor axis of the cross measures 19°, which measures the intersolstitial angle—the angle formed between the positions of the sun at summer and winter solstice sunrise or sunset—at the estimated date of use of the observatory. The

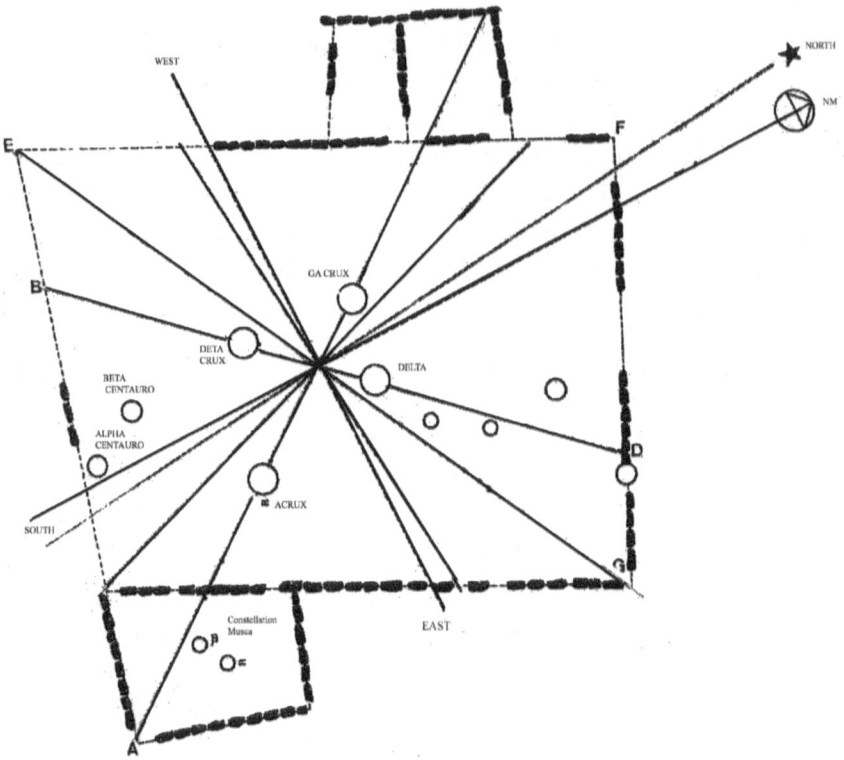

Figure 2.5: Salinas del Chao

angle between the major axis of the cross and the line that reaches from the center of the cross to the southern angle of the quadrangle also measures 19°.

Further analysis of the site of Salinas del Chao shows how the site itself was built on the proportions derived from the Southern Cross. Milla Villena finds the measuring pattern of the Andean Cross inscribed within the structure of the Salinas del Chao to be the minor axis of the Southern Cross (see figure 2.5). The second square is built with the diagonal of the first square corresponding to the major axis of the Southern Cross. The eastern and western edges of the quadrangle (the low walls enclosing the mortars) lie along the lines that correspond to the square that gives the value of π. Thus we can see that the geometrical properties of the geoglyph indicate a knowledge of the squaring of the circle based on the measurement of the Southern Cross—a knowledge that goes back at least to 2000 BC.

What can be seen in the geoglyph of the Salinas del Chao does not constitute isolated evidence. Other geoglyphs represent the Southern Cross. Such is the case for the geoglyph known as *candelabro* (candleholder) in the far north of the peninsula of Paracas on the southern coast of Peru (see figure 2.6). The figure is located on a steep slope, close to the top of the hill on compacted white sand overlooking the Pacific Ocean. The Southern Cross stands upright in the heavens in the same way the candelabra does during the early days of May;[29] which is an important time of the year, marking the beginning of the agricultural calendar.

The base of the candelabra rests on a rectangular pedestal on which is inscribed a small circle that seems to prolong the vertical axis, acting like the basis or pivot of the vertical axis. The Southern Cross rotates around the southern pole, which is what the circle in the rectangle seems to show.

Figure 2.6: Paracas candelabra

The figure can be observed only at a long distance. It cannot be viewed from the north, and even less from the south, given its position in the Paracas peninsula. It can, in fact, be viewed only from farther out on the ocean. This may be the reason why it is also placed toward the top of the incline leading to the hilltop—viewable from afar, compensating for the earth's curvature. The candelabra is in fact visible from the nearby islands of Chincha and is perfectly aligned with them.

The Andean Measuring System

It is becoming apparent that the Andean civilization had a very accurate and sophisticated mathematical/astronomical body of knowledge. Like many other civilizations before and after, in order to discern the unfolding of the seasons and to design their calendars, the Peruvian *amautas* (wise men) needed to divide the circumference of the circle (c)—an operation for which it is necessary to assess the value of π (3.14159...), which links the circle's circumference to its radius (r) since $c = 2\pi r$. When the diameter = 1, then the circumference = π. Knowledge of π and of the sacred proportion thus served the purpose of sacred geometry and the building of the monumental centers. Such knowledge was the revolution upon which rested the Second Age.

Milla Villena's hypothesis is that in order to find the value of π, the *amautas* availed themselves of the most diffused symbol in Andean cosmology, the Andean Cross, which they based upon the pattern of the Southern Cross. The Andean Cross arises out of the so-called squaring of the circle—the attempt to find a square and a circle of equal perimeter, which allows one to obtain geometrically a value for π. To do this, starting from an original square through successive diagonals, we generate four series of squares and enclosing circles that come each time closer to the desired goal (figure 2.7). The *amautas* found π as the value of the diagonal of the three adjacent squares of unit value and came to a value of 3.16. In so doing they obtained the most accurate value possible that could be reached through geometrical means.

Following this initial hypothesis, Milla Villena has discovered that the "Andean operating system of measurement" that allowed measurement of π through the diagonal of the cross also became a system that yielded units, multiples, and submultiples. It served to realize mathematical operations and was utilized for the patterns of design of ceremonial precincts. In essence, all religious symbolism, elements of design, and spatial organization were subjected to this operational system.[30] Knowledge of this operative system survived to the time of the Incas, or was revived by them, as seems obvious from the geographic ordering of their ceremonial centers and temples, to which we will return.

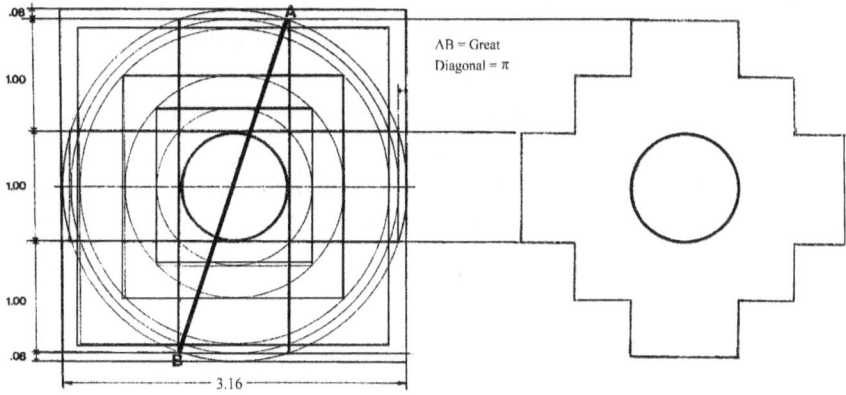

Figure 2.7: Andean cross and its generation

The operative system of measurement (OSM) is geometrical and proportional: its unit patterns are variable. For example, from the unity square, after three operations we obtain the square whose side corresponds to π. This in turn becomes the new unit pattern. At the eighth operation we obtain a second square cross, used to obtain a square whose side will be π^2, or ten times larger than the original square ($\pi^2=10$). The ninth operation (yielding a square of $\pi^2 \sqrt{2}$) forms the limit of the second part of the operative system. In essence four operations were needed for reaching the first Square (Andean) Cross and four other operations to reach the second Square Cross. In eight operations the area of the original square is increased by ten.

The crosses resulting from each successive operation grow in the four directions of space. For practical purposes the *amautas* limited some of the artistic and functional representations (particularly in sculpture) and represented only the first square cross. After that they limited its growth to the vertical dimension.

The Andean system of measurement works first through the "minor diagonal" of the unit square that generates the first Square Cross. The second diagonal is the Great Diagonal that unites the summits of the square cross (three contiguous squares). It has the value of π in the geometric process. The Great Diagonal serves as the main ordering principle of the system. It is used in the floor plan of all the main temples. In relation to this, Maria Scholten d'Ebneth says: "The diagonal is called *chekkaluwa* in Quechua, where the word *ch'ekka* means truth. Thus, overall, for those who devised and realized the great South American operating geographic system, the diagonal may have meant something like 'the path to the truth.'"[31] The Andean cross ruled all dimensions of Andean spiritual life. It was applied at all the levels of magnitude.

The crosses of the first, second, third, and fourth orders served to order and organize the use of space of monoliths and minor surfaces. Beyond that the ordering of space reached larger and larger applications:

FIRST CROSS: generated by the unit square
SECOND CROSS: for operating measurements such as the measuring staff of the *amauta*, equaling 1.117 m (3' 8")
THIRD CROSS: for the category of the monoliths, or unit patterns such as the famous Lanzon of Chavin (see chapter 3)
FOURTH CROSS: for measurement of minor surfaces
FIFTH CROSS: for the scale of the temples and associated ritual surfaces
SIXTH CROSS: for the ceremonial center and the large associated open spaces
SEVENTH CROSS: for itinerant measurements
EIGHTH CROSS: for the organization of urban space, such as the later "*ceque* system" of Cuzco, a system of lines that radiated away from the center of Cuzco (See chapter 9.)
NINTH CROSS: for organizing regional spaces
TENTH CROSS: for the Andean geographic space. An example of it is the "Route of Wirakocha" (See chapter 5.)

The breadth of the application of the Andean system has no known parallel in history. You could say that in the Andean world, religion and ritual had a mathematical origin, or that the *amautas* had a geometric-ritual mind.

The squaring of the circle is only the first part of the operations needed in order for the *amautas* to be able to orient themselves in the dimensions of space and time and to link those two to the eternal. The dimension of space is what the Andean cross addresses. Let us look at the dimension of time and how it affects the *amautas*' worldview.

In all ages and all times, simple observation of the firmament indicated to the initiates and their priesthoods that even the so-called fixed stars are not immobile and constant in the landscape of the heavens. Today we know that this is so, thanks to the knowledge of the precession of the equinoxes, which indicates that every 72 years the sun moves by one degree in the heavens in relation to the fixed stars, so that after 30 x 72 years the sun will rise on the spring equinox in a different zodiacal sign than before. This is why we are waiting for the so-called Age of Aquarius. When that age comes, the sun will be shining at the vernal equinox from the constellation of Aquarius. It takes the sun 72 x 30 x 12, or 25,920 years, to move around the ecliptic and return to the same fixed star in one of the signs of the zodiac. This length of time is called a Platonic Year.

Milla Villena formulated a hypothesis of how the determination of the precession of the equinoxes could have been solved by the Andean initiates. It appears that the Andean priest needed to measure the intersolstitial angle in order to incorporate knowledge of the precession of the equinoxes into the calculations that he could obtain from his astronomical observatories. The intersolstitial angle can be measured from the sun (observations on the day of the equinoxes) or the stars (observations of stars on the nights of the equinoxes). According to Milla Villena, the *amautas* used the stellar intersolstitial angle. This fact would be made manifest in the building of the sunken courts in the angle (width) of their stairs and depth of the inner court. The *amautas* would look at a given marker (star) and observe its position against the topographic background at one of the solstices. They first marked the topographic position, then repeated this operation at the following solstice six months later. The stairway extremes mark the position of a given star at one and the other solstice, thus helping to determine the intersolstitial angle.

As interesting as the theory could be, one can argue that, had the *amautas* known how to locate the solstices, they would not have needed such a difficult technique for calculating the intersolstitial angle. Furthermore, there is no evidence so far that Andean cultures knew of a solar calendar at that time. The first, very isolated evidence has only very recently emerged in the case of the solar observatory of Chankillo in the fourth century AD (see chapter 3). However, the thesis of sunken courts as stellar observatories still has some weight, based on the parallels between Mesoamerica and South America. In both places we are faced with observatories that lost their function in the centuries before the turn of our era. In the case of Mesoamerica, the observatories were the Olmec pyramids in South America, the sunken courts of the Second Age. In the case of Peru, the phenomenon of the precession of the equinoxes probably caused havoc as early as 1000 BC, causing sunken courts to be rebuilt in different locations on the same sites. After a while their use was altogether discontinued. Sunken courts continued to be built only after the turn of our era, in very limited amounts and in cultures of regressive character, particularly the Moche (more about this in chapter 6). It is this author's opinion that the observatories served the purpose of stellar observation, and that the vagaries of their use are due to the shifting position of the stars due to the precession of the equinoxes. The stars could very well be those of the Southern Cross, after all! More research is needed to fully assess this hypothesis.

Let us look at the matter of the sunken courts' demise more closely. There are fourteen sunken courts in the neighboring valleys of Santa and Chao. They present two major variables: the opening angle of the stairs and the depth of the court. On the basis of the above theory we can provide an explanation as to why the observatories would be abandoned when the observatory would not allow the observation of the targeted stars. In such case three things could be done:

- change the opening of the stairway
- abandon the observatory
- build a new observatory and dig deeper than the previous one.[32]

Milla Villena finds no evidence of the first scenario, although the present author surmises this may have been the case in Caral's Hurin sunken court in the example brought forth earlier. The two internal stairways are not aligned to the axis of the pyramid and to the central staircase, but at a slight angle. They face 25° east of north. Historically, the initial design of the stairs was rectangular and later the design was modified to become trapezoidal.[33] The sunken court was originally aligned with the cosmology of the pyramid. Then something happened that negated this cosmology. This independent observation further reinforces Milla Villena's hypothesis of an astronomical function of the courts.

There is evidence for the second and third of the above alternatives in places where there are two sunken courts, used at different times. In this case the second one is dug deeper than the first one. This is what happened in Pampa Yolanda in Santa Valley, Alto Peru de Suchiman, Las Haldas in Casma Valley, Salinas de Chao, and others.[34] After the Moche civilization (~100–600 AD) the sunken courts almost completely disappear. In no instance were they consistently used over time.

We will now move to a plausible hypothesis of the nature of Andean spirituality as it could have been practiced at that time within the precinct of the mysteries in what would have been a purely theocratic society.

The Spiritual-Scientific Background

As the indigenous mind recognizes, evolution does not proceed in a linear fashion, but rather in cycles alternating expansion and contraction, ascent and descent, evolution and decline, etc. Such a view can be reconciled with the scientific method through the work of Rudolf Steiner. This will allow us access to the legends and documents of ancient Mesoamerica.

Lemuria

Spiritual-scientific research recognizes cultural cycles prior to our own. For practical purposes all that will concern us here are the stages designated as Lemuria and Atlantis. Directly preceding Atlantis was the so-called Lemuria that had its center in South Asia, approximately from Southern India to Madagascar. Present Southern Asia and parts of Africa belonged to it.

In Lemuria, the human being, descending from the spiritual world, first underwent the process of incarnation in a physical body. This stage is imaginatively depicted in the Old Testament's myth of the Fall; the same is said in spiritual documents all over the world. The Popol Vuh takes its start from this point in time as well.

In Lemuria the human being had power over his body. He could increase his strength through his will. Men and women had differentiated roles and tasks. Men underwent what can be characterized as a training of the body. They had to undergo dangers, overcome pain, accomplish daring deeds, bear torture. It was a sort of religion of the will: those that held it or practiced it were regarded by others with great awe and veneration, for the power that they held.

The women developed a strong imagination through witnessing the deeds of the men. Women's faculty of imagination became the basis for a higher development of the life of ideas. With the development of the first germs of memory came the capacity to form the first simple moral concepts. Steiner indicates that it was from the spiritual education of the women that the first ideas of good and evil arose. What emanated from men had an effect which was more natural-divine; what women developed was of a more soul-divine nature. The above is the basis of matriarchy, which confirms historical findings; matriarchy preceded patriarchy.

Toward the end of Lemuria, highly developed entities isolated a small group of human beings and designated these to be the ancestors of the coming Atlantean race. This group further divided into smaller groups that the women were put in charge of ordering and consolidating. It was through them that the willful nature and strength of men was educated and ennobled. It was to women that men turned in order to receive advice and interpret the signs of nature. From this state of affairs originated the germs of human religion and the beginning of language in song and dance.

Group Souls in Lemuria and Atlantis

In the earlier part of the Lemurian epoch—before the Fall—the human being was not yet physically condensed, but was developed enough that clairvoyant pictures show the existence of four group-souls: they had something of the image of the bull on one hand, of the lion for the second, of the eagle for the third and something similar to the human for the fourth.[35] In order to become human our ancestors had to pass through four animal group-souls. They felt that they belonged to the group-souls, just like the fingers belong to our body. When they were among spiritual beings they heard the name of what each of them was. "One group heard the word which in the original language was the word for that group; another group heard a different word. Man could not name himself from within; his name sounded into him from without."[36] This situation evolved further in Atlantean times, as we will see below.

Lemurian consciousness still surviving is closely attached to the events of those remote times: such as the descent into incarnation. They have cults ordered according to the phases of the sun and moon. The clan system that results from this is usually accompanied by totemism. Primitive humanity experienced the forces that were later expressed in the signs of the zodiac. They experienced them in the way they were reflected in animals and plants. At present, traces of this early consciousness survive in the dual system patterned on the cosmos generating the subdivision of the village communities in so-called "moieties" (from French for halves).

The matriarchal class-system, marriage rules, and the configuration of villages and cities in moieties are clearly present in the Andes and much of South America. The dual system is the first step in which social life was consciously structured according to the order of the cosmos. The Hanan-Hurin polarity, which survived to the times of the Inca Empire, was already present at the time of development of the earliest Andean cities such as Caral. This is the first layer of Andean culture. To this is added the later Atlantean culture.

Guenther Wachsmuth's research indicates that before Lemuria, South America and Africa were united, and here it was that the first human beings were incarnated. This early stage touched the northern and eastern parts of South America because, at the time, the Andes were still forming and thus unsuitable for settlement. The earlier populations who took no part in Lemurian evolution conceivably later emigrated toward the Andes as well. The later stream from Atlantis was, therefore, added in South America to a much older population substratum than in Mesoamerica or North America.

The end of Lemuria came through volcanic fire. When a colony left the continent in order to found the Atlantean races, they took with themselves the knowledge of the breeding of animals and plants. At the time of Lemuria's end, some of the more advanced groups migrated toward the southern Mysteries of Atlantis and carried there their impulses. The incoming Atlantean influx into the Americas also spread out from the Southern Mysteries of Atlantis. Thus both North and South America have this common element of an early descent into the body as it was present in these Mysteries. In South America this is accentuated by the older populations that were present in the early stages of the continent.

According to the research of Wachsmuth, three groups migrated to the Americas from old Atlantis, starting during the fifth period of Atlantean civilization, around 15,000 BC.[37] Two of them are accounted for in the occupation of the northern continent. The third is most likely the one from which issued the ancient Aymara of the high plateau of Bolivia and Peru. They settled around the Lake Titicaca basin, where the famous Tiwanaku civilization developed, which already had a very complex level of social differentiation.

Atlantean Consciousness

The first Atlantean Mysteries preserved the teachings of the Mysteries of the cosmos connected to the outer planets: Saturn, Jupiter, and Mars. The Planetary Mysteries spread out in different regions. The oracles of the south were Saturn oracles concerned with the Mysteries of Warmth. Warmth forces are the oldest in cosmic evolution. To the north were the Jupiter oracles more concerned with the Mysteries of Light. To the center developed the Mars and Sun oracles. The Mars Mysteries were teachings about the formative forces acting particularly in the watery element. The Sun Mysteries formed a unity of all the other teachings brought to a higher level; they carried all impulses for the future.

The people of the Saturn Mysteries—from which the early Americans originated—were the first to feel the need to bring to birth social forms. In North America this later manifested through the Toltecs; in the east this was initiated by Egyptians and Babylonians. Leadership was assumed by the priest-king who united in himself the male function of rulership with the female quality of revelation. From Southern Atlantis originated the forerunners of Toltecs and other American Indians.

Later on (particularly after the midpoint of Atlantean evolution) were added the oracles connected to the inner planets—Mercury, Venus, Moon, and Vulcan—leading to the development of inner faculties. The Venus Mysteries are those who first gifted humanity its intellectuality. The Mercury spirits were the teachers of the first initiates. The Vulcan Mysteries represented a particular intensification of the other three. In the last stages of Atlantis the cults celebrating the ancestors originated. In these rituals the soul, having lost connection with the divine, sought knowledge of immortality in the continuation of the line of generations.

We need to add here another trait of Atlantean culture, that which marked the evolution of the group souls after the time of Lemuria. In Atlantean time the four types, influenced by the group souls, arose more fully. In the "Bull type" the physical nature became particularly strong and worked in the physical body. In the "Lion type" the etheric left a particularly strong mark. Those in whom the astral body overpowered the physical and etheric were those of the Eagle type. All of the above forces of nature were united and integrated in human beings whose ego had grown stronger. "In this group the clairvoyant has before him what has been preserved in the form of the Sphinx…" The Sphinx is a union of the three: it has eagle wings, bull form and something of the lion body.[38] A parallel movement—

announcing the future differentiation of races of post-Atlantean times—occurred during the second age of Atlantis but also in other regions of the earth. These processes were also the result of geography and environment. Those groups who were strongly influenced by the earthly environment and the bodily functions acquired a darker complexion. Among them were the forerunners of the Native Americans. The stronger earthly influences were played out in the south of Atlantis and in other areas like Africa; the cosmic influences to the north. In the north, human beings were exposed to less intense sunlight and could experience the cosmic influences through the rhythm of the seasons, retaining a lighter skin complexion.

Because of its ancestral roots in Atlantis, the Native American still lives in a type of consciousness that retained many aspects of Atlantean consciousness, the consciousness that is known in the East as Tao. "The wisdom of Atlantis is embodied in water in a drop of dew. The German word *Tau* is nothing more than the old Atlantean sound. So we should look with reverence and devotion at every dewdrop glittering from a blade of grass as a holy legacy from that age in which the connection between man and the Gods was not yet severed," comments Steiner.[39] The T cross—symbol of the Tau—is very widespread in Olmec, Maya, and other American civilizations. It reappears in Inca architecture. The Andean cross itself can be seen as two superposed Tau crosses. What Steiner calls the Tau is what the native-American expresses as "Great Spirit."

The Native Americans still live in the old picture-consciousness of Atlantis. This is because their etheric body is much less connected with the physical body, and this is reflected in the way the Native Americans perceive the world. A very well-known example, reflecting the Atlantean cosmovision, is the image of Turtle Island. This is what the earth is called in North America by the Algonquians and many other groups. This idea is in direct continuation with the way in which the world was seen by early Atlanteans, for whom the gods dwelt in the waters surrounding the continent of Atlantis. For the Atlanteans, and for the Native Americans, ocean and heaven were co-substantial. Among many Maya tribes the same word indicates water, winter, rain, and vegetation. Interestingly, green and blue are also often called by the same name.[40] This reflects of the prevalence of water and air elements over the earth element in old Atlantis.

The closer association of the ether body to the astral body in the Native American is the reason for three other phenomena. The life of feelings was and still is more closely associated with the phenomenon of growth. In early times of Atlantis, and also of the South American continent, the lower astral could influence the growth of the body, which translated into the appearance of giants, dwarves, and other Atlantean human forms. This is also the reason for frequent references to past races of giants in South American lore.

Like the Atlanteans, the South American Natives had, and often still have ‚a prodigious memory—a memory that works differently from our modern memory. This is why what we see in present-day ritual and practices can offer us insights into the religions of ancient times. A final consequence of the Atlantean consciousness of the Native Americans is their easy access to the world of the departed souls and the ancestors. Even at the time of the Incas, much of the ritual life revolved around the preservation of and communication with the departed kings, ancestors of the lines of power that they had formed.

The Evolution of the Mysteries

From times immemorial, the Mysteries were places in which human beings received revelations and instructions from spiritual beings. There were four successive stages of these Mysteries, thus named by Steiner: the Ancient Mysteries, Semi-Ancient, Semi-New, and New Mysteries.[41] The stage in which Andean civilization found itself with the rise of the civilization of the north and central coast formed the transition from the Ancient to the Semi-Ancient Mysteries.

In the early stages of the Mysteries, the gods descending from the spirit world dwelt among human beings, albeit only in an etheric body. Through their representatives they offered their teachings to human beings. For all practical purposes, the participants in the sacred ceremonies perceived no difference between the priests and the gods. At this stage, all sacred ceremonies depended upon and were planned in accordance with certain favorable astrological configurations. Of these Mysteries, nothing historical is preserved.

At the first stage of the Mysteries the ceremonies were carried out under the ground, in caves in the cliffs, and during the act of transubstantiation in the sacred ceremonies, the priest felt his physical organism at one with the whole earth. Guaman Poma confirms that During the Second Age—or Age of the Wan Runa (indigenous people)—human beings abandoned the caves for the first dwellings called *pukullo*.

In the transition to the Semi-Ancient Mysteries, we have at least a few records historically preserved. The gods did not descend anymore but they sent their forces to work in the precinct of the Mysteries. The temples rose to the surface of the earth and a great importance was given to water, through ablution and later baptism. The *cultus* worked with the forces of the etheric body. The beings that worked at that time among humanity were the ancient "Teachers of Wisdom," who have withdrawn to the Sphere of the Moon. They worked among humanity only in etheric bodies.[42] The Semi-Ancient Mysteries were inaugurated after the end of Atlantis.

In the evolution of the Andean Mysteries great cosmological importance is assumed by the Southern Cross. To the north, historical and mythological evidence points to Ursa Polaris and Ursa Major playing a similar role among the Olmecs. The Andean Cross is the astronomical referential of the Great Spirit in the Andes. There isn't as yet a reference to the Sun as the axis of the universe, and that will not appear until the end of the Third Age.

The changes in the nature of the Mysteries were accompanied by a corollary of consequences. The cultural changes that most concern us here are language, writing, and the calendar. In Atlantean time there existed a primal root language common to all. Consonants arose from the need of the soul to convey expression for outer impressions. Vowels mirrored the inner experiences of the soul, such as joy, pleasure, pain, or sadness.

In contrast to spoken language that has a common origin in time for humanity, writing appeared at different points in time in various civilizations and took on very different forms. The need for writing corresponds to the desire to preserve the experience of and connection with the revelation of the spirit. As long as these experiences could be continuously renewed there was no need to preserve memory of them in a fixed form. The pictorial writing of hieroglyphs of Egypt represented the images that were first experienced inwardly. They arose at the beginning of Kali Yuga, the incoming Age of Darkness, whose onset occurred around the third millennium BC. The much more abstract alphabet itself was introduced only much later, around 1500 BC.

Early calendars were tied to the sun and moon, and only later would planetary cycles begin to play a part. The ancient Egyptian Calendar, known as the *Annus Vagus* or "Wandering Year," had 365 days, divided into 12 months of 30 days each, plus 5 extra days at the end of the year. A month consisted of 3 ten-day "weeks." This system was in use by 2400 BC, and possibly before. This same system also appeared among the Toltecs, and parts of it survived in the later Maya calendar.

The experience of time was originally accompanied by a lively feeling for the planetary rhythms reflecting the guidance of the gods. Later on, when this knowledge was lost, time was experienced as the repetition of the same, as a mechanical alternation and recurrence of immutably predetermined laws. This too is discernable in the Toltec Calendar Wheel of recurrent cycles of 52 years. The longer this system survived, the more it acquired a fatalistic and deterministic dimension.

It seems that (contrary to earlier findings) civilization had an earlier start in South America than in Mesoamerica, or at least that the transition from First to Second Age appeared earlier in some parts of the Andes than it did in Mesoamerica. This confirms Wachsmuth's spiritual research that shows South America to have been earlier inhabited than northern America. It also seems that the change of consciousness caused by the "Twilight of the Gods"—the loss of ancient atavistic clairvoyance—took place earlier in South America than it did in the northern continent. A few pointers show it even if only in symptomatic fashion. In the first instance, ceremonial architecture appeared along the north coast much earlier than did Olmec architecture along the Gulf Coast. The second indication has come to surface in the first *khipus* of Caral, pointing to the first possible evidence of counting and possibly writing. Altogether the two elements spell the transition from the consciousness of union with the Godhead to the loss of such intercourse. We can add to this the evidence of the earliest human sacrifices along the north coast already around 3000 BC. The old atavistic clairvoyance, starting to wane, was recovered by the high priests through human sacrifice, but now in a decadent fashion, contrary to the direction of normal evolution.

The Form of Early Andean Spirituality

Very little can be gleaned about the specific nature of the Andean Mysteries, at least directly. What follows has only the value of hypothesis, and is extracted from the work of Grace Cooke who describes from memory of previous lives a process of initiation undergone a few millennia before our time in a society that already knew of agriculture and astrology in South America. She may be referring to the Mysteries that sustained the life of the ceremonial centers of the North Central Coast or similar Mysteries that were present elsewhere along the central Andes, most likely modern Peru. After all, no other cultures of this importance existed anywhere else in the Andes or the whole of South America in the period to which she refers.[43]

The process of initiation was divided into three stages. In the first stage the pupil had to undergo seven years of training of the physical body, tests of strength and endurance. The neophytes had to strengthen both courage and inner readiness.

The second stage concerned first and foremost the observation of natural phenomena over long periods of time. The neophyte was taught the arts of agriculture and animal husbandry, and could then influence nature from within, because the etheric body was far more pliable than at present. Thus the second period was in all degrees a course in natural science as applied to the ordering of human existence.

The last stage corresponded to a further trial of the soul. The pupil had to remain alone in a high mountain cave for a long time of silence and meditation. This is how Grace Cooke remembers it:

"This was the sharpest ordeal ... I had to face legions of elementals and wrestle with them, to overcome or be overcome. Again and again these creatures of the underworld tempted me with all manner of bribes to put myself in their hands, to surrender my faith and trust in God or eternal good: in return for which they would bestow on me power to work the strange magic of the Lucifers, great powers over earth itself and its people, over the people of the inner world even."[44]

After passing this last ordeal the candidate was brought to two different temples. Here he was alternatively exposed to great heat and intense cold. Through his previous training the disciple knew how to protect the flesh from these extremes and how to use the power of thought to heal injuries and illnesses. In women, initiation also promoted the attainment of prophetic vision.

The above processes present many traits typical of Atlantean initiation. Some Lemurian elements continue throughout, particularly the tests of physical endurance or the particular role befalling women. Here, as in the Mexican Mysteries, there most likely was a combination of paths into the macrocosm and journey of the soul conducted simultaneously.

This is as far as we can presently go into the Mysteries of the Second Age of Andean civilization. We will now turn to the seminal civilization of the Third Age, or what archaeology calls the Formative and F. Kauffman Doig calls "Wirakocha movement." This is the culture that had its origin or center in the northern Peruvian sierra at the site of Chavin de Huantar.

CHAPTER 3

The Third Age: Chavin

IN THIS CHAPTER we will look at the civilization that played a role in many ways parallel to the Olmec civilization in Mesoamerica. In addition we will also touch on emblematic developments that took place in the centuries immediately before the time of Christ. Curiously, some of Steiner's assertions about the corollary events surrounding the cardinal events of the life and times of the initiate of the Americas, Ixbalamqué, are better corroborated in South America than in Mesoamerica.

We will first turn to the one that all archaeologists refer to as the main civilization of the time following the Second Age. The major ceremonial center of pre-Christian times in the Andes was Chavin de Huantar. This was the civilization whose apogee followed the demise of the centers of the north-central coast of Peru around the eleventh to tenth centuries BC. The whole period is also referred to as the Formative.

Chavin: In Preparation of the Future

Chavin is located 9800' high in a long valley along a traditional trade route, in the department of Ancash, not far from Huanuco (see map 1, p. 14). The site lies at the junction of the Wacheqsa and Mosna Rivers. Opinions differ as to the time of the onset of Chavin cult. Patterson estimates that Chavin originated around 1300 BC.[1] Others place it back as early as 1500 BC. What is more certain is the time that Chavin's influence ended, roughly in the time preceding what the archaeologists call the Early Intermediate Period, beginning around 200 BC.

With the cult of Chavin appeared the first traces of social stratification, particularly visible in the contents of the burial sites. This stratification affected only a small number of individuals, most likely just the religious elite. Sites that probably held the remains of members of the priesthood are recognizable through the presence of Chavin-style motifs in jewels, breastplates, textiles, etc. Also visible at this time are the gold earplugs that the priests wore, an enduring tradition of the Andes.[2] The influence of Chavin spread to the coast from Lambayeque (Ecuador) to the Ica Valley (southern Peru) and in the highlands from Huanuco to Pacopampa (close to Cajamarca). Apart from Chavin, other temples of the cult existed in Kuntur Wasi (La Copa), Pacopampa, Garagay (north of Lima), Mojeque (Casma Valley, north coast), Cerro Blanco in Nepeña (north coast), etc.

Chavin introduced many artistic innovations: new, complex techniques allowing the treatment of gold and silver for the production of jewels or ceremonial objects; the use of brightly colored textiles; the carving of granite for production of stelae, etc. However, Chavin introduced little in the technological realm and in the way of living of the surrounding populations.

An interesting mythological tradition recorded by Cieza de Leon indicates that Chavin was built by a race of giants, whose portraits could still be seen in large stone sculptures.[3] We have seen other traditions of giants in Mesoamerica and therefore will not dismiss this claim offhand, though this likely refers to strength rather than stature. The second assertion of portraits in large stone sculptures may not be completely unfounded either, although it has not come to light. The contemporary Olmec civilization created the famous colossal heads that archaeologists now believe to be those of priests and leaders. To continue the parallel with Olmec centers, in Chavin too the stone was quarried from distant deposits, at what seems to have been a great expenditure of energy.

There is evidence—which will be analyzed later—that Chavin was a cult of the nature of an oracle, just as the famous Pachacamac was at a later time. This was also the account made by the Jesuit mission at Cajatambo about the function of the site's temple: "a building that is very feared and greatly venerated and they call it the house of huacas [sacred place or object] . . . and [the huacas] spoke and answered the men [who were] their children and [they spoke] to the heads of lineages that exist today among the Indians of this land."[4] This indicates that Chavin cult probably went alongside other local cults and that there was no need for imposing a homogeneous religion throughout its area of influence. This is also confirmed by the survival in time of other local cults in the areas where Chavin influence thrived. It is also reconfirmed by the confined presence of Chavin enclaves in areas of a definitely alien culture. In the necropolis of Paracas, for example, a tomb has been found with more than two hundred pieces of cloth or pottery that do not carry Paracas motifs of the corresponding period (400–200 BC), but rather Chavin iconography. Almost fifty textiles carry the Staff Deity motif that originated in Chavin, and that will play an important part in our later considerations.[5]

Architecture and Iconography

Chavin's site occupies about 32 acres. The main architectural complex is formed by the Old Temple and the New Temple, also called the Castillo. The Old Temple is of modest proportions in relation to the Castillo (figure 3.1).

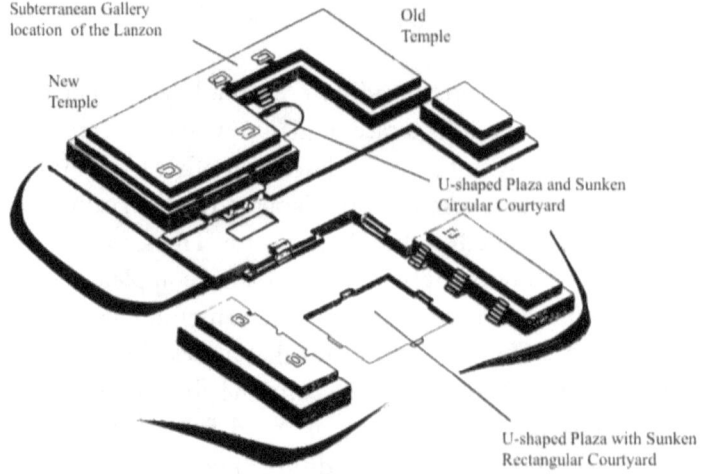

Figure 3.1: Chavin de Huantar

Old Temple

In the Old Temple a core of earth and rock is covered with polished slabs of sandstone, granite, and limestone. The temple is filled with chambers and passageways, and to these were added stairways, vents, and drains that formed a labyrinth. The various structures have been accounted for as labyrinths, monastic cells, ventilation and drainage systems, etc. None of these hypotheses justifies the number of galleries and halls, since the supposed drainage system would have a capacity ten times over what is needed even in unexpected cases.

It has been speculated that this complex system amplified the sound of the waters to make it sound as a thunder-like roar, particularly in the chamber that hosts the famous Lanzon, believed to be the hall of the oracle. Let us look closer at this hypothesis. To achieve sonic effects, it was important to have a sizeable fall of water potential. Being at the confluence of two rivers (Wacheqsa and Mosna) allowed for a height drop of 67' over a distance of 330'. Lumbreras, Gonzalez, and Lietar believe that some of the halls worked as acoustic chambers.[6] The authors hypothesize that the channeling of the water was hidden from view.

Probably the oracle's oldest deity is the Lanzon (Spanish from *lanza* or spear) also called the Great Image, which still occupies its original position (figure 3.2). The tall, elongated carving portrays a human-like form with feet and hands ending in claws. The lifted lips display sharp upper canines. The eyebrows and hair end in snake's heads, and the headdress displays feline heads.

Possible evidence of the nature of the cult comes from the architectural arrangement of the spaces. The sculpture of the Lanzon, the "Smiling Deity" of Chavin, is placed in a dark room. Above the central figure is an opening connecting the lower room with a room above. This may have served to allow the words spoken by the oracle below to be heard in the room above. The roaring waters likely amplified the sound and carried it away.

The Old Temple's side platforms embrace the sunken circular court that is 69' in diameter and 8' deep. The open end of the U-shaped temple—in overall shape similar to the pyramids of the coastal centers—points to the Mosna river and the rising sun. Here we see once again the cult of water and mountain deities that forms a continuity with the practices of the Second Age.

New Temple

At the time of the building of the New Temple (also called Castillo), the Old Temple was probably remodeled and both old and new temples were used simultaneously. In fact the New Temple was created after doubling the size of the south wing of the Old Temple.

The Castillo is formed of three terraces of very similar size. Its walls are covered with polished decorative stones. In its interior it has stone slabs arranged in regular rows. In the center of the eastern façade is a stairway divided in two halves, one decorated with light-hued stones, the other with dark ones. There are two stairways proceeding in the northern and southern directions and arriving at a square landing. The walls were decorated with "tenoned heads," carved heads jutting out of the surface of the wall.

Figure 3.2: The Lanzon

The main rectangular plaza of the temple of 345' x 279' encloses a square sunken court of 164' on a side. Some 1,500 people could have witnessed the ceremonies from courts and plazas further down. Approaching the temple, the plazas become progressively smaller and higher—most likely in order to restrict access to smaller and smaller crowds. The people would witness in the lower plazas, whereas the priesthood alone had access to the galleries, a pattern that was preserved up to the time of the Incas.

John Rowe and other authors had assumed that various parts of the buildings were added to the previous ones without an initial all-encompassing plan, based on the fact that there are discontinuities between structures with newer ones resting against older ones, leaving visible fissures. Kauffman Doig argues for the idea that although parts were built in succession this was done according to an original plan and that the whole had a dimension of iconographic architecture representing a magic religious figure.[7] This could have been the image of a jaguar. Although this is far from clear from what survives of Chavin's architecture, this is a very plausible hypothesis, in fact a feature that persisted throughout the successive periods of Andean civilization, and was still extensively used at the time of the Incas.

One of the most interesting discoveries of Chavin are the heads projecting out of the upper walls of the so-called Old Temple. These represent wrinkled faces and various traits of animal features pointing to a feline (jaguar) or raptorial bird (like the crested eagle). Richard Burger has ordered the heads in a sequence from the most human to the most animal-anthropomorphic form.[8] The result forms a gradual progression from a human wrinkled face to the animal stage representing either jaguar or crested eagle. The intermediate stage is particularly interesting. The bulging eyes and mucus-dripping nostrils faithfully reproduce the effects of modern-day rituals involving the use of psychotropic substances. Discharge of mucus is in effect one of the symptoms of the action of these substances. In this aspect of the shamanic journey we see another parallel with Mesoamerica's Olmec culture.

To the indications of the sculptures we can add the evidence coming from mortars and pestles used for producing the active drugs from the plants. The mortars represent birds or jaguars. Trays, spatulas, spoons, and tubes used in the rituals also reproduce the motif of the San Pedro cactus from which mescaline is extracted.

Rafael Girard points to the fact that many of the animals considered sacred (monkey, lizard, jaguar, etc.) and represented in Chavin and earlier iconography do not originate from the Andes but from Mesoamerica. Elements common to Mesoamerica only point to a common, distant origin in time. Central to all of these is the jaguar motif that we have already seen in the heads of the Old Temple. Chiaki Kano indicates that the jaguar cult was already present in the Wairajirca and Kotosh phases that preceded Chavin.[9] However, the motif evolved from a first purely naturalistic phase in Wairajirca to an anthropomorphized version in the Kotosh and Chavin phases.

The jaguar coat is easily recognizable because it has either quatrefoils (four petal flower patterns), cinquefoils, or star markings. This indicates that it is the jaguar and not a puma. Cats, when they are represented, do not have star markings. The familiar theme of the night god of Mesoamerica, as Girard underlines it, is the same that Chavin has made central to its art. In fact everything divine is referred to the jaguar motif. The mouths of almost any creature, even birds, are represented as a jaguar mouth.

Iconography

We will now move a step further in Chavin iconography. In so doing, our purpose is double. The first is to uncover the major deities of the Chavin civilization and thus characterize its contribution to Andean civilization. Secondarily, we will establish an artistic time sequence, one of the safest means to characterize the evolution in time of the themes of Chavin culture, allowing us to also characterize its phases of evolution and decadence.

John Rowe has studied with keen insight the motifs of Chavin art and determined a series of recognizable traits:

- general use of bilateral symmetry. If the figure is in profile, it is associated with another one that reflects it.
- treatment of twisted geometric figures
- decorative curls
- designs adapting to a framework of parallel lines
- diffuse use of *kennings*. A kenning is an element of comparison, a metaphor. The hair is compared to and treated like snakes; tails, feet, and wings are compared to tongues and therefore emerge from a stylized mouth inserted in the body.

The snakes, as elsewhere in South American native art, are a device for indicating the fields of energy or etheric forces that emanate from the being. Not surprisingly, the most numinous beings we will see are those with countless snakes flowing out of them.

Feline and bird symbolism play a very important role in the symbolism of South America. The jaguar is often associated with the night and the earth; birds with the day and the air. Overall, the jaguar theme predominates in Chavin—especially in relation to the major deities. We will have to wait until after the turn of our era to observe the bird (condor, eagle) theme acquire more importance.

With time, Chavin art evolved a very characteristic style. The decorative curls acquired longer and longer stems; curves were replaced with straight lines; detail was more abundantly repeated; and new, abstract elements were introduced. On the basis of these observations, Rowe distinguished three phases of Chavin art that he named AB, CD, and EF. Based on the above, we can explore the evolution of Chavin religion over time by looking at the three most famous Chavin sculptures: the Lanzon or Smiling God (Phase AB), the Tello Obelisk (Phase CD), and the Raimondi Stela (Phase EF). Rowe's analysis is complemented by that of his follower Peter Roe.[10]

The Lanzon

The Phase AB is the easiest to recognize among the series. The heads of Chavin's court that we mentioned go back to this period. The "agnatic mouth" (without jaw) was the preferred mouth representation. During this phase real animals, without human traits, are more important than in any of the following periods. Human hands are rounded, have long fingernails (not claws) and a correct number of fingers and toes. The so-called collared snake (a snake with a band around its body, just behind the head) seems to be an important motif in this period. The structure of a design during this period is still clearly outlined and immediately apprehended by the mind. All lines tend to be curved.

The Lanzon is the most famous sculpture of Chavin (figure 3.2). It has also been called the Smiling God. Its Spanish name alludes to its elongated form, resembling that of a spear. Only the upper canines protrude from the mouth of an otherwise human figure. The mouth has jaguar fangs, the hair is formed by snakes. One hand points above, the other below. Above the head was a canal that R. Girard believes was used for pouring the liquid offerings to the deity.[11] From its position in the middle of the so-called cruciform gallery, it is clear that the Lanzon was somehow a foundation stone of Chavin. It is a sort of cosmic axis of the temple. The deity has also been represented on other objects such as bones with the shape of a knife or spear. The Lanzon was a figure that only the priests could view. A later version of it is set in a wall of an outside patio and was available for public worship.

The Tello Obelisk

P. Roe divides the phase CD into a C and a CD period. Phase C is defined as a transitional phase in which the famous Tello Obelisk emerges. In this phase we notice the appearance of trophy heads and warriors with weapons. War clubs are represented on the north coast and at Supe. (In the Supe Valley have also been found four skulls fractured from inflicted trauma.) In the iconography we also notice the presence of disembodied eyes with their pupils (at later times they will also appear without pupils).

Phase CD reaches an important stage in the evolution of Chavin. The style turns toward a sort of baroque and convoluted expression at the time of the highest level of expansion of Chavin influence. At the center of this type of expression we find the "flayed-pelt convention" or "split representation" that is one of the causes of the baroque appearance of the artwork of this period. In this perspective the animal or figure is split in two along the axis of symmetry, so that mirror images are reflected on either side of the axis. Additionally the art incorporated more and more detail. Thus, if one compares birds of the CD period with the equivalent ones of the AB period, one can hardly recognize the animal in the CD period counterpart, where the head is split in two and shares a common mouth. The wings are kenned as snakes and extended down to the level of the legs. The whole becomes truly monstrous.

The most important theme of the CD period is the Tello Obelisk (figure 3.3). The obelisk is a motif with two heads: one of a puma, the other of a snake. From the second one emerges a feathered tail that most likely formed the top of the obelisk.

Figure 3.3: Tello Obelisk

The Raimondi Stela: The Staff Deity

During phase EF the complexity of the previous period in terms of compositional elements (flayed-pelt convention, kennings) is accompanied with a simplification at the level of its unit elements. This manifests most of all in the tendency toward rectangularity, leading on the one hand to the highly complex Stela Raimondi and on the other to simplified snake, feline, and human trait elements. After this stage Chavin art went through an abrupt transition, and regional art manifested in a host of different ways.

We can now turn our attention to the later Chavin Staff God of the famous Raimondi Stela of the phase EF (figure 3.4). The Staff God, holding a staff on either hand, seems to have replaced the earlier deities toward the end of Chavin. The serpent motif dominates the figure with a total of thirty. The central head, which looks like two heads in one, is amplified by four heads above it.

Figure 3.4: Raimondi Stela

The fact that the Raimondi Stela is one of the largest slabs found in Chavin indicates the importance of the Staff God. The sacredness of the being is underlined by the repetition of serpent kennings and jaguar mouth motifs. The motif of the stela also appears in a gold plaque of the Rafael Larco Herrera Museum in Lima, where the deity is accompanied by two smaller attendant figures that have a combination of human and bird attributes.

The Staff God is the emerging theme that will accompany much of later South American history. Could it be that Chavin was a place of preparation for future mysteries at the turning point of time? This would explain the name itself. *Chawa* means "in development" or "in preparation."[12] A new form of Staff God, with more clear solar attributes, is the one that we will see at the turning point of time in key civilizations of the Andes. Most significantly, the Staff God is the one that appears in the very famous Gateway of the Sun of the imposing old spiritual capital of the Andean high plateau—Tiwanaku.

At any rate, the adoption of the Staff God was an important step in the evolution of the oracle center. It formed the culmination of the message of Chavin. It marked a time of choice, and it seems that some religious centers cut their ties with Chavin soon after the introduction of the Staff God deity.[13]

The legacy of Chavin brought Andean humanity to a very critical time fraught with trials of the soul. In most instances it was a time of decadence. Signs of it had appeared earlier on. Already during phase C emerged the first iconographic evidence of trophy heads. In the transition from C to CD there is evidence of weapons, specifically atlatl and darts. This is the time of the Tello Obelisk.

The end of the influence of Chavin corresponds with the beginning of the time that archaeologists call the Early Intermediate Period. This was accompanied at first with the building of fortresses and fortified villages throughout Peru, indicating the beginning of a time of strife. The pivotal time of the Early Intermediate is what will occupy us here at the end of this chapter and in the next.

Decadence at the end of Chavin was visible in manifestations that indicate the introduction—or rather reintroduction—of practices of human sacrifice. Such is most likely the case of Cerro Sechin. On the other hand there is also emerging evidence that a new culture was starting to sow the seeds for a "solar revolution."

Chavin's Decadence and Sechin

We will now turn to the famous ruins of Cerro Sechin, a site in which appears abundant evidence of human sacrifice; moreover, of a type that is peculiar to Andean civilization. But first we need to present further evidence of the Chavin artistic time sequence that will allow us to place the phenomenon of human sacrifice in time, and that is far from explicit at first.

We will support our arguments on the artistic time sequence of Rowe and Roe and on the synchronicity of Cerro Sechin with a host of other sites. These two approaches give considerable support for the thesis of the appearance (or resurgence) of human sacrifice at the end of the Chavin civilization. What complicates matters is the fact that Cerro Sechin is a site whose existence spanned over many centuries and our focus turns only to a limited manifestation of the site. In fact three construction phases have been identified that very likely antedate the monoliths that concern us.

Sechin was discovered in 1937 by the famous Peruvian archaeologist J. C. Tello in the Casma Valley in the region of Ancash. The whole complex covers about 12 acres but only 20% has been excavated. The ruins cover a hill called Cerro Sechin, about 2.4 miles from the place where the Casma and Sechin rivers meet. The group has its main access to the north and three passages to east, west, and south. An outer wall built in stone encloses the earlier buildings. This outer wall of the perimeter is embedded with engraved monoliths. Tello catalogued a total of 302 of these.

Most of the monoliths represent bodies or anatomic body parts. Amazingly, no animals nor religious motifs are present and the style is absolutely realistic throughout. This alone indicates a movement toward decadence, moving away from the highly abstract and symbolically charged Chavin style. Among these monoliths appears evidence of human sacrifice in the sculpted images of warriors and prisoners, mutilated human bodies, disemboweled trunks, and body parts from vertebrae to organs, heads, enucleated eyes, pelvis bones, decapitated heads, etc. The mutilated bodies are those of either dead or live victims. From the above evidence, most generally Sechin is believed to have been a center devoted to human sacrifice, at least for what concerns this point of its history.[14]

The artistic quality of the monoliths is, generally speaking, rather inferior; among the monoliths appear some that were reused and others that were corrected in which the previous design can be detected under the later one. However, a very few refined monoliths also appear, almost out of context, leaving the viewer to wonder whether these were earlier, reutilized monoliths.

There are three basic hypotheses concerning the monoliths at Cerro Sechin:[15]

> *1. Sechin antedates Chavin.* Edward Lanning places Sechin no later than the very beginning of the Early Horizon (900–200 BC). L. Samaniego and A. Bueno place it in the fifteenth century BC as an ancestor to Chavin.

> *2. Sechin is a contemporary of Chavin's later stages.* This is the thesis of P. Roe on the basis of the elaborate monolith F of Sechin (figure 3.5). In this design, Roe says, appears a similar motif to the cords that serve to support the severed head of the Head Bearer (*Portador de Cabeza*) of the site of Yurayako. Kauffmann indicates that the eccentric eye and the big long tear (*lagrimon*, a hawk marking) are common to Cupisnique (along the coast) and Chavin. Bonavia and Lathrap agree that Sechin is a final expression of Chavin. What sustains this thesis is the fact that Sechin has none of the allegoric symbols of the earlier Chavin: condor, snake, jaguar, etc.

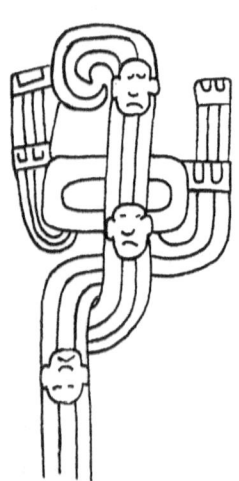

Figure 3.5: Sechin Monolith F

> *3. Sechin comes after Chavin.* Fung and Williams essentially indicate that Sechin is post-Chavin on the basis of the fact that the fishes etched

on an adobe wall of the site have characteristics of Late Chavin. The severed heads are present in pottery examples from the Late Chavin in Tembladera and Chankillo. Note that the third position is not always clearly differentiated from the previous one.

Overall the hypotheses that Sechin follows Chavin have far more support in archaeological circles than the first one. We tend to concur with A. Kroeber who states that Sechin is certainly no culmination of a style. Some simple observations reinforce the second and third hypotheses. Generally, the most decadent art comes at an end of a series, and Sechin clearly points to a period of decadence of a style, both in form and in content.

Let us move deeper into this exploration from an artistic perspective. We will remind the reader of what emerged from previous exploration. During the brief Chavin phase C (which includes the Tello Obelisk) appears the motif of warriors with weapons and of the trophy heads. Another theme briefly emerging is that of disembodied eyes (with pupils). However, this is just a brief interlude, followed by a return to previous themes and abandonment of war-related themes in the following CD phase.

The phase EF is characterized with simplification at the level of its unit elements that manifests most of all in the tendency toward rectangularity and a tendency to local artistic differentiation. The "head-bearer motif"—carrying a trophy head—reappears (figure 3.6). The heads in Sechin are very square and the same is true of hands and feet, another sign of late Chavin art. Severed, square human heads are numerous, although they are not held as trophy heads. All in all Cerro Sechin displays greater similarities with the EF part of the series and only occasionally with the AB. All of the above supports the notion that Sechin comes late in the Chavin sequence rather than early.

Although evidence of human sacrifice appears more clearly than anywhere else in Cerro Sechin, additional evidence shows that this was not a unique manifestation. Artistic evidence from the other four sites that can also be placed at the end of the Chavin period concurs with what has been offered so far.[16] Direct evidence of the kind of human sacrifices practiced at Cerro Sechin is discernable in Puemape during the Salinar occupation (300 BC to 0).[17] In a cemetery of this epoch are found two corpses, both beheaded. One of them also has the phalanges of feet and hands sawed off, just as the Sechin monoliths portray.

The decapitator motif is also found at the same epoch in the south coast in the so-called Oculate Being of Ocucaje (Ica River) traditio. He is an anthropomorphic figure with feline traits, often portrayed in flight. The circular eyes are those of the raptor and the mouth is U-shaped; the body is most often anthropomorphic. In some instances his figure is reduced to the head, which can take the shape of a mask. He often holds a decapitated head and a hafted knife. In addition he may carry a human head in the belly.[18] Historically the figure first appears in the so-called Phase 8 of Ocucaje, a little before the watershed time of the Early Intermediate Period. Like the Decapitator God of the north coast, this is the first iconographic figure that shows little relation to previous Chavin imagery. Not surprisingly we can also see a relationship of this new style with that of Pucara.[19]

Figure 3.6: Head-bearer motif

Ruins and Monoliths

Let us turn now to the wall of the outer perimeter of the site that is the center of our attention in this study. The stones of the wall were held together through the use of large monoliths alternating with smaller ones, small rock, and mortar. The alternation gave major solidity to the artistic work. The perimeter is interrupted to the north in alignment with the previous stairway of access.

Judging by their casual layout, Tello thought that the monoliths of Cerro Sechin had been reused. However, careful observation shows that they follow a master plan. In Sechin, as in Chavin, there is a concern for symmetry, first of all in the compositional flow, then in the arrangement of the stelae, with many paired ones on opposite sides of the main entrance. This dispels Tello's notion of a casual reuse of the monoliths at Cerro Sechin. What led the sacrificers to erect a rampart in stone, so different from the previous adobe constructions? It is likely that the façade was built—among other things—with the intent to intimidate the enemies.

There are many parallel monoliths; most of them are the largest ones, those that are higher than wider. These "dual monoliths" are distributed in an equidistant manner in the N-E and N-W-S walls, from the farthest parts to the north entrance. Between these dual monoliths only details differ.

The warriors look as if they were coming out of the same building from two sides and then returning to the north access. Only the dignitaries at the head of the procession are differentiated from the others by the symbols they display: they wear additional regalia and they hold in their upright hand what looks like a criss-cross of sticks or rays. These criss-cross motifs have been thought of as possible instruments of sacrifice. None of the characters is clearly a priest; most of them look like warriors, and their equality with other figures reinforces this interpretation. Their outfit is minimal and functional, which would have been an asset in conditions of great heat and physical exertion.

Chavin's art is individualized—a piece has value in and of itself. Sechin's monoliths only make sense in the integration of the whole. They give the feeling that the whole was conceived by one person and executed by assistants. Throughout Sechin's wall and neighboring places of the site, one thing is noticeable: the inferior overall quality of the artwork, ensemble care, and arrangement. Thus, six monoliths without motifs have been found, placed on the N-W-S wall in alternation with the severed heads. This leads one to think that this side of the monument was not finished, or that there may have been a rush to finish it. Two of the monoliths in the north wall are of an abstract kind in the form of elongated crosses. Another one of these was set above a lintel over a stone portal. These three monoliths are thematically different from the others, and are the only abstract ones, What was the reason for placing some monoliths—of a clearly different iconography—out of context? Was it a possible ideological justification with past tradition?

The scenes of human sacrifice include figures of the supposed priesthood and soldiers, sectioned bodies, decapitated heads, and anatomic parts. Streams of blood, represented as cords, appear under heads, limbs, trunks. However, there are no explicit trophy heads! It is noticeable that sacrificers and victims all belong to the same ethnic group. The most accepted idea is that the overall theme is that of a battle or—even more so—of a scene of ritual human sacrifice. In fact all the figures appear to be those of proud and haughty sacrificers and submissive and terrorized victims on the other side. Twenty-four upright figures are evenly distributed along the perimeter wall, alternating with the dismembered bodies or body parts. All of them are oriented toward the north, the direction of the central entryway. Sechin's northern orientation divides it into west and east moieties. This idea is reinforced by the twofold stairway of the first adobe building. In fact, the emphasis on the dual aspect goes probably back to the very origin of the building. We have seen this theme at the entrance of Chavin's Castillo. The symbolism of the outer wall points thus to ceremonial battles between the Hurin and Hanan moieties, a theme that continued throughout Andean history, with or without human sacrifice.

Themes of the Monoliths

Among the monoliths we can distinguish three themes:

- group A: high ranking dignitaries or priests
- group B: bodies, body parts, or organs of the sacrificed
- group C: abstract figures

Group A
This is a small percentage of the whole that represents dignitaries; four look to the left, four to the right. They generally hold a scepter, club, or symbol of power that looks rather uniform. They all wear a sort of loincloth. Under the eye, in the form of a U with a half-pupil in the upper part, lies the so-called hawk marking that crosses the whole face. Among all the others, monolith 2 stands out. It displays a stunning symbolic headdress that flows down the body, alternating lines with four small heads (see figure 3.5).

Group B
In this group we see sectioned bodies (without heads, with the torso and head alone, thigh sectioned off, arms cut off at various levels); bodiless heads (the great majority); or anatomic parts. The expression in the faces shows agony and terror as if they had been portrayed alive during the sacrificial act. This is recognizable in the eyes (very wide open), and the contracted mouth. The long thumbnail, broad feline nose, wide mouths showing the teeth, common to both victims and victimizers, are characteristics of animals of prey. This is another indication of the likelihood that the victims were captured in ritual battles.

In the subgroup of sectioned bodies appear desperate victims holding their entrails. Arms are either lowered over the abdomen or raised at the height of the head. Some show the head reclining backward; these are those of dead or recumbent bodies, portrayed in false perspective. The sectioned upper-half bodies' abdomens show inflections or widely serrated edges.

Bodiless heads are the most numerous—some of them without neck. Some of the heads are piled up high (up to twelve) and appear as a more abstract theme. Heads are most often shown in profile, except for those of more abstract nature that are shown frontally.

There are two types of eyes: open eye, or closed eye in a hammock form. The second, that of a dead person, is most predominant. The same design of the eyes appears separated from the head in string sequence. They correspond in all to the design of the eyes in the heads and they look like the open eyes of the mutilated beings. Paredes Ruiz puts forth the hypothesis that the prisoners had their eyes removed in order to avoid their flight at the moment of the sacrifice.[20] The heads are either shaved or only show three hairlocks—those that could serve for carrying the skulls—as representations elsewhere suggest.

Group C
Among these are some very tall banners; they are placed on both sides of the central area close to the stairway. They represent a vertical axis around which a rope is seemingly threaded; the whole sustains a narrow flag decorated with a motif of points and short lines.

Sechin seems to illustrate most clearly what the chronicles call the time of darkness and strife that preceded the Dawning. Historically it corresponds to the end of the Formative or to the first phase of the Early Intermediate Period, according to the views of various authors. Moreover, the monoliths indicate that there were other forms of human sacrifices, such as the ones of which Steiner speaks in relation to Mesoamerica. On the central coast, the priest-sacrificer seemed to have an obsession with occult physiology. Since the same theme appears in other places and other times of Andean history, we could imagine these practices to be associated with the perverted Mercury Mysteries. The progressive Mercury Mysteries on the other hand, appear in the importance that sacred measurement and proportion had, not only in architecture but in sacred geography, and in all of Andean spirituality. More of this will emerge later.

Almost at the same time that human sacrifices gained in ascendancy, a discreet, quiet presence along the Peruvian Coast may have been sowing seeds for the next historical phase. The site of Chankillo, not far from Sechin, may have been one of those places and seeds.

Chankillo: First Solar Culture

In 2007 evidence was brought to light of the existence of the first solar observatory, erected possibly in the fourth century BC. Chankillo is located 250 miles north of Lima in the coastal desert.[21] The observatory is a structure with concentric rings of fortified walls in a site that covers about 1.5 square miles. To the southeast of the site are thirteen towers that form a slightly curved spine embracing the topography of a ridgeline. The towers are regularly spaced at intervals of 16' from each other and are rectangular in shape, varying in surface from 800 to 1350 sq. ft. The ridgeline can be observed from two special towers within the fortress.

Unspecified artifacts found in the area, according to the researchers, indicate the ritualistic nature of the site. The observing points are placed at about 750' from the towers. At either end of the spine stand two towers that mark the solstices. The equinoxes are also marked with equal precision. The site, originally believed to be a fortress, is now recognized as a solar observatory. However, it may well have been fortified, given the time and circumstances in which it was built and its very proximity to Sechin. Chankillo is the first remarkable place where one sees the practice of solar horizon astronomy, the same one practiced much later by the Incas.

The discovery of Chankillo has great importance for later Andean history. If precise solar astrology was already known before the turn of our era, then the disputed claims of Inca solar astrology acquire a deeper foundation, and simply form part of a continuing tradition. More of the tradition of a solar astrology will emerge from our considerations concerning the next historical period, the one known as Early Intermediate Period.

We have come to the terminal phase of the Chavin civilization. It is time to draw the parallels with our Mesoamerican studies. On both sides of the equator we see two civilizations that appear as if out of nowhere; in other words, two spiritual impulses. This is what corresponds to the guidance of the king-priest, surviving later in time in the figure of the shaman. Both ages of the Olmec and Chavin saw the rise of the use of psychotropic substance in the ritual—tobacco, alcohol, coca, San Pedro cactus, etc.

Both civilizations also ushered in prophecies of the future. This appears in the Olmec civilization more clearly than in the South American counterpart through the ritual cultivation of maize and the Sacred Calendar. In Chavin it appears in iconography through the emergence of the Staff God and at the end with the first inklings of solar astronomy. The Andean agricultural calendar most likely originates from this time as well. Both civilizations acted as "missionary centers" out of which impulses were spread, without the need of occupying armies—new meaning was carried through the message enshrined in the portable art of the objects of ritual. In both civilizations, ritualistic traits and deities were superimposed on the local culture, which kept its traditions and integrated the new message. In both, a time of decadence set in before the turning point of time.

SPIRITUAL-SCIENTIFIC CONSIDERATIONS

The initial impetus of Chavin is oracular in nature. It is the civilization of the shaman who has recourse to tobacco, San Pedro cactus, or other hallucinogenics for the shamanic flight. It is the Chavin of the Lanzon god, the oracle of Chavin de Huantar who speaks in the room where the waters roar.

We have recognized some indicative traits of the Chavin civilization and unearthed commonalities with the Mesoamerican Olmec civilization. Eagle and jaguar point to some more primordial elements of Atlantean consciousness. Their symbolism is not exhausted through reference to its natural substratum. Rather, jaguar and eagle are the Lion and Eagle group spirits that worked as human group souls in Lemurian and Atlantean times.[22] For people of the Atlantean-like consciousness that survived throughout the Americas, the group-souls are still a concrete spiritual reality. Here too the parallels with the Olmec civilization continue in quite a remarkable fashion, and independently of cultural contact. As we pointed out in discussion of the Olmec civilization, jaguar and eagle play the role of Guardian of the Threshold, guarding the access of the shaman to the spirit world. The spirit journey is fraught with dangers from which the shaman-priest has to shield himself, and the Guardian tests the disciple's readiness to cross the threshold. However, this stage had to come to an end. The oracle of Chavin was preparing itself to traverse the ordeal of the cultural dark night of the soul. That is what can be detected in the transition from the Lanzon to the Staff God. The civilization of Chavin had the central mission of preparing Andean culture to cross the time of the Twilight of the Gods—the crucible of separation from perception of the divine that all cultures on earth have to cross, each in their own timing.

Another parallel to the Olmec civilization is the periodic resurfacing of human sacrifices. On the central coast, these sacrifices in all likelihood were already present a few millennia before the turning point of time. In Sechin Bajo, and less extensively in other sites along the coast, these sacrifices acquire particularities proper to South American culture. The most striking is the practice of a decadent occult physiology, availing itself of knowledge of the forces present in the organs. Here we see the cult that Steiner describes as the decadent Quetzalcoatl Mysteries, and which are carried out by the Lords of Xibalba in the Popol Vuh.

The theme of human sacrifices is confirmed in the mythological record preserved by later traditions up to the Inca, as we will see in the next chapter. The Ahrimanic deity takes on greater ascendancy in the figure of Ai-Apaec, the Decapitator God. This is in effect the hallmark of the trial that humanity faces with the loss of atavistic clairvoyance. Humanity is no longer protected from those powers that wish to draw it more deeply into matter and force it to forego human freedom. Myths, iconography, and the archaeological record mutually reinforce each other on this issue. The Twilight of the Gods is a time of trial. The loss of atavistic consciousness is a necessary test in which the Chavin civilization, not unlike the Olmec, fell short. The recourse to human sacrifice is the way to regain the lost atavistic consciousness beyond its time, at the cost of human freedom.

The old cosmologies no longer hold true, as it appears by the diminished role of the sunken courts and the cosmic referential of the Southern Cross. The Chavin culture suffered a rapid decline in the few centuries preceding the Early Intermediate Period or Fourth Age, in a way parallel to the Olmecs.

The early Chavin culture stressed the consciousness of the night, of those revelations that reached the priest through the night consciousness. The revolution of the next age is a growing new day-consciousness that is the response that the Andean human being offers to the challenge of the time of twilight. The preparation of this future can be detected in the observatory of Chankillo, where observation of the yearly sun's movement heralds a tentative new cosmology. Here the message of the second part of Chavin—the Raimondi Stela and its Staff God—is carried to a new level, announcing the future of the later civilizations of Gallinazo, Nazca, and Tiwanaku.

CHAPTER 4

Myths of the Collao: The Second Creation

M ANY VERSIONS OF THE CREATION MYTHS have been gathered by the Spanish chroniclers of the sixteenth century. Most of them come from the region around Lake Titicaca called Collao. Other versions come from the regions between Cuzco and Ecuador. We will give an entire rendition of one of the fullest accounts, the one given to us by Juan de Betanzos. This will give us the foundation from which to start our inquiry. To this version we will add the themes of another dozen of generally shorter versions of the same events.

The inhabitants of the Collao were traditional enemies of the Incas. Whereas the first belong to the Aymara ethnicity, the Incas are Quechua. However, all of the myths were collected after the Spanish conquest, and therefore it is unavoidable that some of the facts are colored by later Inca interpretation of the events.

Creation Myth of the Collao[1]

Chapter 1: Which concerns Contiti Viracocha, who they believe was the creator, and how he made the heavens and the earth and the Indian peoples of these provinces of Peru.

In ancient times, they say, the land and the provinces of Peru were dark and neither light nor daylight existed. In this time, there lived certain people who had a lord who ruled over them and to whom they were subject. The name of these people and that of their ruler have been forgotten.

During this time of total night, they say that a lord emerged from a lake in this land of Peru in the province of Collasuyo and that his name was Contiti Viracocha. They say that he brought with him a certain number of people, but they do not remember the number. When he had emerged from the lake he went from there to a place near the lake, where today there is a town called Tiahuanaco in the province of Collao referred to above. When he and his people arrived there, they say that he suddenly made the sun and the day, and ordered the sun to follow the course that it follows. Then, they say, he made the stars and the moon.

They say that this Contiti Viracocha had emerged another time before that one, and that on that first occasion he created the sky and the earth but left everything in darkness. Then he made those people who lived in the time of darkness previously mentioned. These people did some disservice to Viracocha, and since he was angry, he returned, emerging this last time as he had done before. In his anger, he turned to stone those he created first, together with their lord, as a punishment for annoying him. In that very moment, he made the sun and the day and the moon and stars, as we have said.

When this was done, there at Tiahuanaco, he made some people from stone as a kind of model of those that he would produce later. He made a certain number of them from stone in this way, together with a chieftain to govern and rule over them, and many women, some pregnant and others delivered. The babies were in cradles, according to their custom. When he had made all these of stone, he set them aside in a certain place and then made another province of people in the manner described. In this way, he made another people of Peru and of its provinces there in Tiahuanaco, forming them of stones in the way stated.

After he had finished making them, he ordered all those he had there with him to depart, leaving only two in his company. He instructed those who were left to look at the stone likenesses, and he told them the names he had given to each kind of people, pointing to them and saying, "These will be called the so and so and will come out of such and such a spring in such and such a province and will settle there and be increased; and these others will come out of such and such a cave and will be called the thus and so and will settle in such and such a province. Just the way I have painted them and made them of stone thus they must come out of the springs and rivers and caves and mountains in the provinces that I have told you and named, and you will go at once, all of you, in this direction," pointing toward the sunrise, taking each one aside individually and showing him the direction he was to follow.

Chapter 2: Which concerns how the people of this country emerged under the orders of Viracocha and of the viracochas he sent to accomplish this task; how Contiti Viracocha and the two that remained with him left to do the same work, and how Viracocha rejoined his people at last after having finished, and how he put out to sea, never to be seen again.

So these *viracochas* of whom you have heard left and traversed the provinces that Viracocha had told them. When they arrived at the place where they were going in each province, they called on those whom Viracocha had pointed out to them in Tiahuanaco of stone as being the ones who had to emerge in that province. Each *viracocha* stationed himself next to the place where he had been told that these people had to come out, and then said in a loud voice, "So and so, come out and people this land, which is now uninhabited, because Contiti Viracocha, who made the world, has so ordered it." As the *viracochas* called them, the proper people came out of the places that Viracocha had appointed. So they say that these *viracochas* went along, calling and bringing out the people from the caves, rivers and springs, and high sierras, as you have already heard in the previous chapter, peopling the country in the direction where the sun rises.

When Contiti Viracocha had sent out his agents and they had gone in the manner stated, they say that he sent the two who had stayed with him in the town of Tiahuanaco to call and bring out the people in the way you have heard, dividing the two as follows. He sent one to the province of Condesuyo, which is on the left, if you are at Tiahuanaco with your back to the sunrise, so that he could go and do what the first ones had done and call out the Indians and natives of the province of Condesuyo. The other he sent likewise to the province of Andesuyo, which is on the right if you are placed in the manner stated with your back to the sunrise.

After these two had been dispatched, they say that Viracocha himself set out straight ahead toward Cuzco, which is in between these two provinces, traveling by the royal road that goes through the sierra toward Cajamarca. As he went along, he also called and brought out the peoples in the way you have already heard.

When he came to a province that they call Cacha, which belongs to the Canas Indians and is eighteen leagues from the city of Cuzco, Viracocha called out these Canas Indians. They came out armed, however, and did not know Viracocha when they saw him. They all came at him with their arms to kill him. When he saw them coming, he understood what they were coming for and instantly caused fire to fall from heaven, burning a range of mountains near the Indians. When the Indians saw the fire, they feared they would be burned. Throwing their arms to the ground, they went straight to Viracocha and all threw themselves to the ground before him. When he saw them thus, he took a staff in his hands and went where the fire was. He gave it two or three blows with his staff, which put it completely out, whereupon he told the Indians that he was their maker. The Canas Indians built a sumptuous *guaca*, which means a shrine or idol, at the place where he stood when he called the fire from heaven and from which he went to put it out. In this *guaca* they and their descendants offered a great quantity of gold and silver. They set up a stone statue carved from a great stone almost five *varas* in length and one vara in width, more or less, in the *guaca*, in memory of Viracocha and of what had taken place there. This *guaca* has stood there from ancient times until today, and I have seen the burned mountain and the burned stones. The burned area is more than a quarter of a league across.

When I saw this wonder, I called on the oldest Indians and leading men and asked them the explanation of that burned mountain. They told me what you have heard. The *guaca* of Viracocha is a stone's throw in front of the burned area on a plain across a river that runs between the burned area and the *guaca*. Many people have crossed the river and have seen the *guaca* and the stone statue, because they have heard the story from the Indians. I asked the Indians what this Viracocha looked like when the ancients saw him, as far as they have information. They told me that he was a tall man dressed in a white garment that reached to his ankles and was belted at the waist. His hair was short and he had a tonsure like a priest. He went bare-headed and carried in his hands something that seemed to them to resemble the breviaries that priests of today carry. This is the account that I obtained from these Indians. I asked them the name of the personage in whose place the stone was erected, and they said his name was Contiti Viracocha Pacha-yachachic, which means "God, maker of the world" in their language.

Going back to our story, they say that after he had worked this miracle in the province of Cacha, he went on, continuing his work. When he reached the place that is now called the Tambo of Urcos, six leagues from the city of Cuzco, he climbed a high mountain and sat down on the highest point, where they say he ordered the native Indians who now live there to come out of that high place. Because Viracocha sat there, they built a rich and sumptuous *guaca* in that place. Because he had sat down, they made a bench of fine gold and set the statue of Viracocha on it. In the division of spoils that the Christians made when they took Cuzco, this bench was valued at 16,000 or 18,000 pesos of fine gold.

Viracocha went on, making people as you have heard, until he reached Cuzco. Here, they say, he made a lord whom he himself named Alcavicça, and he also gave the name Cuzco to the place where he made this lord. He ordered that the *orejones* should emerge after he had left. He went on, continuing his work, until he reached the province of Puerto Viejo. There he met the others whom he had sent out, as has been said. He went out across the sea with them; they say that he amid his companions walked on water as if on land.

A Comparative Look at the Myths

Veronica Salles-Reese has collected and compared sixteen versions of the cycle of creation myths of the Collao.[2] The following is the average plot of the majority of the myths. During a first creation, Viracocha created the world and within it a race of giants. The creator gave humanity precepts to live by, which over time it started to neglect. Viracocha's wrath brought a punishment upon the human beings, sometimes depicted as the Flood. Five accounts specify clearly that the world was previously wrapped in darkness. The other versions do not deny this. In fact, all of them imply that the second creation involved a passage from darkness into light or from a state of chaos to a new order. Four accounts also refer to humanity as being created twice.

Most of the versions of the creation myth refer to both creations as being the result of the deeds of Viracocha. However, at the time of the second creation, most of them describe him as a human being walking upon earth. Juan de Santacruz Pachacuti Yamqui—one of the native chroniclers most interested in and immersed into aspects of Andean esotericism—differentiates the second Viracocha with the name of Thunupa. Ramos Gavilan says that Thunupa—also called Taapac—was the "Son of the Creator." Finally, according to Cristobal de Molina, Viracocha had two sons by the name of Tocapo Viracocha and Imaymana Viracocha. They both spread their father's message throughout the land, one by traveling along the coast, the other through the mountains. In the version of Betanzos, fully reported above, the two were servants of Viracocha. The terms *sons* or *servants* are spiritually speaking equivalent; the two Viracochas are beings that work in concert with the being who sent them, and therefore can be called sons or servants.

The overall themes of creation of a first world followed by its destruction and the subsequent creation of a new race, or survival of the few elect of the previous race through the deeds of a bodily emanation of the creator, also appear in myths others than the ones we will consider.[3] According to the various versions of the Collao myth, the second creation occurred in either the Island of the Sun—in Lake Titicaca—or in the famous Tiwanaku, situated very close to it to the south.[4] Many renderings of the myth mention a confrontation occurring between Viracocha and the Canas Indians of Cacha, also close to Lake Titicaca. Finally, most of the versions indicate that Viracocha traveled from the southeast to the northwest, disappearing in a kind of apotheosis over the waters of the Pacific Ocean. This peregrination from southeast to northwest reflects the sun's daily and yearly movements. Daily, the sun rises in the east and sets in the west. During the year it is at its strongest at the December solstice, when it shines from the south, and weakest at the June solstice, when it shines from the north. This second movement from south to north is superimposed on the east-west movement in generating the so-called path of Viracocha from Lake Titicaca toward the Pacific Ocean on the northern part of Peru or of Ecuador. This path has deeper meanings that tie in with all of Andean cosmology, as we will discover later.

The being that the Collas called Thunupa, according to Bertonio, was identified in other parts of Peru as Ecaco.[5] One of the possible meanings of Thunupa is "tree of life," or "tree that sustains life."[6] He is also called Taguapaca, Curinaya, or Huariwillca in other parts of the Andes. His name is often related to trees or their fruits, because it was the initiate, according to myths and tradition, who gave the name to plants and taught people about their uses. It is interesting to note in passing that occasionally—in Cristobal de Molina's version as well as the above story of de Betanzos—the envoy of Viracocha is not one but two. This evokes the familiar idea of the Twins, expressed in Mesoamerica and in the southwest United States among the Pueblo Indians.

The God-man Viracocha, or Thunupa—according to the versions of the legend—often appears as a bearded man, wearing a white tunic that reaches his feet, and carrying a staff. His two most prominent gifts are the ability to perform healing and to speak in the tongues of the people he meets. Additionally, he is referred to as a prophet. Among the Aymara, Thunupa is closely associated with thunder. Symbolically he is also associated to the puma. The sky puma (or cat *Ccoa*) is in effect the being that has power over the weather through thunder, lightning, and rain.

It is interesting to note an intriguing, recurring association between the prophet Thunupa, or Viracocha, and a Christian apostle. It is not only the assumption of many chroniclers, all of them of Spanish origin, but also of Santacruz Pachacuti, of Andean origin. The latter comes to the conclusion that the prophet was Saint Thomas—thought to have reached the Americas—on the basis of the spiritual convergence between the message of the Christ and the Prophet's role in the Americas.[7] Others identify this individual as Saint Bartholomew, for example Guaman Poma, or even with Spain's patron Saint, Santiago (Saint James), whom the natives also associated with lightning and with the Milky Way.

Even today there is a surviving tradition of the Prophet's memory in the statuettes of the so-called Thunupa-Ekako.[8] These represent an individual carrying a burden on his back, containing the gifts that the civilizing hero is bringing to his people. The burden on his back is the source of the assimilation with and representation of the being as a hunchback. It is a popular belief that hunchbacks bring luck or are chosen individuals of Thunupa. In archaeological statuettes of the hunchback Thunupa, the prominent sexual organ was an association with the fertility role of the being in relation to the meteorological phenomena of thunder, lightning, and rain that enrich the earth.

Another salient aspect of the creation myths is the simultaneous appearance of the Prophet and the occurrence of the Dawning. In one isolated instance placed in relation to Inca times, we are also told by Cristobal de Molina: "They also declare that when the sun, in the form of a man, was ascending into heaven, very brilliant, it called to the Incas and to Manco Capac."[9] The Sun in the form of a man is a theme that appeared previously in the Popol Vuh. As in North America, the event of the Dawning is accompanied with the idea of differentiation of the tribes and separation of their languages. The myth expresses it with the notion that the

Prophet gives the tribes their distinctive dresses that identify them and separate them from all the others.

Let us review what we have gathered so far. The being who is sent by Viracocha walks the earth as one or two human beings. He comes at a time of a new creation and ushers in the transition from a time of darkness to a time of daylight. He marks the end of an age and a beginning of a qualitatively different one. The sun that rises in the heavens is also said to have the appearance of a man. All of these are the traits that the Popol Vuh describes as the beginning of the Fourth Age, which was found to correspond to the inauguration of the solar calendar and the attainment of the idea of immortality.

The myths of the Collao attribute a central importance to Tiwanaku's civilization whose onset is given by some authors toward the beginning of our era, and by the majority to some centuries later. Many authors also indicate that Tiwanaku inaugurated a transition toward a solar calendar. Stated differently, this means that Chavin civilization dealt with issues very similar to the Olmec civilization in the centuries that followed the progressive diminution of their impulses: the dread of mortality and the "extinction of time"; the probable loss of an astronomical referential point (Ursa Minor and Southern Cross); and a decadence of civilization and the appearance—or reappearance—of human sacrifice.

Other aspects differentiate the South American Dawning from the northern counterpart. An important concept of South American spirituality is the idea of the *paqarin*. Before the luminaries filled the heavens, there appeared a condition of twilight. *Paqarin* means "to be born" or "to dawn." It refers to either the time just before the Dawning or the space on the horizon illuminated by the emerging sun. From these concepts arises the idea that each tribe of the Andes emerged from a particular geographical feature: a cave, a mountain, a lake, spring, a tree, etc. Each one of these tribes witnessed the Dawning from a different place along the Andes. The concept of *paqarin* is therefore closely associated with the Dawning, the place of emergence, and also the star on the horizon or overhead at the time of the Dawning.

We will now turn to the records of archaeology that make the legends fully understandable. To do that we will see how the same reality manifested in different parts of the Andean territory.

CHAPTER 5

Fourth Age: The Time of Thunupa

INFORMATION GATHERED FROM VARIOUS HISTORICAL SOURCES seems partly contradictory. We are told that the Early Intermediate Period (EIP) was, on the one hand, a time of strife; and on the other, a time of cultural development characterized by the differentiation of local cultures. The period of strife was marked by the appearance of fortresses and fortified cities. The motif of the decapitated trophy-heads appeared on the coast where it had previously been rare.[1] What seems most likely is that cultural development followed the period of strife, since renewal could not have been achieved without a large level of free cooperation among tribes and ethnic groups. Examples of it will follow in our study.

The EIP was marked by the spectacular development of cities and technological innovation. Levels of population increased drastically, which corresponded almost everywhere with the founding of new settlements. An example of this comes from the Ayacucho Valley. During the Huarpa period (0–400 AD) the local population had started terracing the mountains. It was also in this period that the first irrigation canals were built, such as the one of Racay Pampa. Between 200 and 400 AD, the population must have expanded, judging by the fact that there were almost three hundred small settlements in the territory.[2] The large ceremonial centers of Cahuachi (Nazca) and Tiwanaku also blossomed at this stage.

Tiwanaku was the center from which spread new ways of farming. Around 500 BC terracing, irrigation, and the techniques of raised beds around the edges of the lake spread in the region of Tiwanaku and Lake Titicaca.[3] It has been estimated that 200,000 acres of irrigated raised beds existed along the western shores of Lake Titicaca alone.[4]

In the artistic realms, both the coast and the high plateau witnessed a time of intense renewal. Artistic innovation, particularly in pottery, gave a rise to distinct new styles on the north coast, with the blossoming of Virú, Vicús, and other local cultures. Art of great beauty was achieved both in Nazca (southern Peru) and Tiwanaku. The same occurred in the northern, central, and southern highlands. By this time the artistic motifs of Chavin had gradually disappeared, and different regions evolved uniquely different types of art.

To illustrate the changes introduced by the EIP we will look at three examples of different cultures or groups of cultures: the north-central coast, Nazca, and Tiwanaku. The latter two offer some of the most spectacular developments of Andean culture at this stage. The example of the north coast offers the clearest indication about the alternating fortunes of the EIP, and the ideological antagonisms that shaped it. Here, more than in other parts of the Andes, it is possible to articulate what was the object at stake at the heart of the "cultural wars" of the age.

The North-Central Coast

In the north coast, Chavin's penetration came later than in most of Peru. During the first half of the first millennium (1000 to 500 BC) there was a noticeable cultural decline in what is known as the Cupisnique culture of the time. The construction of new centers came to a stop and others were left unfinished. Some were abandoned and many places left empty. The coastal populations continued to occupy their settlements, but the farmers moved further inland. Agricultural output suffered, and the displaced populations often moved to higher places close to fortified strongholds. All of this suggests the outbreak of hostilities. This was very likely the result of political centralization, while evidence shows invasions from the highlands. Major ecological disruptions—volcanic activity and tidal waves—took place around 500 BC. By that time at least the southern half of the territory was engulfed in conflict.[5]

At Alto de las Guitarras, in the canyon that connects Moche with Virú Valley, are found many petroglyphs of Classic Cupisnique (1500-1000 BC). The themes constantly represented in this period are either cut heads or decapitators.[6] After 500 BC the north coast region assimilated elements of Chavin culture. There was a replacement of the declining Initial Period

(1000–500 BC) ideology with the new Chavin iconography, and Chavin symbolism merged with the local art. This was accompanied by innovations in weaving and metallurgy. The new influences also brought in the formation of social stratification, particularly detectable in the richness of elite burials. However, the Chavin cultural revival was short lived and came to an end by the third century BC, at which time Chavin itself was being abandoned. What followed was the diversification of local styles and the construction of defensive fortresses at a level heretofore unprecedented.

Archaeologists have found that the transition to the EIP in the north coast was accompanied by the Salinar and Gallinazo horizons. Salinar came to the fore around 200 BC; Gallinazo followed about a century later. Gallinazo later continued alongside the much more famous Moche culture. Salinar, Gallinazo, and Moche, it is now hypothesized, are different cultural manifestations of the same people. However Salinar and Moche were not contemporary. Only the Gallinazo formed a link with the previous Salinar and the later Moche. Interestingly, the Salinar style is what establishes the continuity between the late Chavin themes and the successive Moche tradition. This is more of an ideological link, since Salinar and Moche had little overlap. How this could have happened will become clear in the next chapter.

Salinar culture experienced a time of social unrest, with neighboring tribes attacking each other. This was accompanied by movements away from the lower valleys and the occupation of higher, more easily fortifiable valleys. A clear example of this is present in Cerro Arena of the Moche Valley, the largest documented Salinar site occupying the top of a large ridge. In Cerro Arena appeared the formation of an urban life that had not clearly emerged previously.

The Gallinazo introduced a distinctive, elite pottery, emerging first in the Virú Valley and from there to the neighboring valleys. This culture ushered in great change and introduced a time of social harmony. With the newly introduced stability, people lived again in peace. They returned to their agricultural valleys and extended irrigation channels to new areas. The production of maize, fruits, and vegetables greatly increased. The earlier patterns of close settlements resumed and so did the building of pyramid platforms. The number and size of settlements increased. Very large settlements appeared: Cerro Orejas in the Moche Valley, Licapa in the Chicama Valley, and Huaca Santa in the Santa Valley. Cerro Blanco (lower Moche Valley) ushered in the foundations of what later became the famous Moche capital. To the north the Gallinazo had impressive ceremonial buildings in the Leche Valley, particularly in Paredones. Here the Huaca Latrada platform measured 320' x 190' and 64' high. Overall, the Gallinazo presence was extensive throughout the north coast from the Santa Valley to Ecuador's borders.

In the Virú Valley, the Gallinazo built a town extending over three square miles that was the center of extensive agricultural land. High-ranking individuals were buried with a display of wealth that had not been seen in previous times. The settlements and cultivated areas reached their greatest extent. All of this the Gallinazo leaders could achieve through the recourse to large amounts of organized labor that seemed to have occurred without coercion.

We have briefly touched on the contrast between Late Chavin and Salinar on one hand, and Gallinazo cultures on the other. The same fluid contrast of ideologies was present later in the centuries through the Gallinazo-Moche antagonism. Here too, no clear divergence of ethnic background is visible; rather, an ongoing ideological struggle simmered under the surface before reaching a dangerous pitch. Moche is well-known as the culture that reintroduced human sacrifice earliest among Andean civilizations; in fact, it was the one that ushered in Guaman Poma's decadent Fourth Age earlier than anywhere else in Peru. We will return to this aspect in the next chapter.

The Rise of Tiwanaku

No other ruins in South America have exerted the deep fascination and raised as many questions from scientists as those of Tiwanaku in the Bolivian high plateau (see map 1, p. 14). Macchu Picchu and Cuzco have attained a higher fame with the wider public and presently receive a steady flow of visitors. These two places are part of a later time in history, relatively well understood by researchers. In Tiwanaku lie hidden many questions. The cyclopean dimension of temples and sculptures speaks of people with a very different consciousness from the present. It is very unfortunate that Tiwanaku was ignored and dismantled piece by piece before its value was acknowledged. Thus, many of the original carved blocks now lie at a distance from the old spiritual capital of the southern Andes.

The word Tiwanaku possibly means "the huanaco at the edge of the world" in Aymara, language of the Bolivian high plateau.[7] The huanaco is a camelid, a close relative of the llama. The Aymara civilization flourished before the Quechua that is closely associated with the Incas. In old times Tiwanaku was also known as Taypicala, according to the Spanish chronicles. Its meaning is "Foundation Stone" or "The foundation stone found at the edge of the world."[8] The meanings associated with the two words—Tiwanaku and Taypicala—may not be as contradictory as it seems. The huanaco was identified as the oldest animal species upon which depended pastoral life, consequently a divinity and a foundation stone of civilization. The brothers Elorrieta Salazar point out that aerial photography of the site shows that the outline of the ceremonial center of Tiwanaku has the shape of a huanaco or llama head.[9] This is not the first time that we mention the unique trait of Andean architecture and esotericism—what we could define as sacred landscapes or "fields of power."

As mentioned previously, Tiwanaku played a special role in the development of the new kind of agriculture that propelled the changes introduced during the EIP. All around Lake Titicaca were raised fields—culture beds, artificially raised by removing the soil from the adjacent ditches and piling it up on the beds. The ditches served as irrigation channels. The system could be quite elaborate, as can be seen in Pampa Koani, where the channels were lined with boulders and cobbles and covered with a thick layer of good imported soil.[10] This enormous expenditure of energy was justified for a number of reasons. First, the yields were increased by 100 percent or more over regularly plowed and tilled fields. The standing water has a homeostatic function, serving to minimize temperature fluctuations and temper the effect of frost, thus allowing more crops per year. Nitrogen-fixing plants naturally grow in the ditches and, once drained, these went to periodically enrich the fields. A modern experiment has proven these assertions. The old fields of Pampa Koani have been put under cultivation and the crops survived the 1982–83 drought, thanks to the water from nearby springs that fed the channels. This agricultural innovation offers a first indication of the revolution ushered in by the Tiwanaku civilization.

Various communities were in competition with Tiwanaku: Pucara and Chiripa among them. Tiwanaku held no special advantage over the others; in fact, it could be argued that Chiripa's position, close to the shores of Lake Titicaca, offered it a competitive edge. Scientists are left to wonder why Tiwanaku prevailed over the others. However, a few facts could elucidate the mystery. Tiwanaku's rise was not due to military force. In fact it has been recognized as a center of pilgrimage, a center of spiritual influence that exerted a great appeal far and wide. According to Alan Kolata, the rise of the city to ceremonial center occurred between 100 and 300 AD. By 300 AD it had achieved uncontested preeminence in the region.[11]

Layout of the City

In the pre-Classic phase of its rise to power, Tiwanaku still carried over artistic motifs from Chavin. With time it evolved a unique art characterized by very large, even gigantic, monoliths, and accompanied by a very high level of abstraction. In Tiwanaku also appeared realistic portraits of the human figure.

William Isbell offers a stylistic chronology of Tiwanaku in which he distinguishes phases Tiwanaku I, II, and III. The first two phases do not have clear markers in time; the third goes from 100 to 500 AD.[12] Little is known about the early phases Tiwanaku I and II. At the end of Tiwanaku II was built the so-called semi-subterranean temple. During Tiwanaku III occurred the construction of Kalasasaya and Pumapuncu, each covering more than 2 acres. The two have U-shaped platforms with open ends to the east, a motif that is carried over from earlier ages of Andean civilization. In both buildings, access to the top was reached through a gateway and immediately behind it was a sunken court. There probably was a monolith in front of each court. Another important building, the Akapana pyramid, covered almost 8 acres.

Tiwanaku stood at the center of a hierarchy of geographical space. The arrangement of the city's monuments was mirrored throughout the neighboring territory in other secondary cities from 6 to 12 miles away. At Qallamarca, 7 miles from Tiwanaku, there was a smaller temple similar to Kalasasaya; in Chiripa, on the shore of Lake Titicaca, a ceremonial center with a temple similar to the semi-subterranean temple; in Wankani there was a platform like that of the Kalasasaya.[13]

The Akapana remained Tiwanaku's singular and unique monument. In fact Tiwanaku was built from the center formed by the Akapana, one of the largest structures and its spiritual heart. The Akapana is a very unique pyramid of about 650' x 650', of a very distinct bilateral symmetry, that surges in seven stages toward a superior sunken court. (Figure 5.1) Most of it is crumbled at present. It is a recent discovery that the Akapana is in fact an entirely human-made construction. The pyramid forms half of an Andean Cross, which actually corresponds to the important symbol of the TAU, relating to the Great Spirit. The upper terraces were adorned with carved, painted

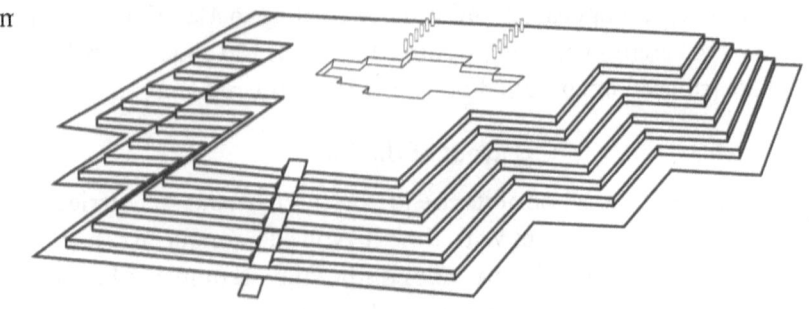

Figure 5.1: Reconstructed Akapana

The sunken court, filled with water, may have carried some of the large monoliths that have rendered Tiwanaku famous. The Akapana mimics a mountain, particularly a mountain in relation to its springs and waters. This is emphasized by the complex drainage system that starts at the top, draining the central sunken court. This system drained water from the upper terrace to the next lower one. From one terrace to the other the water resurfaced for a while before sinking to the next level. So there was a system of surface water alternating with deep drainage at every step until the water emerged at the base of the pyramid and then discharged in the Tiwanaku River.[14] There is speculation that the court may have been filled with water to a constant level, since an evacuation water channel is recognizable. It is also conceivable that there could have been a temporary lake around the pyramid, as Miranda Luizaga claims. In fact, in the site of Lukurmata there was clearly an island core of the site.[15] As in Chavin, there may have been an additional acoustic effect of the waters raging through the channels during a storm, and imitating the thunderstorm.

The Akapana's drainage system does not correspond to any utilitarian need and is far too complex for that function alone, just as we saw previously in Chavin's Old Temple. It actually imitates the flow of water in the Quimsachata mountains, where surface streams alternate with subterranean streams. This was an important geographical feature since the raised fields of the altiplano depended on the water coming from it.

F. and E. Elorrieta Salazar have studied the etymology of the word *Akapana*. Its most likely meaning is something like "the multi-colored breaking through of the sun at dawn." What appears from this word is the Akapana's relation to a new age, a new beginning, and possibly its relation to the time of the Dawning, the Second Creation. It is significant in this relation that the Akapana very likely bore a miniature lake on its top. This could have served as another commemoration of the most celebrated site of emergence, the sacred rock on the Titicaca's Island of the Sun.

Everywhere throughout Tiwanaku can be discerned the natives' knowledge of the golden mean, and the Fibonacci series that derives from it. According to Miranda Luizaga, the Akapana forms in effect the center around which are arranged, according to a higher order, other monuments and even cities. Four other monuments are arranged equidistant from the Akapana: the pyramid of Puma Punku (the Pyramid of the Moon), the Pantheon, Tunti Lluri, and the temple of Wila Pukara (figure 5.2).[16] After drawing a circle around these four points we can build the next square according to the proportion of the golden mean (a:b = b:c). This gives four points that Miranda Luizaga identifies as the farthest edges of the city, its outer confines. Repeating the process once more we find four cities of Oruro, Santa Ana, Tacna, and Pucara at the vertices of the square (not shown on the map. This application of the Andean cross measuring system also shows the cultural continuity with the previous ages of Andean cultural development.

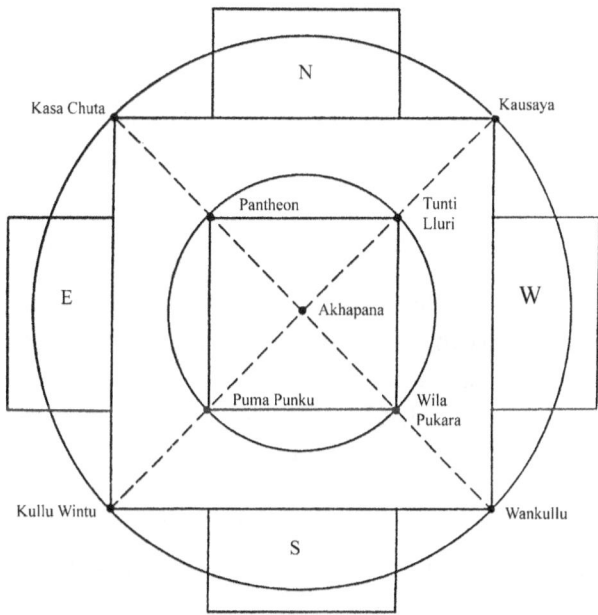

Figure 5.2: Quadripartition of Tiwanaku and surroundings

The general plan of Tiwanaku would be a circle within a square (quadripartition). The Akapana would have been the core of the northern moiety and Puma Punku the center for the southern moiety, according to A. Kolata and C. Ponce Sangines.[17] Puma Punku—pyramid of the Moon—was the lynchpin of the southern ceremonial complex in the city. Akapana and Puma Punku's doorways face the east. Both of them also had staircases to the west. This novel east-west orientation was also shared by Kalasasaya, Chunchukala, and Putuni buildings. The western staircases are significantly smaller than the eastern ones.

The new east-west axis and cosmology played a major role in the city. The center was occupied by the Sacred Mountain, the stepped pyramid of the Akapana. The three peaks of Mount Illimani are to the east, the lake to the west. Both are visible only from the summit of the pyramid. Only from the top was the sun path completely visible.

The east-west orientation is further accentuated by topography. The ceremonial core of Tiwanaku was surrounded by an immense artificial moat that restricted access to the sacred city. It made the center look like an island, like the mythic site of Atlantean world creation and emergence. Thus moving from the outside in was like entering a sacred space. There were also two additional moats to the east of the primary moat. The movement from the east toward the center marked progressive hierarchical demarcations. This is a theme that preceded Tiwanaku and that continued later through the centuries.

Tiwanaku Iconography

Tiwanaku's art is very abstract. There is practically no narrative. The basic unit of iconography is something like a glyph that is used and repeated more or less in a standard form. The glyph is part of a limited repertory, very tied to formal convention. Curiously, the art is modeled around the sensitivity, skill, and limitations present in the art of weaving. The process used in forming the figure is in all very similar to what can be seen in the textiles, like those of Paracas in the southern Peruvian coast.

The following are some of the main glyphs: feline head, condor head, fish head, threefold feather, feather with (solar) disc, pedestal with an oval disc on top, shell, meander, and concentric circle sign (*cocha*). Three figures play a very central role. The fish head has been recognized as a symbol for water, the feline associated with the night and the earth, and the bird with the day and the air. This list is completed with some more elaborate exceptional signs, such as those prominent in the motifs of the famous Gateway of the Sun. Some examples are: trumpeter, bi-headed arch with fish in the middle, double crown, fantastic bird with head of a fish, fantastic feline head, and paired birds with very long wings.

A further iconographic differentiation is achieved through the use of figures in either a frontal or profile position. Among these we find: anthropomorphic figures, bird anthropomorphs, feline anthropomorphs, snail anthropomorphs, and camelids (llamas, huanacos). The orientation of the personage (frontal or profile) does not determine who the figure is, as has long been believed. The difference is probably a matter of hierarchy, with the frontal one being the more important. The identity is expressed by the appearance (e.g., whether purely human or anthropomorph), the signs and glyphs that decorate the vestments, or the headdress of the being. The frontal deity can be represented as a whole figure or just as a head over a step-podium. All supernaturals wear diadems of feathers with appendices. The spiritual character is underlined by the radiating headdress, or the big tear under and around the eye. The radiating headdress itself is clearly the fruit of the introduction of a new solar symbolism.

Chief among all the monoliths of the altiplano capital the so-called gateways stand out, and particularly the Gateway of the Sun. The fullness of its symbolism is only partly replicated in other Tiwanaku monoliths. Its location is puzzling, because it has been proven that such an architectural element was meant to be part of a larger structure and was not destined to be free-standing as it is at present. The Gateway of the Sun may have been part of a project that was never finished. It was found in the northeast corner of the great ceremonial enclosure called Kalasasaya, north of the Akapana pyramid. There is another gateway called Gateway of the Moon whose original location is not known either. The two gateways have similar elements such as friezes of stepped pedestals that form meanders, radiating faces, the Staff God, etc.

The central figure of the gateway, which we can call a Thunupa-Sun God, is the most discussed of the deities of Tiwanaku—variously known as the Gateway God, the Great Image, or the Staff God. The free-standing monolith measures 9' high and 12' wide. All the sculpted material is found longitudinally above the portal. The central motif of the Gateway God stands out by its size and the three-dimensionality that separates it from the rest of the low-relief carvings. The deity represented by a human figure holds a staff in either hand. Here we clearly see further elaborated—and with a new solar connotation—the motif that first appeared in Chavin with the Stela Raimondi (see figure 3.4, p. 65).

To each side of the main figure are found twenty-four winged attendants in three rows of eight. Under the deity can be seen what has been called a "solar meander" with the Staff God in the central position and an additional eleven solar faces (See half of the solar meander in figure 5.3). What unites these faces to the central Gateway God is the meander formed by the bicephalic serpent, a motif already known from Chavin. However, in Tiwanaku the heads are represented by profiles of the royal condor, a reference to the powers of air and light, whereas in Chavin, the serpent was closely associated with the puma. This indicates once again an important change of consciousness.

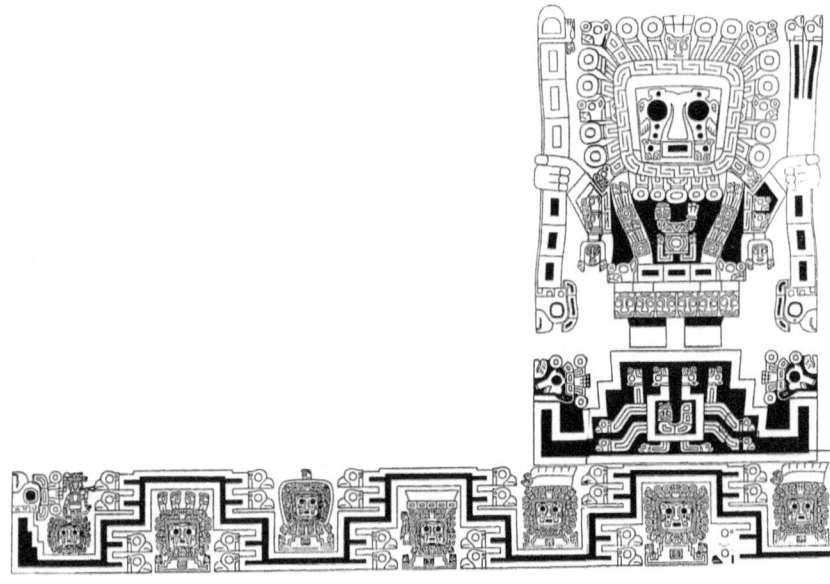

Figure 5.3: Left half of the Sun's Gateway solar meander

The Sun Calendar of the Gateway

One of the pioneers of Tiwanaku studies, A. Posnanski, considered the Gateway of the Sun to be a solar calendar. The eleven faces plus the central deity formed in his view the twelve months of the year. Ibarra

Grasso confirmed Posnanski, adding that the calendar year was achieved through the sum of twelve thirty-day months and an additional five to six days of a ritual month. Many others support the hypothesis with different variations. The main idea has been further elaborated in recent times by Krzysztof Makowski Hanula.[18]

Not only is the new radiating gesture highly indicative of the Sun, but so are the disc symbols attached at the end of the feathers. If the central image is that of the Sun, then the other ones must be variants of it, since they all share the same posture. A first indication of the likelihood of the hypothesis is that the majority of the headdresses have twenty-four feathers. If, as many researchers have agreed, the complex alternating and repetition of frontal figures represent calendrical aspects of the Sun, we should be able to find the position of solstices, equinoxes, and zenith within a sequence of twelve solar months.

There are seven variations of the solar motif: the great central staff deity, five pairs in the solar meander, and the last, nonmatching one, standing below the Staff God (figure 5.3). The differences among the variants consist in figurative details: the type of feathers in the headdress and larger associated designs (double birds, trumpeter, arch motif, etc.)

The Great Image (Staff God) of the Gateway is the most central and most complex, as well as the one with the most glyphs. From an overall study of all Tiwanaku's monoliths, Krzysztof Makowski Hanula has ascertained that the beings that stand on a podium decorated with felines are higher ranked than the ones with bird podiums. The five podiums of the upper part of the meander are adorned with feline heads, whereas the four of the lower half have bird heads. On the basis of the symbolism we have already explored, the upper half would represent the rainy season (feline, fishes); the lower half the dry season (birds); the Great Image, standing on the top, would then represent the December solstice of the rainy season and the central face just underneath would signify the June Solstice of the dry season. At the far ends of the frieze are the two special heads with the trumpeter motif—these would be those of the equinoxes, announcing the beginning and end of the rainy season. It is interesting that these do not have podiums and may indicate that the Sun is closer on the horizon and far from its solstitial seats. The findings are summarized in table 1.

Notice that although seven heads are presented on one side (above) and five on the other in table 1, two are intermediary signs (trumpeters), and do not correspond to either side, nor do they stand on podiums.

TABLE 1: Disposition of the twelve figures on the solar meander (adapted from a table of Krzysztof Makowski Hanula)[19]

Month	Figures of the lower half on Step-podiums with birds	Figures of the upper half on Step-podiums with felines	Month
September	Trumpeter (no podium)		
		Fishes	October
August	Bi-headed bird arch		
		Fish / birds	November
July	Big birds motif		
June	Central Face		
		Great Image	December
May	Big Birds Motif		
		Fish / birds	January
April	Bi-headed bird arch		
		Fishes	February
March	Trumpeter (no podium)		

Miranda Luizaga reaches similar conclusions to the above according to slightly different premises. His critique of the earlier authors is that their specific conclusions were not based on archaeological findings correlated to present-day or known past cosmology. His analysis looks at the precise composition of the figure and the motifs that are found in the solar rays, above them or to the sides, and in the pedestal that supports the solar face: the motifs of pumas, fishes, and condors. On the basis of the symbols present in the meander, and the numerical equivalence he assigns to them, Miranda Luizaga reaches the conclusion that there were nine months of 30 days, two months of 28, and a month of 39 days, the one corresponding to the central motif of the Gateway God. The total is 365 days.[20] Notice that the unusual month of 39 days may be the one that contains the five to six extra days. The author concludes that the calendar is actually a complex solar-lunar calendar. Even from slightly different premises, this conclusion is not dissimilar from the one mentioned earlier.

The Gateway God is most likely the equivalent of the man-god Thunupa, overshadowed by the solar being. It is interesting to look closely at the staves. The one on the left hand is bicephalic (one condor head on one side, two on the other) and represents the thunderbolt. The right-hand staff has a small head-hook in the form of a condor; it represents the sling. Under the eye the deity has a rain/hail tear that takes the form of a puma. Most of the rays that emanate from the head end in solar disks.

The Staff God is a close equivalent of the Maya Ixbalamqué—the initiate who presides over the cycle of the agrarian calendar. Like its Maya counterpart, it operates on the meteorological phenomena through thunder and lightning. It is fitting that the Sun-overshadowed Thunupa appears most strongly during the rainy season that has its apex at the December solstice. This is the exact parallel of Maya cosmology. At the opposite time of the year stands a Sun without body. For the Maya, the solar part of the year (after the time of the Sacred Calendar) reached its highest point at the December solstice; this is the time of the June solstice in the southern hemisphere. A new solar calendar explains why the monuments of the altiplano capital also reflected this new solar orientation (east-west), an element that also appears in the civilization of Nazca.

Andean Cosmology and the Mystery of the Nazca Lines

Nazca is a small modern town in the southern coastal desert of Peru, 250 miles south of Lima (see map, p. 14). The dry desert climate of the coast has allowed the preservation through the centuries of a myriad of lines and other geometric figures that criss-cross the surface of the so-called pampas—the Nazca plains. Even more puzzling than the lines are the animal and plant geoglyphs that are concentrated north of the lines. Modern people are puzzled by the source of knowledge that allowed for the building of such figures at the remarkable level of precision to which they were achieved. Speculations have attributed such feats even to aliens from outer space. Others have depicted the forms as elaborate representations of constellations. When all is told, modern research actually puts forward a simpler explanation to the puzzle. The Nazca lines naturally insert themselves in a continuing cosmological tradition original to the Andes. They are actually part of a tradition that continued for centuries after them, and partly still survives.

The Nazca culture flourished between 2,000 and 1,200 years ago. The first large settlements in the area date back to the La Puntilla Period, a phase influenced by the Chavin civilization. Settlements grew wherever water was available, not in the middle valleys. This came to an end in a period of conflict, after which the Nazca culture emerged.[21] The nearby coastline is one of the richest fishing grounds in the world. The valleys offered the best conditions for the cultivation of maize, manioc, sweet potato, and other crops, provided they were irrigated. The first traces of sedentary farming go back to 200 BC. Anthony Aveni indicates that before the beginning of our era, fortified villages outnumbered the pyramids and ceremonial plazas, a pattern that we have encountered before.[22]

In the south coast the alternation between the Paracas (with its own variations) and Nazca cultures forms a pattern of overlapping and competing cultures, somehow similar to that of the north coast, where we found the Salinar, Gallinazo, and Moche. The original Paracas culture (Paracas Cavernas) flourished between the valleys of Cañete and Nazca from the fourth and third centuries BC. Its oldest centers were located in the Ica Valley. There was a change inaugurated in the second century BC with the construction of imposing ceremonial buildings, comparable in size to those of Moche and Gallinazo cultures, particularly in the Ica Valley. The art of this culture differs both from the previous one (Paracas Cavernas) and the following, Nazca. The elegant style that resulted has been called Topará (Paracas Necropolis). Topará diffused from the centers of Chincha and Cañete toward the south, to Paracas, Ica, and even Nazca. The presence in Nazca lasted only until before the rise of the important ceremonial center of Cahuachi in the first century BC. Thus, the three traditions—Paracas, Topará, and Nazca partly coexisted and competed for hegemony in the south-central coast, roughly from the second century BC to part of the first century AD.[23] Nazca continued after that. Central to the development of its culture was the ceremonial center of Cahuachi.

Cahuachi: Ceremonial Center at the Turn of Our Age

The area of the desert that interests us is framed by the Ingenio River to the north, the Nazca River to the south, and the Andean foothills to the east. The pampas are elevated dry plains occupying about one hundred square miles. The animal forms or geoglyphs are concentrated to the north, in the pampa that bears a variety of names: Pampa de los Incas, Pampa Jumana, Pampa San Jose, etc. The western zone is called Pampa

Majuelos; the southeastern, Pampa Cinco Cruces. At the other extreme, on the southern bank of the Nazca River, is the monumental center of Cahuachi, composed of more than forty mounds. We will now look at the rich symbolism of the ceremonial center, its lines and geoglyphs, before turning to what Nazca art can add to the whole.

Cahuachi is located on the southern edge of Rio Nazca, with Rio Ingenio to the north. The site extends to 1.2 miles on a side and covers approximately 370 acres. The location is unique for its geology and hydrology. The trail leading to Cahuachi from the north (Camino de Leguia) crosses the Nazca Valley in a place where there are permanent springs. There are many other water aquifers—*puquios*—in other areas around the center. Although most of the geoglyphs and the longest lines are found in the pampa of San Jose, immediately to the north, there are also lines south of Cahuachi, in the pampa of Atarco, and they are oriented to the most notable architecture of the site. Researchers thus agree that the site played a role in conjunction with the geoglyphs.

Apart from the presence of a limited supply of water, Cahuachi presents a very poor choice for economic reasons. The waters tend to periodically flood the underlying valley; the soil tends to accumulate salinity, and the hills are hardly fit for cultivation. In addition, violent wind storms are frequent.

The site's platforms were built over natural hills by terracing them and containing them with adobe walls. The hills determined the form of the platforms themselves; however, an additional effort was used in making them face north. On the mounds one can see evidence of labyrinths, rooms, and hallways modified over time. It seems that the mounds were built by different social groups. Helaine Silverman hypothesizes that various *ayllus*—the basic Andean social unit—were responsible for the building of their own mounds.[24] In between those are natural and artificially defined open spaces.

Throughout the site, there is no evidence of structures used for large storage of food. Likewise, there were few or no domestic dwellings during the epochs of its occupation. Pottery with elaborate iconography far outnumbers utilitarian objects during the site's main occupation period. The presence of postholes without structure, serving a temporary need, and of refuse accumulated in construction fills without there being permanent settlements, attests to a temporary use of the site.[25]

Cahuachi was most likely a site used for pilgrimages and cyclical rituals. Each *ayllu* performed its own rituals and played a part in the whole.

Thus there was only a temporary, larger hierarchy that returned in between times to a local autonomous hierarchy. The above is reflected in the type of architecture found. The basic unit is the repetition of mound or *kancha* (plaza). The site is covered by identical structural units that vary in size. This indicates with high probability that each *ayllu* built and maintained their own mounds and plazas. At the same time this was a very fluid situation; groups could be reaching their apogee while others were dissolving. This explains why there is no master plan in the way the site is built, no homogeneity between the mounds, nor a visible regulating control factor. In other words, little is visible of a centralized authority. Some mounds could be on the way out while others continued to be built up. For the same reason, there are no clear boundaries to the site; the pattern just seems to fade out. However, two separate, large walls define the two most important areas of the center of the site. This sort of acropolis is formed by Temples 1, 2, 8, and 9. Unit 2 has been called the "Great Temple," and is significantly different and centrally located.[26]

Cahuachi was a sacred center from the earliest Nazca period (phase Nazca 1). In the Great Temple hundreds of broken vases, ceramics of the phases 2 and 3, have been found, as well as numerous remains of llamas, bird feathers, and other evidence of sacrifices. The burials are most often found on the mounds' tops, at least during the time of the site's apogee, and from the areas in between the mounds later on.[27] In addition to serving as a pilgrimage center, some historians believe the site could also have served for the enactment of social dramas, such as ritual battles, when the tension accumulated between one village and another. In fact Cahuachi may have been the testing ground for the vitality of the *ayllu*, the place where it found its strength or was challenged for its survival.

The site declined at the onset of stage 5, a time that saw the rise of a new kind of art with the recurrent presence of the trophy head symbolism, and other symbolism of warfare. Around 400 AD there were serious droughts, and the rivers carried little water to the sea. The water disappeared further upstream, obliging people to move toward the mountains. This is the time in which people decided to turn to the use of the aqueducts called *puquios*, since their flow was more predictable than that of the rivers. However, the use of the *puquios* could be controlled and restricted by few, hence the evidence of increased conflicts. This is reflected in an increase of the warrior theme in Nazca 5 and the fact that communities fragmented and rose against each other.[28]

Nazca's Geoglyphs

From the north to the south (toward Cahuachi) we have this succession of signs: geoglyphs—which are for the most part separated from the lines—then the lines, with their highest concentration to the south toward the ceremonial center of Cahuachi.

The dating of the pottery shards found all over the pampas yielded dates ranging from 200 to 1450 AD. The animal figures, also called biomorphs, date from 200 to 600 AD. Most of the animal lines lie under later straight lines, indicating that they preceded them. On this most of the scientists agree. Of the lines a small fraction belonged to the Early Intermediate Period, whereas the majority of them dated from the so-called Middle Intermediate Horizon (600–1000 AD) and Late Intermediate Horizon (1000–1450 AD). A correction factor could be due to the seeming habit of removing earlier potsherds, indicating that the construction of the lines may have started earlier than the evidence indicates.[29] The unique system of subterranean aqueducts at the eastern end of the pampa yielded dates around 360 AD.[30]

Let us now turn our attention to the geoglyphs. What at first sight appears as replicas of animals is in fact the depiction of a supernatural being. None of the animals portrayed are faithful replicas of their close relatives, but rather mythical counterparts, although they may closely resemble them. We see monkeys with spiraling tails, birds with overextended bills and zig-zag necks, unrecognizable plant-like structures or even a flower, and many other forms that have animal-like appendages or components. Aveni identifies eighteen birds, four fish, two lizards, one fox, one monkey, one spider, one insect, and many composite figures. All of the figures have in common the fact that they each were drawn with a single, continuous line. These are some of the dimensions: the frigate bird covers 5 football fields and has a bill 900' long, the lizard measures 510', the condor's wings span is 450', and the hummingbird measures 300'.

Let us hear the observations of R. Girard, as usual full of deep insight. What do the animal figures indicate? Birds and serpents were animals of the rain, as they were in Maya and other American cultures. The serpent motif often represents the lightning. The largest biomorph, the one identified as the frigate bird, has a bill larger than its body. It is pointing toward the rising sun on the June Solstice, a date of cardinal importance in Andean astrology and spirituality, presently still known as the celebration of the Inti-Raymi. Another large bird, with a highly pronounced bill, points this time toward the December Solstice sun.[31]

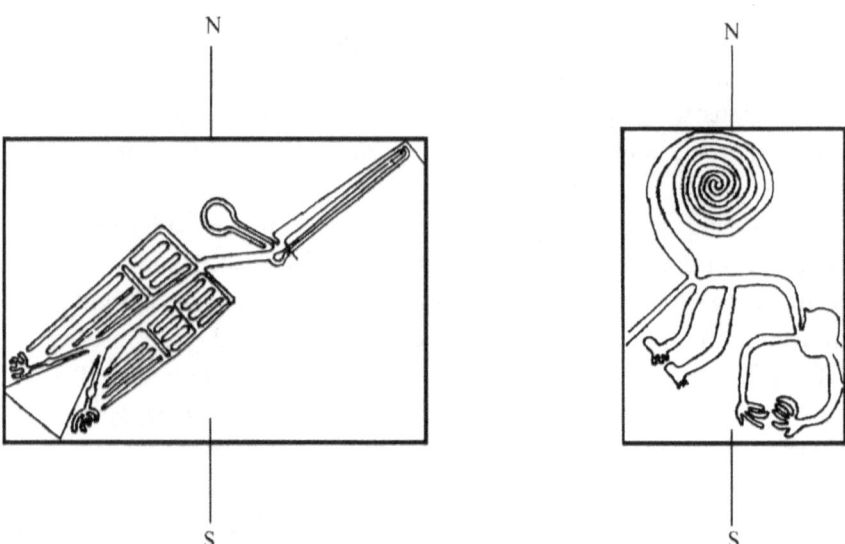

Figure 5.4: Nazca geoglyph orientation

The new importance of the sun appears in a more pervasive manner. M. Scholten d'Ebneth discovered that the pampa geoglyphs are oriented to the cardinal directions, and therefore to the sun's east-west axis, just as the monuments in Tiwanaku are. All geoglyphs are found to be contained within a rectangle oriented to the cardinal directions (see figure 5.4).[32]

On the whole, the pampa south of the river Ingenio, where the geoglyphs are found, is like a gigantic replica of the drama of the storm. Birds and snakes repeat on the ground the phenomenon that had a paramount importance in the life of the desert and of its people. Among the plant forms is a very archetypal symmetrical, tapering form that Girard identifies as the Tree of Life. Together with other plant-like forms, it completes the tableau of the ritual of fertilization that rain and thunder bring about on earth. The pampa geoglyphs are like a gigantic invocation; they form an altar to the gods of the heavens. M. Scholten d'Ebneth indicates that many of the animal forms are associated with a ceremonial trapezoid or triangle landing. Since the geomorphs are traced with one single line, the landings could have been the places of departure and arrival for a ceremonial walking of the figures, resembling what we know of the use of labyrinths in the European Middle Ages. These ceremonies most likely invoked the propitiation of the rain deities for the cycle of the yearly agricultural operations. If that were the case, then each tribe or *ayllu* may have contributed its rituals to the ceremonial agricultural year. Scholten d'Ebneth agrees with Paul Kosok that the mythic animals could also have been representations of totemic clan symbols.[33]

Nazca could give the false impression of being a unique and separate manifestation of Andean culture. Not only are the geoglyphs much more widespread in the region but they also form a continuing tradition throughout the centuries, and we have seen their first traces in the Second Age on the north coast. The chapters on Inca culture will provide ample documentation about this cultural continuity.

In the pampa just north of Nazca is found the figure of a sixty-feet-tall owl-man. Another one found in Palpa, north of Nazca, most likely represents the Staff God with a staff in either hand. It seems to be contemporary with the figures of Nazca. In Peru's province of Chiclayo (close to the coast in northern Peru) is found on top of a hill a figure built with lines of stones. It represents an anthropomorphic bird having a head 49' in diameter and a wingspan of 272'.[34] The work of Johan Reinhard has brought to light the existence of other large geoglyphs as far south as northern Chile. In Cerro Unitas, close to the coastal town of Iquique, can be seen an anthropomorphic representation 295' high, one of the world's largest anthropomorphic geoglyphs.[35] Similar to one of Nazca's representations, it has a square frontal head, solar rays emanating from it, and rectangular eyes and mouth. The figure of a feline is closely associated to the left of this figure. A. Aveni adds another very similar example from the Atacama desert of northern Chile (Figure 5.5).[36] Finally, it should be noted that although sacred landscapes attained their most spectacular expression in the Andes, even North America has preserved examples of them. The most famous is the Great Serpent Mound of Ohio.

In Nazca the lines and some other geometric figures are much more common and widespread than the geoglyphs. Aveni has estimated that there are more than one thousand lines across the pampas. The first useful observation is the fact that at least eight hundred of these lines emanate from one of about sixty centers variously interconnected to one another. In total, Aveni found 62 ray centers connecting 762 straight lines. Each of these centers is positioned on natural hills. Drawing the geoglyphs or the lines is not the gigantic undertaking that it is usually thought to be. Johan Reinhard estimates that all of the geoglyphs could have been executed by one thousand people over three weeks. It has also been demonstrated that the desert figures could just have been amplified from scale models with rudimentary tools and techniques.[37]

Figure 5.5: Geoglyph from Chile's Atacama desert

Other than lines there also are trapezoid forms, zigzags, and spirals. Zigzags may have represented the lightning and rivers, whereas spirals may symbolize shells and therefore the ocean, or more simply different forms of etheric energy. The lines can be as long as a few miles; trapezoids can be 1.25 miles. Some of the trapezoids, at least, result from alignments of the longer sides with human-made structures, such as the central mounds of Cahuachi.[38] Very often a trapezoid ends in a line that continues for about half a mile before terminating in a spiral or zigzag. This pattern is also found in many irrigation canals along the coast.

Archaeologist Toribio Mejia Xesspe believes that the lines were once walked on. This would explain the high concentration of lines found around the ceremonial center of Cahuachi, to the south of the pampa. If that were the case, we could surmise that the lines were already present at the times when Cahuachi was first built (the first century AD) and that they were continuously maintained throughout the centuries by removing all previous potsherds. In view of all that has been said above, the word *Cachahui* acquires a particular interest, since its meaning is "that which makes them see" or "that which lets them foretell bad luck"—hence, the likelihood that the priests observed from here natural and heavenly events. There are hypotheses that this is what allowed agricultural operations in conjunction with a lunar calendar. Evidence of this can be found on a famous weaving of Nazca period 2 held in the Brooklyn Museum. In it one can see a month of thirty days, divided in two periods of fifteen days.[39] This author believes, in light of all the later discoveries, that it may have been a solar calendar. More will be said about this as we return to the conclusions.

Looking at the statistical orientation of the lines has not borne out any significant correlation with astronomical points of reference. Fifty percent of the lines are oriented toward the azimuth 100–105 (east). This is the direction that the sun reaches between October 22 and November 2. The latter is the date of the first zenith passage of the sun in Nazca, and the time in which water starts to discharge in the irrigation canals, which even today is considered the single most important event of the year. This confirms the strong correlation of the lines with water phenomena. The principal local deity was a mountain of sand—Cerro Blanco—associated with the highest mountain in the eastern horizon, Illa-kata; with the distant, snowy peak of Carhuarazo; and with the mountain Tunga near the coast. It was believed that a lake inside Cerro Blanco fed all the underground irrigation channels. With the trapezoids it has been found that often the thinner end of the narrow figure connects to a source of water, whereas the trapezoid axes are often parallel to the flow of water. This gives rise to the hypothesis that the trapezoids, too, may have been ritual space for ceremonies.

In conclusion, lines and geoglyphs may have served any of the following purposes, either together or separately. The geoglyphs may have been used as ceremonial paths and places of worship, and they may have served as places of convergence. The lines may have functioned as the *ceques* did at the time of the Incas when they were walked ceremonially. (We will touch on *ceques* shortly) They also mapped underground water and its aquifers (*puquios*).

Aveni, Reinhard, Girard, and other scientists' findings have finally elucidated the origin and reason for the lines and geoglyphs. The traditions probably inaugurated in the Second Age have persisted into modern times. Conversely, what appears from the observation of present-day practices sheds more light on the traditions of the past. Straight footpaths leading to a rock cairn among the Chipaya Indians of Bolivia are still used at present. The pilgrims walk the straight lines to the rock cairn with no regard to the topography. They bring their bowls and shatter them at the shrines where they give offerings. The same is done in two other villages of Bolivia, where the villagers walk, following the lines and offering devotions and dances to the mountain gods.[40] Both in Bolivia and Chile, the straight lines lead to hill or mountain tops, often themselves used for worshipping higher mountains. Lower mountains and lakes are believed to be the wives of higher mountains that fertilize them. These beliefs coincide with the ecological role of mountains that are the origin of rivers and act as sources for the condensation of water from the consequent rains.

In Inca times, straight lines were called *ceques*. Their characteristics have been reported and studied by the chroniclers and have been further studied by the modern science of archaeoastrology. We consequently know that these *ceques* also had a rich calendrical function. To round off our understanding of Nazca cosmology let us now look at the testimony of its art.

Nazca Art and Iconography

Nazca art is known primarily through its pottery. A documented sequence allows for the recognition of artistic motifs that evolved from about 100 BC to 800 AD. They form a sequence from Nazca 1 to Nazca 9. At the beginning of the sequence, the ceramic is often decorated with mythical creatures. In the middle of the sequence, more naturalistic themes are introduced. Finally, toward the end there is a return in a new way to the fantastic. This time masks of demons are found on human bodies; military themes appear closely associated with disjointed human figures. Condor-warriors and the theme of the trophy heads—pointing to human sacrifice—complete the picture. Besides the pottery, Nazca has also left us finely woven textiles.

Nazca iconography allows us to cast a glance at their deities and rituals, and hence, further understand their cosmology, particularly in relation to the geoglyphs and lines. This art is very ornate and rich. It had frequent recourse to the idea of hybridization, combining in very startling fashion parts of animals, plants, and human beings in ritual vestments. Examples of this are: the frontal part of the headdress transformed into the flower of a yucca; bird feathers transformed into darts; a feline that gives birth to a tree, etc. Among these is one that recurs with great frequency: appendiges that emerge as snakes/slugs or plant sprouts from inside a body of human appearance. The individuals portrayed performing a ritual transform themselves into spiritual beings when their bodies present appendiges. In all likelihood, the more of these, the higher is the personage.

Tongues emerging from heads and snake/slug motifs represent the flow of energy, what we could call etheric energy. The head is the origin of these flows. The appendiges, described as the snake/slug motif, that appear wherever the dead gives birth to the living (e.g., from the body or from the earth) stand as a symbol of the special powers of the supernatural, in relation to what is the source of life and fertility. The motif has many precedents, such as Chavin, where it is the omnipresent snake. There too, head motifs were used abundantly in all parts of the body.

In Nazca iconography there is no clear boundary between the natural and the supernatural. It is not always easy to distinguish between human beings dressed as a priest or a spiritual being. In later Nazca phases, we see more scenes with human beings, and these are also more figurative. Likewise, there are few or no representations of daily life in Nazca art. The vestments of individuals mark differences between ceremonial activities. Plants and animals that are part of a mythical context adopt human parts, e.g., heads, feet, and hands. Animals can even adopt other animal characteristics: birds have jaguar heads or their bodies resemble that of insects.

In representations of rituals, such as those that most likely rep-resent harvest festivals, men dance with food staples in their hands. There is no difference in the attire among individuals. Consequently, there is no clarity of whether the rituals were conducted by dedicated priests or ad hoc celebrants, such as members of the various *ayllus*. In Cahuachi there are deposits where one can find the vestments, masks, and objects for the ritual; another indication that participation in the ritual offered sacred status to the participants and that there was no official priesthood. Among the paraphernalia for the cult one can find gold ornaments for mouth and forehead, fine pottery, gourds sculpted and singed, engraved stone cups, and musical instruments. Textiles were also very important. After being used they were buried ceremonially

There is ample evidence that music was played as part of a choral language. Among the instruments were trumpets, drums, and *antaras*— pan pipes built of clay. *Antaras* appear everywhere in the archeological record. Traditionally they are played in pairs; one *antara* leader takes priority over the follower. The leader *antara* is associated with the east, upper world and the masculine; the follower with the west, the lower world and the feminine.

Burial sites must have been very special areas even though they lacked surface markers. They were conceived of as houses. The place of burial, conceived as house, serves as the physical representation of a lineage. These burials most often come from the mound tops, at least during the time of Cahuachi's apogee, or from the areas in between the mounds later on.

When all evidence is reviewed, the system of geoglyphs and lines, seen in conjunction with the rituals held there and those held in Cahuachi, was a system of water-use through rituals to the water and mountain deities, in conjunction with a cult to the ancestors who had a hold on the land, as we can understand from the record of Nazca art and from their prominent position in the cosmology of Cahuachi.

Everything we have described and interpreted so far in relation to the north coast, Tiwanaku, and Nazca has a twofold tendency. On the one hand, it continues the traditions that were inaugurated two thousand years earlier during the Late Archaic (Second Age). On the other hand, new tendencies emerge, underlining the solar revolution that Andean society underwent under the renewing impulse of Thunupa, the initiate of the Andes.

Thunupa

It is surprising how South American myth describes events that are strictly correlated with the events of the Popol Vuh. However, South American mythology has a more fragmentary nature. This could be due to the fact that Tiwanaku was not the central stage of the confrontation with the initiate of the Americas. According to Steiner, that confrontation occurred in Central America, and the previous research has identified the center of it in the region of the Mexican Soconusco and the site of Izapa.

Let us review similarities and differences between the continents. The deeds of the Twins and Wirakocha/Thunupa bring about in both instances the birth of a new world through the central event of the Dawning, or Second Creation. The event has been described in similar ways in North and South America. Cristobal de Molina also specified that it was the "Sun in the form of a man" that rose in the heavens at the time of the Second Creation. This is another parallel with the Popol Vuh. Both the Twins and Wirakocha/Thunupa usher in a new age. There is no strict correspondence between these two sets of beings and the Maya Twins. Wirakocha corresponds to the North American Great Spirit and the Maya Seven Ahpus, whereas Hunahpu is the solar spirit. Thunupa seems to correspond to the Twin called Ixbalamqué. In the Gateway of the Sun he appears as the initiate overshadowed by the power of the Christ Sun, signified by the solar headdress and the solar calendar meander. To unravel the apparent differences between north and south more fully, we will need to wait until the description of the time of the Incas, who continued this tradition and rendered it more explicit.

The north-south parallelism is reflected in many ways through the changes brought in the ensuing civilization. Similarly to Central America, the Second Creation brings in momentous changes of consciousness. The Maya introduced a new astronomy in their civilization and acquired a new sense of time. There is every reason to believe that Tiwanaku introduced a new solar calendar, as the evidence of the Gateway of the Sun indicates. Changes in the Nazca worldview also reflect the introduction of a solar revolution. Admittedly, it is hard to place this event in a precise chronology in South America. However, it is recognized by archaeologists that many of the most significant changes of civilization occurred during the initial stage of the Early Intermediate Period, sometime between 200 BC and 200 AD.

Thunupa's Confrontation with Evil

Let us now look more closely at the being Wirakocha/Thunupa. He has been described as a prophet, a preacher of a new message, and a healer. He is clearly human, although overshadowed in the narratives by the qualities of the creator-deity Wirakocha. It is interesting to note the feelings and reactions of those chroniclers who had a foot in both Spanish and Andean cultures, chief among them Santa Cruz Pachacuti.

The man who went by the full name of Juan de Santa Cruz Pachacuti Yamqui Salcamaygua was familiar with Inca and Spanish cultures. Even his name gathers cosmologies of both worlds; *Santa Cruz* for "Holy Cross" and *Pachacuti* for "world change." He indicated being the descendent of the *curacas* (local chiefs) of the village of Santiago of Guayua Canchi, in the area around the Lake Titicaca. These chiefs had been converted to Christianity since the early part of the Conquest. Santa Cruz Pachacuti, as he is generally known, had a keen interest in both Andean and Christian spirituality. He is, in fact, the individual who has left us the most complete account about Inca worldview. His *Relacion de antiguedades deste reyno del Piru* (An account of the antiquities of Peru) shows Santa Cruz Pachacuti's desire to bring about a rapprochement between Christian and Inca worldviews. It could be argued that he could hardly have written anything different from this, given the political climate established by the Conquest. Nevertheless, the proof of his genuineness lies in the quality of the insights that he offers to our exploration, not in a mechanical juxtaposition of creeds.

In a few paragraphs Santa Cruz Pachacuti provides a condensed view of the events preceding and following the Dawning. This spiritual blueprint is very much in harmony with the historical record. Before the arrival of Thunupa, a time is described in which fortresses were built, strife reigned supreme, and the *hapi-ñuños*—demons—carried away men, women, and children. So far this reflects historical facts known to be associated with part of the Early Intermediate Period, or immediately preceding it, according to the various chronologies that set different start dates for the EIP. These times saw the documented rise of human sacrifices in other parts of the country.

Calancha mentions that the individual called Makuri, chief of the Umasuyus, desired to rid himself of Thunupa/Wirakocha. Makuri had been admonished by Thunupa for his cruelty and his warrior habits. In his absence, his daughter had been converted by Thunupa's disciples. The chief retaliated by putting them to death.[41] Santa Cruz Pachacuti also indicates that Thunupa was driven out of the town of Yamquisupa. He was put in prison near the lake of Carapucu (part of Lake Titicaca). He had been condemned to a cruel death, but together with a youth he escaped and entered the lake borne up by his mantle as if it were a boat. From there it is said he went to Tiwanaku.[42]

The above are just a few indications of Thunupa and his disciples' confrontation with another cult, a cult of antithetical nature to his teachings. Where did these events take place? Do they coincide with the episode most often quoted by the chronicles: the confrontation with the Canas Indians at Cacha? Cacha is the place where Wirakocha/Thunupa caused the lava to flow down from the mountain.[43]

For Cristobal de Molina, the "rain of fire" occurred in Pucara. Pedro Sarmiento de Gamboa refers to Pucara as the place where could be seen the people transformed into stone that had perished during the Flood, another event placed in close association with the time preceding the Dawning. Finally, Santacruz Pachacuti mentions that on the hill of Cacha-Pucara was the idol of a woman to whom were offered human sacrifices. Cacha and Pucara are in fact two neighboring sites. In memory of the deed of the initiate in Cacha, the Incas had elevated a temple that was one of the major shrines of the empire. Let us now turn to the historical dimension of Pucara.

The city of Pucara was situated seventy-five miles northwest of Lake Titicaca. It was a major secular and religious center that seems to have been in competition or open hostility with Tiwanaku. Its historical duration was short, going from 200 BC to 200 AD. Stelae and sculptures in full round were found on site. It is also in Pucara that was found the figure of the "sacrificer," which sometimes wears a collar of trophy heads, and at other times is depicted carrying a trophy head. There is no similarity in the artistic motifs of the deities represented in Tiwanaku and Pucara, apart from the Pachamama, the earth mother, in spite of the geographical proximity. The themes familiar to Pucara, like the trophy heads, only reemerged in Tiwanaku after the end of the EIP.[44]

After describing the defeat of the demons through the teachings of Thunupa, Santa Cruz Pachacuti says, "By this it must be understood that the devils were conquered by Jesus Christ our Lord on the cross on Mount Calvary," an astonishing comment that clothes in Christian Andean terms the statements of Steiner about the Mexican Mysteries. It is not surprising therefore that Santa Cruz Pachacuti, as well as Guaman Poma—another native chronicler—and many others, identified Thunupa with one of the apostles. Ramos Gavilan describes a legend in which the apostle is St. Thomas; Garcilaso says the mestizos of Cuzco identified him with Saint Bartholomew; for Valera, Thunupa/Viracocha was the Christ himself. For others, as in Mesoamerica, he was Santiago, Saint James. These are deep intuitions that cannot be resolved without turning to spiritual science. There is truth in seeing Thunupa as both Christ and as human being, and that is what the Popol Vuh does with the esoteric device of the Twins—the initiate overshadowed by the power of the Sun deity. This is a theme that can be exhausted only by looking at many different versions of the myths.

Another sign of cultural decline appears clearly in the Paracas peninsula at the end of the Early Intermediate Period through the widespread practice of mummification. Before the onset of the Kali Yuga (Twilight of the Gods), the initiates could converse with the Moon beings who had a great part in the guidance of humankind. As evolution progressed this was becoming no longer possible, particularly so since the onset of the

Egyptian culture. This state of affairs progressed and continued until the turn of our era. Ever since the third millennium BC, Moon beings could not reach human beings during the hours of daytime. Only during night could they do so, but the initiates found a way to influence human souls during the day.[45] Through their practice of mummification, they provided a dwelling for the Moon beings in the mummies they held in their burial places. Thus, they could come down to Earth, even though this was no longer their task. The mummified corpses allowed the descent of the Moon beings, now turned Luciferic. Through these mummies around them, the initiates could study and understand animals, plants, and minerals; what initiates before them had been able to draw from nature and life. This was a first step in the direction of natural science at a time in which the human being could not make use of his intellect, nor could he retain his old clairvoyance.

However, through mummification, the initiates retained the souls of the departed captive to their bodies for a time after death. They did so by altering their natural destiny. This was a sign of a declining culture, all the more so since this practice opened up new possibilities for those who wanted to mislead their followers for their own gain.[46] Part of this lay in the fact that through the use of the mummies, the priests wrested knowledge of the forces acting in the organs.[47]

We can further add to the practice of mummification the widespread evidence in the Paracas necropolis sites of cranial deformation, another means for retaining atavistic consciousness. It is interesting to note in passing that mummification also was the practice of the old Egyptians at the time of their Twilight of the Gods. Egypt too was close to the surviving influences of the end of Lemuria when migrations took place through Africa in the direction of the emerging culture of Atlantis. In Egypt as in the Andes, the Mysteries of the South are concerned with the physical body and with the Mystery concerned with the gates of death.

Our exploration, spread out among many chronicles, has brought to light many of the same elements that accompanied the life and deeds of the Twins in Mesoamerica. South American human sacrifice is most often represented with the trophy head, a motif that is preserved in many places and over many centuries and millennia all over Peru. As it appears from our explorations, the chronicles do in fact elucidate part of the answer that archaeologists seek. Why did Tiwanaku prevail over the other centers, Pucara in particular? The answer, it seems, is not to be found in geographic, political, or economic factors but rather at the spiritual level. Tiwanaku introduced a more successful spiritual impulse.

The new spiritual impulse of the EIP is signified by the development of important pilgrimage centers such as those of Tuwanaku and Cahuachi. We have more documentation about the latter, in which we can detect a departure from the oracular nature of Chavin. In the Nazca civilization a new impulse emerges in the integration of the ritual functions of the *ayllus* that carry the whole of the ritual year. We can surmise that the function of the shaman of the Third Age came to an end. Oracles of later times— e.g. Pachacamac—have a more regressive nature. We will see later that Pachacamac revived the antagonism of the *wakas* at the time in which the Incas reintroduced unity in diversity through the cult of Inti—the Sun.

Teachings of Thunupa

Thunupa's legacy, mirrored in the events that followed the Dawning, modeled all of Andean history for centuries to come. The Incas revived it and evolved it further after it had undergone a time of darkness and oblivion. Looking at how the Incas reconnected themselves to the message of the Prophet will further allow us to elucidate aspects that now seem unclear.

The event of the Dawning formed a watershed between prehistoric and historic times. After the Dawning the tribes traced their descent according to their *paqarinas*, their place of origin or emergence. It can be said that each tribe saw itself attached to that place where it first witnessed the event of the Dawning and therefore the teachings of the initiate of the Andes. In this case the *paqarinas*—literally "places of Dawning"—relate to parts of the landscape, considered sacred because they were associated to the event of the Dawning, as it was experienced by the particular tribe. The paqarinas were also linked with some particular stars on the horizon. It is as if each star of the heavens were reflected on earth by the tribes, an important and recurrent motif present in Andean cosmology. The Andes can be seen as the reflection of the Milky Way on earth, a concept that the Inca literally carved in stone in the landscape of their Sacred Valley, as we will see later.

Closely associated to the *paqarinas* are the lineage *wakas*. These are a variety of sacred objects, such as the mummy or stone that commemorates the first ancestor at the time of the Dawning, or parts of the landscape. They were, and still are, considered sacred. In this way the lineage *wakas* were a reminder for the tribes of their common descent from the momentous time of the Dawning. This is how these correlations are described by Cristobal de Molina:

> The Creator began to raise up the people and nations that are in that region, making one of each nation of clay, and painting the dresses that each one was to wear. Those that were to wear their hair, with hair; and those that were to be shorn, with hair cut; and to each nation was given the language that was to be spoken, and the songs to be sung, and the seeds and food that they were to sow. When the Creator had finished painting and making the said nations and figures of clay, he gave life and soul to each one, as well as men and women, and ordered that they should pass under the earth. Thence each nation came up in the places to which he ordered them to go. Thus they say some came out of caves, others issued from hills, others from fountains, others from the trunks of trees. From this cause, and owing to having come forth and commenced to multiply, from those places, and to having had their beginning of their lineage in them, they made *wakas* and places of worship of them in memory of the origin of their lineage which proceeded from them. Thus, each nation uses the dress with which they invest their *waka*; and they say that the first that was born from that place was there turned into stones, condors, and other animals and birds. Hence the *wakas* they use and worship are in different shapes.[48]

Molina ties together the new creation after the Dawning with the origin of the tribes and the lineage *wakas*. The *wakas* were a reminder of unity in diversity. They could be either objects, stones, mummies, or features of the landscape, as Molina mentions above. Through the *wakas* was celebrated the message of the initiate of the Andes. These objects were therefore sacred intermediaries or intercessors. What Santa Cruz Pachacuti defines as idolatry is the belief that the *waka* had a magic power of its own, that it was independent from the whole and therefore from the teachings of Thunupa and the Sun deity. This theme is one that we will find in many instances of later history.

The lineage wakas are closely associated with heavenly constellations, often with stars and constellations of the Milky Way. It can be said that the transition into a more historical consciousness gave origin to the present social form of the so-called *ayllu*. To be more exact, the *ayllu* was most likely preexistent; the prophet introduced the *ayllu* that works according to a mixed matrilineal and patrilineal line of descent and harkens back to the lineage *wakas* of the time of the Dawning.

There is an additional important element in most of the myths. Before accompanying the *ayllus* in the emergence at the time of the Dawning, the progenitors of the lineages travel underground. The myth of Puquio (Ayacucho) is similar to the one described by Molina above. It states that "the ancestors created the lakes and opened the earth. The ancestors of Puquio traveled along the cavities of subterranean water that are the veins of the mountains, toward the water springs carrying golden drums on their heads."[49] This view corresponds to the way in which Andean culture saw the circulation of water. The sea water that surrounds the solid world emerges to give rise to lakes. The lakes feed underground water veins from which originate smaller lakes, ponds, creeks, springs, and hence the water flows back to the ocean. This also explains why the majority of *paqarinas* are lakes, rivers, creeks, and springs! In this way the myth links the ancestors and the cosmic circulation of the waters and source of life of the tribes to the time of the Dawning. The Dawning relates the tribes to the Sun God and to the Great Spirit Wirakocha as well.

The EIP continued the trend established by Chavin. Each civilization that Chavin touched superseded the teachings of the spiritual center to its own, cementing the union of the *wakas* and their subordination to a larger message. This is why the separate cults could continue, while Chavin symbolism and spiritual contents appeared alongside. Now, at the time of the Dawning another step was taken. The wakas were subordinated to the new Sun deity. This was no longer the preparation of something future for which Chavin stood, but the concrete realization of a new step of civilization. A complete break from the Second Age was completed. And there was another step that showed the qualitative nature of the change.

As in Mesoamerica, the Dawning introduced a major change in the structure of society. Earlier Andean social structures had been based upon matriarchy. The Dawning introduced patriarchy among the Maya. In the Andes, a new social structure superseded matriarchy, a structure bearing equally on the male as on the female side of descent. This passage from matriarchy to a mixed patriarchy-matriarchy is possibly what is referred to in a striking image that closely follows the Dawning in some versions of the creation myth. There, it is said that the moon was too bright, in fact, brighter than the sun. The sun had to dim it by throwing ashes over her face.[50] The dimming of the feminine principle corresponds here with the time of the formation of the *ayllu*, or its evolution into mixed patrilineal and matrilineal lines of descent.

The *ayllus* trace all descent, whether male or female. Therefore they tend to be overlapping, non-discrete groups. This leaves individuals the choice of which line to affiliate with, and the decision can be changed for what is perceived as the individual's interest. Although hierarchical, the *ayllu* is a highly flexible form of kinship-based social organization. Much resides in the inherent capacity of the leader in implementing and maintaining highly generous reciprocal relationships. That not being the case, the individuals have the choice to leave the group for the other side of their kinship.

The *ayllu* was, and in many instances still is, the center of social and economic integration and of the practice of mutual help. Each farmer receives help at critical times (sowing, harvest, etc.) and is likewise bound to offer help to others. The *ayllu* is in fact the main protagonist of Andean social life, not the individual.

Researchers have placed in evidence the role of the *ayllus*, particularly in Nazca. Here we can see that they had a role of coequals in the temporary hierarchy of the ceremonies held in Cahuachi. They each had their sacred mounds. Each one of the *ayllus* played a part in the maintenance of the lines and geoglyphs and of the ceremonies held there. Performance of rituals and the course of the agricultural year were inextricably bound together to the point that it would be hard to separate what is economic and agricultural from its ritual counterpart. In fact, researchers speak of the ritual obligations in the context of what is known as *mit'a*, the notion of collective duty, or tribute, of the *ayllu*. *Mit'a* is an important concept that will reappear clearly articulated later among the Inca. It stands at the heart of the Andean "reciprocity" ideal.

Reciprocity concerns a view of the "justice" of the interchange of goods, feelings, people, and even religious values or simple information. Reciprocity is the guarantee of the right level of interchange among human beings and nature, humanity and God, the living and the dead. Reciprocity affects humans and their environment. Human beings depend on their environment and have the power to modify it in productive ways. Terracing sustains a growth that the natural environment alone would not be able to produce. In turn this modification of the environment allows a growth of population in full respect of the environment. Human beings also depend upon each other in offering mutual help, either within the *ayllu* or between the *ayllus*. All individuals offer help to those in need through the agency of the *ayllu*, and they can likewise expect to be offered help in case of need.

On another level, the gods depend on human beings, and vice-versa. Human beings have an active co-creator role in the world. Finally, the living depend on the dead. All of the living are actively connected to their lineage ancestor, whom they honor and serve. From the ancestors the living have received the knowledge that allows them to reap the fruits of the earth. Even in the present, the dead still play an active role in the society of the living.

Reciprocity is the central nexus of all Andean ethics, and the support of its economic life. It is a principle of cosmic justice. This worldview goes beyond the individual and the present generation. Natural disasters are considered the result of lack of reciprocity. The same is true of human-made calamities. Communities may have to shoulder the guilt of an individual, indeed even later generations may have to do the same. God inflicts a chastisement in order to allow the correction of the cosmic imbalance. It is not seen as a gratuitous punishment. A great part of reciprocity regulates the relationship of humanity (community) and the divine. In this case reciprocity is fulfilled through symbolic offering. Andean humanity comes to the divine not as a supplicant but with something to offer (soul and physical offering). Without reciprocity, the earth itself would not be fertile.

The multifaceted changes that arose in the Andes and South America through the deeds of Thunupa amount to the forming of a new historic consciousness. It may not have been as clearly articulated as it was among the Maya. However, there was much more to it than history usually records. One aspect at least that has already partly emerged is the cosmological Sun revolution introduced by the Andean initiate.

The "Path of Wirakocha"

The transition of the EIP can be defined as a shift from the Andean Cross / Southern Cross / Chakana cosmological reference to the new Sun orientation. This does not mean that the Southern Cross was abandoned; rather, it was subordinated to the new Sun cosmology that the initiate inaugurated.

Maria Scholten d'Ebneth confirms in Nazca what Milla Villena had found through his study of the Southern Cross in Andean cosmology;

namely, that Andean civilization continued to use as a base for its geometry the square and its diagonal, and therefore the relationship 1 to $\sqrt{2}$.[51]

Scholten d'Ebneth confirms all the following basic dimensions that Maria Reiche—the Nazca pioneer researcher—finds over and again in the Nazca pampa in meters, their decimal multiples or fractions: 6.64 and 3.32 corresponding to 2 and 1 Andean Units (AU); 4.7 = $\sqrt{2}$ AU, 13.36 = 4 AU, and 26 = 8 AU. All the figures of the pampas have been built upon the AU through the patterns of enlargement based upon the 1 to $\sqrt{2}$ progression.

M. Scholten d'Ebneth points out that the pampa geoglyphs are contained within a rectangle oriented to the cardinal directions. Moreover, the measure of the "boxes" that contain the figures are expressed in the relationships of AU and its patterns of 1 to $\sqrt{2}$ or 7 to 8 relationships. For example the large bird "box" measures 28 AU by 32 AU (7 to 8 relationship).

Everything, from the patterns of the textiles to the positioning of cities in the landscape, was subjected by Andean civilization to the ordering principles of number and proportion. As already mentioned, an equivalent way to extend the 1 to $\sqrt{2}$ relationship was through using the 7 to 8 proportion. M. Scholten d'Ebneth has found it to be omnipresent in textiles, sculptures, and the horizontal surface of temples and buildings.[52]

All of the above is not new to Andean culture. Rather, it is the continuation of the cosmology of the Andean Cross, based on the Southern Cross. However, the emphasis on the Sun as a cosmic reference point is new. We can surmise that its preparation had been lying in wait for some time—at least from the isolated evidence of the astronomical Sun-observatory of Chankillo in the fourth century BC.

From the traditions of the previous twenty centuries, it is not surprising that the Sun initiate Thunupa completely unifies in himself the notion of measurement of space and time. He is the initiate who measures time and space, which gives a particular coloration to the Andean Mysteries.

One of the other names for Thunupa, according to Scholten d'Ebneth, is Tarapaca. *Tara* is a tree from which magic wands were cut; *paca* is a secret hidden thing. Thus *Tarapaca* could mean "the hidden, secret staff."[53] The staff is the attribute of the creator god, of his servants and their descendents. With the staff the initiate measures the world. Once more, measuring and knowledge are made synonymous. This is why Thunupa, the initiate par excellence, is represented with the two measuring staffs, as is the case in Tiwanaku's Gateway of the Sun. With the sinking of the staff more than a millennium later, Manco Capac of the Incas founded Cuzco.

Fourth Age: The Time of Thunupa 121

The important acts of measuring and truth itself are made synonymous. The truth in Quechua is called *chekka*. *Chekkaluwa* is the diagonal that directs itself to the opposite corners of a figure or field. Thus the diagonal was for the Quechua the "line of truth." This notion is carried to the extreme in the myth of the Dawning in what has been called the "Route of Wirakocha."

In Cristobal de Molina's narrative, Wirakocha sends his son to Pukara so that he can "set in place" or "reorder" the solstices. One emissary went to the west and the other to the north, whereas Wirakocha went to Cuzco, following the exact southwest to northeast direction from Tiwanaku or the Island of the Sun (figure 5.6). Further on the way, Wirakocha sends his older son to Pachacamac and continues his progression toward Cajamarca. This Tiwanaku-Cajamarca axis is the Route of Wirakocha, the great diagonal that crosses the whole continent.

Figure 5.6: Path of Wirakocha

Tiwanaku and Cuzco are connected through a line that forms a 45° angle with the east-west axis. Pukara is situated exactly midway.[54] The same line continues toward Cajamarca and the coast of Ecuador. The other sites mentioned in the legends—Pachacamac and Puerto Viejo—are placed at an angle of 28° 57' on both sides of the axis. In Cajamarca, Wirakocha takes the route toward the north—not straight on the same line but toward Puerto Viejo. This is the direction that closely matches the elongation of the winter solstice sun.

The Being of Thunupa: Esoteric Considerations

The Sun initiate confirms the central content of the myth of the Fourth Age, the Dawning. It is no coincidence that the new Sun emerges from Titicaca, that the lineages emerge from their *paqarinas* and that a cultural revolution follows in the creation of the new *ayllu* with its intricate matripatrilineal structure. It is no coincidence that the cosmic orientation pivots around two central elements—the Andean Cross and the Sun—around the turning of our era. However, the prevalence of the Southern Cross or Andean Cross cosmology comes to an end. Sunken courts had to be dug deeper and deeper or were discontinued because of the difficulty of keeping this cosmic reference accurate in the changed conditions of the times. The latest continued use of sunken courts are those of the Moche in the fifth century; very isolated examples survived later in the Wari and Chimú cultures. Significantly, all of these were rather decadent societies. It is not surprising that a culture like Moche, that preserved an earlier cosmology, did so with the equally regressive ritualism of human sacrifice. The same is true, though in minor scale, of Wari and Chimú.

The Sun revolution represents the shift toward a new consciousness, from the deities of the night, Southern Cross, and Moon, to the new day-consciousness of the Dawning and the Sun. This does not mean that all previous cosmology comes to an end. The pattern of the Andean Cross still continues to play an important part in all sacred geometry. We have given examples above of how that occurred. However, the Andean Cross becomes clearly subordinated to the new Sun-Christ orientation.

Tiwanaku and Nazca—most clearly among the civilizations of the EIP—display a clear Sun orientation of their ceremonial centers. The intuition of the use of a solar calendar, emerging from various independent sources, is another step in the confirmation of the revolution inaugurated by the Sun initiate. It is not too surprising that some South American authors have dubbed Thunupa "the South American Christ" and others called him St. Thomas, St. Bartholomew or St. James. Behind these flashes of intuition stands a deeper truth of occult history that only Steiner has ever referred to, of which more below.

The myths of the Andes speak of the same Sun-hero that is called "the Twins" in the Popol Vuh. He is the one who blots out the fear of the end of time and of the soul's mortality, the one who brings to America the knowledge that the earth has been revivified by the deed of the Solar God. No doubt the Andean *amautas* could perceive the renewed aura of the Earth at the time of the deed of Golgotha, just as this had been perceived by the initiates of Hibernia, the primeval Ireland. Of the Mysteries of Hibernia and their offshoots, Steiner's research offers that while the Mystery of Golgotha occurred on earth, on the island of Hibernia the events were experienced in imaginations at the same time in which they occurred.

The spiritual confrontation that took place at the turning point of time has been placed in the context of the Mysteries of Izapa in *Spiritual Turning Points of North American History*. This event is mirrored in all the pertinent mythologies of the continent. Most cultures of the Americas speak of a civilizing hero who altered the fate of the societies of North and South America. This being is called "the Twins" in the Popol Vuh and among the Pueblo of the Southwest United States, among the Caribs, and among various tribes of the Amazon such as the Amwesha; Manabhozo or Glooskap on the East Coast of the United States; Paruxti among the Pawnees; Waicomah by the Dakota; Tacoma by the Yakima, etc.[55] Oftentimes, as is the case in the Popol Vuh, the Twins undergo an apotheosis in the transformation into Sun and Moon. The underlying unifying element of these legends is a single event that affected the Americas from the far north to the far south. No historical record can point to the nature of this event, nor is there any other modern esoteric record than that of Rudolf Steiner in this matter. His findings form a complete parallel to the language of the Popol Vuh in the chapter concerning the descent of the Twins to the Underworld.[56]

All populations of the Americas revere a being whom we can call the Great Spirit or Tao. This is the embodiment of the creative spirits known in the Bible as Elohim or in Western esoteric tradition as Exusiai. The Atlantean transplants to the New World preserved the memory of the working of the undivided being of the Elohim even in post-Atlantean times in America, in effect preserving the memory of their essence in the concept of the Great Spirit. In the West, according to Steiner's spiritual research, arose one who was an opponent of the Great Spirit—Tao—but, nevertheless, connected to it. His name sounded something like Taotl. Given the strong geomagnetic forces prevailing in America, the Ahrimanic influences of this Taotl were stronger than they ever were in the Europe or the Middle East at the time of Christ. The Popol Vuh calls this being under the collective name of 1 Camé and 7 Camé, thereby manifesting its link with the Great Spirit, which is called 1 Ahpu and 7 Ahpu. Steiner also refers to another regressive spirit, known under the name of Quetzalcoatl: "His symbol was similar to the Mercury staff found in the Eastern Hemisphere, the spirit who could disseminate malignant diseases through certain magic forces. He could inflict them upon those he wished to injure in order to separate them from the relatively good god, Tezcatlipoca."[57] He is described as a Mephistophelean being, which is to say, essentially Ahrimanic. The esoteric cult of Quetzalcoatl contributed to the furtherance of the Ahrimanic impulses in America. The Popol Vuh confirms the presence of this being with the portrayal of the Lords of Xibalba, each of them described according to the diseases that he can inflict upon humanity.[58] The Taotl and Quetzalcoatl Mysteries were opposed by the cult of Tezcatlipoca, a being of a much lower hierarchy than Taotl, partly connected to the Yahweh God, one of the Elohim. The cult was a sort of parallel to the religion that was then developing in Palestine. However, it soon lost its strength and became purely exoteric.

Central to the decadent Mexican Mysteries was the performance of human sacrifice through excision of the stomach from a live individual. The victim's soul relinquished the desire to incarnate and bear a human ego, and, at the moment of dying, drew the initiate with itself into the realm that was to be found beyond earth. The high priest of the Mexican Mysteries acquired mastery over the forces of death, using them over everything living on earth. Steiner concludes: "The earth would gradually have become desolate, having upon it only the force of death, whereas any living souls would have departed to found another planet under the leadership of Lucifer and Ahriman."[59]

Knowledge of the decadent Mysteries has not survived in the legends of South America in the same way it has been preserved in the narrative of the Popol Vuh. Nevertheless, the chroniclers speak of the early time of the

EIP (second and first century BC) as the time of the demons and also refer to black magicians. Moreover, curiously, evidence of human sacrifice with organ removal is preserved in the artistic record of Sechin of which we spoke in chapter 3, while no such record has been recovered unequivocally in Mesoamerica.

Over and against the decadent Mysteries worked the initiate whom Steiner called Vitzliputzli, who was born in the year 1 AD. Steiner confirms the tradition of Vitzliputzli's virgin birth. It is a "feathered being," an etheric entity, who has impregnated the mother; in the case of the Popol Vuh this is the virgin Ixquic, daughter of one of the Lords of the Underworld, and mother of the Twins. Steiner characterizes Vitzliputzli both as an initiate and as a "supersensible being in a human form."[60] Vitzliputzli lived in America between the years 1 and 33 AD, at the same time as Jesus Christ's life in Palestine. In the year 30 the initiate underwent a three-year confrontation with the high priest-magician of the decadent Mexican Mysteries. At the end of the three years the magician was crucified. The crucifixion was enacted so that at his death the knowledge he possessed could be obliterated. Through this act the evil unleashed by the super-magician would no longer reign unrestrained. It recovered its rightful place in world evolution.

In his two lectures of 1916 Steiner characterized the decadent mysteries far more than the progressive Mexican Mysteries of Vitzliputzli. However, this is what he says of them in a lecture of the cycle "Karmic Relationships": "These [Mexican] Mysteries had at one time been a factor of great significance in America but had then become decadent, with the result that conceptions of the rites, and their ritual enactment, had become thoroughly childish in comparison with the grandeur of earlier times [at the turn of our era]."[61]

There is a puzzling parallel between Mesoamerica and the Andes. Izapa and Island of the Sun are counterparts in the northern and southern hemisphere where they play a central role in relation to the event of the Dawning. Izapa is situated at latitude 14° north, the Island of the Sun at latitude 15° south, within a degree of each other on opposite hemispheres. Izapa is that place situated in a particular relationship to the American oceans. The region that begins with the isthmus of Tehuantepec is a place in the Americas in which the land is aligned differently from the rest of the continent in relation to its oceans. Whereas these run north to south everywhere in the Americas, here and in parts of Central America, they run east to west. Added to this, the surrounding region of Soconusco is a very particular region for its exceptional climate and the presence of volcanoes. The Island of the Sun presents a polar opposite image. It is situated in an island but in the heart of an altiplano and therefore surrounded by high mountains, in a unique configuration for the whole of South America. It is located in the only large lake of the continent and at very high elevation in an exceptional climate that allows human settlement. According to Marko Pogacnik, who has done extensive practical geomantic work around the globe, one of the most important continental energy channels runs across the Andes, from the Pacific Ocean across Lake Titicaca toward the Amazonian basin.[62] This is not too surprising in light of the unique configuration of the altiplano. To the immediate north lies the Vilcanota knot where three mountain ranges converge. To the south of the altiplano, the Andes are formed by one single mountain range.

The next chapters will explore the alternating cosmic drama played out in the Americas. After the vanquishing of the Mysteries of Taotl, Steiner tells us, "Nothing survived from these regions of what might have lived on if the mysteries of Taotl had borne fruit. The forces left over from the impulses that lived in these Mysteries survived only in the etheric world. They still exist subsensibly, belonging to what would be seen if, in the sphere of the spirit, one could light a paper over a solfatara."[63]

Later on in the same lecture cycle the thought is thus completed: "Nevertheless, so much force remained that a further attack could have been made upon the fifth epoch, having as its aim so to mechanize the earth that the resulting culture would not only have culminated in a mass of purely mechanical contrivances but would have made human beings themselves into such pure homunculi that their egos would have departed."[64]

To outer history it is known that the Maya calendar was devised very closely around the time of the events of Christ's ministry in Palestine. It was the first solar calendar that was no longer cyclical, unlike the preceding Calendar Round of fifty-two years. We have seen that the Andes offer the strong indications of a solar revolution in Chankillo first, and later in Tiwanaku and Nazca. Confirmation of the Sun revolution will come later through the Incas, whose civilization can be characterized as a restoration of the values of the Dawning, of the central point in time. In between the first time of the Prophet in the first few centuries that followed his deeds, and the renewal of his message by the Incas, an "Age of Darkness" ensued that has been referred to as the time of the Auka Runa, "people of the times of war," by Guaman Poma. As in Mesoamerica, ages of light and darkness alternated with each other. Andean culture went through a period of turmoil in which the new Sun-oriented cosmology alternated with times of cultural decline. We will point to some of these tendencies in the next chapter.

PART II

Cultural Decline and the Inca Spiritual Revolution

CHAPTER 1

THE AGE OF THE WARRIORS AND CULTURAL DECLINE

THE NATIVE CHRONICLER GUAMAN POMA calls the Fourth Age the age of the *Auka Runa*—the "people of the times of war." Everywhere sprung up fortified cities, interestingly called *pukaras*, a term that reminds us of the town that was Tiwanaku's spiritual antagonist. The farmers left the lowlands to take refuge on the ridgetops. Although called a Fourth Age, it is in reality a stage of decadence of the Third Age.

Guaman Poma's Third Age—the Fourth Age in this book—had been a time of great cultural development and demographic expansion. It was a time of prolonged peace, at least in most places. Without that peace it would have been impossible for the communities to build imposing ceremonial centers, expand irrigation work, and exploit the agricultural colonies or enclaves that were often situated at great distances from the main centers.

To fully cover the second part of the Fourth Age or "Age of the Warriors," we will look at the most significant cultures that covered the span between the later part of the Early Intermediate Period (EIP) and the expansion of the Inca Empire. In archaeological terms, this span of time is subdivided into a short Middle (Intermediate) Horizon, going from 600 to 1000 AD, and a Late (Intermediate) Horizon, coming to a symbolic end with the Inca occupation of Ica in 1476. In light of a dating that keeps in mind spiritual turning points, 1438—the estimated date of Pachacuti's accession to power—seems a better estimate for the ending of the period and a significant new beginning.

The EIP set in place important changes throughout the Andes. The Middle Intermediate Horizon was brought about by a watershed natural catastrophe, the prolonged drought that went from 562 to 594 AD. The most prominent civilization of this epoch was the Wari Empire. The Late Intermediate Horizon began around 1000 AD, after the fall of Wari. We will look at these epochs in some detail, since they set the stage for the situation at the turning point of time of the fifth post–Atlantean epoch, closely coinciding with the advent of the Inca Empire. In order to paint a full picture we will first look at the Moche culture, which most clearly reinstated the practice of human sacrifice.

Our exploration will take us back and forth between the north coast and the area of Ayacucho in the central sierra. It was on the north coast that human sacrifice and its associated ideology returned earlier and with more force in what we know of as the Moche civilization. At a time corresponding with its decline, but independently from it, the Wari regime, spreading from Ayacucho, in the central sierra, reached the highest spread and influence all over the Peruvian Andes. Later in time another large empire took the place of what had been Moche on the north Coast: Chimú or Chimor. Finally we will return to the region of Ayacucho in which, after the Wari collapse, the Chanca alliance took place, which was threatening the emergent Inca nation.

Among all these cultures we will devote a particular attention to the Moche because they have a more extensive archaeological record and are the most studied and understood.

Moche Culture

The Moche were contemporaries of Gallinazo cultures that we have previously mentioned as those who formed the transition to the times of the Dawning, following the Salinar culture. We have characterized previously how the Gallinazo brought a time of peace and expansion after the strife that had accompanied the Salinar culture. In order to look at the interactions between Moche and Gallinazo cultures, we must first be able to establish a timeline; this can more easily be done on the basis of Moche culture.

Moche is the generally accepted name of the civilization; Mochica is what the Spaniards called the language of the Chimús, their cultural successors. Therefore, most scholars refer to Moche rather than *Mochica*. The civilization covers the span from 200–300 to 700. The super El Niño that hit shortly before the year 600 gave it a fatal blow. However, the civilization survived in a modified form for another one to two centuries.

Evolution of Moche and Gallinazo Cultures

The methodology allowing us to reconstruct the sequential chronological development of Moche civilization is based upon the ceramic typology. It was developed primarily by Rafael Larco Hoyle on the basis of the evolution of the iconography painted on the vases.[1] The thick-line drawing of simple motifs in the so-called Moche I and II phases gave way to fine-line, more descriptive drawing of narrative scenes during Moche III and IV. This further evolved into ever more complex and busy imagery in phase V. Larco Hoyle's sequence has been further elaborated by Christopher Connan, who subdivided Larco's phase III in A, B, and C subphases. There is no exact time correlation for each phase due to the independent evolution of the styles in the diverse valleys of the north coast, except possibly for Moche V, inaugurated around 600 AD, and corresponding already to the Middle Horizon. Moche artistic sequences are based exclusively on goods retrieved from graves and therefore on almost exclusively religious art. The sequence emphasizes abrupt changes rather than a possible continuity. On the basis of iconography, we can subdivide Moche culture into the following larger periods:

- Early Period: Moche I and II
- Middle Period: Moche III and IV
- Late Period: Moche V

The Moche inhabited the valleys of Moche, Chicama, Jequetepeque, Lambayeque, and Piura, and to the south Virú, Santa, and Nepeña, and maybe even Casma. They cohabited with the Gallinazo in most if not all of these areas. It is only in the Moche and Chicama Valleys that there is a visible transition from the end of Gallinazo influence to the beginning of Moche culture.[2] Both Moche and Gallinazo buried their representatives within their platform mounds.

Recent scholars do not see clear dividing lines between Gallinazo and Moche; in fact no racial differences have been detected. What distinguishes them most is their ideology, particularly in their artistic expression. Moche iconography is richer, especially that associated with the pottery vessels, the textiles, and metals associated with the burial of elite figures—in short, all of the symbolism associated with power.

Apart from the Moche heartland, the Gallinazo culture survived alongside the Moche to the north and to the south. In the Virú Valley, Gallinazo persisted until about 350. It continued undisturbed even longer in the northern area.

The Rise of Moche Culture

The main center of early Moche civilization lay in the Moche and Chicama Valleys. Only one site close to Cerro Blanco (Moche Valley) can be attributed to Moche I, whereas Gallinazo occupation is far more widespread. The same was true in the neighboring Virú Valley. It was only in the Phase III that Moche became widespread.[3] It is believed that in Moche III, around 350–400, the Virú Valley and its neighbors were invaded.

Although some other authors see little cultural importance in the early Moche phases, G. Bawden underlines that the ceremonial art found in burials already marked the emergence of a new ideology.[4] These traces were rather subtle at first; they hardly indicated the practice of human sacrifice that was to follow.

Moche culture flowed into the continuity of previous monumental ceremonial complexes. The construction techniques continued unaltered. The Gallinazo had developed the imposing ceremonial centers. The platforms and pyramids dominated a dispersed pattern of settlement. Concentration into more urbanized centers followed in the Moche period, especially from Phase V on. As for the architecture, the major irrigation systems used by the Moche were for the most part inherited from the Gallinazo culture. Likewise, the pottery used for cooking, storage, or serving continued the Gallinazo tradition. Even ceremonial vessels evolved from Gallinazo precedents, both in form and often in the use of artistic motifs.

In conclusion, Moche was not, by and large, a foreign cultural invasion but rather a new ideology developed by people of the same ethnic background as the Gallinazo. Some external triggers, such as natural disasters, may have created the material ground for its growing strength. Such seems to have been the case in the Piura region, where Moche ideology followed a major flood that had partially destroyed parts of the Gallinazo complex of Cerro Ñañañique. Moche emerged in various places at different times and expressed itself variably according to the local culture. It is quite likely that Gallinazo persisted, especially in valleys north of the Chicama Valley, throughout the EIP. Only during the Middle Horizon—Moche Phase V—was the local Gallinazo culture overpowered. The valleys of the south resisted the change forced upon them during Moche III and IV, and were conquered. It is of some interest to look at the differences between the north and south of Moche territory, since this difference forms a pattern that subsisted for centuries afterwards.

Moche in the Northern Area

Generally, Gallinazo settlements were located in the lower valleys and by the sea; Moche occupied the inland, and the relationship between the two was peaceful even for part of the Middle Horizon.

In some places Moche and Gallinazo offerings are even found in the same burials, as is the case in Pacatnamú in the Jequetepeque Valley. In the Middle La Leche Valley, Gallinazo and Moche occupied the same ceremonial center and a center for the production of ceramics, a fact that implies the highest level of peaceful cohabitation seen heretofore. There is also little evidence of Moche Phase IV in the stylistic sequence, both in the Upper Piura and in the Jequetepeque Valley. However, this does not mean that Moche ideology was not as fully developed. In San Jose (Jequetepeque Valley) were found some of the richest Moche burials of the north coast; here were buried women who officiated as priestesses in the sacrifice ritual, even though Phase IV Moche evidence hasn't been found. This picture does not support the idea of an extensive and unified Moche Empire, but rather various territorial, centralized units.

The ideological presence of Moche in the Lambayeque Valley is even more impressive than in the Moche heartland. The display of wealth at the tombs of Sipan surpasses even what is visible in the Moche capital. Clearly this wasn't a subordinate center. However, in this region Gallinazo and Moche coexisted. Archaeologists suspect that the two cultures' coexistence in the northern territory may be due to the fact that there was a large agricultural capacity, able to support all societies present, thus no competition for limited resources.

The upper Piura presents a complex picture. During the EIP, evidence shows that some communities adopted the Moche worldview while others retained their earlier Gallinazo orientation. In fact in the Piura-Tumbes region, little evidence of Moche ideology is present during the whole of the EIP. Over time Moche started prevailing and functioning as a unifying culture among the various communities. In the Upper Piura Moche culture expressed itself in sophisticated metalwork rather than with effigy vessels. This suggests once more an independent adoption of Moche symbolism by local communities, rather than a model imposed from the outside.

Representations of the ritual of sacrifice, particularly high-ranking individuals portrayed holding a trophy head in one hand and a sacrificial knife in the other—the so-called decapitator motif—appeared particularly in Sipan and San José during the Middle and Late Moche.

Moche in the Southern Valleys

Things stand differently in the Virú Valley and further south, where the Gallinazo cultural influence was suddenly disrupted and replaced by Moche standards of culture. Invasion and subjugation is the most generally accepted hypothesis. Gallinazo ceremonial centers were abandoned and replaced by new centers. There was a movement of expanded agricultural activity from the north side—the one cultivated by the Gallinazo—to the south side of the Virú Valley.

In the Huancaco site, presence of defensive walls indicates that Moche presence was not peaceful.[5] The conquest of the Virú Valley involved some displacement of indigenous population together with the influx of people from Moche and Chicama Valleys. Finally this involved the building of Moche platforms. In the Santa Valley (closer to Virú), there is evidence of massive Moche intervention accompanied with displacement of the previous population toward the lower valley with a resulting 500 percent increase of population.[6] This valley was an important food supplier and offers a confirmation that the Moche's reason for expansion lay in the limited resources of its heartland.

At the southern edge Moche culture interfaced with Recuay highland culture. The relationships between Recuay and Gallinazo had been mostly peaceful. This changed with the advent of Moche polity; it turned to distrust and often open enmity, and resulted in a pattern of Recuay occupation of the upper valleys and the Moche holding on to mid-valleys and coastline. Fortresses were present at the demarcation line.

Moche Society and Ideology

Moche social organization was very strictly vertical. There was a clear division between the nobility and the masses. The ruling class is most often portrayed with a haughty attitude, faraway look, and tyrannical gestures. Its members wore very large golden ear plugs and also nose rings. In their tombs the bodies of dignitaries had metal pieces covering their eyes, nose, and chin.

The Moche lived in a continuous state of warfare among themselves, even between groups of the same valley. Historians suspect that much of the fighting was done in a ritual manner. In fact Moche art most often describes ritual battles, processions of captives, and ritual human sacrifice. However, there is no suggestion of permanent standing armies. The absence of armies and of a clear model for political control rendered Moche occupation precarious.

Centralization of power manifested itself, among other things, with the formation of a class of artisans that specialized in the production of the symbols of power, objects that were destined solely for the elite. The "portrait vessels" are the clearest illustration of this proposition and one of the most admired artistic expressions of Peru. Almost all of the portrait vessels have been found in the central valleys. In those vessels the individuals are recognizable through their articles of clothing and especially their headdresses. These articles were clearly reserved for the use of individuals with specific positions of power in the sacrifice ritual.

The Moche reached high achievements in their architecture. The most famous specimens are the so-called Waka de la Luna and Waka del Sol. Sun and Moon are later epithets, probably superposed by the Incas and do not bear any known relationship to fact! Waka del Sol may have been more administrative in function, Waka de la Luna more ceremonial. The Waka del Sol measured some 130' and had a 525' x 1130' base. It was the largest in the Americas, but has since been partly washed away. There were eight stages of construction, most of which were concluded by 450 AD.

Waka de la Luna measures 950' x 690' at the base and rises to 105'. It counts six construction stages spanning over six hundred years. It is located in front of Waka del Sol at the foot of Cerro Blanco. Here are found polychromatic murals in relief that have high symbolic value. They are part of late Moche art. Some of them have been introduced through later influence, or adoption of, ideas from the Wari empire.

Through the art of the portrait vessels, and especially what is present in the major ceremonial centers, we can have a fair idea of Moche religion and of their main deity, Ai–Apaec. The early Moche representations of Ai–Apaec, the God of Water, show him as a feline crowned with an emblem of rows of wave-crests. Later, Ai–Apaec is represented by a human body and predominantly human head with a feline mouth and an avian crest and sometimes wings. At other times only the head is shown (figure 1.1). The deity feeds on decapitated heads in order to ensure the fertilizing role of water.

Figure 1.1: Ai-apaec

Around the waist Ai-Apaec wears a snake belt. He always displays large ear plugs and in many instances holds a *tumi*—a ceremonial half-moon knife—in front of a potential victim, or is decapitating him. In Sipan the decapitator is represented as an anthropomorphic spider with fanged mouth and double ear spools. Some artistic pieces show the victims thrown off from a mountain summit, Ai-Apaec's symbolic abode.

Other significant aspects give us a further view of Moche ritual life. The first are the ceramics depicting different forms of sexual intercourse, especially in sculptural pottery. These themes are unique among Peruvian civilization. At times they clearly represent sexual relationships between the living and the dead. Sexual acts are portrayed in the most diverse positions and types: autoerotism, fellatio, homosexuality, anal sex, etc. Autoeroticism and the heterosexual are very commonly portrayed. Also represented are "anthropofalluses" and "anthropovulvas." F. Kauffman Doig believes that the majority of sexual scenes correspond to ritual context in relation to earth fertility.

The Moche also portray—especially in Phase V—the myth of the advent of eternal night. The absence of the sun is coupled to the theme of the rebellion of human artifacts, a theme that was widespread throughout the whole of Peru and that echoes the episode of the Popol Vuh at the end of the Mesoamerican Third Age. The theme appears in the Waka de la Luna, in the mural painting known as *the Rebellion of Domestic Implements* that covers the walls of what seems to have been a temple. It shows individuals who try to save themselves from objects with arms and legs—especially cooking utensils—attacking them. In the neighboring Lambayeque Valley's monument of La Mayanga (or Huaca Facho) this mythological scene is recognizable through the motif of the humanized and winged clubs and shields.

Human Sacrifice

Everything we have discussed above has gradually introduced us to Moche's central ritual, the Sacrifice Ceremony. This is the theme already introduced through Ai–Apaec, the Decapitator God.

Fine-line drawings on portrait vessels often portray Moche warriors in procession, probably marching to the battlefield. Combat most likely took place in set aside areas, away from cultivated fields and from inhabited settlements. Depictions show what seems to be the desert. No regular troops or army units are portrayed; only individuals in one-on-one combat. Fighters were overcome by hitting them on the head or body with a war-club. Obviously, capture was sought, not death. The defeated enemy lost his headdress and other parts of his uniform—used as a trophy—and the opponent removed his nose ornament and slapped him in the face and /or grabbed him by the hair. After that all clothing was removed and the captive was led with a rope tied around his neck. The prisoners were then presented to a high authority atop a pyramid. Sometimes the captives are depicted as anthropomorphized deer with ropes around their necks. The captor himself can be represented as an anthropomorphized feline. The above warrior combats and sacrifices appear frequently portrayed in the phases Moche III and IV.

Many themes we are evoking are reminiscent of what we have previously found to be true of Cerro Sechin—before our era—although in a different art style. The "hawk marking" theme—the eye line across the warriors' eyes—has been carried further by the Moche. Otherwise, we can also find a parallel in later Aztec "flower" wars that were carried out in a similar manner and for the same intentions.

The sacrifice itself was carried out through the slitting of the throat. The prisoner was then dismembered and hands, feet, and head tied together with ropes to create a trophy. The captive's blood was taken for ritual consumption as one can see in many effigy vessels in the figure of the Priest Warrior taking a cup of blood. Sacrifice ceremonies are abundantly portrayed in Moche art. In the so-called Mural Bonavia, one can recognize a priestly hierarchy comprising the Warrior Priest, the Bird Priest, the Priestess, and another assistant priest. In the background of these representations are often visible fruits that have the shape of a curved pear or large drop. This is most likely the fruit called *ulluchu* that is believed to have kept the blood from coagulating.

The specific participants in the sacrifice ceremony do not appear at all in Phases Moche I and II. However, the decapitator motif is already present in early Moche art, particularly in Upper Piura to the north. In the oldest of the Sipan burials, the high priest is buried with articles that portray the decapitator but nothing that makes the sacrifice ceremony recognizable. Everything points to the conclusion that the sacrifice ceremony, specific to Moche III phase, had been secretly prepared in earlier phases. The new importance of the ceremony corresponds in time with Moche territorial expansionism.

In Sipan we can trace the development of the sacrifice ceremony in a manner that confirms the hypotheses put forward thus far. Here have been found the likely tombs of the high priests that followed each other in time. They allow us to retrace the development of Moche ideology to the ideological culmination of the sacrifice ceremony.

Tomb 3 is an early tomb that hosts the remains of the "Old Lord of Sipan" who had died at the dawn of Moche civilization, some 200 years earlier (~0 to 100 AD) than the more famous but later "Lord of Sipan."[7] It likely belongs to what Larco calls Moche I or II. In it Moche ideology is not yet fully established. The tomb was found 16' below the surface of the pyramid, therefore in the latter's earliest phase of construction. As in the later Tombs 1 and 2 the individual was buried with rich offerings. Among the objects placed atop him was found a gold necklace of circular beads representing the motif of the spider with the human head as its body. Further in the pile was a feline head of gilded copper with a very striking, ferocious expression and a double-headed serpent motif on its forehead. The figure's legs and arms spread out in a menacing gesture with clawed hands and feet. The whole composition measures 2' high. It seems that the objects had been intentionally broken before burial. In the tomb were found a golden and a silver scepter. The silver one shows a warrior with a rack above his head from which hang two heads. An anthropomorphized crab in gilded copper is another representation of the Decapitator God. Above the pelvis of the old lord lay sets of bells and so-called backflaps (which hang from the waist), portraying the decapitator holding a knife in one hand and a human head on the other.

Tomb 3 pre-announces the elements that are later developed further in Tomb 1. Almost all the steps of the sacred sacrifice are portrayed in the objects of Tomb 1 on what is most likely the tomb of the warrior priest.

Together with the Warrior Priest there is another figure buried together with a dog. On the warrior's backflaps is portrayed the Decapitator God, the supernatural who holds a crescent-bladed knife on one hand, and on the other the human head held from its hair. The Decapitator is an anthropomorphized spider. Spiders are apt symbols for a ceremony in which the prisoner is captured, tied, and his blood extracted.

It seems that in some places or in some stages of the ceremony a special role also devolved to a priestess. This is what has been found in San José del Moro in the Jequetepeque valley, not far from Sipan. Here the singular casket of a priestess is outwardly decorated with metal laminas that mirror the corresponding parts of her body and portray the figure as if she were flying, accentuated by the ritual wings above her head. In the same site another two tombs were found. In one of these is present a ceramic chalice decorated with scenes that portray how it was used for human sacrifice. Other specimens portray cruel scenes of sacrifice. The whole points to the important part that the priestess played in the rituals. In the mural of Pañamarca, described by Bonavia, there is also a feminine figure holding a cup in her hand in a sacrificial context.

Symbolism of sacrifice holds the central place in Moche ritualism. It is also developed in the themes of the ritual combat and the ritual hunt. Scenes that portray ritual combats contain combinations of human combatants, mythical beings, and anthropomorphic birds and animals, encompassing thus both the physical and the supernatural worlds. We have already seen the dimensions of human combat and what they teach us of the historical component of it. Supernatural combat preceded the human combat in time. In a "confrontation theme" portrayed by Luis Jaime Castillo, a cultural hero with Moche elite traits battles a fantastic animal.[8] Both hold in their hands a *tumi* and a severed head. In what looks like a narrative, the hero appears in the final depictions holding the head of the monster in the so-called Decapitator pose.

The sacred hunt, as it is portrayed in pottery, was led by a restricted elite group and depicted in association with religious symbolism. The hunters wore elaborate feather headdresses indicating that this was an exclusive activity of the elite. The dead deer is sometimes portrayed in the position of the sacrificial captive, seated upright, with a rope around the neck and limbs. These traditions persisted in later times in the northern highlands where they were part of religious and sacrificial ceremonies, of which we have a historical record.[9]

Middle Intermediate Horizon and the End of Moche Civilization

In the years 562–594, drought accompanied by exceptionally erosive flood events—maybe also earthquakes—caused major changes all over Peru and particularly on the north coast, following an El Niño event of eighteen months or more. This was in fact one of the longest droughts in history. Since the water table lowered, irrigation was less available and the drier soil was more easily eroded. Water and sanitation systems were probably destroyed. Strong winds, blowing from the ocean, caused the formation of sand dunes with consequent loss of productive land, and pushed the farming population to the hinterlands. The capital of Cerro Blanco was evacuated at the close of Phase IV. Fishing, however, was not equally affected.

Added to this, and especially along Moche's southern border, was the added pressure exerted from the Wari empire. Its influence, felt over a large part of the territory, is most clearly visible in the record of the pottery between the sixth and eighth centuries. However, there is no evidence of Wari direct occupation of the north coast.

Moche individual expression of power, with its strong social inequalities, was the innate source of social stress. To this tension were added external pressures, particularly in the south that had been conquered beforehand. It was at this time that the important center of Pachacamac (close to Lima) acquired growing importance, indicating that the recourse to oracles, harkening back to Chavin times, found a resurgence in time of crises.

The so-called Moche Phase V, that marks the beginning of the Middle Horizon, takes its start from around 600, after the above events. It is recognizable through the erection of *pukaras* and fortified settlements. The southern valleys—from Huarmey through Virú—separated themselves from the Moche heartland. No Moche V phase is detectable there. The capital of Cerro Blanco was abandoned and so was much of the cultivated land in the central and northern valleys.

The Moche capital moved to Cerro Galindo on the north side of the valley neck, in a place important for strategic and defensive purposes, beginning as a fortified hillside. The capital had little in terms of monumental buildings. Interestingly however, it had a rectangular sunken court, one of the last of the surviving tradition.

In the north, the new capital was Pampa Grande in the Lambayeque Valley. Here, gigantic pyramids survived. The north and south continued to differentiate in a way that holds interest for our further analysis. This contrast is most visible in the complementary aspects of Galindo and Pampa Grande, the most important cities.

Galindo

Even though the site of Cerro Blanco was abandoned, the Waka de la Luna was continually in use until the Late Period without a break. The new Moche Valley center was Galindo, on the north shore of the river, twenty miles from the ocean in a position that was more easily defendable. Galindo was essentially a newly developed town, even though there had been a modest settlement previously. In Galindo what strikes the eye most are the elements of geographical, social, and architecturally functional segregation. The lower-status occupants of the steep slopes were separated by a wall from the rest of the population and from access to water. High walls also enclosed administrative buildings, and a whole area built on the terraces of a spur of Mount Galindo that was used for storage of subsistence goods. That an entire section of the city is devoted to one-room structures used for storage of staples, indicates the degree of concern for survival. It is clear that the rulers feared a time of scarcity, following the many previous natural catastrophes, and did not trust the support of the population at large.

In Galindo there was a notable change in architectural functions. The platforms receded both in function and size. Moreover they were located toward the periphery. In the center the platform was replaced by the *cercadura*—a structured enclosure. Toward the outside, the *cercadura* presented high perimeter walls. Inside, it was divided into small enclosed spaces, kept remote and hidden from public view. This leads archaeologists to believe that Galindo abandoned the public ceremonies of the platforms. This is a pattern that survived until the time of the Incas throughout Middle and Late Horizons.

A new complex appeared that enclosed a burial platform, surrounded by high walls and connected to the outside through a small gateway. Probably the burial platform was used only by one ruler and his family. This too survived in later times, particularly in Chimú culture.

Pampa Grande

In the north I. Shimada suggests that the Moche conquered the local Gallinazo culture that had survived side by side with it until then.[10] In fact, the largest segment of the population was probably formed by the subjected Gallinazo.

In the northern valleys there was more continuity than in Moche. However, here too the establishment of Pampa Grande occurred over a relatively short time. It was established like Galindo at the neck of the valley, where there was little previous settlement. However, the town is different in some aspects from its southern counterpart. Like Galindo the core administrative functional center of the city is also functionally and formally compartimentalized. Added to this were highly organized workshop spaces for specialized crafts, where access was limited and controlled. The city is dominated by Waka Grande, or Waka Fortaleza, one of the largest platforms of the pre-Columbian New World. It is 125' high, and covers an area of 885' x 590'. What is unique about its construction is the fact that it was not built of successive additions, covering the previous ones. It made recourse to the chamber and fill construction method, which allowed a fast construction pace. Thus, like Galindo, Pampa Grande was built hastily.

Moche V overall is characterized by the struggle for ideological adjustment. G. Bawden sees this adjustment occurring most successfully in the Jequetepeque Valley with its enduring focus on the Sacrifice Ceremony.[11] It was in Galindo that iconographic changes show the most. Radical changes appear here in the burial practices, where the *cercaduras* replaced the traditional platforms. The burial platforms suggest the new practice of deifying the ruler.

New symbolism also appeared in the artistic realm. Shortly before this time the Waka de la Luna was ornamented with a polychrome mural that displayed a large anthropomorphic being resembling the motif of the Staff God of the Gateway of the Sun at Tiwanaku—the *Mural of the Figure with Scepters*, found buried by later paintings. This shows a human figure with arms outstretched, holding staffs that have a snake-like appearance and end in feline heads. From comparative analyses, these heads could represent lightning. The new figure shows analogies with the Tiwanaku Gateway of the Sun and the figure of Chavin's Stela Raimondi. The new deity probably reached Moche via the Wari culture, who had imported it from Tiwanaku's later phases. It seems that at the time, the Moche culture was struggling to reinvigorate its ideology by creating links with the past that would offer it new legitimacy.

Another theme closely related to the previous one is that of the Tule Boat, portraying the arrival of newcomers from far-off maritime origins.

The leader is surrounded by a circle of feline rays. The boat carries bound captives. This looks like an attempt to merge two sets of symbols: the first of the Prophet coming at the time of the Dawning, the second of the sacrificing priesthood. Thus, even with new symbolism, the old message is continued. This is the same theme of the Lambayeque and Taycanamo legends that originated in the north coast. Is has not been clearly established, however, whether the Naymlap legend precedes or follows the Moche.

Middle Intermediate Horizon and the Emergence of Wari

The beginning of the Middle Horizon gives rise to a disruption of the previous state of affairs. The outward trigger was very likely the prolonged drought from 562 to 594, as can be seen from indications gained through ice cores taken from Andean glaciers.[12] At this time in the central sierra, in the region of Ayacucho, grew the political power of Wari (see map 1, p. 14), the most powerful political entity of the "Age of the Peoples of War."

Two types of organizations emerged during the Middle Period: *intensive* and *extensive* ones. Coastal Moche was an intensive solution, a cultural presence that took over administrative functions, at least in the southern part. The extensive approach lies in the practice of establishing colonies or satellite communities to integrate the economy in diverse environments. When the state reinforced its structure, these "islands" became administrative nodes and connected with strengthened communication systems of roads, places of storage, networks of distribution, etc. In this approach there was no need to control the territory in between. M. Moseley believes that the Wari model was more extensive than intensive.[13] However, he sees direct military evidence of Wari presence in some places, as in the fortified colony of Cerro Baúl, placed atop a very steep summit, close to the Moquequa River, in the direction of Tiwanaku. The same could be said for the area of Nazca.

Before the time of the Middle Horizon, in the valley of Ayacucho towns coexisted peacefully. Thus, for example, in the most productive bottomlands there were three towns and five villages that co-existed within a circle of 3.5 miles with no evidence of fortifications.[14] The Huarpa people of the Ayacucho area, who were among the first ones to irrigate and terrace mountain territory, had built a very large and innovative agricultural system. This preexisting infrastructure gave Wari the ability to withstand droughts better than their neighbors. Since the concentrated pattern of settlement in the valley could not support itself on the basis of local resources, there must have been exploitation of distant colonies in mutual agreement between different groups, coexisting in peace. This peaceful cohabitation is also reflected in the valley through what appears as a rather homogeneous art style.

One example of Ayacucho's distant exploitation of resources at the end of the EIP appears in the Nazca Valley, as can be evidenced through the presence there of Ayacucho ceramics.[15] In the valley are three settlements placed on a straight line, parallel to the coast, on major tributaries of the Nazca drainage system. The strategic placement of the colonies may already have marked an intentional move toward a more centralized control of the territory. In later epochs, the Wari expanded first toward the north to Cañete and Chincha, and successively to the south. This gives an indication that in some places the Wari directly occupied territory, whereas in others they were content with more indirect forms of control.

There are indications showing that Wari attacked Tiwanaku but did not stay, probably because of the ongoing drought that afflicted the altiplano. However, the occupiers took back with them Tiwanaku architects, builders, and laborers to build monuments in their new imperial capital. Some of these artisans were captives in urban *mitimaes* (colonies that offered their labor as tribute). Apart from the Tiwanaku, the Wari people had also brought back to the capital the goldsmiths and metal workers of Callejon de Huaylas and Cajamarca.[16]

Wari was situated on a steep slope between 8,800' and 10,200' on the eastern ridge of the Ayacucho Valley. It quickly grew during the early Middle Horizon (600 to 700) and survived until about 1000. The growth of the empire was accompanied with migrations of population from the periphery. Estimates of the capital's population go from a conservative range of 10,000 to 20,000 to a probably overestimated evaluation of 50,000 to 100,000.[17] The change toward the rise of empire occurred quite abruptly. Large-scale construction was performed where previous buildings were destroyed. During Middle Horizon 1 (AD 600–700) there was a phase of construction of temples that was abandoned in the epoch of the Middle Horizon 2 (700 to 800) and the temples left unfinished. In the emerging state organization the building of an imperial structure followed, and Wari grew into a city of about 1,000 acres.

A distinguishing element of the city is its massive walls that run parallel or perpendicular to the contour lines; some of them up to 16' wide. However, the perimeter of the city was not fortified, indicating that protection was directed to internal sources rather than external threats.

The empire extended its political control to the north up to Cajamarca and to the south, as far as Nazca's coast. Wari's presence is recognizable by the layout of Wari's distinctive architecture carefully replicated throughout the territory. Wari administrative centers were scattered across the cordillera from Pikillaqta in the south near Cuzco, to Cajamarca in the north. Evidence of the coexistence of Wari with other independent ethnic groups is most obvious in the Carahuarazo Valley, where at the time was a strong independent state with a capital in Marcahuamachuco, less than 2 miles away from the important Wari complex of Viracochapampa.[18]

Wari's influence spread as far as the north coast. However, here it was more present through its ideology than through physical presence. Elements of Wari iconography diffused north to the Moche, who adopted Wari's version of the Staff God at the Waka de la Luna; it went as far north as Batan Grande in the Leche Valley of the Lambayeque basin.

The empire expanded quite rapidly in a period of one hundred and fifty years and declined in the period going from 800 to 1000. Its collapse was quite abrupt, as is illustrated by a phase of monumental building in the city of Wari that was left unfinished prior to the city's abandonment. After Wari's end, a pattern emerged of a multitude of warring cities and villages that were built and fortified on top of mountain ridges. One of these was the Chanca nation, of which more will be said below.

Wari's Architecture and Art

Wari's most symptomatic legacy speaks through the special form of its architecture defined by W. Isbell as "orthogonal cellular style."[19] The main architectural unit of the city is what could be called a "walled enclosure." This structure conforms to different patterns. One of these consists of tight-nested rooms around a circular or D-shaped courtyard. Another, probably later pattern, was made of rectangular enclosures divided into square or rectangular patios, with rooms on three or four of its sides. These were residential units—in fact families lived in units similar to an apartment. W. H. Isbell indicates that this pattern, especially in its original form, repeats the arrangement of rooms around sunken courts at Pucara on the Titicaca high plateau.[20]

For a time archaeologists were puzzled by the use of these architectural forms. It is now clear that they were actually inhabited, not just storage places or garrisons, as it was initially believed. Some of the striking features of Wari architecture include: streets and roads bordered by high, parallel stone walls; narrow gates and doorways restricting flow; architectural units of standard forms; almost complete lack of drainage, water supply, or gardens; use of walls to isolate entire parts of a city; and sealed chambers hiding funerary or offering deposits located under floors, behind walls, or in independent buildings. The latter often take the form of pits under the floor, carelessly built, where among other things have been found human figurines, human bones, and skulls.

Overall, a mood of confinement hovers above Wari's squarely laid cities. The emergence of this kind of architecture is a very abrupt phenomenon. There are no previous similar structures in Ayacucho's valley, where Wari was first established. However, there is a certain functional analogy with Moche's late phase in the city of Galindo, and with Chimú architecture of which we will speak later.

There is no more fitting comparison and contrast than between Tiwanaku's EIP phase and Wari's architecture. Tiwanaku's early architecture emphasized public space and openness, vast views over the horizon. The logarithmic progression of lines, walls, and single motifs gave a harmonious feeling of integration with the environment. The beautifully carved architrave is a symptomatic expression of this architecture, an element that is completely absent from Wari, and one that disappears in the late Tiwanaku polity that converged toward Wari's ideological themes.

Only at the beginning did Wari build megalithic chambers for funerary purposes, resembling those of Tiwanaku. However, they were completely shut, and in this differed from their political and ideological counterpart. Wari completely emphasized closed spaces and the principles of subdivision in smaller units. Buildings were not adapted to the environment. They followed straight lines regardless of the topography, as is clearly visible in Pikillacta, near Cuzco. Everything gives the feeling of enclosure and exclusion; no space was devoted to public ceremonies. In fact, movement from one place to the next must have been difficult. One has the impression that these cities were bureaucratically planned.

Tiwanaku and Wari played two opposite roles in spreading their influence. The former, earlier, spiritual capital was a center of pilgrimage, where ceremonies were performed publicly. Tiwanaku had regional temples within a radius of 36 miles. Whereas Wari's architecture spread 621 miles from the capital, no temples accompanied it.

The architectural record reveals something else. In the capital, under a later building archaeologists have discovered a spectacular rectangular sunken court. Carbon dating of material associated with it has yielded a date of 580 +/− 60, corresponding to the city's early stage.[21] The court was used over a long time, and just as in previous ages, the floors were periodically renewed. This is a first indication of the ideology of the Southern Cross continued past its time.

We may complete the image of Wari ideology from another angle yet. In this regard its interaction with Late Tiwanaku is very revealing. In effect, in the early stages of Wari's development Tiwanaku influences emerged in the architecture as we just saw above. Some archaeologists speculate that there were Wari pilgrimages to Tiwanaku. Others suggest that there were missionaries from the Titicaca capital coming to Ayacucho.[22] The incipient Wari borrowed ideological themes from Tiwanaku at a point in which the altiplano capital had moved to a new cultural stage. At the end of Tiwanaku phase 3 or beginning of phase 4, new religious symbolism surfaced that has been designated as "Tiwanakoid." Its defining figures also appear contemporaneously in Conchopata, 6 miles from Wari. The main theme is that of a frontal figure with arms raised, with a headdress that terminates with rays—stalk-like projections—that end in animal heads. There are two versions of this being; one with a long tunic and a belt; the other with the same garment but without the belt. It may be that the first is a male version, the other a female one. The same being can be accompanied by an angel or one or more rows of angels to its right and left. The main character is often called the "front-face deity." This much resembles the Staff God of Tiwanaku's Gateway of the Sun. However there is another constant element: trophy heads endlessly repeated.

Together with these themes, in the Tiwanaku altiplano we notice the presence of wooden articles in the form of shallow trays, found in conjunction with snuffing tubes carved in bone, used for ritual snuffing of hallucinogenic powders. These are replaced in the Ayacucho area by the *kero*-shaped goblets that have the same Tiwanakoid designs. Isbell believes that this may be the functional equivalent for hallucinogenics taken in the liquid form.[23] W. H. Isbell concludes: "There can be little doubt that Tiwanakoid iconography belongs to a mythical tradition with its roots in the late Chavin culture." The front-face deity is a modified version of the Raimondi stone.

There is a style that continues the Chavin tradition in the time between the two cultures—Pukara, where we find a small sculpture of the front-face deity with staffs, headdress, and other attributes matching Tiwanakoid elements. The trophy heads are also abundantly portrayed there. Isbell thinks that Tiwanakoid iconography was derived from Pucara and spread simultaneously to Tiwanaku and Wari.[24] However, Pucara was abandoned around 200 and the Tiwanakoid style reemerged around 500. Since no historical continuity has been established, we believe that this is a cultural resurgence of a theme that had emerged during the time of Chavin's decadence. So, we can only speak of a cultural thread, not a historical one. Note that this is a repeated pattern we have already found in the Salinar-Moche continuity, which also does not correspond to a historical continuity.

Finally, we can complete the picture from yet another side. The center of Pachacamac was established during the Middle Horizon. Some scholars believe that it was an independent center from Wari, developing its own symbolism, particularly recognizable in the symbol of the "Pachacamac griffin." This same motif, however, has also been found in excavations in the site of Wari, together with other trademarks of Pachacamac symbolism.[25] The use of the shamanistic methods associated with hallucinogens, recourse to oracles, and the ideology of trophy heads all indicate a return to decadent Chavin times.

As the record shows, Wari's iconography shared little with early Tiwanaku. Instead it returned to themes that were common before the EIP that returned in vigor in the late phases of Tiwanaku. This is the case particularly with Wari's new version of the Staff God. The god went from being a solar deity to expressing himself as an agrarian fertility god. The solar rays of the headdress were replaced by ears of corn. In many other instances the staffs carry trophy heads at their ends. A. Cook calls Wari's deity the sacrificer rather than the Staff God because of the distinguishing motif of the trophy head and axe that he holds in the right hand, and the additional trophy heads around the eyes.[26]

The deity often holds a tethered llama, an animal that served as a symbolic analogy for the subjugated foe, who could be sacrificed in a similar manner to the deer, a theme already encountered in Moche culture. The sacrificer theme evolved in time toward simpler versions, particularly from the whole body to a simple head, another theme that we have seen in Moche culture among others.

Wari Ideology

We can now try to draw some conclusions as to Wari's ideology, although only tentatively, given the fragmentary nature of present day research. Wari was the first Andean entity to introduce an organized collection of tribute taken from a centrally organized state. This consisted in tribute in labor rather than in goods. For this to be possible, the state had to organize a whole infrastructure of roads and system of distribution of goods. The Wari empire put in place a system of administrative centers scattered throughout the territory with networks of roads and *tampus*—places of rest and for storing food and goods. The Incas continued this tradition centuries later, even reutilizing part of the surviving Wari infrastructure. The Incas however, did this under an ideology quite different from Wari's.

Administrative centers are found in Jincamoco, Viracocha-pampa, and Pikillacta (near Cuzco), the most studied among various others. These contain evidence of barracks-like quarters, community kitchens, and warehouses, and what would have been residential facilities for the local leader and his attendants. These three centers, and others like them, served for the coordination of the effort of manpower for agricultural or crafts production. Here we find large kitchens and earthenware obviously used for serving a large amount of people. In this scheme of affairs, Pikillakta or Viracochapampa may have served the use of second-order capitals in the Wari empire.

Wari's power could not have been merely political. Its spiritual doctrine is harder to identify and reconcile with the fact that in many places Wari granted quite a high degree of local autonomy. Some archaeological discoveries may serve to shed some light. Wari's link with the cult of Pachacamac will highlight a complementary aspect.

One of the most instructive discoveries of Wari's cult comes from the contents of two of the subfloor caches of the site of Pikillacta. In each cache forty figures were found arranged in a circle and prostrated in an act of submission around a bronze rod (a scepter or war-club). Each of the figures, differently dressed, represented the archetypal totality of the number 40, meaning a totality of the tribes. One of them has been recognized as a representative of Tiwanaku. What the caches most likely represented was the result of a ritual to bring all the other tribes to submission through magic.

In Collao (altiplano) folklore, Wari—or Lari—is the puma, invoked by the magician, from whose eyes flash tongues of fire.[27] The initiate of the

Andes is the one often represented, especially later by the Incas, as the one who has domesticated the puma; he has subjugated its forces for his own purposes. The image of the puma of fire accompanies all of Andean tradition, representing the untamed forces of the night deity that preceded the Dawning; forces that have now become regressive and are used by the sacrificer.

Another important source of power could have been Wari's link with the local and most important *wakas*, such as the oracle of Pachacamac, previously mentioned. This is an oracle cult that most likely originated from late Moche culture. Apart from playing an important part during the Wari Empire, the cult still cast a large shadow in the later stages of the Inca Empire.

A later particularity of Andean *wakas* was that of having relationships of different degrees among them. This practice originated under Wari, according to Maria Rostworowski.[28] The "family relationship" had an eminent economic function, since it gave the priests of the "mother *waka*" access to the lands of the related *wakas*. This translated into the request of tribute from the periphery toward the center. The goods of the harvest and other tributes were accumulated at the location of the high temple of the divinity. Each *waka* possessed land dedicated to the cult, such as the land needed to produce maize for the fermented corn *chicha* for its celebrations. The size of the land was proportional to the importance of the particular *waka*. This is a notion that is still fully visible, although in a completely modified way, in later Inca history.

Let us now look at the deity itself. Pachacamac was the god of the depth of the earth; he was the one who controlled the forces of the earth. His importance stemmed from the impact that earthquakes had all over the territory. According to the chronicler Avila, this was how he manifested his disapproval of human conduct. He could produce tremors of the earth through the least of the movements of his head. If he rose up, a cataclysm would ensue. Fear of earthquakes served as an incentive for offerings that would appease the god. According to Pizarro, in earlier times in Pachacamac the vultures and condors of the cult received anchovies and sardines daily, because of their use in human sacrifices.[29] In his myth, Pachacamac offered his mother to the carrion birds. Later she was buried and resurrected.

Pachacamac's temple was located close to Lima on the central coast at the time of the Incas. It was the site of an oracle and the pilgrimage for people of the coast who sought his divinations. According to Jorge Zevallos

Quiñones, the Great Waka del Sol of Moche was called Capujaida. In later Wari times, the original name was substituted with that of Pachacamac.[30] During Inca times the *waka* was named Waka of the Sun in accordance with Inca cosmology, since it was the largest. However, the name *Pachacamac* continued to be current among the local population, according to the chroniclers Cristobal Castro and Diego de Ortega Morejon, who said the local population did not adore the Sun but the *wakas* and the oracles.[31] Santa Cruz Pachacuti indicates that when the Inca emperor Wayna Capac arrived in Pachacamac, the priests of the sanctuary asked that he move their *waka* to Chimú.

With this latter information we have an element of speculation about the nature of Wari's power. Could the capital of the empire have central control over all the *wakas* under its territory, in the same way that the single *waka* extended its own control through its related *wakas*, and required tribute from the local populations? Could Wari's sacrificer have been the central *waka* to which all other *wakas* were related? With what we have from the archaeological record, it is too soon to draw a conclusion. Without anticipating too much, we can argue with certainty that the Inca endeavor adopted some similar forms, but radically opposite intentions.

With the Moche and Wari regimes, the legacy of the Prophet and its solar revelation were fading into the background—none of its constitutive elements were preserved. This tendency continued into the Late Horizon. It acquired different forms in the Chimú and Chanca societies. The second was the greatest opponent of the Inca Empire at its incipient stages. Chimú was the most vehement ideological and military opponent when the Inca attained their maximum expansion.

Late Intermediate Horizon and the Chimú Kingdom

The Late Intermediate Horizon is sometimes called the "Protohistoric Period." Let us look at the developments that accompanied this period in various regions of Peru.

In the high plateaus were the powerful Aymara kingdoms of the Lupaqa and Colla nations, to the southwest and northwest borders of Lake Titicaca, respectively. Other groups were the Cana, Umasuyo, Canchi, Charca, Pacaje, etc. The Inca accounts relate that these nations were constantly at war with each other. These assertions are confirmed by the evidence of fortified cities and differences of styles among the groups. In the Lupaqa region, after the demise of Tiwanaku the settlements moved away from the lower areas near the lake to hilltop locations above 13,000'. Most, or all of them, were surrounded by defensive walls. Since the ridged fields of the lowlands had been rendered inoperative, there was a return to a more pastoral lifestyle. At the same time all previous architecture disappeared: there is no presence of platform mounds, sunken courts, or gateways like the Gateway of the Sun. In contrast there was the innovation of the *chullpa* (or *"waka sepulturas"*), large burial towers for ruling families. The commoners were buried in circular pits.

In the southern sierra, the early settlements of the greater Urubamba region were characterized by hilltop fortified settlements. However, Cuzco's region presented an exception. The valley had a stronger, unified political structure under the first Incas or just before them. When the Incas came to power and started to expand, they shifted the population out of the hilltops toward the lower areas. This actually happened earlier in the Sacred Valley.[32]

In the central sierra there was the powerful ethnic group of the Wankas. Here too, low-lying sites were abandoned and the population moved to fortified hilltop settlements. On the north coast the situation developed that progressively led to the kingdom of Chimú.

Chimú Legends and History

The legends giving the genealogy of the Chimú rulers, according to Garcilaso de la Vega, harkened back to Tacaynamo, the civilizing hero of the north coast. R. Ravines sees in it a cultural continuity with the earlier Naymlap-Lambayeque legend.[33] This latter has interesting elements reminiscent of the figure of Thunupa, but there isn't sufficient evidence to ascertain its origin in time. Most of modern authors believe the Lambayeque legend refers to the events that took place after the Moche abandoned their capital at Pampa Grande, somewhere between 700 and 900. Others point to its connections with the Early Intermediate Period.

There is a difference between Tacaynamo and Naymlap legends. The latter applies to a political confederacy; the Taycanamo one refers to centralized rule. Differences notwithstanding, it seems likely that the Chimú tried to align themselves on this ideological precedent. The Chimú culture differentiated sometime around the tenth century AD. It was one of the most important political entities of the central Andes by 1450. Historically it seems that Chimú may have absorbed some of Wari's cultural patterns in the region around 750–900. However, there is no historical continuity between the two cultures.[34]

The historical references don't agree with each other, but at present, archaeological research indicates that Chimú influence spread in the coastal area up to the Andean piedmont in the latitudes between 3° 30' to 10° 50' south. This corresponds to a stretch of 620 miles of Pacific coastland and two-thirds of all irrigated lands along the desert.[35]

Central to Chimú's history is the El Niño event of A1100 that conditioned Chimú expansionism. In Phase 1 (900–1100), the focus of the state lay in developing the local canal networks. Agricultural production formed the primary wealth of the kingdom. Chimú Phase 2 (1100–1400) was inaugurated by the catastrophic episode of El Niño that brought flooding and caused havoc to part of the irrigation system. This was followed by Chimú's military expansionism, of which we know from the chronicles. The state turned to the collection of tribute, rather than the extraction of its own resources. This was seen in Chan Chan with the building of the Tello Ciudadela and its annexes, and Ciudadela Laberinto. In the latter (dated 1150–1200) appear the first large number of storerooms, likely used to store the influx of tribute taken from the conquered peoples. At the same time there was an attempt to restore the damaged irrigation system through the building of the La Cumbre canal that, however, failed. By Late Chimú 2 (1400) the local irrigation system was hardly functional.

A second campaign of conquest toward the north (Lambayeque) started between 1300 and 1370. This was reflected in the city of Chan Chan with a new expansion of construction. Kolata sees at this phase a possible change in the nature of the goods stored at Chan Chan.[36] Before that time there were also large storerooms that may have been used for agricultural products, whereas the smaller ones were probably reserved for objects of higher value. After 1300–1350 the storerooms were all of a standard size. Kolata sees confirmation of these data of the nature of Chimú expansion and of the simultaneous reduction of agricultural irrigation.

In summary, there was an initial phase in which the state relied on agricultural production, followed by a dual economy depending on local production and tribute levied from the empire, and finally a complete dependence upon tribute. In later times, no fishermen or farmers lived in the city, which had been completely turned into a place of governance.

The above phenomena went hand in hand with increasing social differentiation. The king acquired more and more status and authority, and the nobility expanded, creating an increasingly complex structure. The above was reflected in the evolving form of the so-called *ciudadelas* in the city of Chan Chan.

Chimú Architecture

Historical record, as well as legends, indicate that Chimú conquered Lambayeque, to the north, only very late. This is the source of the marked differences between south and north, continuing to echo the polarity we saw between Galindo to the south and Pampa Grande to the north in the Moche epoch. This polarity, however, inserts itself within a larger homogeneous tendency and unifying cosmology.

Chan Chan, the kingdom's capital, is dwarfed in the comparison with Lambayeque Valley's monuments. Although there was Chimú occupation, the absence of real Chimú centers indicates that the region enjoyed political autonomy to quite a degree.

During the Chimú period, pyramids were built with one terrace and one or two enclosures. They are generally oriented to the north, generally truncated, with a rectangular base, and with a frontal access ramp. Among these, one of the most important was likely the one at Pacatnamú (Jequetepeque Valley) to the north. This has been considered a pilgrimage site for the cult to the Moon, of which we know from historical sources. It was a place that had a role similar to the Pachacamac oracle. Such oracles were cosmopolitan places of worship that were respected across political boundaries.

South Chimú: Chan Chan

The unique pattern of Chan Chan (see map 1, p. 14) was never replicated elsewhere. It was one of the largest cities of the New World in its time, with estimates of its population varying from ten thousand to one hundred thousand. The name Chan Chan could derive from Sian, or Shian, meaning the Moon, an important pointer to the nature of its cults.[37] The marking characteristic of the city's architecture are its individual compounds, called *ciudadelas*, standing for citadel or small fortress. These are vast enclosures whose walls, often very high and thick, indicate a defensive function, although not from outside attackers, since there are no outer walls surrounding the city. In most if not all of the *ciudadelas*, there was only one access point from the north. In the city there is no central plaza pointing to a unified state or common ritual, nor a main street. In fact, in this city the parts seem more important than the whole.

The high walls of the *ciudadelas* indicate that there was great fear of theft. From the chronicles we know in fact that thieves were severely punished.[38] In some places walls reach more than 30' high and 2300' long. At times there are two and even three walls! Overall, however, the walls far exceed a defensive scope and may in fact denote an additional focus on status and the desire to impress.

Many images referring to the use of Chimú architecture have survived in ceramics, particularly in relation to the temple mounds. But no images were left of the capital Chan Chan and its own particular structures. This may indicate that what occurred in the *ciudadelas* was more private in nature.

The *ciudadelas* are threefold structures (Figure 1.2). In the central sectors of the enclosures—separated from the front *audiencias* (audience chambers) to the north—was carried the administrative function. The central sector became more and more the private domain of the king, his wives, and maybe a few court attendants. Added to these two parts is the funerary platform, a raised structure with a north-south orientation, with internal compartments designed for burials accompanied with offerings. The access to the cells was offered through lateral ramps of access to the north. Among the cells there was a larger one in the form of a T, most often situated centrally in the platform.

In the Ciudadela Laberinto, the platform has a central T-cell with twenty-four smaller cells around it. The cells contained offerings of high quality: pottery, fine weavings, sculpted wooden objects, metalwork, and Spondylus shell—a distinguishing material for royalty—both whole or ground. In this platform it seems that each cell would have twenty-four bodies buried. Whenever gender was recognizable, these were adolescent or young females.

This *ciudadela* with the enclosed funerary platform was not the early architectural pattern of the city; it became prominent in the later stages of Chimú civilization. The most likely hypothesis for the platforms is that they served as burials for important individuals. Evidence shows that the platform was the last component built in the *ciudadelas*. The platform was used at the death of the important individual, whose death may have been the occasion for rituals extended over time. A part of these ceremonies would have been the sacrifices of the women found in the accompanying cells. Nothing else would explain their selective presence. Specific burials for young women would contain far more bodies than the platforms do. In addition to the main burials, in at least five instances a new, smaller structure was added against the platform. Two of them have an additional T-cell, suggesting that important individuals, related to the main one, were buried there.

From all of the above Moseley concludes that the individuals buried were Chimú kings.[39] This is confirmed by these three conditions concerning the distribution and manner of construction of the *ciudadelas*:

- rarity. There are only nine *ciudadelas* in Chan Chan. Two of them seem to have been razed intentionally; Moseley believes this was a way to rewrite history by eliminating the existing evidence. Incidentally, the nine kings of the nine *ciudadelas* may be the very ones mentioned in the Taycanamu legend.
- sequential construction.
- prestige of the offerings and the highest form of treatment of any Chimú burial. Moreover, one can see the presence of ground Spondylus, privilege of the royalty.[40]

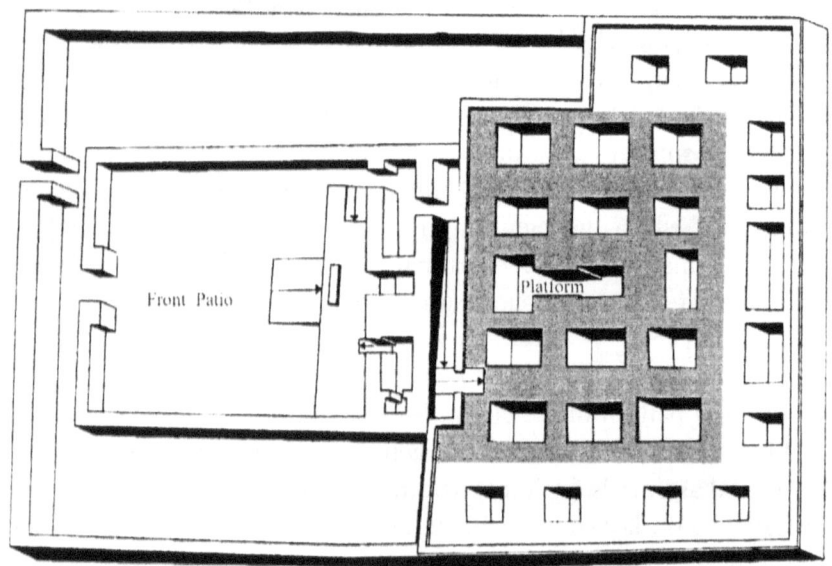

Figure 1.2: Structure of a Ciudadela

In fact the step taken by Chan Chan was to place the king at the top of the pyramid—never the case before—and thus enshrine his divinity. Kolata sees that divine kingship was crystallized at the time of the conquest of Lambayeque, when access to the inner court of the ciudadela was severely limited.[41]

In a sense, the *ciudadelas* were posthumous palaces for the kings. Thus Chan Chan's pattern was the sequence king/palace/funerary platform. Each sovereign built his palace, culminating in the funerary platform. The new institution of divine kingship gave the sovereign sanction for new conquest. This was the king's sacred function.

Let us now look at Chan Chan's northern counterpart.

North Chimú: Pacatnamu

The cosmology of Pacatnamu is deeply rooted in Moche Valley artistic precedent. Practically all mounds have the same orientation toward the local mountains, the Cerros de Catalina. *Ceque* lines converge on a focal point in front of the mountains. The only exception is Waka 38, close to the ocean at the end of the peninsula, which faces the ocean. It is possible that it was an early *waka*, following an earlier cosmology.

The Waka 1 Complex dates from the Chimú occupation stage. This is recognizable by the fact that it was built with standard Chimú bricks. Radiocarbon dating further confirms the above.[42] Interestingly, Waka 1 has a sunken courtyard to the east, very likely the latest survivor of the early Andean cult. On top of the mound is a very small U-shaped room, built in a form familiar to those of the Moche Valley. The structure with access progressively restricted from the north to the south, points to a likely use as palace. The ceremonial public area was in the front; the palace proper to the rear with circuitous access leading to it.

The primary entrance to the *waka* is once again to the north, similar to the pattern of Chan Chan. The access is through a causeway above a trench and further through a small door placed between massive walls. At the entrance to the pyramid in a large courtyard are two altars with a low flat top, both oriented east-west.

It seems that Waka 1 was used for ceremonial purposes primarily. Part of the ceremonies would likely be seen by a large number of people. However, we saw that further access was very restricted. Once inside, access to places is not only restricted, but at times also long and convoluted. In many instances there are two accesses; such is the case from the primary entrance to the various parts of the complex. When there are two paths, the one that goes to the right (west) is generally larger, more highly decorated, and executed in massive structures. The left (east) access is often smaller, narrow, irregular, and poorly built. Spaces reached by the right-hand path indicate access to ceremonial or administrative functions. Spaces reached through the left are associated with refuse and indicate domestic functions or food preparations. This right-left dichotomy is also seen in the access to the summit of Waka 1 and to other *wakas*.

The major quadrangle of Waka 1 complex is an enclosed area like the *ciudadelas* of Chan Chan. Both *waka* and *ciudadelas* are oriented north-south with a small entrance near the center of the north wall. In both instances we also find massive walls, walled enclosures divided into many rooms and courtyards, long corridors, and blind hallways.

Whereas the Chan Chan *ciudadelas* have various *audiencias* situated in their central section associated with storage rooms, in the Waka 1 complex there is only one *audiencia* without storage space next to it. Neither is there evidence of burial platforms in Pacatnamu. Conversely, no altars like the ones of the Waka 1 complex have been observed in Chan Chan.

The motifs of *waka* and wall carried over from the Moche are clearly reversed in Chan Chan. The walls are gigantic; the U-shaped forms are very limited in size and function. The peripheral walls have openings to the north only. In summary, the sacred U-shaped temple was rendered more secular, and the wall was rendered sacred. The compounds of Chan Chan have in common with Wari and late Moche architecture the idea of excluding and placing obstacles. From the above, we can conclude that the step taken by Chan Chan was to place the king at the top of the pyramid and enshrine his divinity, while on the whole reflecting a tendency toward secularization.

Chimú Cosmology

Chimú ceramics have very scant references to sacred or mythic imagery. Most have naturalistic representations of fish, crustaceans, or birds. The only attribute that has a supernatural connotation is the ruler's headdress, says F. Kauffman Doig.[43] There is no visible presence of a higher deity such as with Ai-Apaec during the Moche period. The main motifs found in the city of Chan Chan are adobe friezes with themes of the ocean and ocean creatures, motifs that had first emerged in the last stages of Moche culture.

According to the chronicler Antonio de la Calancha, the main cult of Chimú was devoted to the Moon. The planet was considered more powerful than the Sun, because it was visible both at night and sometimes in the day. Solar eclipses were considered victories of the moon over the sun; lunar eclipses were occasions for mourning. Lunar worship was apparently widespread over the whole of the Peruvian coast through the avian deity that was considered the patron of fishermen. Its attributes are stylized feathers from a marine or nocturnal bird that represent this divinity all along the Peruvian coast.

The Chimú also worshipped the ocean, Ni, to which they offered cornmeal and red ochre earth. In addition they had stone idols, considered the lineage progenitors; originally they were sons of the Sun and they were turned into stone for killing their mother.[44] Finally, in passing, Calancha mentions the worship of four stars, considered progenitors of the social classes. Two of these were more brilliant (for the chiefs and nobility) and two small ones for the commoners. This is a possible reference to the Southern Cross.

The cult of the dead occurred through burials and funereal dances, but especially burial offerings. The major devotion was given to the *munaos*—heads of lineages. Of special importance was the treatment of the corpse. This was certainly the case for the rulers, but possibly also for the family ancestors. Calancha indicates that the dead were buried on the fifth day after death. They were wrapped with their clothes, together with their most beloved objects; then covered with animal skins and wrapped with a layer of leaves, grasses, or seaweed; and finally wrapped in a cloth. In the early Chimú period (900–1100) burial grounds were irregular pits in the sand, or in irregular floors, or they were placed in the platforms of mounds that had been built in the Moche period. Burials of the following period (1100–1250) were dug in the walls and platforms of adobe of the Moche pyramids. Here, as in other instances, we see an emphasis in the continuation of the Moche tradition.

Of all Moche influences, the Chimú held the closest with the tenets of Moche V period and with the influences that had spread out of Galindo. Like the Moche of Phase V, the Chimú restored the role of walls and separation that had been the hallmark of Galindo, Moche's southern capital during Phase V. Other holdovers of this epoch were the themes of the ocean and ocean creatures, mostly used in the adobe friezes and the continued presence of sunken courts, even in their very diminished importance. However, the major difference is that Ai-Apaec did no longer figure in the pantheon of the gods. By this time a cult of the Moon, and generally speaking, of the deities of the night, had gained ascendancy.

More evidence of the Chimú-Late Moche continuity appears especially in the later stages of Pacatnamu to the north. The remains of fourteen young males were found in 1994, buried in three groups just outside the entrance to Waka 1, the main ceremonial complex of the city. They appear to have been ritually mutilated and sacrificed in three separate instances before burial.[45] Radiocarbon dating of the skeletons (confirmed by associated ceramic style) points to 1270 +/- 110. It seems likely that they were executed and sacrificed in situ, or very close to it. Analysis shows that the bodies range in age between fifteen and thirty-five, with an average of twenty-one. They all show strong bodily configuration and frequently traces of previous injuries in their skeletons that had healed. This points to people or professions that implied hazards, and most likely soldiers; hence the hypothesis of prisoners of war. In the groups of the second and third burials are individuals showing evidence of decapitation, opening of the chest, and dismemberment. In group 2 the left leg is often missing; in group 3 the hips are disarticulated.

Ritual sacrifice and mutilation show commonalities between Chimú and Moche cultures. The wooden figurines found at Waka Dragon (also called Waka Arco Iris) in Moche Valley may point to these sacrifices. Some of these figurines have their hands tied behind their backs, and one of them has holes pierced in the upper left side of the chest and another in the lower back. Both holes are painted red on their margins.[46] There is further ideological connection with Moche tradition. In groups 2 and 3 mentioned earlier, a vulture skeleton has been found in association with the remains. These are the skeletons of Black Vultures (*Coragyps atratus*).[47] One of the two vultures shows evidence of having been intentionally killed before burial through a penetrating fracture in the skull area of the eye. The particular vulture of these burials is an aggressive species known to attack prey that is still alive. These birds are found in flocks of up to a hundred and do not fear human beings. When they attack a prey they first peck at the eyes, then the anus, pulling the intestines through the opening. They often do the same with genitals and tongue in order to create openings on the body.

Black vultures are often represented in Moche art in fine-line drawings in the vessels of Phase V in connection with ritual sacrifice, always in the upper left portion of the drawings. The captives were tied to a rack and left to the vultures. One of these drawings also suggests that the practice of vulture sacrifice was followed by the burial of the vulture.

At the time in which the Incas conquered Chimú, its cultural impulse had veered further and further away from the legacy of the EIP, closer to the direction taken by the Moche, maybe even returning to earlier forms of human sacrifice. It is no wonder, therefore, that they formed the bitterest rivals to Inca expansion. Chimú was not only the strongest and most organized nation, but also had the most antithetical ideology. The Incas did not confront Chimú until much later phases of their expansion. Another adversary presented a formidable challenge to the man who single-handedly contributed to the formation of the Inca Empire, Pachacuti Inca. These were the Chancas.

The Chancas

Although they were one of the most important nations between 1100 and 1400, little is known about the Chancas. They flourished in the same area where the Wari had founded their capital—the Valley of Ayacucho. Here they established their cities on the mountaintops or places easy to defend. M. Rostorowski hypothesizes that they had a part in the downfall of the Wari empire.[48] In contrast, others see the Chancas as what was left of the old Wari empire.[49] In any case, their expansion occurred soon after Wari's collapse in 1100 and continued until the mid 1400s. Under the reign of the Inca Capac Yupanqui, the Chancas formed a confederacy and aimed at expanding in the direction of Cuzco. At the death of the Inca, they took advantage of the confusion to annex the province of Andahuaylas, peopled by Quechuas allied to the Incas.

The Chancas had the lagoon of Choclococha as their *paqarina* at an altitude of 16,000', not far from Ayacucho to the northwest. They claimed descent from the puma and used its mask to cover their heads when they danced.[50] Chanca art displays numerous representations of priests covered with capes decorated with mythical grotesque animals, holding the severed trophy heads of their enemies.[51]

Nothing was found in Chanca ruins that would denote the use of temple structures, nor religious artifacts with specialized use. However, they had a multitude of *wakas* and they commemorated their ancestors

Usco Vilca and Anco Vilca (founders of Hanan Chanca and Hurin Chanca respectively) with stone *wakas* that they would cover with cloths.[52] Regardless of the nature of their links with the Wari, it appears that they carried further, in a more primitive fashion, the spiritual thread of the Age of the Warriors.

Conclusions

The Middle and Late Intermediate Horizon Periods marked a prolonged return to ideologies in many degrees similar to those that preceded the EIP, superimposed with new patterns. This happened first of all in the Moche culture, three to four centuries after the time of Thunupa. Here we witness a return to human sacrifice in a way that is reminiscent of the north coast precedent of Sechin. Human sacrifice with consumption of blood forms the central ritual of Moche society. Organ removal from a live victim was not likely, since there are no representations matching those of Cerro Sechin. With time Moche itself toned down its ideology or returned to more moderate versions of pre-EIP ideology. The rise of competing empires and ideologies may have contributed to this state of affairs.

With the Wari, a new ideology came to the fore. It dipped its roots in similar fashion into Late Chavin ideology. Its contribution to Andean civilization lies in the formation of its first large-scale political entity. The Wari continued Tiwanaku's culture but in its late, modified version, with motifs that point more to Pucara's ideology than to the altiplano's capital original message.

Chimú arose at the end of Wari and independently from it in the north coast. It adopted Wari's administrative model and continued its trajectory. In its later stages it returned, at least in part, to Moche precedents. It can be said thus that the whole period was predominantly marked by a readoption of Chavin ideology at a time when it had ceased serving the progressive aims of evolution. The rise of oracles, such as Pachacamac, Lurin, and Andahuaylas marks a clear return to the priesthood of the Third Age.

The late Moche, Wari, and Chimú continued the traditions of the times preceding the Dawning, of the deities of the night consciousness that preceded the turning point of time. The persistence—even though marginal—of sunken courts in all three cultures points in this direction. Most clearly, the complete lack of reference to a solar deity is the conspicuous thread uniting all of these cultures, their differences notwithstanding. The Staff God of Wari is altogether a new version of the old deity. Solar references have been displaced in favor of references to trophy heads and human sacrifice. The abandonment of the message of the Prophet is accompanied with a general trend toward secularization, coexistent with the elevation of the monarch to the status of a god. Wari and Chimú architecture and art become more and more secular—a new characteristic of this age.

Behind the outer manifestations of the culture we can at least generally surmise the tendency of the subordination of the regional *wakas* to the *wakas* of higher order, of which Pachacamac was an example. The return to the oracular nature of the Third Age cult marked a departure from the original message of Chavin. Whereas the spiritual capital upheld the equality of the *wakas,* the Middle and Late Intermediate Horizons placed the *wakas* in competition with each other. When empire developed, as in the case of Wari, we can imagine that the central *waka* of the empire gained ascendancy over all others. This movement is in part similar to what occurred in Mesoamerica with the Toltecs in Tula and Chichen Itza. It is what we have called the resurgence of the Quetzalcoatl Mysteries, a prelude to the resurfacing of human sacrifice with organ removal. We will return to this point in our final considerations, in placing South America in contrast to North America.

Another symptomatic development is the ubiquitous note of an architecture of confinement and separation, enshrining marked social differences. The rising of the first South American cities accompanied this development. Concurrent with the rise of the cities we find two side developments: the extraction of tribute in food and/or artifacts; and the progressive abandonment of irrigated land, raised fields, terracing, etc. For many groups that also meant the return to a mainly pastoral lifestyle and the abandonment of the precepts of reciprocity between different cultures.

The Chancas of the central sierra were a rather minor civilization that did not attain a level comparable to the previously mentioned groups. They carried on the themes of the Age of the Warriors and represented a threat to the new cultural message emerging from Cuzco.

One could imagine that what awaited Andean civilization could only have been an accentuation of the tendency toward the full reinstatement of human sacrifice with organ removal as its cornerstone, had there not been the Inca cultural revolution. The incipient Inca nation encountered a major challenge in the changed conditions of the time. How could irreversible trends—particularly the formation of large political entities—be continued in such a way as to encompass and renew the message of Thunupa? How could the idea of reciprocity that the Andes saw from their earliest civilizations be reinstated in new ways? How could the *wakas*—representatives of the lineages—find coexistence in equality in such a way that could ensure peace? These were the challenges faced by the future Inca, Pachacuti.

CHAPTER 2

Inca Foundation Myths

There are at least sixteen different versions of the myths concerning the founding of Cuzco by the Incas. They were compiled between 1552 and 1653. Some authors, like Garcilaso de la Vega or Bernabé Cobo, collected more than one version. The myths reconnect Inca origin with the myths of creation through the Inca association with the Lake Titicaca or with Tiwanaku. Is this to be understood literally or is this a claim of spiritual descent?

The Myth

Among all the versions, we will offer Pedro Sarmiento Gamboa's rendition. Although tainted by a certain attitude of disbelief toward the indigenous myths, its merit lies in a full and extensive rendering of the events.[1]

I. The Fable of the Origins of the Incas of Cuzco

All the native Indians of this land relate and affirm that the Incas Capac originated in this way. Six leagues south-southwest of Cuzco by the road that the Incas made, there is a place called Paccari-tampu, which means "the house of production,"[2] at which there is a hill called Tampu-tocco, meaning "the house of windows." It is certain that in this hill there are three windows, one called Maras-tocco, the other Sutic-tocco, while that which is in the middle, between these two, was known as Capac-tocco, which means "the rich window," because they say that it was ornamented with gold and other treasures. From the window called Maras-tocco came forth, without parentage, a tribe of Indians called Maras. There are still some of them in Cuzco. From the Sutic-tocco came Indians called Tampus, who settled round the same hill, and there are also men of this lineage still in Cuzco. From the chief window of Capac-tocco, came four men and four women, called *brethren*. These knew no father nor mother, beyond the story they told that they were created and came out of the said window by order of Ticci Wirakocha, and they declared that Wirakocha created them to be lords. For this reason they took the name of *Inca*, which is the same as "lord." They took *Capac* as an additional name because they came out of the window Capac-tocco, which means "rich," although afterward they used this term to denote the chief lord over many.

The names of the eight brethren were as follows: The eldest of the men and the one with the most authority was named Manco Capac, the second Ayar Auca, the third Ayar Cachi, the fourth Ayar Uchu. Of the women, the eldest was called Mama Occlo, the second Mama Huaco, the third Mama Ipacura (or, as others say, Mama Cura), the fourth Mama Raua.

The eight brethren, called Incas, said: "We are born strong and wise, and with the people who will here join us, we shall be powerful. We will go forth from this place to seek fertile lands and when we find them we will subjugate the people and take the lands, making war on all those who do not receive us as their lords." This, as they relate, was said by Mama Huaco, one of the women, who was fierce and cruel. Manco Capac, her brother, was also cruel and atrocious. This being agreed upon between the eight, they began to move the people who lived near the hill, putting it to them that their reward would be to become rich and to receive the lands and estates of those who were conquered and subjugated. For these objectives, they moved ten tribes or *ayllus*, which means among these barbarians "lineages" or "parties"; the names of which are as follows:

I. CHAUIN CUZCO AYLLU of the lineage of AYAR CACHI, of which there are still some in Cuzco, the chiefs being MARTIN CHUCUMBI, and DON DIEGO HUAMAN PAUCAR.
II. ARAYRACA AYLLU CUZCO-CALLAN. At present there are of this *ayllu* JUAN PIZARRO YUPANQUI, DON FRANCISCO QUISPI, ALONSO TARMA YUPANQUI of the lineage of AYAR UCHU.
III. TARPUNTAY AYLLU. Of this there are now some in Cuzco.
IV. *WAKAYTAQUI* AYLLU. Some still living in Cuzco.
V. SAÑOC AYLLU. Some still in Cuzco.

The above five lineages are HANAN-CUZCO, which means the party of Upper Cuzco.

VI. SUTIC-TOCCO AYLLU is the lineage that came out of one of the windows called SUTIC-TOCCO, as has been before explained. Of these there are still some in Cuzco, the chiefs being DON FRANCISCO AVCA MICHO AVRI SUTIC, and DON ALONSO HUALPA.

VII. MARAS AYLLU. These are of the men who came forth from the window MARAS-TOCCO. There are some of these now in Cuzco, the chiefs being DON ALONSO LLAMA OCA, and DON GONZALO AMPURA LLAMA OCA.

VIII. CUYC USA AYLLU. Of these there are still some in Cuzco, the chief being CRISTOVAL ACLLARI.

IX. MASCA AYLLU. Of this there is in Cuzco JUAN QUISPI.

X. ORO AYLLU. Of this lineage is DON PEDRO YUCAY.

I say that all these *ayllus* have preserved their records in such a way that the memory of them has not been lost. There are more of them than are given above, for I only insert the chiefs who are the protectors and heads of the lineages, under whose guidance they are preserved. Each chief has the duty and obligation to protect the rest, and to know the history of his ancestors. Although I say that these live in Cuzco, the truth is that they are in a suburb of the city that the Indians call Cayocache and that is known to us as Belem, from the church of that parish which is that of our Lady of Belem.

Returning to our subject, all these followers mentioned above marched with Manco Capac and the other brethren to seek for land (and to tyrannize over those who did no harm to them, nor gave them any excuse for war, and without any right or title beyond what has been stated). To be prepared for war they chose for their leaders Manco Capac and Mama Huaco, and with this arrangement the companies of the hill of Tamputocco set out, to put their design into execution.

II. The Road That These Companies of the Incas Took to the Valley of Cuzco, and of the Fables That Are Mixed with Their History

The Incas and the rest of the companies or *ayllus* set out from their homes at Tampu-tocco, taking with them their property and arms, in sufficient numbers to form a good squadron, having for their chiefs the said Manco Capac and Mama Huaco. Manco Capac took with him a bird like a falcon, called *indi*, which they all worshipped and feared as a sacred, or, as some say, an enchanted thing, for they thought that this bird made Manco Capac their lord, and obliged the people to follow him. It was thus that Manco Capac gave them to understand, and it was carried in *vahidos*, always kept in a covered hamper of straw, like a box, with much care. He left it as an heirloom to his son, and the Incas had it down to the time of Inca Yupanqui. In his hand he carried with him a staff of gold, to test the lands that they would come to.

Marching together they came to a place called Huana-cancha, four leagues from the valley of Cuzco, where they remained for some time, sowing and seeking for fertile land. Here Manco Capac had connection with his sister Mama Occlo, and she became pregnant by him. As this place did not appear able to sustain them, being barren, they advanced to another place called Tampu-quiro, where Mama Occlo begot a son named Sinchi Rocca. Having celebrated the natal feasts of the infant, they set out in search of fertile land, and came to another place called Pallata, which is almost contiguous to Tampu-quiro, and there they remained for some years.

Not content with this land, they came to another called Hays-quisro, a quarter of a league further on. Here they consulted together over what ought to be done respecting their journey, and over the best way of getting rid of Ayar Cachi, one of the four brothers. Ayar Cachi was fierce and strong, and very dexterous with the sling. He committed great cruelties and was oppressive both among the natives of the places they passed, and among his own people. The other brothers were afraid that the conduct of Ayar Cachi would cause their companies to disband and desert, and that they would be left alone. As Manco Capac was prudent, he concurred with the opinion of the others that they should secure their object by deceit. They called Ayar Cachi and said to him, "Brother! Know that in Capac-tocco we have forgotten the golden vases called *tupac-cusi* and certain seeds, and the *napa*, which is our principal ensign of sovereignty." The *napa* is a sheep of the country, the color white, with a red body cloth, on the top earrings of gold, and on the breast a plate with red badges such as was worn by rich Incas when they went abroad; carried in front of all on a pole with a cross of plumes of feathers. This was called *suntur-paucar*. They said that it would be for the good of all, if he would go back and fetch them.

When Ayar Cachi refused to return, his sister Mama Huaco, raising her foot, rebuked him with furious words, saying; "How is it that there should be such cowardice in so strong a youth as you are? Get ready for the journey, and do not fail to go to Tampu-tocco, and do what you are ordered." Ayar Cachi was shamed by these words. He obeyed and started to carry out his orders. They gave him, as a companion, one of those who had come with them, named Tampu-chacay, to whom they gave secret orders to kill Ayar Cachi at Tampu-tocco, and not to return with him. With these orders they both arrived at Tampu-tocco. They had scarcely arrived when Ayar Cachi entered through the window Capac-tocco, to get the things for which he had been sent. He was no sooner inside than Tampu-chacay, with great celerity, put a rock against the opening of the window and sat upon it, that Ayar Cachi might remain inside and die there. When Ayar Cachi turned to the opening and found it closed, he understood the treason of which the traitor Tampu-chacay had been guilty, and determined to get out if it was possible, to take vengeance. To force an opening, he used such force and shouted so loud that he made the mountain tremble. With a loud voice he spoke these words to Tampu-chacay; "Thou traitor! thou who hast done me so much harm, thinkest thou to convey the news of my mortal imprisonment? That shall never happen. For thy treason thou shalt remain outside, turned into a stone." So it was done, and to this day they show the stone on one side of the window Capac-tocco. Turn we now to the seven brethren who had remained at Hays-quisro. The death of Ayar Cachi being known, they were very sorry for what they had done, for, as he was valiant, they regretted much to be without him when the time came to make war on any one. So they mourned for him. This Ayar Cachi was so dexterous with a sling and so strong that with each shot he pulled down a mountain and filled up a ravine. They say that the ravines, which we now see on their line of march, were made by Ayar Cachi in hurling stones.

The seven Incas and their companions left this place and came to another called Quirirmanta at the foot of a hill, which was afterward called Huanacauri. In this place they consulted together how they should divide the duties of the enterprise among themselves, so that there should be distinctions between them. They agreed that as Manco Capac had had a child by his sister, they should be married and have children to continue the lineage, and that he should be the leader. Ayar Uchu was to remain as a *waka* for the sake of religion. Ayar Auca, from the position they should select, was to take possession of the land set apart for him to people.

Leaving this place they came to a hill at a distance of two leagues, a little more or less, from Cuzco. Ascending the hill they saw a rainbow, which the natives call *huana-cauri*. Holding it to be a fortunate sign, Manco Capac said: "Take this for a sign that the world will not be destroyed by water. We shall arrive and from hence we shall select where we shall found our city." Then, first casting lots, they saw that the signs were good for doing so, and for exploring the land from that point and becoming lords of it. Before they got to the height where the rainbow was, they saw a *waka* that was a place of worship in human shape, near the rainbow. They determined among themselves to seize it and take it away from there. Ayar Uchu offered himself to go to it, for they said that he was very like it. When Ayar Uchu came to the statue or *waka*, with great courage he sat upon it, asking it what it did there. At these words the *waka* turned its head to see who spoke, but, owing to the weight upon it, it could not see. Presently, when Ayar Uchu wanted to get off he was not able, for he found that the soles of his feet were fastened to the shoulders of the *waka*. The six brethren, seeing that he was a prisoner, came to succor him. But Ayar Uchu, finding himself thus transformed, and that his brethren could not release him, said to them: "O Brothers, an evil work you have wrought for me. It was for your sakes that I came where I must remain forever, apart from your company. Go! go! happy brethren, I announce to you that you will be great lords. I, therefore, pray that in recognition of the desire I have always had to please you, you will honor and venerate me in all your festivals and ceremonies, and that I shall be the first to whom you make offerings. For I remain here for your sakes. When you celebrate the *huarachico* (which is the arming of the sons as knights) you shall adore me as their father, for I shall remain here for ever."

Manco Capac answered that he would do so, for that it was his will and that it should be so ordered. Ayar Uchu promised for the youths that he would bestow on them the gifts of valor, nobility, and knighthood, and with these last words he remained, turned into stone. They constituted him the *waka* of the Incas, giving it the name of Ayar Uchu Huanacauri. And so it always was, until the arrival of the Spaniards, the most venerated *waka*, and the one that received the most offerings of any in the kingdom. Here the Incas went to arm the young knights until about twenty years ago, when the Christians abolished this ceremony. It was religiously done, because there were many abuses and idolatrous practices, offensive and contrary to the ordinances of God our Lord.

III. Entry of the Incas into the Valley of Cuzco, and the Fables They Relate Concerning It

The six brethren were sad at the loss of Ayar Uchu, and at the loss of Ayar Cachi; and, owing to the death of Ayar Cachi, those of the lineage of the Incas, from that time to this day, always fear to go to Tampu-tocco, lest they should have to remain there like Ayar Cachi.

They went down to the foot of the hill, whence they began their entry into the valley of Cuzco, arriving at a place called Matahua, where they stopped and built huts, intending to remain there some time. Here they armed as knight the son of Manco Capac and of Mama Occlo, named Sinchi Rocca, and they bored his ears, a ceremony that is called *huarachico*, being the insignia of his knighthood and nobility, like the custom known among ourselves. On this occasion they indulged in great rejoicings, drinking for many days, and at intervals mourning for the loss of their brother Ayar Uchu. It was here that they invented the mourning sound for the dead, like the cooing of a dove. Then they performed the dance called *Capac Raymi*, a ceremony of the royal or great lords. It is danced, in long purple robes, at the ceremonies they call *quicochico*, which is when girls come to maturity, and the *huarachico*, when they bore the ears of the Incas, and the *rutuchico*, when the Inca's hair is cut the first time, and the *ayuscay*, which is when a child is born, and they drink continuously for four or five days.

After this they were in Matahua for two years, waiting to pass on to the upper valley to seek good and fertile land. Mama Huaco, who was very strong and dexterous, took two wands of gold and hurled them toward the north. One fell, at two shots of an arquebus, into a ploughed field called Colcapampa and did not drive in well, the soil being loose and not terraced. By this they knew that the soil was not fertile. The other went further, to near Cuzco, and fixed well in the territory called Huanaypata, where they knew the land to be fertile. Others say that this proof was made by Manco Capac with the staff of gold that he carried himself, and that thus they knew of the fertility of the land, when the staff sank in the land called Huanaypata, two shots of an arquebus from Cuzco. They knew the crust of the soil to be rich and close, so that it could only be broken by using much force.

Let it be by one way or the other, for all agree that they went trying the land with a pole or staff until they arrived at this Huanaypata, when they were satisfied. They were sure of its fertility, because after sowing perpetually, it always yielded abundantly, giving more the more it was sown. They determined to usurp that land by force, in spite of the natural owners, and to do with it as they chose. So they returned to Matahua.

From that place Manco Capac saw a heap of stones near the site of the present monastery of Santo Domingo at Cuzco. Pointing it out to his brother Ayar Auca, he said, "Brother! You remember how it was arranged between us, that you should go to take possession of the land where we are to settle. Well! Look at that stone." Pointing out the stone he continued, "Go thither flying," for they say that Ayar Auca had developed some wings, "and seating yourself there, take possession of land seen from that heap of stones. We will presently come to settle and reside."

When Ayar Auca heard the words of his brother, he opened his wings and flew to that place which Manco Capac had pointed out. Seating himself there, he was presently turned into stone, and was made the stone of possession. In the ancient language of this valley, the heap was called *cosco*, whence that site has had the name of Cuzco to this day. From this circumstance the Incas had a proverb which said, "Ayar Auca cuzco huanca," or, "Ayar Auca a heap of marble." Others say that Manco Capac gave the name of Cuzco because he wept in that place where he buried his brother Ayar Cachi. Owing to his sorrow and to the fertility, he gave that name which in the ancient language of that time signified "sad" as well as "fertile." The first version must be the correct one because Ayar Cachi was not buried at Cuzco, having died at Capac-tocco as has been narrated before. And this is generally affirmed by Incas and natives.

Myths and Inca Origin

The great majority of the myths agree on the Titicaca as the point of departure of the Inca odyssey and Cuzco as the place of arrival. All the versions also identify Pacaritanpu as an intermediate stage of the journey. Pacaritanpu's meaning is "Inn of the Dawning." We are therefore faced with the apparent contradiction of both Titicaca and Pacaritanpu as the place of the Dawning for the Incas. Molina and Cobo (in two versions) describe an underground journey from Titicaca to Pacaritanpu, the Inca place of emergence. This manner of characterizing the emergence of the Incas aligns itself with the myths of the Second Creation studied previously, in which Wirakocha sends his disciples to awaken each tribe at their *paqarina*. This double origin may also be the myths' way to claim both a particular origin, and a spiritual link and continuity. In this case, the physical place of origin is different from the spiritual place of origin, Lake Titicaca. It is the being of Thunupa who links the one to the other.

The chronicles can be divided in three main types. The simple and more prosaic of them describe only one hero: Manco Capac. Others, for example Garcilaso de la Vega's, associate the hero with his sister-wife Mama Occlo. They are the divine pair sent forth by the Sun God. In eight versions, as in the one given in full above, there are four brothers and four sisters.

Let us turn to some historical considerations resulting from recent research before we turn our attention to the mythical content again. The meaning of Pacaritanpu, the Inn (Temple) of the Dawning, is also the "temple where one was born," which we could further clarify as "temple whence one emerged."[3] Tanpu is in fact the place of rest or place for storing food and goods. It has both a general meaning given to all places of rest and a specific meaning that makes it equivalent to Pacaritanpu. The chronicles mention another locality within Pacaritampu, the place called Tanputoco, literally "place of the window," which is also how Sarmiento de Gamboa translates it in his chronicle.

That a place of the window exists close to the Inn of the Dawning is a recent revelation of Inca spirituality. This is situated in Ollantaytanpu, city of the Sacred Valley. Its rich esoteric tradition has been explored by E. and F. E. Elorrieta Salazar.[4] However, we are faced with an apparent contradiction. While, on the one hand Pacaritampu refers to the famous place in the Sacred Valley, on the other hand most of the chronicles situate Pacaritampu at the same distance from Cuzco but in the opposite direction from the Sacred Valley, to the south. Let us review a few considerations about this riddle before looking at all the evidence.

The research done by E. and E. F. Elorrieta Salazar is astounding and demonstrates that the Inca and their descendents managed to hide the knowledge and preserve the existence of their most sacred monuments. It is not surprising that scant evidence appears in the chronicles about the gigantic enterprises undertaken in the Sacred Valley. Nevertheless some of it appears, and we will return to it. At another level however, it is clear that Inca cosmology covers different levels of complexity; the existence of the two Pacaritampu may indeed correspond to different levels of the myth, as we will see further on.

In the Inca Sacred Valley of the river Vilcanota (or Urubamba) can be detected a gigantic pyramid, concealed to the unsuspecting tourist. Here lies one of the most incredible discoveries of Inca spirituality: a three-sided pyramid that has lain undetected for centuries, although it covers 370 acres (150 hectares) and is 110' (34 m) high, and its base measures 1630' x 850' (498 X 261 m) (figure 2.1). Ignorance of its location was possible because it is in fact an asymmetric pyramid that is visible only from certain angles of the landscape. The flat top is called Rimac Pampa, "the Place Where it is Spoken." An irrigation system originates from this skewed top that rests against the side of the mountain. Its water is distributed down a system of nine terraces where maize and quinoa are cultivated.

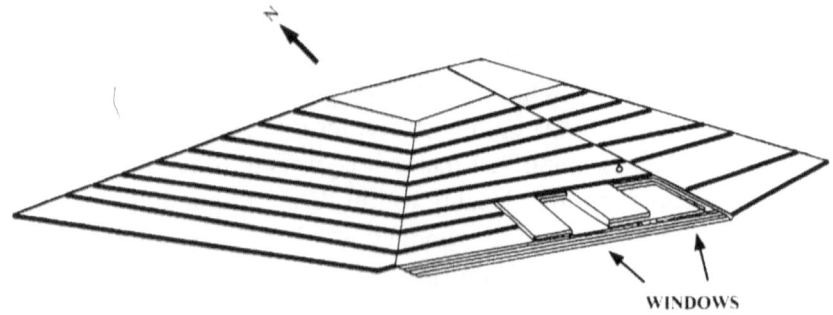

Figure 2.1: Sacred pyramid of Ollantaytanpu

The pyramid of the place called Ollantaytanpu surpasses in its volume all other known pyramids. It was an initiatic monument undetectable to the novice. Inca secrecy about these matters may explain why, although Bernabe Cobo situates Pacaritampu in the Sacred Valley, all other chroniclers indicate the right distance from Cuzco but give the opposite direction.[5] Can the knowledge of the place of origin have been carefully concealed, just as the pyramid was, in spite of its massive size?

What purpose did the pyramid serve? The answer to this question lies in the pyramid itself and in the host of monuments that is enshrined in the landscape of the Sacred Valley. We will return to the farthest aspects of the cosmology of the Sacred Valley in chapter 9. For now, we will confine ourselves to the many layers of meaning encoded in the pyramid.

The middle side of the pyramid has the stylized shape of a hand. At the base of this side lie two rectangular, depressed enclosures bordered by three close, consecutive terraces. These depressions are there to portray the windows mentioned by the Inca myths of the origins. That only two of the three windows depicted in some versions of the myth are illustrated is not an invalidation of the myth. The third window, Maras-tocco, appears when the pyramid is looked at from a larger perspective. We can see at the base of the pyramid of Pacaritanpu the two windows of Sutic-tocco and

Capac-tocco. The third window of Maras-tocco, or "Window of the Great Tree" will appear once we enlarge the perspective of the sacred geography of Ollantaytambo and come to realize that the pyramid itself is part of a larger geomantic unit (figure 2.1). One fact worth noting at present is that on June 21–22, the date of the important festival of the Sun, Inti-Raymi, the rising sun, sends a shaft of light to illumine the window identified as Capac-tocco before the rest of the pyramid is illumined, reinforcing the special meaning given to that window as the place of emergence at the time of the Dawning.[6]

Let us look at the third window, the so-called Maras-toco, in its relation to the Sacred Tree.[7] This last feature is not as immediately recognizable by its shape. The tree's crown overlaps the pyramid. The trunk is formed of parallel terraces on either side of the river Patacancha, an effluent of the Sacred River. The third window (Maras-tocco) is present not far from the other two at a place that has a special connotation in relation to the old Inca city of Ollantaytanpu. The zone called Kanaquelca represents the roots of the sacred tree and has a *waka* where was celebrated a specific cult to the root. On the terraces only quinoa and maize were cultivated. The canopy itself was framed by the light effects on the evenings of the solstices.[8]

The whole geomantic feature acquires fuller meaning when we appreciate what the tree stands for. The term coca refers to all trees in general. The term *mallqui coca* refers to all kinds of cultivated trees. *Mallqui* also refers to the mummies of the ruling class. Through the tree were symbolized the roots into the past (ancestors) and the *ayllu*. The ancestors were the mediators between the living and the gods or the forces of the earth.

Let us now turn to another landscape sculpture that is closely associated to the theme of the Dawning and placed just above the tree on the hill Pinkuylluna. On the part of this hill called Viracocchan Orcco (Wirakocha's envoy) is visible the figure of a gigantic countenance. What is most noticeable are the flowing beard and the large ears. On what would correspond to the region of the shoulders, the individuality carries a burden. This is where we still find the remains of old warehouses (*collcas*) for the storage of seeds and food. Over the head is built an observatory in the form of a four-cornered hat, reminiscent of the *chuku*, the hat worn by the priest-astronomer. The sunlight illuminates this observatory at the Summer Solstice (December 22) sunrise, the date of the Capac Raymi— Feast of the Kings—an important date of the Inca calendar. In this way the illuminated initiate shows his kinship with the kings that follow him, a theme that parallels the kinship of the initiate Ixbalamqué with the

Maya kings, who are considered his brothers. In addition, every day the light of the sun illuminates the eye between 2:30 and 3:30 p.m. From a nearby astronomical observatory, the sun also shines on the east, top, and west facades of the mountain on the dates of the June solstice, during the month of August, and at the December solstice, respectively.[9]

On the side of the mountain, this gigantic sculpture reunites all the traits that we have seen associated with Thunupa—this is also E. F and E. Elorrieta Salazar's conclusion. In this representation Thunupa appears both as the priest-astronomer and as the bearded pilgrim that carries on his shoulders the gifts of civilization that he freely gives to his people. He is in fact reminiscent of the hunchback Thunupa-Ekako statuettes studied by C. Ponce Sangines. It is highly significant that it is the initiate who overlooks the whole of the sacred tree and the pyramid with the windows of emergence. This is more reason to believe that the place of origin of the Incas is more likely to be found in the Sacred Valley than to the south of Cuzco.

That Ollantaytanpu is very likely the actual Pacaritanpu of the famed origins is also confirmed in another way by the chronicles. Garcilaso de la Vega indicates that the Incas of this central section of the Sacred Valley played a special role. The Incas of Urcos (Calca), Y'ucay, and Tanpu could open their ears more widely—through the insertion of ear plugs—than all other Incas and only less than the emperor. To this particular group of Inkas of Tanpu, Bernabe Cobo also attributed the tradition of the use of a special language of their own. The enlarging of the ears that brought to the Incas the epithet *Orejones* (big ears) was a practice that denoted initiation back to the times of Tiwanaku and other Andean civilizations, presumably even Chavin.

Why would the Incas reunite in one place as important as the Sacred Valley both a monument of their place of emergence and a reminder of the initiate of the Americas? This must have been one of their most guarded secrets, even though once it has been discovered it speaks unmistakably of the continuity that the Incas desired to establish between their emerging empire, the Dawning on Lake Titicaca, and the initiate of the Andes.

The Four Brothers

It seems that the Inca myths condense a long differentiation, which occurred over the centuries, in the idea of the four brothers and four sisters. The brothers can be understood as the different people that originated at the different epochs of South American humanity—and as the groups of people of different horizons that were present in Cuzco at the time the Incas arrived. In fact they can be a mixture of the two, representing both the levels of consciousness and the mythical ages.

Garcilaso de la Vega offers us a key in pointing out that each of the brothers has a particular meaning. *Cachi* means "salt" and would also mean "natural life," and is thought of as masculine. *Uchu* is the *ají*, the hot pepper, and stands for the feminine. *Sauca* (or *Auca*) means "rejoicing," "satisfaction," "delight," and "sexual pleasure." At Capac Raymi, when they specifically commemorated the saga of their origins, the Incas refrained from salt, hot pepper, and sexual pleasure, recapitulating thus elements of their mytho-history. The three brothers constitute the three primary *wakas* of the Incas. A historical confirmation of the above comes from the studies of Maria Rostworowski and Burr Cartwright Brundage. According to Indian sources at the time of the Conquest, the first to arrive to Cuzco were the Sauasiray, descendents of Ayar Cachi, then those of Ayar Auca, from whom derived the *ayllu* of the Antasaya, and finally the Alcabizas, descendents of Ayar Uchu.[10] The last ones to arrive were the descendents of Manco Capac. It is to be noted that the second and third brothers are often reversed in the chronicles.

The *wakas* of the three brothers form a progression from the Sacred Valley to Cuzco. The Ayar brothers were turned into stone in Pacaritanpu (21 miles from Cuzco), in Huanacauri (9 miles from Cuzco), and in the center of Cuzco. The *waka* of Ayar Auca, an isolated stone, was called Cuzco Huanca, and located close to Tanpu Kancha, the palace of Manco Capac. The descendants of the three Ayar form the so-called original *ayllus*. The very first of the original *ayllus* is called Chahuan, meaning "half raw, half cooked." It corresponds to the lineage of the most primitive of the brothers, Ayar Cachi.

The Sauasiray's (Ayar Cachi) cave of origination was most likely the Sutic-tocco. A mountain of Paruro, close to the southern Pacaritanpu, bears that name. The Sauasiray were also connected to that quarter of Cuzco called Cuntisuyu, corresponding to the direction of the south. Here once more we see how the two Pacaritanpu may be reconciled: the one to the south as the primordial place of origin, that of the first brother; the one to the north as the real place of origin of the Incas. This type of conundrum is not at all uncommon in the Inca worldview.

The Antasaya's (descendents of Ayar Auca) origination is most likely the Anta Basin to the northwest of Cuzco. Both Sauasiray (Ayar Cachi) and

Antasaya (Ayar Auca) were called *Cuzcos* in contrast with the descendents of Manco Capac who called themselves *Tanpus*. The Incas, descendents of Apu-Tanpu and Manco Capac, naturally attributed to themselves the Capactocco. The Alcavizas (Ayar Uchu) formed the Ayar Ucho *ayllu* and were the last to be incorporated. They offered a long resistance to the Incas, so much so that the emperor Pachacuti banished them from Cuzco. They are not specifically referred to a window in the sacred landscape of Ollantaytanpu.

The three first brothers repeat the Ages preceding the Incas. The first time of "natural life" preceded the Second Age and the matriarchy of the Third Age. Then followed the Fourth Age, identified as the time of equality between the sexes. The Fourth Age is that of Manco Capac, the disciple of Thunupa to which the Incas hearken back, at least in the myth. To sum up, Manco Capac and the other brothers represent lineages and representatives of Andean humanity, having attained different degrees of evolution. Ayar Cachi is the man of the First Age, or First Man; Ayar Uchu, the Second Man; Ayar Auca, the Third Man. Manco Capac is the Man of the Fourth Age, as is made clear by his relationship to Thunupa.

Ayar Cachi has some of the traits of Zipacna, the representative of First Man in the Popol Vuh. He can bring down mountains. He is also overcome in the same way as Zipacna in the Popol Vuh, by bringing the mountain down on him. A confirmation of the myth of the transformation of Ayar Cachi into a *waka* is found in the Sacred Valley in the monument Waka del Condor, a mountain chosen for its resemblance to a condor. Under the head and bill is found an altar. On December 21, date of the solstice, the shadow from the bill falls on the middle point of the altar where is positioned a gnomon that allows the date to be determined with precision.[11] The Waka of the Condor too is located close to the Sacred Pyramid and Tree.

The second and third brothers are turned into stone by turning to the wrong kind of worship. They are fastened to a *waka*—made captive of it. Joan de Santa Cruz Pachacuti adds important information about the death of the second brother, whom he calls "younger brother." That he is the second brother we can infer by the fact that this episode occurs after the appearance of the rainbow, as in Gamboa's myth rendered above. Santa Cruz Pachacuti's insight is very valuable because he is the one who has the most distance from the events and highest interest in the esoteric content of the material he shares. Unfortunately, his account is not very complete. In any case, he refers to the event of the so-called Waka of Sañuc.[12] Here, in addition to the other chroniclers, he tells us that both the younger brother and one of his sisters remained captive of the *waka*. He adds that the two brothers had sinned. Interestingly, Santa Cruz Pahacuti calls the event *pitusuray/sauasuray*, meaning "one person fastened on top of the other." The third brother is turned into the stone of possession—a foundation stone or *taypicala*—thus reiterating the concept that was familiar to Tiwanaku at the time of the Fourth Age. Manco Capac could overcome the opposing power of the *waka* through the gift of the golden rod—the *tupa-yauri*.

Finally, let us turn to the last, most important brother, the mythical founder of the Inca state. The three first brothers perform courageous feats and use powers of magic; they can destroy mountains, open the earth, fly, or change themselves into idols. In comparison, Manco Capac is the most utterly human. Let us come closer to his identity through what we can gather from the chronicles. Montesinos reports, "But the truth, the ultimate truth is, that Pirhua Manco was the first one to rule in Cuzco. Pirhua Manco and [his son] Manco Capac . . . are sons of the Sun and therefore they have the full happiness, *and I have seen this first lord measuring by his steps the whole earth*, and therefore his descendants will be favored by happy fortune" (author's translation).[13] Montesinos adds that the Fourth Sun was completed forty-three years after Christ's birth in Bethlehem, and this corresponded to the second year of the reign of Manco Capac, the third Peruvian king to bear that name. The same Pirhua Manco is also called Apotanpu. And Santa Cruz Pachacuti tells us that Apotanpu received from the great Thunupa a part of his staff (the staff is also compared to a ray of the sun), because he was the one who listened to his teachings with love.[14] Garcilaso indicates that Thunupa gave Apotampu a staff of half length and two fingers thick.[15] In this instance the giver is considered as the unity, the receiver as half of it. At the birth of Manco Capac, the staff is miraculously transformed into gold. The legends take us back once again to the time of the Dawning. They claim that Manco Capac is the initiate of the Sun, and place Inca civilization in the cultural heritage of Thunupa. Is this a vain claim or is it substantiated by Inca history?

The Incas and the Memory of Thunupa

It is once more Santa Cruz Pachacuti who offers us the keenest insight into the nature of the changes introduced by the Incas. In many ways the Inca foundation myths legitimize a continuity with the legacy of Thunupa. That this is certainly the case is the object of the rest of our explorations in the next chapters. The Incas did in fact bring this process a step further into the new times.

Santa Cruz Pachacuti shows the thread leading back from Thunupa to Manco Capac. The *tupac-yauri* is the staff that Manco Capac inherited from his father Apotanpu. The latter had received a staff from Thunupa. It was only at his death, when the staff passed into the hands of Manco Capac, that it turned into a golden staff. It is clear from this imaginative language that Manco Capac is the one who embraces the message of the prophet. S. C. Pachacuti also specifies that Manco Capac was the one who fought against the idolatry of the *wakas*.

Here it is easy to become confused by the terms that S. C. Pachacuti uses. Up until that point he has talked about the *wakas* as intermediaries between humanity and the gods. They are in fact the direct link to the time of Thunupa and the universal message that renewed Andean civilization. What S. C. Pachacuti considers idolatry is the belief in an autonomous power of the *wakas* and their use as independent oracles. This point is made clear in relation to Wayna Capac, the Inca sovereign whom S. C. Pachacuti reproaches to have made recourse to the oracle of Pachacamac. To this he refers when he describes the demons working through the *wakas*. Accompanying the use of the oracles was, in some instances at least, the practice of human sacrifice. Thus, in speaking of later Inca sovereigns, the native chronicler refers to Capac Yupanqui in his fight against the so-called practice of human sacrifice of Capaucha-Cocuy, involving the burial of live virgin boys with silver and gold.

One must not forget that the *wakas*, at least in the case of the mummies, were the locus for the preservation of life forces that connected to the past; in many instances at least, to the past of the initiate Thunupa. They were actual sacred objects that could be put to the use of progressive or regressive spiritual beings. When the mummies were taken out on the occasion of festive celebrations, the priests or other officials could narrate the history of the deceased emperor by reliving the events that the presence of the *waka* made spiritually visible or understandable. The ancestor that has been transformed into stone is the *waka* that still accompanies the life of its people. We will see this illustration of Inca spirituality in yet another instance in the Legend of the Chancas in the next chapter.

The above ideas—concerning Thunupa's confrontation with the

opposing forces—are restated in Inca art that commemorates the deeds of the initiate at the time of Christ. We will look first at the monument of the Waka of Ticci Wirakocha found in Urcos. In this place are found megalithic ruins of Inca origin.[16]

The sanctuary comprises:

- a puma sculpture of 31' x 10' (9.4 x 3m)
- a group of buildings on either side of it
- a system of terraces and irrigation channels
- a tower built of stone and mortar

Among many other interesting archaeological remains there are:

- the vestige of an artificial pond or reservoir, used for baths or for raising fish
- a throne of the Inca cut into a megalithic block of remarkable dimensions. It looks to the north, in the direction of the aqueduct.

Let us look at the language of the monument, first of all at the puma. His very realistic head is oriented to the east and is 10' (3 m) wide. The eyes are circular and surmounted by brows, the snout angular, the ears small and round. Around the neck there is the trace of a collar. The spine of the animal is arched as if he were to pounce on a prey. Behind the head there is a circular excavation that was used for pouring liquid sacrifices. From the circular cavity behind the head, the blood of the offerings, mixed with the water coming from the Kan Kan lagoon, flowed into a tail in zig-zag form that ends in the head of a snake. The animal is enclosed in a corral where there are three sides, no east side, and no roof. The head of the puma rises higher than the walls. The whole gives the impression of an imprisoned animal, reinforced by the presence of the collar.

Della Santa reports the local traditions of the legend of the Inca Urco Huaranqa's promising his daughter to the one who would build a channel that could bring water to the Tanpu of Urcos.[17] In a time past, there lived in this community a man by the name of Inka Urco Huaranqa, who had a very beautiful daughter by the name of Paucarilla. The princess was the object of contention from many local chiefs. Due to the scarcity of water, the Inca offered his daughter's hand to the first who would canalize the water to the village. The winner, Rumi Maqui ("stone hand"), was not loved by the young princess, who called on the gods and fled with her beloved chief, Uska Paucar ("flowered"). Together they ran up the mountain, where they were transformed into stone. The water was brought down through an aqueduct from the mountain lagoon of Kan Kan. At present there are two channels in the site of Urcos; one of them comes from the mountain lake of Kan Kan, fed by the glacier of the Pitusiray.

In Santa Cruz Pachacuti's chronicle, an episode referring to a site called Sauasiray/Pitusiray takes place within the myth of emergence of the Incas. It portrays the fight against the Waka of Sañuc. Two of Manco Capac's brothers (one of them is later called "sister") are defeated and transformed into stone by the *waka*. Manco confronts the *waka* and defeats it with his tupa-yauri, the golden staff. Pachacuti mentions that the brothers had sinned. This theme mirrors the idea that Manco Capac's first and second brothers are turned into stone by turning to the wrong kind of worship mentioned above. They are fastened to a *waka*—made captive of it. The legend of Urcos may indicate that the daughter committed a transgression by turning to a man who used forces from the past, rather than embracing the message of the initiate. Poma de Ayala, describing the cult to the mountain Pitusiray, reports the belief that an Inca had been transformed into a puma.[18]

According to Pedro Sarmiento de Gamboa, the Urcos building was erected to commemorate the passing of Thunupa through Urcos.[19] Wirakocha Inca had another temple built in Cacha in which stood a statue to Ticci-Wirakocha. Note that this was the place in which Thunupa had subdued the fire magicians. We can see a similarity and a recurring theme between the symbolism of Urcos and Cacha.

The persistent tradition of the Puma of Fire will throw light on the further meanings of the legend. Among the Guaro Indians (Indians of San Martin de Guarocondor, close to Cuzco), the magicians (called Yacarca) possessed the gift of ubiquity and could assume different forms. To do this, according to Archbishop Villagomez, the magician had to drink human blood.[20] The puma depicted in the sculpture could be therefore the puma of fire tamed by the white "fire magician" Thunupa. The symbolism of the temple indicates that a magician-initiate has subdued the puma of fire and the fire magicians that worked with him. Thunupa himself was another kind of magician, one who did not draw his strength from the Puma of Fire and from human sacrifice.

Early Inca History

Very little is known of the origins of the Incas and of their links to the time of the Early Intermediate Period. It is difficult to bring historical evidence of their connection with the culture that established itself around Lake Titicaca and the individuality of the Andean initiate. However, a link of cultural and spiritual continuity exists between the civilization of Tiwanaku and the forming of the Inca Empire. It is the whole object of the second part of this work. A historical link may also exist. What follows is not proof of it; rather, some circumstantial evidence.

More and more evidence indicates that the Sacred Valley may indeed have been the route through which the Incas arrived at Cuzco. Basing themselves on the Colla myths of origins, given by Garcilaso de la Vega, the brothers Elorrieta Salazar hypothesize that part of the Collas, the population of Aymara descent of the Titicaca basin, emigrated toward the headwaters of the Vilcanota (Urubamba). What follows is the result of their research.[21] The Colla met with the resistance of the Canchis, and of their spiritual enemies, the Canas of the area around Pucara, and were obliged to take the route of the mountains, taking refuge in areas similar to the original *punas* of the high plateau. After a time of warfare against the neighboring tribes, they were finally able to occupy the territories at the origin of the Vilcanota River and the area of Paucartanpu, to the east of it.

The traces they may have left are visible in the ruins of Ninamarca, Tocra (Paucartanpu), Ancashmarca, Aukani, and Choquechancha (Calca). Finally, Ollantaytanpu became their primary residence. The community of Q'ero (district of Paucartanpu, east of Ollantaytanpu in the mountain) preserves myths indicating the successive attempts of the Colla in penetrating the valley. Of particular interest is the part of the legend that refers to the creation of Inkari and Qollari, wise man and woman. The reference to Inka and Colla is obvious. To Inkari was given the gold staff, and to Colla a weaver's distaff. As in the more well-known Inca myth of origin, Inkari had been entrusted with the task of finding fertile ground that he would have recognized by being able to sink the staff. Q'ero was a first step along the way of Inkari's peregrinations: here, the staff fell obliquely. Ollantaytanpu was the following, definitive one. Having accomplished his task, Inkari returned to Titicaca.

Ollantatytanpu gathered all the ideal conditions and a spiritual geography reminiscent of Copacabana (on the shores of Lake Titicaca) and Tiwanaku. Ollantaytanpu also gathers the ideal conditions for the growing of maize (as it is still done on the terraces of the sacred pyramid), and the proximity of the *punas* for the llama herds. Near Ollantaytanpu are found the very ancient sites of Qorywayrachina and Llukumarca. In the mountains around Ollantaytanpu rises a peak called Huanacauri, carrying the same name of the mountain near Cuzco that is the city's first *waka*! On its summit are the ruins of an old temple with a trapezoidal base. On the slopes of the mountain called Tamboqhasa—against which leans the pyramid of Ollantatytambo—is found the temple of Pumaorco, whose construction denotes the architectural technology of Tiwanaku.[22]

Let us finally turn to the only chronicle that explores the earliest origins of the Incas, the much debated Montesinos version that lists the kings of the many dynasties that preceded the Incas. What has made Montesinos's version controversial are his fantastic theories associating the events of his chronicle with mythical events taken from the Bible. An example of this is found in the first page of the chronicle, where mention is given of Ophir who settled America after the Flood. Ophir was Noah's descendent who populated Peru with Armenians, according to the chronicler.

There are similarities between the accounts of Montesinos and those of Blas de Valera. Both of them were Jesuits. It appears that Montesinos borrowed the knowledge of the genealogies from Blas de Valera without acknowledging him, when he was in La Paz. Blas de Valera, the now presumed "anonymous Jesuit," wrote a work entitled *De los Indios del Peru sus costumbres y pacificacion (About the Indians of Peru, their traditions and their cultural assimilation)*.[23] More about Blas de Valera will be discussed in a following chapter, "The Rewriting of History by the Spaniards."

When we turn to the so-called historical Incas, facts are not established with great clarity. The first seven Incas of Cuzco hover in a place between legend and history. Little is known about their lives, although the succession of their names is consistent in most of the chronicles. The first five rulers belonged to Hurin Cuzco.

Under Manco Capac, the first of the Inca dynasty, the Incas captured the Sauasiray (Ayar Cachi) chief and took possession of the Alcabizas' (Ayar Uchu) land. Manco Capac and his descendents occupied the Temple of the Sun according to all the chroniclers. The first ruler founded the higher part of Cuzco, the so-called *Hanan Cuzco*, Mama Occlo the lower, *Hurin Cuzco*.

Manco's son, Sinchi Roca, was born in Ollantaytanpu. He is the first truly historical sovereign. The name *sinchi* indicates that he was a war chief. He married Mama Coca, and managed to form a confederation of tribes based on the principle of mutual aid.

Under the reign of the next sovereign, Lloque Yupanqui, the Ayarmacas were defeated. His successor, Mayta Capac, is remembered as a prodigy for his precocity. Under his reign the Alcabizas rebelled but were subjugated anew. Mayta Capac also managed to defend his realm against the Condesuyus. Under the reign of Capac Yupanqui, the Chancas of the valley of Ayacucho formed a confederacy. The Quechuas of Andahuaylas, feeling threatened, sought an alliance with the Incas. This did not stop the Chancas from annexing them at the death of the Inca.

The sixth emperor, Inca Roca, arrived to power through a palace coup. He was the first ruler belonging to Hanan Cuzco. He had to face the revolt of Hurin Cuzco and the *ayllus* that had allied with them. He was also the first Inca to face the Chanca threat by invading their territory and inflicting a defeat on them. No territorial occupation followed, however. He expanded territorially in a modest way toward the east, and is known to have spent time and energy improving the city of Cuzco.

The last ruler of the pre-empire period was Inca Yupanqui. His rulership forms a very confused episode of Inca history. The Condesuyus organized a rebellion after a betrayal in which the Inca was killed, and the Chancas took advantage of the occasion to expand territorially.

The above short episodes of the life of the first seven Incas show some of the patterns of what Guaman Poma qualified as the Fourth Age, a time of continuous warfare between local chiefs whose power extended over a rather limited territory—at least after the time of Wari. It was a time of precarious alliances and federations. However, the Cuzco region represented a partial exception. This indicates that the valley had a stronger politically unified structure even under the first emperors.

What allowed the leap from the dimension of a larger warring local chiefdom to the empire that rose within a century, encompassing a territory extending from Ecuador to northern Chile? The transformation of Inca rulership is the acknowledged work of the ninth Inca, Pachacutic. However, from a spiritual perspective, the stage was set in two consecutive steps, first by Wirakocha Inca, then by Pachacuti, his son.

CHAPTER 3

Inca Empire and the Fifth Age

Most historians attribute the qualitative changes that ushered in the sudden expansion of the Inca Empire to the reforms of the ninth emperor, Pachacuti. The transition from Wirakocha Inca to Pachacuti, his son, forms a confusing picture in the chronicles. Events overlap between one sovereign and another. Feats attributed to one Inca in one chronicle are said to be the deed of the other sovereign in a second chronicle. Part of these discrepancies may lie in the autonomous sources of power formed by the *panaqas*, the royal *ayllus* that celebrated the memory of their respective sovereign founder. According to the sympathies of the chronicler or to the sources he consulted, one Inca shines at the expense of the other. In between the two sovereigns there may even have been the short inter-reign of Urcos, another of Wirakocha Inca's sons.

According to the majority of the chronicles, however, it is Pachacuti who was the major protagonist in the meteoric rise of the Inca empire. It is not this view that is questioned. However, the present work proposes to offer a complementary approach to the purely historical-scientific viewpoint. Our focus will turn toward three aspects of the spiritual turning point that gave rise to the Inca empire: the spiritual experiences undergone respectively by Wirakocha Inca and by Pachacuti, and the threat posed by the attack of the Inca rivals, the Chancas. Each of these builds upon the other and forms a coherent picture that supports the significance of the historical change.

The Chancas posed a spiritual threat to the Incas because of their antithetical spiritual views. Against this threat arose a spiritual response formulated by the two sovereigns. To understand the nature of this response, we need to turn to their biographies and to the spiritual experiences that formed the pivotal points of their lives. We will follow the historical timeline that leads from Wirakocha Inca to the Chanca invasion and finally to the response offered by Pachacuti. One has the feeling that the Chanca threat was the litmus test from which emerged the Inca Empire. To the threat of the continuation of the decadent Age of the Warriors, the Incas brought forth the spiritual response that inaugurated a new civilizing impulse, a true South American Fifth Age.

Wirakocha Inca and the Vision at Urcos

Bernabe Cobo indicates that the young prince's wild and proud behavior motivated his father Yahuar Huacac to send him to Chita (not far from Urcos in the Sacred Valley) to curb his spirit by entrusting to him the task of guarding the llamas of the Sun. Garcilaso de la Vega goes a step further in describing the prince's behavior. He describes a streak of "black malice and lack of humanity" in his conduct. He mentions that he liked to beat on his comrades. His father relegated him to Chita for three years when the young man had reached age nineteen. Polo de Ondegardo also confirms the banishment of the young heir.[1]

The youth of Wirakocha Inca did not form a promising debut. It is his famous vision that brought forth a spiritual conversion, and therefore also a change in the qualitative tenor of his life. This vision occurred in the Sacred Valley at Urcos, a place that has already been mentioned previously in relation to its ruins and surviving legends. Cobo indicates that the young prince saw an aged and bearded man, standing for the being named Wirakocha-Yachachic. He asked the youth to inaugurate a cult for his being and authorized him to bear his name. Cobo is one of the few chroniclers who links this turning point to the decisive battle and defeat of the Chancas. Garcilaso de la Vega confirms the vision and adds that the figure held an animal on a leash. Both he and Cobo call the figure a "ghost." Garcilaso specifies that the figure called himself "son of the Sun" and "brother of Manco Capac."[2] He adds that he was sent by the Sun. Sarmiento de Gamboa and Santa Cruz Pachacuti also believe in the reality of the vision. For Polo de Ondegardo and Acosta it was a dream. According to the historians it is most likely in response to the vision that Wirakocha Inca built the Quisar-cancha.

All of the above elements have a specific frame of reference in the context of Urcos. If we refer this context to what we know of Urcos from our previous explorations, a clearer picture will emerge. Urcos, like Cacha on the Titicaca altiplano, was the place of an important Inca place of worship. It commemorated places where Wirakocha/Thunupa had stopped in his peregrinations along the Andes. Both places are commemorated for Thunupa's fights against decadent magical practices. Finally, both of them had temples that showed the deed of the initiate in the taming of the Fire Puma, the vehicle of inspiration of the deity that directed South American civilization in the times preceding the Dawning—later to become decadent. All these elements together indicate quite clearly the being that Wirakocha Inca saw in his vision.

It may not be surprising, then, to find out that Wirakocha Inca grew a beard, something that was not common among the Incas. According to Garcilaso he also liked to impersonate the apparition of the "ghost."[3] The same author indicates that Wirakocha Inca initially made a distinction between the being that he had witnessed and himself. Later he gave way to the temptation of placing himself on the same footing. These facts may be the source of confusion between the mythical Wirakocha/Thunupa and the historical Wirakocha Inca in the chronicles of Molina and Murua.[4] From all of the above, we can say that Wirakocha Inca formed an important spiritual transition in the recovery of the knowledge of the role of Thunupa that had been lost in the time of decadence of the Age of the Warriors. However, it also brought in an element of confusion between Wirakocha (the Great Spirit and Creator God) and Thunupa, the initiate that Pachacuti would later call with the name of Illapa. A clear understanding could only be restored in relation to a third deity, the Sun God, Inti. It was Pachacuti who brought an answer to the burning question of Inti and his relation to Wirakocha and to the initiate Illapa/Thunupa. Pachacuti's later vision was intimately intertwined with the destiny of the Incas and with the impending invasion of the Chancas. That is why we will turn to the legend of the Chancas before looking specifically at Pachacuti's life and spiritual experiences.

Pachacuti and the Legend of the Chancas

We have seen how the Chanca culture inserted itself within the thread of the Wari, although as a culture of minor import in relation to the first. The

Chanca's far superior force now threatened the unfolding of a new spiritual impulse that wanted to enter the Inca nation through the person of Pachacuti. The following narrative, concerning the Inca emperor (originally called Cusi Yupanqui or Inca Yupanqui before his spiritual experience) is taken from the chronicle of Juan Betanzos.[5]

Concerning the character and virtues of Inca Yupanque and how he isolated himself from his companions, went into prayer, and, according to what the authors say, had a revelation from heaven; how he was aided, went into battle with Uscovilca, captured and killed him, along with other events that took place.

As a young man, Inca Yupanque was virtuous and affable in his conversation. He spoke little for such a young man, and he did not laugh in an exaggerated way but, rather, with discretion. He was fond of helping the weak. He was a chaste young man who was never heard to have been with a woman, nor did those of his times ever find him telling lies or not keeping his word. He had these qualities of a virtuous and valiant lord, though still a young man, and he was very courageous. As his father thought over the character of his son Inca Yupanque, he was filled with envy and detested him. His father wished that his eldest son, named Inca Urco, had Inca Yupanque's character. Since his father saw Inca Yupanque's strength of character, he did not allow Inca Yupanque to come before him, nor did he give anyone any hint that he loved Inca Yupanque. Since his father noticed that Inca Yupanque had so many good qualities, he feared that after his days the lords of Cuzco and the rest of the community would take him for their lord; and that even if he left the title of lord to Inca Urco, these lords would take it away from him on seeing that Inca Urco was rather simpleminded and lacked the capacity and character of Inca Yupanque, whom everyone loved very much, as you have heard. After his days, their father wanted to leave his title to Inca Urco. Therefore, Wirakocha Inca made the lords of Cuzco and the rest of the people treat Inca Urco with the same deference and respect accorded to himself. Thus Wirakocha Inca had the lords of Cuzco serve Inca Urco with the royal insignias used for him personally. No one was allowed to appear before him with shoes on, no matter how important a lord he might be, not even his brothers; rather, they came barefooted with their heads bowed all the time they were speaking before him or bringing him a message. He always ate alone, without anyone daring to touch the food he was eating. Lords carried him in a litter on their shoulders. If he went out to the square, he sat on a golden seat under a parasol made of ostrich feathers dyed red. He drank from golden tumblers, and all the other service dishes of his household were of gold. He had a great many women. Inca Yupanque had no part of any of this because, as you have heard, he was detested by his father, who loved Inca Urco. When Wirakocha Inca saw that Inca Yupanque had remained in the city of Cuzco, it pleased him. He thought Inca Yupanque would end his days there. When Inca Yupanque sent for the help about which you have already heard, Wirakocha Inca refused to come to his aid.

Inca Yupanque left his companions the night already mentioned to you [the night preceding the Chanca attack]; in this account they say that he went to a place where none of his followers could see him, a distance of about two shots with a sling from the city of Cuzco. There he started praying to the creator of all things whom they call Wirakocha Pachayachachic. Inca Yupanque was saying a prayer in the following words: "Lord God who created me and gave me the form of a man, come to my aid in this difficulty in which I find myself. You are my father who created me and gave me the form of a man. Do not allow me to be killed by my enemies. Give me help against them. Do not allow them to make me their subject. You made me free and your subject only. Do not allow me to be a subject of these people who want to subdue me this way and put me in bondage. Lord, give me the strength to resist them. Make of me whatever you will, for I am yours." When Inca Yupanque was saying this prayer, he was crying with all his heart. And still praying, he fell asleep, overcome by fatigue. As he was sleeping, Wirakocha came to him in the form of a man and spoke to him: "My son, do not be distressed. The day that you go into battle with your enemies, I will send soldiers to you with whom you will defeat your enemies, and you will enjoy victory."

When Inca Yupanque remembered this happy dream, he took heart, returned to his followers, and told them to be happy, as he was. They should not be afraid, for they would not be defeated by their enemies. He would have soldiers in the time of need, but he refused to say more about what, how, or where, although they asked him. From then on, every night Inca Yupanque would go away from his companions to the place where he had said his prayer, where he always said it exactly as he had the first time, but not so that he would have the same dream as the first night.

However, the last night while he was praying, Wirakocha came to him in the form of a man, and while Inca Yupanque was awake, said to him: "My son, tomorrow your enemies will come to do battle. I will come to your aid with soldiers so that you will defeat your enemies and enjoy victory." And they say that the next morning Uscovilca was coming with his soldiers down through Carmenga, which is a hill on the side of town toward the city of Los Reyes. As Uscovilca was coming down with all his forces and soldiers, there appeared twenty squadrons of soldiers never seen or known to Inca Yupanque or his followers. These soldiers appeared on the Collasuyo quarter, on the road to Accha, and on the Condesuyo road. As these soldiers came up to him, Inca Yupanque and his companions were watching their enemies descend toward them. As the enemies approached, those who came to Inca Yupanque's aid surrounded him saying: "Let us go, our only king, and we will defeat your enemies, whom you will take prisoner today." And so they went up to Uscovilca's soldiers who, full of fury, were coming down the hills. As they met, they unleashed their battle, fighting from morning, which was when they started, until noon. The battle turned out in such a way that large numbers of Uscovilca's soldiers died and not one entered into combat without dying. In that battle Uscovilca was taken prisoner and killed. When his followers saw him dead and saw the great slaughter that was being made of them, they agreed not to wait any longer. Returning by the road on which they had come, they fled until they reached the town of Jaquijahuana, where they stopped to rest and recover.

Having escaped this defeat, some of Uscovilca's captains sent this news right away to their land asking for aid. They also sent the news to the captains Malma and Rapa, who had gone on a campaign of conquest across the province of Condesuyo up to the province of the Chichas, as you have already been told in this account. These captains were already returning as victors, triumphant over the provinces that they had conquered. They came with great wealth, bringing their spoils. At this time, the defeated captains who were conferring together in Jaquijahuana sent their messengers to the other two captains, whom Uscovilca had also sent from the town of Paucaray to discover and conquer whatever provinces and towns they could find. These captains had gone across the province of the Andes and had conquered up to the land of the Chiriguana, which is more than two hundred leagues to where they reached back to Paucaray. As these captains Yanavilca and Tecllovilca were returning as victors with great spoils, the messengers met them. When they found out about the death of Uscovilca, how he had been defeated and the way it was done, they all made their way as fast as they could to join the captains who had escaped from Uscovilca's defeat to confer at Jaquijahuana, as you have already heard. We will now leave them all together and speak again about Inca Yupanque, who was victorious.

* * *

There is a consistent pattern in the chronicles. Those chroniclers that devote most of their attention to Wirakocha Inca also attribute to him the resistance offered against the Chancas: Bernabe Cobo and Garcilaso de la Vega. Cobo explains that the invasion happened soon after Wirakocha Inca's vision. However, Maria Rowstorowski claims that twelve chroniclers attribute the defeat of the Chancas to Pachacuti.[6] Among them are names we have often heard so far: Polo de Ondegardo, Sarmiento de Gamboa, Cieza de Leon, Acosta, Santa Cruz Pachacuti, and Juan Betanzos. This is therefore the version of the facts most often acknowledged by historians. Gamboa and Betanzos indicate that the young prince had reached somewhere between age twenty and twenty-three when the Chancas invaded Cuzco. In fact, this may have been one of many attacks.

The legend of the Chancas is intimately intertwined with Pachacuti's experience in Susurpuquio (close to Cuzco). So let us turn to the individuality of the young Cusi Yupanqui up to the point when he would assume the momentous name of Pachacuti, which means "world change," or "inaugurator of a new age." The young Cusi Yupanqui was the third or fourth son of Wirakocha Inca and his first wife Mama Runta. We saw that Betanzos attributes many virtues to the young Inca. He was affable, chaste, fond of helping the weak, sincere, and courageous. Santa Cruz Pachacuti confirms that he had a special predilection toward the dwarves and hunchbacks, and that he offered them a house and special care once he became sovereign. To all appearances we have here to do with a special individuality even before his spiritual conversion. Some of his traits are reminiscent of the folklore attached to Thunupa.

The vision of Susurpuquio had a particular background to it that distinguishes it from Wirakocha Inca's vision at Urcos. It was certainly young Cusi Yupanqui's vision; however, in more than one way it was also a message to the young Inca nation. Cusi Yupanqui had made a desperate stand when few, including himself, had any hope that the Incas could resist the Chanca threat. Although he had called to the Incas and other nations for help, little had been offered. Betanzos explains that Cusi Yupanqui went to pray in a state similar to despair. "He was crying with all his heart" and fell asleep overcome by fatigue. Let us quote some of the chroniclers in order to approach the nature of the vision and of the being who approached Cusi Yupanqui. Gathering the content of different chronicles, we are told of an anthropomorphic figure with impressive attributes: puma heads projecting from his torso, serpents twisted about his arms, golden rays about his face (Polo de Ondegardo, Cobo, Molina, Betanzos). In Betanzos's version—although after the facts and further in the text—we are told the following: "He took into account that the one he had seen there, whom he called Wirakocha, he saw with great brightness, as they say. And so much so that it seemed to him that the whole day was there before him, and its light, which he saw before him, they say gave him a great fright. And he was never told who it was. As he was planning on building this house [the Temple of the Sun], he judged by the brightness of the one he saw that it must have been the Sun, and on coming near the first word he spoke, 'Child, fear not'; thus his people called him 'child of the Sun.' Taking into account what you have heard, he decided to make this house of the Sun." Gamboa confirms the epithet "child of the Sun" three times. Nor is Betanzos's version the only one to describe the traits of this being in the same way. Sarmiento de Gamboa indicates that it was a "personage like the Sun." Cristobal de Molina attributed this sentence to the being who appears to Pachacuti: "Come my child, fear not. I am the Sun, your Father, and know that you will subjugate many nations." (author's translation)[7] It was from this experience that Pachacuti proceeded to give the Sun the central cult of the empire. Although in Betanzos's version Pachacuti first describes the being as Wirakocha, a little like Wirakocha Inca had done, when the description is given at length (later in the chapter) and compared with what other chroniclers say, it appears that it is a solar being. This is also abundantly borne out by later history and by the central importance given to the cult of the Sun in the empire founded by Pachacuti.

Who are then the helpers that the Sun being sends to Cusi Yupanqui? Gamboa says that the Chancas suddenly saw a multitude of men coming down from the hill who had been sent by Wirakocha. These miraculous soldiers are called *pururaucas*. The word has the meaning of "hidden bandit" or "hidden archer." The tradition persisted at the time of the Spanish Conquest that the *pururaucas* were rocks found around Cuzco. Thus seven were found in the north quarter (Chinchasuyu), four in the south quarter (Collasuyu), and fifteen to the west (Cuntisuyu).

We can now attempt to reach the deeper meaning of the legend of the Chancas. A spiritual battle was engaged between the heirs of the decadent Fourth Age and the new spiritual impulse partly reinaugurated by Wirakocha Inca. The old emperor had reestablished the connection of the Inca Empire with the deeds of Wirakocha/Thunupa. This is made clear by many little indications. He is the being who appears bearded, accompanied by a tame animal on a leash. The imagery and the geographic placement of Urcos tie the apparition to the being who had supposedly guided the Incas from the Titicaca region to the Sacred Valley and later to Cuzco. This is therefore the being of Thunupa. This is only the first step of the restoration and new evolution of the Andean heritage that had been lost to the Age of the Warriors. After all, the staff deity was still known, albeit in a distorted fashion, even among the Wari. It may have been this time of decadence itself that brought forth the confusion between the supreme being, Wirakocha, and its envoy Thunupa. In fact much indicates that Wirakocha Inca partly succumbed to the temptation of identifying himself with the supreme being Wirakocha.

Inca Yupanqui really inaugurated a new age, as the meaning of his adopted name—Pachacuti—indicates. After him the Inca called themselves the men of the Fifth Age. Martin de Murua refers to the Fifth Sun, indicating that this was the Sun whose symbol stood in the Qori-cancha—the House of the Sun.[8]

The being that Pachacuti experiences is the very same inspiration that shines behind Wirakocha/Thunupa. It is the solar being "in the form of a man," the Christ himself. It is this important distinction that prevented Pachacuti from confusing his personal role with the role of the supreme deity. As an initiate, the emperor was brother to Thunupa, whom he called Illapa. He was truly a "son of the Sun," much like the initiate at the time of Christ. In so doing, he had reestablished the link between Thunupa and Wirakocha (Great Spirit) and the being of Inti, the Sun God or Christ. This allowed him to keep from identifying with either Sun or Supreme Being. The statues of the emperors that he placed in the Inti-Cancha looked away from the Sun at least until the time of Wayna Capac. Pachacuti himself took in battle the effigy of Illapa, his *huaoqui*, or brother.

The *pururaucas* are a well-known symbol to the people of the Third Age, to whom they represent the immortal souls of the dead. This was also known through the mummies, or the lineage *wakas* in the form of stones. Pachacuti in his despair had stood hopelessly against the invading Chancas. The solar being had shown to him that in fighting in his name, he was rallying the heritage and the help of the lineage *wakas*, of all the lineages established by Thunupa at the time of the Christ. The *pururaucas*, once they performed their function, reverted into stone. This is the same idea expressed in the legend of the four brothers founding Cuzco. Although at one point their mission comes to an end and they are transformed into stone, they do not stop being present in spirit.

It was the spiritual assurance of the support of all the dead and of the lineage *wakas* that gave Pachacuti the courage needed to fend off the Chanca invasion. It was in final acknowledgment of this fact that his father Wirakocha Inca reputedly gave him the name Pachacuti, after bowing to him as a vassal, in recognition of his previous lack of appreciation.

Wirakocha Inca had needed to subdue a rebellious nature. This had been possible in the meeting with the Lower Guardian at Urcos—a meeting in which he clearly saw all his failings. Pachacuti Inca had an otherwise more exalted nature than his father. It appears through the chronicles by many telling symptoms. Although aware of his father's deception and attempt to divest him of authority in favor of his other son Urcos, Pachacuti offered his victory against the Chancas to his father, since he still was the legal ruler at the time of the events, in spite of the fact that Wirakocha Inca had fled the invading Chancas. Pachacuti's turning to the spiritual world is also the humble gesture of the one who has lost any hope, any of the supports offered by the lower ego. He has to place all trust in his higher self and find it in the figure of the Christ that supports and sustains it. Pachacuti's conversion is an initiation in and through the Christ.

Pachacuti assumed a role in all ways equal to that of Manco Capac and Thunupa. The spread of the cult of the Sun and the resulting meteoric ascent of the Inca empire lay down the basis of a cultura-spiritual revolution of an unprecedented nature, truly a Fifth Age, as we will see now.

The Birth of Empire

Pachacuti's political expansion was the direct result of a spiritual revolution. Therefore, our attention will be directed first of all to some aspects pertaining to cult and spirituality before we turn to a brief review of the religious, political, and economic reforms. Political and social reforms, new religious practices, architectural and artistic innovations, and practically all changes that ushered in the time of the Inca empire point to the individuality of Pachacuti. This is truly surprising, and a confirmation of the initiatic knowledge of the ninth emperor. In him is found the link with the legacy of Thunupa, the resurrection of traditions that probably lay buried for centuries, and their adaptation to the changed conditions of the times.

First, let us see how the emperor understood his person in relation to the gods, in particular the triad of the Creator God, Wirakocha; the Sun God; and Thunupa/Illapa. After the victory against the Chancas, Pachacuti established the precedence of the Creator God over Sun and Illapa. The greatest majority of the chroniclers, except Garcilaso, agree that Creator God, Sun God, and Illapa shared the main altar in the Qoricancha.[9]

We have seen that the Emperor had been called "Child of the Sun." It is not surprising then that in the Temple of the Sun, all the statues of the former emperors after Pachacuti were arranged around the Sun, but looking away from it. According to Sarmiento de Gamboa, next to the Sun was also present the statue of the idol representing the thunder and lightning, the one called Illapa, and sometimes also Inti-Illapa. Illapa had a temple built by Pachacuti, and situated opposite to his palace on the other side of the River Sapi. Here was kept the image in solid gold of his double, which he called Inti-Illapa. Another important clue offered by Molina is the fact that such a figure wore ear plugs, a distinctive sign of the initiate priest for millennia in the Andes.

The Creator God, Wirakocha—the Great Spirit—was represented in the Qoricancha and in its own temple of the Quisar-cancha. Molina describes the statue as the golden figure of a man the size of a ten-year-old boy with a raised right arm in the gesture of command. Cobo confirms this.

Pachacuti could direct himself to Thunupa/Illapa as his equal, to the Sun as His son, and with the deepest reverence to Wirakocha. Chief among all of the temples that reflected Pachacuti's spiritual experience at Susurpuquio was the Qoricancha. Pachacuti had enlarged the garden where appeared animals and plants made of or covered with gold. The Sun was represented in two aspects: as the Lord-Sun he was represented by a golden male adult figure; as the Son-Sun (Punchao, the day) his effigy was a golden face surrounded by rays. In fact there were even three suns, as we will see later in more detail.

Molina offers an image of the Sun's golden icon in the Qori-cancha in a description that fits, all in all, with the description of Pachacuti's vision at Susurpuquio. In its head it wore a *llauto*—the headband of the Inca king—and had perforated ears with earplugs. The head emerged from a lion placed between the legs, and in his shoulders he had another lion. A snake encircles his shoulders and back. Antonio de Vega described the deity's representation, probably taken down secondhand in 1590. He too stresses that it was the image of the royal Inca. He adds that from the shoulders and upper back radiated massive golden rays. At his sides the idol had two golden snakes and two golden lions. A third report, that of the Toledo Viceroy in 1572, confirms some of the above details.[10]

From the fragments of these explorations, some elements may emerge more clearly. Wirakocha Inca most likely recognized Thunupa in his vision, but he may have confused him with the Creator. This may explain why he was tempted to identify himself with him and ascertain the authority of the Inca as the authority of a god. In doing so, he had relapsed into the grandiose temptation of his youth. Pachacuti Inca restored the legacy of Thunupa more fully. This can be done only by separating the First Creation of Wirakocha from the part that Thunupa played in the Dawning or Second Creation. Thunupa is identified with the Staff God, with the guardian being that holds the thunder and lightning. He is therefore called Illapa or Inti-Illapa, in order to remind us of his human-divine nature through which the Sun being expresses Himself. In effect, the emperor had been initiated through the vision and the trial of fire of the Chanca invasion. Like Thunupa he had come to inaugurate a new age. He too was a Child of the Sun, an initiate of Christ. However, he could only turn to Inti or to the Creator Wirakocha with the highest reverence.

Understanding the import of Pachacuti's reforms is like disassembling and reassembling a complex puzzle. His legacy is composed of so many parts, all intricately interwoven, that reassembling the whole puzzle after taking it apart is all the more challenging. We will attempt to look at the interconnection of the parts and their coherent subordination to the whole in a way that maintains and highlights the intention of the builder.

Reform of the Calendar, Religion, and Political Power

Pachacuti is most aptly remembered for the reforms in the cultural and political realm that enabled the expansion of a vast empire, as if overnight.

Most chroniclers agree that he instated the most important reforms in the ritual and the calendar. He most likely made the calendar start at the December Solstice—a return to the cosmology of Tiwanaku. Around this time occurred the ceremonies of the Capac Raymi, in which the Inca youths were initiated into their knighthood rituals. This is what conferred upon them the title of Inca.

At the opposite time of the year was the important festival of the Inti Raymi, the festival of the Sun, celebrated at the June Solstice. Only the Incas and the Virgins of the Sun could partake of the ceremonies. This included ceremonies in the Qoricancha and sacrifices offered in the high mountains toward the rising sun. After other ceremonies that took them out of the capital, the Incas returned to celebrate in Cuzco to the Aucaypata, the main plaza.

The polarity of Inti Raymi and Capac Raymi underlines once again the principles that have emerged from the spirituality that Pachacuti restored and renovated. To one part of the year, the rainy season, corresponded the time of initiation. This is what conferred upon the Inca the spiritual and moral authority that enabled him to govern. Pachacuti had in fact restored the principle of initiation as the source of authority of the emperor and of all other political figures. However, the Sun deity had a cult all its own at the opposite time of the year, at the June Solstice. The Inca could then bow to the very source of the initiation that conferred power on him. Betanzos and Cieza de Leon indicate that it was Pachacuti who presided over the forming of the orders of "big ears" or knights, as well as the Huaccha Ccuyac brotherhood of the "Friends of the Poor." The first was instated in memory of the victory over the Chancas.[11]

An interesting addition on the nature of the polarity between Capac and Inti Raymi comes from Guaman Poma's commentary and illustrations concerning the two festivals. At the December solstice (Capac Raymi) the sun is at its strongest. It shines from the north and is close to the zenith. Guaman Poma represents it as large and with a beard. In comparison, the Sun at the June solstice is smaller and without any particular attributes. This reflects the fact that the sun is more distant at that time of the year. The December sun of the rainy season is the one that grows larger from drinking from the swollen Sacred River of the Vilcamayu. During the dry season the sun shrinks due to the little water present in the Vilcamayu. This is a symbolism that dips its roots in Tiwanaku symbolism of the time of Thunupa. In chapter 5 we discussed the Gateway of the Sun. The upper half represents the rainy season and the so-called Great Image has been recognized as the Sun of the December solstice of the rainy season. Just below it, much smaller, stands the central face of the June solstice, the sun of the dry season.

The Capac Raymi reminded the Incas of their own history, their arrival in Cuzco, the time of initiation and a time that harkened back to the (bearded) initiate, hence the bearded sun. The Inti Raymi was a celebration of a larger history, that of the Sun deity, Inti. This is why during the June solstice there was a pilgrimage to Lake Titicaca, to the celebrated place of origin and time of the Dawning. The two times of the year form the significant, omnipresent division between the political and the spiritual.

The Inti Raymi comprised various ceremonies of Thanksgiving for the harvests and a pilgrimage to the Sun's spiritual origin toward the southeast. The ceremonies of Thanksgiving, called Yahuarincha Aymoray, were celebrated in Rimac Pampa (modern Limac Pampa). The festivities lasted for ten days and started with the first sunrise. After a long period of silence and expectation, the emperor was the first to address the Sun in chanting. Offerings were given to Inti and the *curacas* of the empire brought their tribute to the Inca and rendered an account of the state of affairs of their administration. Complaints could be brought to the ear of the supreme authority. The *ñustas*, daughters of Inca blood, were given in marriage to the young knights. The *wakas* were all taken out of the Qoricancha and assembled on Rimac Pampa, where each of their priests would prophesy for the year to come. The previous year's prophecies would be evaluated and the *wakas* put to test for their truthfulness.

However, the most significant part of the festival was the pilgrimage to the source of the Sacred River (Vilcamayu or Urubamba). This is the route that, according to the Inca myths, the ancestors had followed from Lake Titicaca. The priests directed themselves from Cuzco to La Raya mountain pass.[12] They returned from La Raya following the Sacred River. In following the southeast to northwest route, they were repeating the mythical path of Thunupa/Wirakocha. This is also the path that the sun follows from the east to the west and from the south (weakest) to the north (strongest). Thus this pilgrimage recapitulated Inca mythology and reputed history, the sacred journey of the initiate of the Andes, and the sun's path. While the priests retraced the route of the sun and of the initiate and returned through the Sacred Valley, the emperor consecrated the bond that united each part of the empire and its *wakas* with Cuzco and their common origin at the time of the Dawning.

A review of Inca festivals would not be complete without the link of the two previous festivals to the supreme deity Wirakocha at its festival of Citua. This occurred during the month of *Qoya* Raimy (Festival of the Queen, meaning also the Moon Goddess) in August or September, according to the years. This was still the time of the dry season, soon after the new seeds had been sown. It was the time of waiting for the rains and of the new agricultural year. In preparation, Cuzco celebrated the festival of the Great Spirit Wirakocha and offered itself in ritual cleansing of purification. Before the celebrations, all foreigners and foreign *wakas* were removed from Cuzco and placed beyond a six-mile limit. The first day of celebration started in Cuzco's spiritual center of the Qoricancha. All deities were there assembled; those that resided elsewhere were taken from their shrines. To the gathering came also all the lineage *wakas* of the previous emperors, their mummies, and the *ayllus* carrying the *wakas* of their lineage ancestors. They all divided into their respective upper (Hanan) and lower moieties (Hurin).

The festival started with a ritual "laundry list" of all the wrongs committed by the members of *ayllus* and *panaqas* in civil, criminal, or ceremonial matters. After hearing these, the *huchacamayoc*, or highest judge, inflicted the fines or penalties that were appropriate. This was a first stage of the cleansing. After the first celebrations, an army of four hundred chosen Incas erupted into a simulated fight with evils and demons, driving them out of the city in the four directions of its quadrants, or *suyus*. At their approach all other Inca citizens and their servants started a ceremonial driving-out of their evil spirits with ceremonial fumigation, using torches of ichu grass. The above ended in the cleansing of individuals, *wakas*, and objects in the waters of springs, or tanks placed in the *ceques* of each corresponding *ayllu* and *panaqa*.

On the third day all the population partook of a meal of sacred cornmeal bread—the *yahuar sanco*—moistened by the blood of the sacrificial llamas. This was seen as a further stage of purification of the soul. The same communion was repeated with the *wakas*, mummies, and deities, and was followed the next day with celebrations offered to the Sun, sacred dances, and prayers. Finally, during the last day all the *wakas* of the empire returned to the city. There were further sacrifices of llamas and once more the sacred *yahuar sanco* bread was offered, but this time more specifically to the foreign *wakas*. The celebration ended in dances and feasting between Incas and the other residents of Cuzco.

Inti Raymi and Capac Raymi mirror the division of the year by the Maya. Naturally this occurs at the opposite times of the year. The Maya turned to the Great Spirit/Ahpus during the time of the rainy season. This was the time of the agricultural operations and of everything that was turned toward the earth via the knowledge of the stars. It is the initiate Ixbalamqué that guards this time of the year. The transition into the dry season occurred at Yaxkin, the commemoration of the Dawning. After November 1, the calendar entered into the solar year, the time of Hunahpu/Solar God, culminating at the December solstice. It is also the time devoted to the political authority, historical commemorations, and so on.

The terms are reversed in the Andes. The rainy season precedes and includes the time of the Capac Raymi. Initiation occurs in this period of the year. Interestingly, the sun of the corresponding time of the year (Capac Raymi) is represented as bearded. The Inti Raymi occurs during the time of the dry season, extending from April to October at the latitude of Cuzco.

The two festivals plus Citua—the festival of Wirakocha, the Great Spirit—played a central role in Inca worldview. They further defined the many aspects of their Sun deity throughout the year. We have already seen this expressed in the way Guaman Poma portrayed a large sun with a beard when the sun shines from closer to the zenith during the rainy season (Capac Raymi: December solstice and rainy season) and a small sun at the opposite time of the year (Inti Raymi: June Solstice and dry season). There were in fact three images of the Sun. These were in order of importance: Wayna Punchao, adolescent Sun; Punchao Inca, young Sun; Apu Inti (or Apin Punchao), adult Sun.[13] During Capac Raymi (November/December) Wuayna Punchao (adolescent Sun) presided over the initiation of the young Inca and the time of growth of maize and potatoes.

The Inti Raymi (May/June) was celebrated in honor of Punchao Inca ("daily Sun" and young Sun). This was the ritual that celebrated the return of the sun in the heavens after the rainy season. During Citua (August September) Apin Punchao (mature Sun) presided over the end of a cycle and the beginning of a new one.

In summary, the year is divided into the following intervals:

> Citua to Capac Raymi: four months at the beginning of the agricultural year, the time of the adolescent Sun

Capac Raymi to Inti Raymi: six months, the time of the young Sun
Inti Raymi to Citua: two months, the time of the adult Sun

It is worth reviewing these festivals with some added detail. The last day of Capac Raymi (the day of the December solstice) the statue of Wayna Punchao (adolescent Sun) was moved in the opposite direction to the temple of the Puquin Hill. Before it, went one pair of llama statues of metal.

Just before the June solstice of Inti Raymi, the statue of Punchao Inca (young Sun), the two statues of the women Palpasillo and Incasillo, and the figures of two pairs of llamas (two of gold and two of silver) were transported to the hill called Mantocal.

Citua celebrated the beginning of the agricultural year. During this festival the Inca, the queen, and priests accompanied the image of Apu Punchao (mature Sun) and the two golden images of the women Inca Occlo and Palpa Occlo. There is no mention of llamas. The statues were transported from the Qoricancha to the nearby square of Aucaypata. In this feast came also the priests of Illapa and of the sacred hill Huanacauri—the first Inca *waka*—and all the *panaqas* with the ancestors of both sexes.

From the above we see that in each festival the Sun deity had a different name and the celebrations involved different sacred objects. This is summarized in the following table (from Krzysztof Makowski, slightly modified):[14]

FESTIVAL	NAME OF idol	PLACE	DIRECTION of movement	FEMALE figures	LLAMAS (number)
Capac Raymi	Wayna Punchao (adol. Sun)	Hurin Cuzco SW	From West to center	None	2 pairs
Inti Raymi	Punchao Inca (Young Sun)	Hanan Cuzco NE	Center to East	Palpasillo Incasillo	1 pair
Citua	Apu Punchao (mature Sun)	Hurin Cuzco Center	Center/Hurin	Inca Occlo Palpa Occlo	none

More can be learned about the specific way that political power had been linked to initiation in Pachacuti's vision by looking to the ceremonies held at the Sacred Rock, a symbol par excellence of the Dawning. These are very indicative of the relationships between political and spiritual authorities.

The Island of the Sun had a very sacred character. In fact, even the isthmus of Copacabana leading to it was the object of special observances at the temples by the pilgrims coming to worship at the Sacred Rock. Part of the isthmus was separated by a wall that conferred sacred character to it. From Copacabana the pilgrims arrived in stages from the south to the northern extreme of the island, where are located the rock and the most sacred shrines. Gavilan indicates that the pilgrims had to pass through three gateways, delineating three spaces.[15] At each one of them they had an audience with a priest. The first gate was called Pumapuncu, the Gate of the Moon in front of which the mythical puma stood guard. A stone lion was said to guard the entrance. The pilgrims had to offer confession of their sins before entering. The general population most likely stopped at this stage and worshipped the Sacred Rock from a platform from where it was visible. The second gateway was called Kentipuncu, or Gate of the Hummingbird. Interestingly, it was also called Intipuncu—Gate of the Sun. Three stone steps presently indicate the location of the gate. Here again the pilgrims (presumably *curacas* and dignitaries) had to undergo a ritual confession. The final gateway was called Pillcopuncu. The *pillco* is a bird with brilliant green feathers. Figuratively, the name meant "Door of Hope." Only the highest Inca nobility and priesthood could gain proximity to the rock. The others had to leave their offer-ings in front of the third gate and the priests would bring them in.

The process that is made most physically visible in the Island of the Sun was also repeated in the rituals of the Qoricancha in Cuzco. The process of initiation of the Inca is made graphically visible by having to pass first the Gateway of the Moon, entrance to the soul world; then the Gateway of the Sun, entrance to the spiritual world; and finally, as it were, the entrance into the highest spiritual world offered only to the highest nobility that had been educated through a process of initiation. These successive stages are intimated in the progression between Capac Raymi, Inti Raymi, and Citua or between the equivalent deities: Illapa, Inti, and Wirakocha.

The reader may have noticed the similarities between the sacred architecture of Tiwanaku and the Inca sacred rock, particularly in the succession of ritual spaces, one of which is specifically called Puma Punku or

Gate of the Moon in both instances. Tiwanaku also harbors a Gate of the Sun that was subsequently moved from its original location. We saw that Tiwanaku's ceremonial center was surrounded by an artificial moat and there were two additional moats to the east of it. Going from the east toward the center marked progressive spiritual thresholds, similar to those found in the Island of the Sun.

Pachacuti visited Tiwanaku before his son Topa Inca. According to Cobo he was so impressed by the architecture of Puma Punku that he sought to emulate it in Cuzco and in the rest of the empire.[16] Through architecture Pachacuti marked a return to the past that could only have been integrated through the fruits of initiation. Inca architecture pointed back to the megalithic architecture of the time of Tiwanaku. It was a new refinement of an old art that had been lost. Cobo and Betanzos confirm this by referring to legends that attribute to the emperor the establishment of canons of Inca architectural style.[17] Cieza de Leon follows this further by telling us that the monarch personally drew the plans for the construction of the cities and the placement of key temples and buildings.[18]

The architecture of Cuzco and other places that has astounded the Spaniards and all subsequent tourists—in particular the way to cut complex, polygonal rocks and assemble them together with no in-between spaces—remains for the most part a mystery for modern man. However, the technique itself is further surpassed by the cosmology embodied in Inca architecture. This facet of Andean civilization forms a fascinating and complex topic that will be illustrated in the next chapter.

The Inca resurrected the monumental use of the landscape already seen in the Nazca geoglyphs, although this had to be done differently in the mountainous region of the sierra than it could have been done on the desert floor. An eloquent testimony of how the Incas considered themselves the heirs of Thunupa is the gigantic bearded face found in the Sacred Valley of the Urubamba, close to Ollantaytanpu, on the mountain called Pinkuylluna that we have previously mentioned in chapter 7.

We have come back full circle from Pachacuti to the legacy of the initiate of the Americas. However, much more lay in store with the reforms of Pachacuti than a mere restoration of the past.

Cuzco and the Periphery

Another unique feature of Pachacuti's reforms was the particular role played by Cuzco. Commoners did not live within it! Strict laws governed access to the city and the behavior allowed therein. It was not a city in the sense we give the name. It really stood for the center of the Inca cosmos. In the Aucaypata (central plaza) stood the Capa Usno—throne and symbolic pyramid—which only the Inca could ascend. It was the center of that world, together with the Qoricancha, its spiritual counterpart.

Cuzco was a sacred city. The city was divided, as elsewhere in the Andes, into an upper, Hanan city and a lower, Hurin city. Hanan Cuzco was oriented to the north, Hurin Cuzco to the south. According to the myths Manco Capac gave origin to Hanan Cuzco, Mama Occlo to Hurin Cuzco.

All the conquered nations of the empire brought to Cuzco their *wakas*. One or more priests from the nation came to Cuzco to offer the same adoration to the *waka* that it would have received in its place of origin. They were in fact placed among the Inca *wakas*. Once more the principle of the common origin of the *wakas* shines through the idea of their cohabitation in Cuzco. Additionally, this served an undeniable political purpose. In case of rebellion of the province, the *waka* was publicly exposed and ritually flogged.

The local chiefs, *curacas*, had to reside part of the year in Cuzco. Here they were given an Inca wife of the nobility. The conquered people retained their own cults and rituals. The cult to the Sun was superimposed onto all the others. However, practices of human sacrifices were barred. To this it may be objected that the Incas still practiced some residual sacrifices, particularly of youth. However, these very limited sacrifices occurred at very particular and exceptional times, as in the rites of succession of the Capa Chucha.[19] At that time all the nations of the empire, Incas included, sacrificed a small number of youths. Apart from its rarity, this kind of human sacrifice did not make recourse to ritual battles, organ extraction, or capture of enemies.

We could ask ourselves: How could this overarching political transformation be carried out effectively? Pachacuti amplified the process of schooling for adolescent boys. This was given to both the young Incas and the sons of the *curacas* in the so-called Yacha-Huasi. The instruction started at age fifteen and lasted for what some believe to have been four years. The first stage was the teaching of the Runa Simi or Quechua language. In the second year doctrine, religion, and cult rituals were taught. The third year taught the use of *khipus* through which was stored all the accounting information, and at least according to some chronicles and to a growing section of modern research, also writing. Finally, the youth was told in the fourth year about history, facts of war, use of oratory, etc. The initiation of the Capac Raymi was then the culmination of a long process; it concerned not only the Incas but also populations subjected to the empire.

In order to strengthen what has become known as "the administration of generosity," Pachacuti had ordered the building of *acclahuasi* with the purpose of hosting and educating the chosen women that would be offered to the local *curacas*. There were many types of *acclas*. The *guayrur acclas* served the Sun and the Moon. *Uayror acclas* served the most important *wakas*. Others specialized in the weaving of textiles or in the work in the fields. Essentially the *acclas* served at least three major purposes: serving the cult, educating women to become the wives of *curacas* and warriors, and producing textiles and other products. The textiles were very much desired, and the marriage of the *curacas* to Inca women was more than a simple "exchange of favors"; witness the fact that the *acclas* were highly cultured Inca women. They were the first link in exporting Inca culture. The second link was their sons, who already could claim more Inca blood.

The Incas wanted to spread their spirituality throughout the extent of their empire. The best suited son of an important *curaca* was sent to Cuzco to be educated in Inca administration practices, and actually to receive Inca initiation. At his accession to power he was likely to spread Inca values. The Inca requested much the same of other relatives of the *curaca*. The *curacas* themselves had to reside in Cuzco part of the year and participate in Inca military expeditions. The education of the lords played a central role in Inca policy—understandably, since the heirs were to succeed the local *curacas*, and exposure to Inca ways would reinforce the links of Cuzco with the provinces. The Cuzco residents were also to be used as hostages if needed.

In the conquered land the Incas introduced a reform in the division of land and the offering of tribute. Lands were divided into lands of the Sun, lands of the Inca, and lands of the *runas* (common people). The products of the lands of the Sun went to the priesthood, and made possible the life of the sanctuaries and the numerous sacrifices of animals. The temples of the Sun sprouted next to the *wakas*' cults that the local population retained. The land of the Inca served the administrative bodies of the empire and the supplying of the army. They also sustained the needs of the workers during public works (so they would not deplete local resources) and provided help in case of calamities. Warehouses on this land stored large amounts of ropes, weapons, and goods in major part for the army, removing the need for looting in times of war, at least in theory. Part of the wealth generated from this land supported the administration of Cuzco. Tribute was offered in labor or, when that was not possible, from the result of one's labor (e.g., fishermen and craftsmen). Part of what made the above possible was the fact that the Incas inaugurated a new time of peaceful collaboration among the nations. Additional land placed under cultivation through terracing and irrigation allowed for the lands of the Inca and of the Sun without depriving the local population of its own land. It is known that the Incas colonized marginal territory that could not have previously been used because of its not being defensible.

Reform of the Ayllus and Creation of the Panaqas

We have seen what part the *ayllus* played at the time of Christ if not earlier. The new, mixed social form was and still is called *ayllu*. This structure is a system of double descent from both mother and father. It has been described as a "vague and extended family by common agreement." Marriage is generally exogamous, occurring outside of one's *ayllu*. The *ayllu* operates as a system of mutual aid in agricultural work, construction of houses, all sorts of public work, the care of the orphans and widows, etc. This social form extends at present from the north of Peru to the south of Argentina.

The way in which the *ayllu* is formulated is reflected in the shared importance of male and female roles in Andean society. Men and women work side by side in the fields. The man prepares the furrow with the foot-plow and the woman plants the seed. The integration of male and female also reflects of the integration of female pastoralism of the preceding ages with the agricultural/male knowledge. It was the peaceful coexistence of nomad shepherd societies and sedentary farmers, we may remember, that allowed the integration of the so-called vertical archipelago.

In the different ways explained above the male/female archetypal connotations are visible in the lineage *wakas*. The male descent is associated with the male generative power of the lightning. It is found in the lightning stone, in the idea of the ancestor turned into stone. Female descent, as reaffirmed by Santa Cruz Pachacuti, comes from the tree of origin—the Tree of Mother Earth and from the mummy. It is interesting to note that *mallqui* signifies both tree and mummified ancestor in Quechua.

The *ayllus* are a reflection of the heavens on earth. Individually they are like a single star or constellation, living on earth, a constellation that found its place on earth at the time of the Dawning. As all the constellations form the unity of the heavens, so do the *ayllus* form a unity on earth, all of them linked to the time of the Dawning and the teachings of the initiate of the Andes. Unity and diversity are consecrated in the concept of the *ayllu*. The *ayllu*'s *waka* therefore acquires its sacredness not out of an inherent magical power, but in relation to all the other *wakas* and to their common origin.

The refounding of Cuzco's system of *ayllus* was one of the deeds attributed to Inca Pachacuti. According to Sarmiento de Gamboa there were ten original *ayllus*, five Hanan and five Hurin. The original *ayllus* were those descending from the old companions of Manco Capac, the Ayar brothers, as we have seen previously. Each of them was associated with a royal *ayllu*, or *panaqa*.

The *panaqa* is a special form of *ayllu*; this, too, was a creation of Pachacuti. By the time the Spaniards arrived there were eleven *panaqas*: five belonging to Hurin and six to Hanan. *Pana* is the way in which a man calls his sister. Traditionally the founder of the *panaqa* was the second son of the living emperor, or the descendent of the second son of a deceased emperor. The *panaqa* started to operate at the death of the emperor. The idea of the *panaqa* enshrined the continuation of the influence of the dead emperor through the intermediary of his mummy or his *huaoqui* (literally "brother"), a stone, or other object that served in lieu of the mummy. Members of these groups had responsibilities in the state administration, in the priesthood, and in the army. The women played an important role as priestesses of the Moon, and as wives and mothers of potential heirs.

No emperor inherited the property of his forerunner. The property passed to the descendants who formed the *panaqa*. Upon ascending to the throne, the ruler had to find ways to secure property and goods for his kin. The first way to do this was to incorporate new lands to the kingdom or place new land under exploitation. Another was to take over the care of a *waka*.

Polarity Between Political and Religious Powers

There is little knowledge of the Inca political system obtainable from the chronicles. It seems that the chroniclers turned most of their interest toward Inca religion, perhaps because they often were men of the cloth. In addition, many assumptions crept into the chronicles since most of the individuals could not conceive of a system of succession other than the

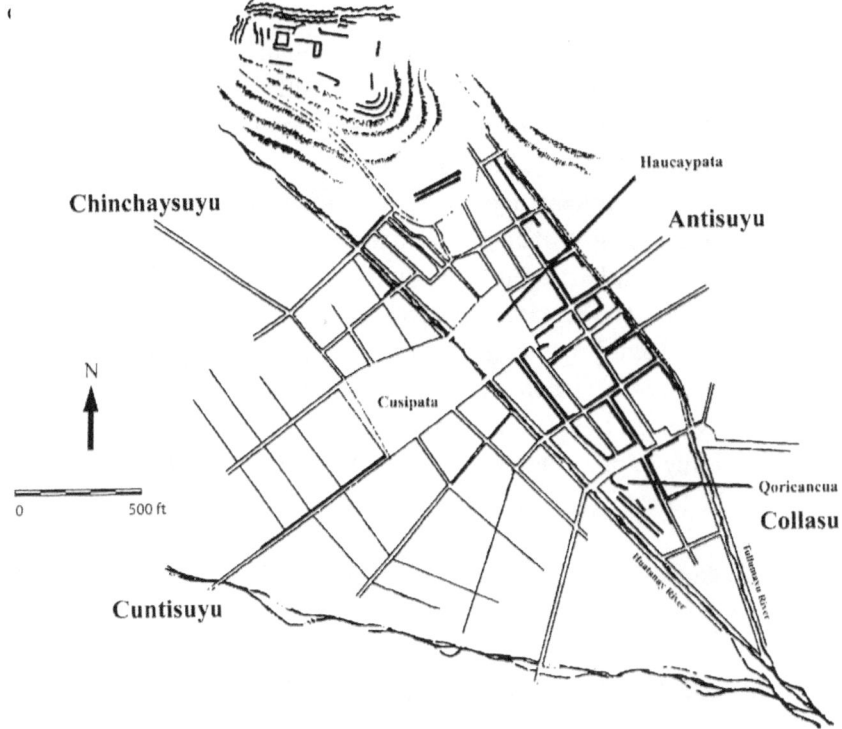

Figure 3.1: Quadripartition of Cuzco

To understand the political system and its relation to the religious system we must look at Andean quadripartition and tripartition, respectively. The empire was called Tawantiunsuyu, the "Land of the Four Quarters." The empire was divided in four quarters or *suyus*. Whether this corresponded to a functional or symbolic quadripartition is a matter open to debate because there is as yet no clear evidence that these four quarters corresponded to clearly individuated political entities, or that a governor existed who wielded power over each separate *suyu*. However, there is another way to look at quadripartition from the perspective of Cuzco (see figure 3.1).

Each moiety—Hanan and Hurin—was further subdivided in two. To the north (Hanan) lay the Chinchaysuyu (north-west) and Antisuyu (north-east), to the South (Hurin) lay the Collasuyu (east, south-east) and the Cuntisuyu (south, south-west). The four roads separating the *suyus* were roughly oriented toward the intersolstitial cross. A matter of importance lay in the relative territorial and population importance of the *suyus*. The most populated of the *suyus* was the Chinchaysuyu, extending all the way to Ecuador. The largest one was the Collasuyu going toward Chili and Argentina, followed by the Chinchaysuyu.

Apart from the fundamental duality of Hanan and Hurin, Marti Pärssinen and others believe that there may have been further Hanan and Hurin subdivisions. Pärssinen takes support for this thesis from a document of the trial of Francisco Toledo against some Incas of Cuzco and Vilcabamba.[20] According to this document Hanan Cuzco was divided into a Hurin sector and a Hanan sector. The author surmises that the Collasuyu may have been the Hanan sector of Hurin Cuzco, since it was much more politically important than the Cuntisuyu. The division of the sectors accorded the following order of importance

Hanan Cuzco Chinchaysuyu (Suyu1?) Antisuyu (Suyu 2)
Ha/Ha (1) Hu/Ha (2)

Hurin Cuzco Collasuyu (Suyu 3) Cuntisuyu (Suyu 4)
Hu/Hu (3) Ha/Hu (4)

This sequence presents three patterns of opposition:

opposition Hanan (above: 1 and 2) and Hurin (below: 3 and 4)
opposition between two internal Hurin sectors (2 and 3)
opposition between two internal Hanan sectors (2 and 4)

The four suyus were further subdivided in *ceques*. *Ceque*'s closest meaning is "line." We have seen that a *ceque* was walked as a straight line in the examples quoted in the chapter about Nazca, and it had a religious/calendrical function. More about this will be said in the next chapter. The *ceque* was and is walked as a straight line regardless of the topography. The *ceque* system was another of the reforms introduced—or rather reintroduced and further elaborated—by Pachacuti.

There were 328 *wakas* along the Cuzco *ceques* as Polo de Ondegardo transmitted them to us. They were recorded in a *khipu*, the set of knotted strings that conveys coded information. The chronicler records that Cuzco was divided into twelve parts and that the king had given each one of them the name of a month. Cobo enumerates the names of the twelve groups, adding that each of them was associated with a group of three *ceques*. Three *ceques* formed a month, nine of them a season. However, the total number of *ceques* was 41 or 42 and not 36 as expected, because of the fact that there were 14 or 15 *ceques* in the Cuntisuyu, instead of 9. This is the first indication that although the Cuntisuyu was the last of the *suyus* for political importance, it nevertheless played an important role for purposes other than political.

Each group of three *ceques* was ordered according to criteria of importance and subordination:

first: *qollana*, excellent
middle or second: *payan*, close relation
last: *kayaw*, of the origin

This threefold division is found in many places and in many ways in Inca thought, and is oftentimes closely associated with the quadripartition. Sarmiento's version of the myth of origin speaks of three parts among the indigenous of Cuzco, and three parts among the newcomers. The well-known myth of origin refers to three windows. The Men of the First Epoch are called *qollana*; in *payan* is placed the Second Man and in *kayaw* the Third Man. Each epoch itself is divided in three classes. Thus in the third epoch, the three windows and the people that emerge from them are ordered in the following manner: *qollana*: Maras-toco (Maras); *payan*: Sutic-toco (Tambos); *kayaw*: Capac-toco (Incas). Note that according to this classification, the Incas would be last in the order of hierarchy.

The above is confirmed in the hierarchy of the generations, where the parent and child generations were called *kayaw*; the grandparents and their descendents were *payan*; the great-grandparents and their descendents, *qollana*. However, from the point of view of prestige—hence the political—the reverse of the above was true. According to the order of prestige the Incas were the *qollana* group.

Lineal triads, as expressed in the order of time, are not the only way to express tripartition. There are also concentric triads, such as have already appeared in the example of the windows. These three correspond to *qollana* (center), *payan* (right side), and *kayaw* (left side). In the myth of origin from the left (Maras-toco) emerge the Maras; from the right (Sutic-toco) emerge the Tambos; from the central one (Capac-toco) emerged the four brothers and sisters. The most important window in this case is the Capac-toco, the one situated in the middle.

In Guaman Poma's *Nueva Coronica*, the triadic structure appears in the way he portrays the deceased Inca (*qollana*), the queen (*payan*), and their descendant (*kayaw*). To these also correspond Sun, Moon, and Venus and their metals: gold, silver, copper. In a parallel way of expressing threefoldness, Santa Cruz Pachacuti shows the idols of the Qoricancha:

SUN / WIRACKOCHA (Creator) MOON

Guaman Poma does something similar in placing the Christian Father God in the center between man and woman.

MAN / FATHER GOD / WOMAN

It is interesting to see the contrast between duality and threefoldness and how it expresses itself. When Inca and *qoya* are present alone, the Inca stands to the right (in the example: Topa Inca) and the *qoya* to the left. However, when the dead Inca appears then the spatial relationships change. The dead Inca stands to the center (he is the most important from a spiritual perspective); his queen (*qoya*) to the left; the succeeding Inca (*auqui*) to the right, and much smaller than the deceased. The dead Inca had great importance in religious thinking. In concluding, we can say that the linear triad corresponded more to political thinking; the concentric triad more to religious thinking.

This assertion is reflected in the way the Incas saw the succession of the rulers. The center (ego) of the system was the living Inca. This Inca was the last in the chronological, spiritual order. However, he and his father were the first in order of prestige. This was a dynamic system.

In terms of history, the order was such at the time of Pachacuti:

Time flow: 1 2 3 P 1 2 3 P = Pachacuti

At the death of the Inca, the whole system was reclassified thus:

Time flow:1 2 3 P 1 2 3 P = Pachacuti (IX emperor)
1 2 3 T 1 2 3T = Topa Inca (X)
1 2 3 H 1 2 3 H= Wayna Capac (XI)

This agrees with the chronological/mytholgical order of importance: the farther ancestors are *qollana*! However, in political terms (prestige) the exact reverse was true:

Time flow: 3 2 1 P 1 2 3 P = Pachacuti (IX emperor)
3 2 1 T 1 2 3T = Topa Inca (X)
3 2 1 H 1 2 3 H = Wayna Capac (XI)

The political ordering included four generations. The first two (father and sons) were *qollana*. The third was that of the *auquis*. After the fourth generation, the descendents belonged now to a lesser category called *yngas* or *yngas caballeros*.

To return to the ordering of the *suyus*, we find there that the tripartition is superposed to the quadripartition. In spite of there being four *suyus*, the political power is shared among the first three ones. Cuntisuyu (*suyu* 4) has little political importance.

The Chinchaysuyu (Ha/Ha) comprised the following *panaqas*:
Inca Roca (Sixth Inca)—Pachacuti (Ninth Inca)—Topa Inca (Tenth Inca)

The Antisuyu (Hu/Ha) comprised the following *panaqas*:
Wirakocha (Eighth Inca)—Yahuar Huacac (Seventh Inca)—

In the Collasuyu (Ha/Hu) were placed the *panaqas* of the following rulers:
Lloque Yupanqui (Third Inca)—Capac Yupanqui (Fifth Inca)—Mayta Capac (Fourth Inca)

In the Cuntisuyu (Hu/Hu) one *panaqa* alone is mentioned:
Manco Capac (First Inca)

Sinchi Roca (Second Inca) may have belonged to the Collasuyu, according to some authors; to the Cuntisuyu, according to others.

Considering that Pachacuti and his descendents were the most important Incas and that those who preceded him were least important, we see reflected in the ordering of the *panaqas* the political importance of the four *suyus* in the way we have already shown previously:

Cinchaysuyu 1—Antisuyu 2—Collasuyu 3—Cuntisuyu 4

The first three *suyus* were organized in similar fashion and were most prominent in political matters. The Cuntisuyu was the Hurin/Hurin sector, and that is a way to separate it from the other three, all of whom have at least a Hanan component. This is an example of how tripartition was embedded in the quadripartition. However, the last *suyu* had more *ceques*, spelling a more important role in religious matters, in a way that is congruent with its Hurin nature. The importance of the solar year is reflected in the way in which the *ceques* were ordered in the Cuntisuyu, as it will appear in the next chapter. Even before going this far we can point to other ways in which the religious importance of the last *suyu* is made manifest.

The Cuntisuyu may be the last of the *suyus*, but this is where the Anahuarque *ceque* lay, comprising fifteen *wakas*, more *wakas* than in any other *ceque*. This *suyu* also includes Mount Huanacauri, which commemorated the death and transformation of Ayar Uchu, the progenitor of the Second Age. It was the oldest *waka* in Cuzco, and had a very strong relationship to the Sun and Wirakocha. It served as intermediary between the founders of the Inca dynasty (Manco Capac) and the three principal deities.[21] Huanacauri had its own priesthood that played an important part during Citua and during the rites of initiation of the Capac Raymi. It also played a role in an additional way. We have seen previously that Tiwanaku and Cuzco are connected through a line that forms a 45° angle with the east-west axis. These directions (northeast to southwest) meet respectively the ruins of Tiwanaku and the Huanacauri hill that is sacred to the Incas. This is why Cuzco was in reality founded on Huanacauri.[22]

If the above were not sufficient to underline the Cuntisuyu's religious importance, let us notice that in the Cuntisuyu lies the *panaqa* of Manco Capac who was the priest-initiate that inaugurated the Inca civilization, at least from a mythic perspective. From that perspective he was the first, just as Pachacuti and later Incas were the first in order of political importance. Moreover, Manco Capac was the one who inherited his mission directly from Thunupa. It is also interesting to note that many of the recognized *wakas* of Wirakocha, Inti, and Illapa lie in the Cuntisuyu, and that almost all of them are situated in Antisuyu and Cuntisuyu, the Hurin subsections of Hanan and Hurin Cuzco.[23]

The conclusions thus reached fully explain the complementary aspects of Hanan and Hurin Cuzco. What is true from the perspective of

Hanan becomes reversed from the perspective of Hurin. From the political perspective of Hanan, Chinchaysuyu (suyu 1) is the most recent and the most politically important; from the religious perspective, Cuntisuyu (suyu 4) is the oldest and most important. Finally, from this perspective the dilemma of the two places of origin could also find a resolution. Ollantaytanpu, the place of the pyramid and the place dear to Pachacuti, is situated to the north in the Chinchaysuyu, the *suyu* of highest political importance. The other mysterious place of origin, to the southwest—Paqaritanpu—is then the place of origin of the first ancestors ("First Man"); it lies in the Cuntisuyu that also has the Huanacauri mountain, commemorating the death of the ancestor of the Second Age.

Finally, let us notice that the *suyus* reflect the double ordering that we have seen in the succession of the emperors and in the succession of the Ages. From a political perspective the last ones—hence the Incas—are the most important, and this is reflected in the ordering of the *suyus* where the Chinchaysuyu (Suyu 1) is the most important. From the religious perspective the older Ages and ancestors are the most important, and that is reflected in the religious importance of the Cuntisuyu, the *suyu* of the mythic progenitor Manco Capac. Theocracy corresponds to earlier ages. It is present in Inca times, with the importance given to initiation, in political matters throughout the territory. The Incas preserved the importance of initiation through the introductoin of a revolutionary political system. They were the last in the ordering of the theocracy, the first in political terms. The ideas of the previous theocracies were preserved and furthered, thanks to the political system devised by the initiate Pachacuti. This is how the spiritual and the political were closely intermeshed. The Hanan classes were associated with empire and warfare; Hurin with religion. During the Capac Raymi, the Inca received the instruction of the priesthood for their initiation rituals. This constant division between the political and the religious was present in the occupation of new territories conquered by the Incas; some lands were devoted to the Inca and others to the Sun priesthood.

If the above were not enough, we also know that the high priest of the Sun played a very important role in the empire and in the naming of the future Inca. The high priest of the Sun was probably the second most important person of the empire, and his office was initiated during Pachacuti's reign.[24] The high priest position was filled by a royal kinsman, a collateral relative of the emperor who belonged to a different *panaqa*. Part of his importance lay in his role in confirming the selection of the new emperor. Consider in this relation the problems encountered by Wayna Capac, who was repeatedly rebuffed by the high priest before gaining access to the throne. This explains why he wanted to invest both roles in his own person, so that he might ensure his own succession! He signified this change by placing his effigy in the Coricancha in such a way that it faced directly towartd the Sun, unlike any of the previous rulers.

Political Organization

It is clear that the Inca gathered in his hands considerable powers. How he was chosen and how he shared his powers with the *panaqas* or with the religious powers does not appear clearly from the chronicles. This is a matter that will emerge more clearly at the end of our explorations, especially after highlighting the importance of spiritual authority. We will look at present at how the Inca was chosen and how the hierarchy of power moved and operated under him.

Maria Rostworowski has studied at length all the colonial sources in the matter of how the Incas or other local authorities were chosen.[25] What emerges from the sources is in this regard quite homogeneous. The paramount criteria of selection were a mix of heredity and ability. As a general rule in Andean tradition, the power went to either of the following: the brothers of the departed, one of the sons, or a son of the sister.

Garcilaso de la Vega indicates that it was "the son most wanted by the subjects." This may point to an ideal, but we know that this was often not the case. Las Casas offers that the succession went to the most able person and that the sons were given first choice. He also indicates that the successor had to give proof of ability during the life of the previous ruler, a fact confirmed in many instances in Inca history. It is well known that Pachacuti intended to leave power to Topa Amaru, but later opted for Topa Inca because the former had more inclination for the priestly office. Betanzos indicates that the son of the *qoya* (queen) was chosen, but in his absence sons of the royal consorts were chosen. He also stresses personal skills as a deciding factor.

Guaman Poma relates that it was the son of the *qoya* and that he had to be "chosen by the Sun." This points once more to the importance of the process of initiation and to the role of the high priest of the Sun. Morua and Cobo say much the same and add that if such a prince was not suited for the task, another was chosen among the sons of other consorts of the king.

Sarmiento de Gamboa indicates that those who had the right to elect the king were members of the *"ayllus custodios"* (non-royal, original *ayllus*) and members of the *panaqas*. He says that the *ayllus custodios* had a part in the naming of the emperors Inca Roca and Yahuar Huacac. Cieza de Leon also indicates that Wirakocha Inca acceded to power through an election.

Other key players had a role in the election of the king or direction in which the process may have moved. One of these were the *panaqas*. Rowe hypothesizes that one of the Upper Cuzco royal kinship groups may have shifted to Lower Cuzco every two generations in order to preserve balance between the moieties. Terence N. D'Altroy seconds the idea.[26]

The queen had an important power. A *qoya* mother could apparently veto the marriage of her daughter to the king. Similarly the prospective *qoya* could refuse! This happened to both Washkar and Wayna Capac, at least temporarily. Women had a role to play in promoting a son as a royal successor. The lineage of the candidates' mother played an important role, since sitting rulers did not belong to their father's kin group. They founded their own *panaqa* and identified closely with their mother's lineage.

Succession and marriage times were the pivotal times for political intrigue. Another reason for this was the Andean tradition that favored vigorous leadership. In reality, there were no rightful and legal heirs; this is more of a Western notion superimposed onto Inca ideology.

Two changes in the marriage and succession practices came later in time. The first was to select a principal wife from whose offspring would be selected the future king. The second was marriage with the full sister. Topa Inca may have been the first to do so in order to exert a closer control on the succession and also in order to limit the influence of the competing *panaqas*. This is in keeping with other measures he took, particularly in granting power to regional *wakas* in independence from the cult of the Sun.

It is to be remembered that no emperor inherited the property of his forerunner. This was another way to ensure collaboration between the *panaqas* and prevent excessive accumulation of power through wealth in the hand of the ruling Inca. Another balance of power was exerted in the relationship between political and spiritual authorities as has already been pointed out. Spiritual power will be looked at in the following chapter. Without going further, we will just mention that the cult of the Sun occupied a very extended and important administrative role. Additionally, there may have been a council of the four *suyus*. Finally, it is very likely that the Inca balanced power with two other coregents of lesser import, in the scheme of the so-called triarchy. Let us look at both elements of the quadripartition and tripartition, and later at an idea that will further reconcile them.

The chroniclers don't offer much information about the division of the empire in its four *suyus*. Many scholars believe that the king governed with the four *capac apus* of the *suyus* and that together they formed the Supreme Council of the Tawantinsuyu. The sources that mention this council are the *khipocamayocs*, those entrusted to keep accounts and records. Las Casas, Cieza, Betanzos, and Sarmiento concur but do not give the council a permanent or special status. Those who refer to a council of three *capac apus* are Falcon, Murua, Garcilaso, and Cobo.[27] Some authors speak of a larger council that included three governors for the Chinchaysuyu (largest *suyu*), two for the Cuntisuyu (very small), and one for Antisuyu (small and sparsely populated). Guaman Poma speaks of a council of sixteen: two for Hanan Cuzco, two for Hurin Cuzco, four for Chinchaysuyu (largest province), two for Antisuyu (small), four for Collasuyu (large), and two for Cuntisuyu (small). The above representation reflects partly the order of prestige of the *suyus*, but more so, the order of importance (territory and population).

Diarchy or Triarchy?

For quite some time there has been a hotly debated theory of an Inca diarchy; lately, even the idea of a triarchy has been advanced. Pärssinen has found that when the *khipocamayocs* Cieza and Garcilaso speak about the conquests of Capac Yupanqui, these are actually described as the very same conquests attributed to Pachacuti. The same is true when Garcilaso, Guaman Poma, and Oliva speak of the conquests of Sinchi Roca. They are possibly referring to the half brother of Wayna Capac who ruled Cuzco when Wayna Capac was in Chachapoya. Cieza de Leon puts out (tentatively) that he heard that there were two rulers: one for each side of Cuzco. This is why Duviols and Zuidema hypothesized a diarchy.[28] According to Zuidema, every Inca of Hurin and Hanan Cuzco is a symbolic representative of the ancestor of the different social classes. However, this theory has little evidence to support it.

Oddly enough, a triarchy seems more likely than the diarchy. This is the conclusion reached by Pärssinen on the basis of the results of genealogical research and the reports of the chronicles, especially in regard to iconography. This did not mean three people with equal power; but rather two adjunct rulers with specific, limited power, primarily in the administration of Cuzco and in military matters. The triarchy is a scheme that is also found elsewhere in the administration of the provinces, many of which were subdivided into three subsections.

The first confirmation of the likelihood of this hypothesis comes from iconography, particularly in the way the king and the supposed second and third person were portrayed. Habitually, the emperor wore a headband of braided cloth called *llauto*, sometimes with added feathers. Out of this headband, a thick tassel, a *machapaycha*, covered his forehead. He also wore very large ear spools, symbol of initiation. The Incas in the Herrera portraits, published in 1615, have three types of *machaypachas*.[29] In the first group are Huascar, Wayna Capac, Topa Inca, Pachacuti Inca, and Inca Urco; in the second group are Wirakocha Inca, Yahuar Huacac, and Capac Yupanqui; in the third group Mayta Capac, Lloque Yupanqui, and Sinchi Roca. Las Casas confirms that the Incas had "tres diferencias de cabezas" (three differences of heads) that distinguished them from each other. Pärssinen finishes by saying that Cuzco was governed by the first *suyus*. The above poses some puzzling questions in regard to genealogy and the succession of the Inca emperors. The following is the evidence in relation to two successive rulers.

Epoch of Pachacuti

According to the *khipocamayocs*, Wirakocha Inca had three sons: the elder son was Inca Yupanqui (Pachacuti); the younger ones Inca Urco and Inca Mayta (likely the same Mayta Capac). In the system of the *ceques*, Mayta Capac is placed in the *kayaw* position (Collasuyu) and Pachacuti Inca in the Chinchaysuyu (*qollana*). Inca Urco could have been either Chinchaysuyu (*qollana*) or Antisuyu (*payan*). Confirmation of this is offered by the fact that Inca Urco is shown to wear a *machapaycha*, like Pachacuti and Topa Inca in the portraits of Incas published by Herrera. The royal position of Inca Urco is confirmed by Cieza de Leon; although he was later eliminated from the record of the *khipus* and from Inca ballads.

Epoch of Topa Inca

The accession to the throne of Topa Inca can be defined in two stages: the first in which he shared the throne with his father during his lifetime, and a second after Pachacuti's death. When the chronicler Santa Cruz Pachacuti speaks of the first part of his reign, he describes that Pachatuci Inca, Topa Inca, and Amaro Topa were seated in three equal golden thrones and the three wore the royal *machapaicha*. However, he expresses the difference of importance between the three in their scepters.[30]

In referring to later times, the document called *Probanza de los Incas nietos de los Conquistadores* shows that the descendents of Topa Inca, Amaro Topa, and Topa Yupanqui all belonged to the same royal *panaqa*, divided in three. He indicates that at the death of Pachacuti, the order had been changed and Topa Yupanqui had been added to the triarchy.[31] Topa Inca belonged to the *qollana ayllu*; Amaro Topa to the *payan*, and Topa Yupanqui to the *kayaw ayllu*. Other sources confirming the successions of the kings are the *khipocamayocs*. According to them Pachacuti had three "sons": Topa Inca Yupanqui, the elder; Topa Yupanqui, the younger; and Topa Inca.

If the first scenario is true, then Topa Inca was the "second person" of Pachacuti Inca and Amaro Topa the third. The chroniclers also indicate that before the choice fell on Topa Inca, Amaro Topa was the first candidate to the succession of Pachacuti. This means that probably the status of the two was reversed. To add weight to this is the recorded mention by some chroniclers that in the absence of Topa Inca, it was Amaro Topa who governed Cuzco. In support of the second scenario, there is a recorded mention by Don Martin (son of Topa Yupanqui) claiming that Topa Yupanqui governed the empire (not just Cuzco) for Topa Inca. The above line of reasoning holds true from the record of the successive ruler, Wayna Capac.[32]

In summing up, the triarchy was most likely a symbolic disposition in recognition of the power of the three *suyus* (*suyus* 1 to 3). It was limited to the administration of Cuzco and to military matters in the absence of the emperor. We know that principles of hierarchy, duality, tripartition, and quadripartition ordered Andean sociopolitical organization. What is less clear is how these worked together and intermeshed. In looking at how political work was carried even after the time of the Incas on the north coast of Peru, Michael E. Moseley and Alana Cordy-Collins shed light on an important principle of cooperation between moieties and submoieties, down to the lower levels of the administration of power.

"Conciliar Politics" [33]

The idea of "conciliar politics" is far removed from the way power is conceived of in the Western world and may shed much light on what we do not yet understand about Andean political systems.

According to the scheme there were various levels of authority; we will call them level 1, level 2, level 3, etc. At level 1, a lord alone had authority. However, at the second level he shared the power with a second chief, thus having only 50 percent direct control. At the third level he only had 25 percent direct control; at the fourth only 12.5 percent, and so on. Chief B (of the second level) had 50 percent at the second level; 25 percent at the third level; 12.5 percent at the fourth, etc. (table 1).

Let us see how the above could have worked at the level of the empire. In the example above, Lord A would be the emperor or king. At the military level, he alone had power. At level 2 the emperor heads the highest ranking moiety; Lord B heads the second moiety. At level 3 the moieties are each further subdivided into a total of four. Lord A—emperor—heads the higher ranking, the Hanan submoiety. Lord B is the ruler of the higher-ranking subdivision of his Hurin moiety. At level 4 there are eight subdivisions and eight lords. Lords A and B head only one of these respectively. At level 5 there are sixteen lords. Lords A and B now yield a very low marginal power (two out of sixteen).

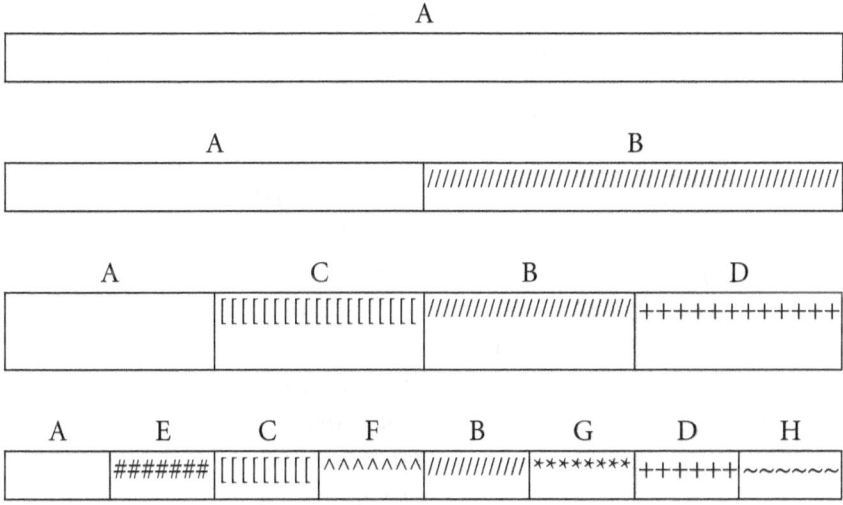

Table 1: "Conciliar" political organization

We can see now how this applied to the north coast. The higher-ranking moiety was placed on the northern shore of the river. The second, lower-ranking moiety was on the southern bank. Then each moiety was further subdivided into two, four, eight, etc. There may have been six such organizational levels in total. Reflecting the above disposition, the irrigation system was subdivided into four main sections and lower-level units.

The authors of the study conclude: "Most economic activities required ritual participation by the lords or they would not have been carried out. Furthermore, the lords' position as living ancestors, as the link between the living and the dead, the present and the non-present, greatly enhanced their power."

Let us go back with this in mind to the example of the empire and the *suyus*. It is clear that the Inca was alone at the first level. He, the ruler, representing *suyu* 1, had 100 percent of the power at Level 1. At level 2 he shared this power with Lord 2 of the Antisuyu (*suyu* 2: Hu/Ha), each sharing 50 percent. At level 3 there were four lords, each with 25 percent of control. From this perspective the prominence of Hanan over Hurin power decreased exactly as it has been said, from *suyu* 1 to *suyu* 2 to *suyu* 3 and *suyu* 4, which is exactly how things stood from the political perspective. Other levels of authority were devised at the provincial levels, but historical records are not clear on this account.[34]

In addition to ternary or quaternary divisions, decimal organization was often superimposed on the previous one. The latter, it is now becoming clearer, played an important, if not an exclusive role, in economic matters.

Decimal Organization and the Economy

The decimal system was used in the army and in the *mit'a*, tribute offered in labor. It was also an important tool of determination in the politics of reciprocity. This system even continued in certain areas (e.g., Lupaca) under the colonial system. Catherine J. Julien has studied an Inca *khipu* (later used by the Spaniards) that offered a census of Aymara population.[35] The *khipu* established how to subdivide the total of five hundred miners needed for the *mit'a* in the mines of Potosi. Pärssinen establishes convincingly how this system was used by the Incas on the basis of simple proportions: one of a hundred, two of a hundred, etc. The amounts in the *khipu* correspond very closely to the theorized ones, if one approximates to the hundredth unity above (e.g., 1234 = 1300). According to this calculation, the previous example shows almost exactly that the Incas took three *mit'ayocs* (people devoted to the *mit'a*) out of a hundred of each community for work in the Potosi area.

From the above we can conclude that the administrative divisions according to the decimal system were devised in order to divide the weight of tribute equitably among the diverse ethnic or regional groups. This decimal system allowed the creation of an easy determination without having to change the local administration. In other words, decimal organization was superimposed on the existing administration. In some cases the two coincided at some level or another.

The terminology of the decimal system was the following:

Hunu: 10,000; Pisca Guaranga: 5,000; Guaranga: 1,000;
Pisca Pachaca: 500; Pachaca: 100; Pisca Chunga: 50; Chunga:10

The unity of reference is the domestic unity. The chiefs of each level were called *huno curaca; pisca guaranga curaca, guaranga curaca,* etc.

All of the above were not so much political units as units of calculation in order to ascertain the dimension of a province, the importance of its ruler and the contribution for the *mit'a*. In reality the idea of the amount of family units in each decimal unit was approximate. Thus, the *hunu* level went from around 6,000 in some places to 12,000 in other places. In some places (e.g., Cuntisuyu) the *guarangas* were quite large (150 to 280 units), which reflected the local triadic tradition. This also reflected the reality that here villages were much larger than in most other areas.

The *mit'a* tribute involved specific number of days' labor in the army, public works projects, in service to the emperor or state officials, or agricultural work in fields of royal corporations or fields of the Sun. This was done by resettling the population into ecological enclaves. However, the resettled population retained ties with their original communities; they did not respond to local *curacas*. When newcomers were integrated into the local administration, they formed part of the upper moiety. Allies could be settled in frontier areas to promote allegiance to the emperor. Or, vice-versa, hostile groups could be dispersed away from their original areas.

The *mit'a* resumed the idea of the vertical archipelago, or self-sufficient, island-like specialized communities whose economy was integrated with the larger economy through reciprocity and redistribution mechanisms. The Incas' attempt to restore the use of the land that had been disrupted by the wars of the Fourth Age meant an extensive recolonization of valleys—previously judged unsafe from a strategic perspective—or the construction of terraces in marginal mountain lands. This was done by partially depopulating a certain land and then sending colonies of *mitimaes* of mixed ethnic origin. This was also a means to spread the use of Quechua language. In all, this was a return, in a new way, to the practice of the vertical archipelago that existed ever since the Archaic period of the Second Age. This new economy started at the epoch of Pachacuti. Since this practice had already been a practice of the past, the Incas developed it considerably in areas where the tradition had already existed. In practice, interestingly, this means that the heavier Inca presence was felt in the poorest, rather than in the richest areas.[36] Many old, fortified settlements were transferred to the lower-lying, more fertile areas.

The work in the *mitimaes* was a way to forge new identity, loosen ethnic ties, deepen the penetration of Quechua language, exploit new ecosystems, extend the reach of and integrate the local economy, benefit the local populations, and accumulate surpluses for draughts and famines. It was the means for allowing local lords access to enclaves that they could not have otherwise reached, and thus to goods they could not have produced.

There were many kinds of *mitimaes*: economic, sociopolitical, military, and artisan. Some of the *mitimaes*, especially in fortresses in the border areas, were for the army. Some were specialized in agricultural production. Thus, the *mitimaes* in the Cochabamba Valley of Bolivia were devoted on a grand scale to the production of maize used for state purposes, under the reign of Wayna Capac. At one point the Incas started to establish colonies of artisans to produce the things that were needed for the *mit'a* itself, the festivities, the *curacas*, or for the army. Some *mitimaes* had a sociopolitical function. In some instances, Inca nobles formed part of faraway colonies, perhaps integrated with other populations. Interestingly, in these situations the two groups most often responded to either Inca administration (for the nobles) or local authority (for the local groups).

Administration of the System of Reciprocity

The interchange of women and gifts was determined as a function of the importance of the chief, and his importance depended on the amount of people he ruled over. An example: a *hunu curaca* (10,000 family units) could offer to the Inca a daughter in marriage and in exchange receive a noble woman and concubines from Cuzco.

The rapid Inca expansion was achieved thanks to the links created between the local *curacas* and the Incas. However, these relationships had to be renewed at the death of each emperor. The links had to be reconfirmed periodically through reciprocal gifts to the ethnic chiefs. Transitions were delicate times in which the center feared centripetal tendencies from the periphery.

Among the most prestigious gifts *curacas* could receive were textiles and metalwork. These were after all the proof of the cultural renewal that went hand in hand with core Inca spirituality. Other prized gifts were regional specialties. Thus, llamas and alpacas were numerous in the southern Collasuyu and prized in the northern Chinchaysuyu. The spondylus shell (*mullu*) found off the coast of Ecuador was extremely prized in the Collasuyu. The shell was collected by *mit'ayocs* along the coast of Ecuador. From there it was sent to Cuzco were it was used for decorating *uncus* (tunics), and these were redistributed to the various parts of the empire, especially to the Collasuyu. In this system of redistribution, the gifts always came from the lords of Cuzco. The Incas converted mere economic capital into gifts of high symbolic value. It was a way to create interdependence and gratitude. This practice has been dubbed the "administration of generosity."

The most appreciated gift was the women that the *curacas* could get from Cuzco. The more important the *curaca*, the more women he received in reciprocal exchange with the Inca. The women were instrumental in forging links of kinship between the Incas and the periphery. The more important the local lords, the closer were the women to the Inca nobility and the sovereign. This policy was also a means of strengthening Inca blood among the subjected nations. The reverse movement was also true: the Incas would take as secondary wives the sisters or daughters of the local *curacas*.

That the Incas devoted much care to the preparation of the women indicated that this was also a way to export Inca culture to the periphery. In order to strengthen the administration of generosity, Pachacuti had ordered the building of *acclahuasi* with the purpose of hosting and educating the chosen women—*acclas*—that would be offered to the local *curacas*. They were ambassadors of Inca culture to the periphery.

The *mit'a* is part of a much larger idea that in the Andes is given the name of reciprocity. Andean ethics command that the individual/group work at the maintenance and up-building of the cosmic relationships, thus avoiding causing a disturbance in the order of the cosmos. Humanity is a co-redeemer of the cosmos, and ritual is the ethical necessity of Andean life that accompanies the task of redemption. Andean ethics place a boundary between what applies to the *ayllu*, to the Quechua, and to the world. The ethical obligation decreases along that axis.

Reciprocity concerns a view of the justice of the interchange of goods, people, religious values, feelings, etc. Reciprocity has a great place not only in the realm of work and the economy. It is the guarantee of the right level of interchange among human beings, human beings and nature, humanity and God, the living and the dead.

Reciprocity is also a principle of cosmic justice. It goes beyond the individual and the present generation. Communities may have to shoulder the guilt of an individua; indeed, even posterity may have to do the same. God inflicts a chastisement in order to allow the correction of the cosmic imbalance. It is not seen as a gratuitous punishment, but rather a chance for compensation.

A great part of reciprocity regulates the relationship of humanity (community) and nature. Without reciprocity, the earth would not be fertile. This is mediated by the human being turning to the divine, as a participant. Practically, reciprocity means bringing an offering: coming to the divine not as a supplicant but with something to offer (a soul offering). Consequently, natural disasters are considered the result of lack of reciprocity. This explains the paramount importance of ritual for the achievement of concrete goals.

CHAPTER 4

Inca Esoteric Knowledge

In the previous chapters we have analyzed the nature of the spiritual revolution undergone by Andean civilization at the hands of Wirakocha Inca, and more important, Pachacuti, the ninth emperor. The results of such a revolution were felt with the tremendous political, social, and spiritual changes that followed the expansion of the Inca empire. Now that Pachacuti's spiritual experience has received some plausible hypotheses as to its nature, it becomes evident that between Pachacuti's vision—the motor of the social changes—and the achievement of Inca empire, lay a whole new concept of the world, a very rich body of knowledge that made possible the achievement of Pachacuti's dream. In other words, Pachacuti did not just receive a vision that gave him the strength to repel the Chanca invasion. Together with it, Pachacuti opened his inner eye to initiatic knowledge. Through this knowledge, the Inca reestablished a conscious link with the time of the Dawning—and therefore the being of Thunupa and the inspiration of the Christ—and looked forward to the impulses of the incipient Fifth Age. Elements of this knowledge are to be found in the things we have already seen: the central festivals of Capac Raymi and Inti Raymi, rituals of initiation of the Inca nobility, the system of *ceques* of Cuzco and elsewhere, and the reintroduction of titanic architecture (e.g., Sacsayhuaman, Cuzco). In addition to these we will also find a precise knowledge of the solar calendar, the geomantic sacred landscapes, and the use of the *khipus* as a system for storage of information and for writing. These additional elements have come to light from revelations made public in the 1990s.

How could this evidence have been buried for centuries and finally resurface at present? To history, Spanish occupation of Peru and Andean countries represents a notorious time of brutal social repression, genocide, and an attempt at complete eradication of religion, native attire, and identity. Nevertheless, the Spaniards never completely succeeded in their attempts, partly because many of the very same people who were supposed to carry them out could not help but be fascinated by the depth, beauty, and power of Inca civilization.

The Rewriting of History by the Spaniards

Recently the academic world of Inca historians, archaeologists, and other specialists has been rocked by the revelations of the so-called Miccinelli manuscripts. The documents assert that the Spaniards poisoned Atahualpa's generals and obliterated, or attempted to obliterate, all evidence of Inca writing.

The manuscripts owe their name to the person who found them and first exposed them to the public in 1984, Clara Miccinelli. After deciphering them, together with the journalist Carlo Animato, she published a book titled *Quipu, I nodi parlanti dei misteriosi Inca* (Khipu, the Talking Knots of the Mysterious Inca) in 1989. The book was addressed to the general public in a way that could certainly raise the eyebrows of the academic world, particularly for its way of juxtaposing topics that bear no immediate connection to each other. The book did not have the expected impact and would have left the scientific world unruffled, had it not been for the subsequent rediscovery of Miccinelli's book by Laura Laurencich Minelli, professor of indigenous civilizations of the Americas at the University of Bologna. The professor saw the value of these discoveries and wanted to verify the authenticity of the documents. She reached the conclusion that they were authentic and published *Il linguaggio dei numeri e dei fili nel mondo degli Inca*.[1]

The astonishing origin of the documents and the no less astounding revelations about Inca civilization put many things in question that many scientists had thought definitely answered. The fact that these revelations find their origin outside the academic world may be no less disturbing to some. The documents have been called modern forgeries. They most likely are a mix of truth and forgery. Unwittingly, they reveal how much was at stake for the hierarchies of church and state in the public perception of Andean civilization. In this sense they serve a purpose for our study, once we are able to separate truth from fiction and winnow the important contributions from the spurious claims.

Assessment of the Miccinelli Documents

R. T. Zuidema, Juan Ossio, and Father Borja de Medina (a Jesuit) claim "the Naples documents" are forgeries dating back to the seventeenth or eighteenth centuries. Juan Carlos Estenssoro and others have argued that the documents are a modern forgery. This charge has been easily refuted. Proofs have come out in favor of their authenticity in time through evidence of the materials used and through archival evidence pointing to documents quoted in the Miccinelli documents. Central to these documents is the figure of Blas Valera, an "indigenist Jesuit" and ardent defender of Inca culture, and two documents that carry his signature: *Exsul Immeritus* (Undeserving Exile) and *Historia et Rudimenta* (History and Rudiments).

The paper, ink, and other materials used in the manuscript effectively belong to the seventeenth century. Radiocarbon dating, spectroscope analysis of colors and inks, and microanalysis of the metal content confirm this; the authenticity of the handwriting of some of the authors has been proven, and the manuscripts reveal historical facts about Blas de Valera's life that were only released later in time. The important exception is Blas de Valera's handwriting, which does not correspond to other examples of his hand.

Although this disposes of the idea that the letters are modern forgeries, it does not mean that what the Naples documents claim is entirely correct. The hypothesis with most weight is the following. Some Jesuits with grudges of their own may have had reasons to vindicate Valera's death because of their sympathy with the Jesuit's views. One of these in particular would have been Juan Anello Oliva, whose work was heavily censored by the Jesuits. Oliva had an unstable character and left a questionable record in the charge of the Jesuit College in Callao (close to Lima). A telling sign is the fact that the chronicler was well versed in apocalyptic literature and that the latter emerges in the presumed Valera's *Exsul Immeritus*, although it does not seem to have been part of Valera's thinking. Anello Oliva had spent twenty-three years preparing his writings, but the publication of his work was forbidden. This may have been the motive that pushed him to identify with the fate of Valera. Blas de Valera's signature (but only the signature) in the *Historia et Rudimenta*, and handwriting and signature in the *Exsul Immeritus* do not match other samples of his handwriting.

Sabine Hyland concludes that Valera's signatures and handwriting in the two documents attributed to Valera were forged and believes she has found by whom. It is likely that Juan Anello Oliva wrote *Exsul Immeritus* and *Historia et Rudimenta*.[2]

Let us first look at the central author and other figures who took part in the writing of the Miccinelli manuscripts. This is a parenthesis that we feel is necessary in order to lend credit to documents that are at the center of passionate debates and often times virulent prejudice. Later we will turn to the nature of the revelations purported by the authors, and finally to the evidence that lends support to the Miccinelli manuscripts, or to various parts of them. We will spend some time relating the biography of Blas de Valera, whom some have compared to Bartolomé de las Casas, the individual who accomplished the most in the defense of the native populations of Mesoamerica. We will refer to the work of Sabine Hyland, who has researched Valera's life without using the Miccinelli documents. The importance of the chronicler lay in the fact that he was a significant representative of a whole movement.

Blas de Valera, the Anonymous Jesuit?[3]

Scholars have speculated that Valera's mother—Francisca Perez [her Christian name]—had Inca ancestry. There are in fact some indications pointing to her belonging to the court of the last emperor, Atahualpa. She most likely taught Quechua to Blas, whose fluency was well known. This may also explain why Valera was strongly in favor of Atahualpa and against Huascar, the latter's rival to the throne before the Spaniards' arrival.

Valera entered the novitiate in 1568 at the age of twenty-four, ended his studies in 1570, and was probably ordained in 1573. He was first sent to the mission of Huarochiri in 1570. In that year the local Jesuits consented to a Corpus Christi celebration that incorporated indigenous dances, poetry, and costumes. The report of the Jesuits states, among other things: "And asking where they took [the verses], they stated that the same [lyrics] that the ancient gave to the Sun and to their king were converted to the praise of Jesus Christ [by] taking material from that which they had heard preached [by the missionaries]." The mission, however, was abandoned in 1572, partly because the Jesuits distrusted religious syncretism, while Valera was very supportive of it.

Most likely in 1572 Valera was sent to the mission of Santiago del Cercado, near Lima, a year before being ordained. Santiago was a place to which all the natives from hamlets in the area had been forced to relocate. This was done with the intent of control and instruction into the Christian way. As a result of this policy, Valera witnessed many natives die of diseases.

In 1576 Valera was transferred again, this time to Cuzco, whose Jesuit house had been founded in 1571. Here he met Gonzalo Ruiz, one of the founders of the house, and an earlier friend from Blas' home town. The Jesuits had installed themselves in the former Amaru Cancha, where they had placed the tabernacle on the altar upon which once stood the snake idol. Here Valera became the spiritual advisor of the confraternity of the "Nombre de Jesus," among which were many important noble Inca. And here he began to formulate his radical religious views about the spiritual concordance of Christianity and Inca spirituality. The natives, especially the members of the Nombre de Jesus, protested when Valera was asked to transfer. As a result he was delayed for a time by these appeals.

By 1577 Valera was in Juli by Lake Titicaca. On this site there had been a Dominican mission where the friars had committed much abuse; therefore, hostility against Christianity was strong. This must have been a very harsh experience for Valera, especially witnessing the climate of disillusion, resentment, and radicalization between the two sides. Two years later Valera was transferred to Potosi, then one of the largest cities in the world.

In 1582 Valera was brought back to Lima to work on translating the Catholic catechism into Quechua. Here he entered into close contact with Jose Acosta, the Jesuit provincial. At this time Valera's thoughts were coming under close scrutiny as heretical, especially in a context of growing radicalization and distrust in the ability of the natives to come to Christianity. Publicly there were charges that Valera had been incriminated by the Inquisition for sexual crimes. However, documents in the Inquisition archives prove that he was not in trouble with the Inquisition but rather with the Jesuits themselves—and not because of moral misconduct, but for heresy. Letters of that time indicate that the Jesuits were reticent to indicate the nature of the "crime" in writing.

The punishments given to other Jesuits, even repeat offenders in matters of sexual misconduct, were in fact rather minor.[4] The punishment inflicted upon Valera is quite different from theirs. Whereas the former cases are repeatedly mentioned in the Inquisition papers, Valera is never mentioned as a suspect.

Valera was specifically barred from teaching grammar (and that included his Quechua teaching) and given the option of leaving the Jesuits for another order. Valera had used grammar to specifically point to the similarities between the Christian and Inca religions. In 1583 he was confined to a prison cell, forced to fast and pray, and was flogged weekly. It was said that he had added other mortifications to the ones imposed upon him, and that after release he continued to practice weekly fasts and recite the seven penitential psalms. His health suffered from the years in prison until 1587, when he was placed under house arrest for six years.

About Valera's crime, the Jesuit general Aquaviva states in a letter, "If it is judged appropriate to dismiss Father Blas Valera, take as the reason that which he did with the woman and dismiss him; and if not, then keep him [in prison]." Anello Oliva and Joan Antonio Cumis in the Naples documents assert that Valera had been kept in prison because of what appeared in his writings. This is also what has emerged from documents of the Spanish Inquisition kept in Madrid.[5]

In 1594 Valera was allowed to travel to Spain, but serious health problems detained him in Quito and then Cartagena for almost two years. In Quito, Valera wrote *Relacion de las costumbres antiguas de los naturales del Pirú* (*Account of the Ancient Customs of the Natives of Peru*). By 1596 he was in Cadiz, Spain, where the Andalusian provincial allowed him to teach humanities; but once again, on orders from General Aquaviva, he was barred from teaching grammar. In late 1596 the English pirate Robert Devereux sacked the city of Cadiz. His men went on a rampage upon the population, and Valera was one of their victims. Wounded, he died in April of the following year, and is listed among the deceased in the College of Malaga.

Two of the Naples documents assert that Valera's death was faked by the Jesuits. After 1597 he would have returned to Peru where he would have written the *Nueva Coronica*, presently attributed to Guaman Poma. He would have left Spain for Peru in June of 1598, arriving first in Cartagena, and traveling by land first to Quito and then to Cuzco. In Cuzco his fellow mestizo Gonzalo Ruiz allegedly hid him among the natives of the city. And there, he would have written *Nueva Coronica*, choosing Guaman Poma as a conduit for his work, since he could not present it openly.

The above is very likely untrue. Sabine Hyland has now given weight to the hypothesis that the exaltation of the life of Blas de Valera was the work of Juan Anello Oliva, whose life and purposes matched in some level Valera's; not the means, however. The fabrication of the documents was an underhanded stratagem devised by Anello Oliva to revalue and restore the weight of Inca knowledge that the Jesuits and the church systematically undermined, with results that carry consequences to the present.

Hispanic Obliteration of History and Validity of the Documents

A disputed contention of the Miccinelli documents is the alleged poisoning of Atahualpa's generals by Pizarro with the help of the Dominican friars Vicente Valverde, Juan de Yepes, and Reginaldo de Pedraza. Arsenic would have been diluted in three barrels of wine that had been offered to the generals and other leaders of Atahualpa's army in Cajamarca, on November 16, 1532. The veracity of this alleged episode has been undermined by the research of Sabine Hyland, who has ascertained that, although such letters claiming to the alleged facts exist, there is little evidence that they refer to actual events, and much suspicion that these were vengeful and unfounded allegations.[6]

The above episode has limited interest, per se, in our research. It is another important claim that attracts our attention. Just as the Spaniards needed to lend the façade of disinterested work of evangelization of the natives, so did they need to prove that the Inca effectively needed such an intervention in their life because of the evident lack of the rudiments of civilization. The lie that the Miccinelli documents try to uncover is the assertion that the Inca had no form of writing. This is in effect the central content around which revolve the documents and the major debate generated around them. The various authors bring much evidence to the assertion that the Spanish conquistadores systematically destroyed all traces of a certain kind of *khipu*, the literary or "royal *khipu*."

The weight that the Miccinelli authors add to these assertions is the illustration of how these literary *khipus* were conceived and used. If the Spanish needed to erase the major evidence of the high degree of Inca civilization, it is quite obvious that they could do this by concealing one of the major proofs of their achievements: writing.

Among the indigenist Jesuits, Valera—because of his Inca heritage—had reached a deeper understanding of Inca culture and had spent his life trying to bring it to light. His intent went deeper than a matter of pure recognition. He had also intuited the deeper convergence between the Christian message and what the Inca carried forth in the Fifth Age from the heritage of Thunupa. Valera's intuitions and those of Santa Cruz Pachacuti, which are very similar, were not given credence in their time. Ultimately they can be validated only through the results of spiritual-scientific research.

The Miccinelli documents are undergoing close scrutiny. According to graphologist Luigi Altamura, the writing of the so-called JAO corresponds to that of Juan Anello Oliva, as does Blas de Valera's writing in *Exsul Immeritus* correspond to what is found in other documents penned by his hand and preserved in Lima and Rome. Gonzalo Ruiz's writing corresponds to what appears in much of *Nueva Coronica*.[7] The destruction of the royal *khipus* that the Miccinelli documents refer to are confirmed by letters addressed to the Spanish Viceroy in Naples (1610–1616) from Mexico and Peru.[8] On the other hand, it is becoming more and more obvious that the Inca had writing. Spiritual science's knowledge of the laws of human evolution confirms it all the more.

Inca Historical Consciousness and Writing

Inca theology and cosmology remain a mystery even for those who have studied them most closely. Gary Urton, a leading scholar concludes: "There is something in their way of thinking that is very alien to us. Most of your natural intuitions don't serve you well looking at Inca sites. It's hard for us to know how they thought."[9] It is not surprising that the same Gary Urton has studied the *khipus* and tried to find their correlation with the mystery of writing.

Whether or not the Inca possessed writing is a matter that has remained impenetrable until the present. The Miccinelli documents seem to finally offer evidence that should help establish this matter beyond doubt. However, other well-known authors have come to similar conclusions through independent research, among them Gary Urton, R. Larco Hoyle, and W. Burns Glynn. The chroniclers themselves left contradictory statements about the *khipus* as tools for written communication. Not only are the references contradictory; sometimes, even the same author contradicts himself on the matter!

Garcilaso declares: "The *khipucamayocs* were assigned by the *curacas* and nobles of their respective provinces to the preservation of historical facts that had been transmitted by their predecessors or of all other events worthy of mention that occurred in such or such district; and the *khipucamayocs*, in guise of writers and historians, preserved the records, which, as we have said, were the *khipus* or 'annals'" (author's translation).[10] Contradicting himself, in other places Garcilaso asserts that "the knot indicates the number, not the word" (Book 6). Polo de Ondegardo indicates, "In that city there were many officials of the Inca, both in charge of religion and of government, and something else which I would not believe if I had not seen it, that through strings and knots are preserved the laws and statutes of this and that, and the succession of the kings, and there was even some clarity about the statutes that had been instituted in the time of each one of them [kings]" (author's translation). Domingo de Santo Tomas (1560) affirms that the Indians did not use writing but rather "an ingenious means." This statement is reinforced by J. de Acosta who asserts that the Indians made up for their lack of writing with paintings and *khipus*. Cabello de Balboa indicates that, upon dying, Wayna Capac drew lines of different colors that expressed his last wishes on a post. These were translated into *khipus* and further studied by the *khipucamayocs*. The friar Martin de Murua indicates that the *khipu* was the equivalent of a book. He adds that the use of the *khipu* was admirable but quite obscure, and that from the *khipu* all sort of information was extracted.[11] Another explicit reference to *khipus* as books is present in the thirty-seventh chapter of the Third Session of the Provincial Council of Lima, celebrated in the cathedral of Ciudad de los Reyes on September 23, 1583. The council declared that it was necessary to destroy these *khipus*.[12] Other chroniclers who confirm various aspects of these statements are: Pedro Cieza de Leon, Cristobal de Molina, Sarmiento de Gamboa, the anonymous Jesuit, Anello Oliva, and Antonio de Calancha.[13] Finally, Spanish amnesia about Inca writing seems hard to justify in light of the fact that even the Spaniards used them at some point. The Mercederians—a missionary order—used *khipus* extensively in their effort to evangelize Peru in the middle to late 1580s. The missionaries obliged the natives to write down the major Catholic prayers. The friars also encouraged the natives to record the Christian year in *khipus* and use these for recording the will of the deceased.[14]

Khipu means "knot" and counting through knots. The *khipus* consisted of a string with a series of knots; the many strings were placed together around a main string in a sequential fashion (figure 4.1).

The material used was of either animal origin (llama, alpaca, and vicuña) with its natural hues, or of dyed cotton; in some cases even human hair or threads of gold and silver were used. Valera illustrates how the royal *khipus* were used. He filled five pages of his manuscript with drawings of royal *khipus*. He also mentions a system of translation from the royal *khipus* to the numerical ones. Interestingly, the translation was also done in relation to the *yupana*—the abacus of the Incas.

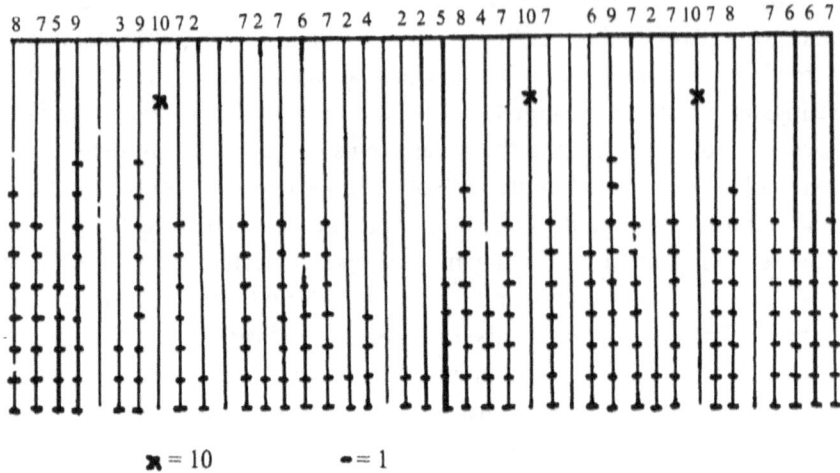

Figure 4.1: Numerical khipu

Sabine Hyland gives the hypothesis that the literary *khipus* may have been the invention of Blas de Valera, a little like the Cherokee syllabary was the invention of Sequoyah. Once more her objections are based on her refutation of possible concordances between Inca and Christian symbolism. She comes to the conclusion that this system was devised by Valera because of:

- Aristotelian quadripartition of fire/air/water/earth in relation to the depiction of Pachacamac, the godhead.
- The correspondence with Western concepts of the gods; the Christlike quality of Wirakocha, described as the god incarnate.

To this it can be countered that at the time of the Conquest, the Aristotelian conception of things was more alive in the Andes than in Europe, in fact more natural to the *amauta* than to the friar. The convergence of symbolism is a de facto phenomenon that can be understood only from a spiritual perspective. Hyland points out that no royal *khipus* have been found, but two factors could have contributed to this state of affairs: the systematic destruction of the *khipus* and the natives' desire to hide them for preservation. After all, larger things have been hidden from view, and for centuries.

Juan Anello Oliva (Book JAO II of the Miccinelli documents) reveals that the woolen *khipu* of Acatanga (site located below Tiwanaku)—

attached to the manuscript *Historia et Rudimenta*—is about the song "*Sumac ñusta*."[15] The song reads: "Beautiful princess, your brother broke your urn, Pachacama sends back your sap in rain." Anello Oliva adds the drawing of a royal *khipu* in which once again appears the song "Sumac ñusta" (figure 4.2).

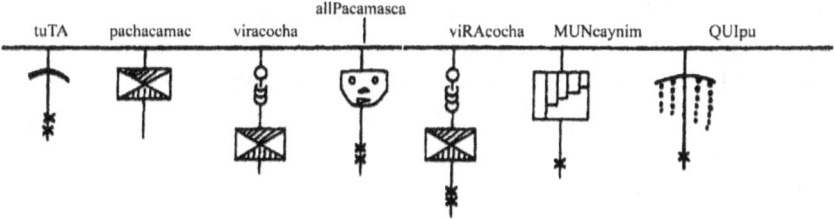

Figure 4.2: Literary khipu

Valera offers us a valuable insight into the origin of the *khipus*. According to the knowledge he received, they went back to the time of Manco Capac. In the *khipu* Manco Capac invented a writing that imitated the rays of the sun, the colors of the *quychu* grass and the contours of the mountains. He used wool (of the llamas) and cotton and he devised three kinds of *khipus*. Note, in passing, that the various sources point to either two or three kinds of *khipus*. The third kind may be the one referred to by Burns Glynn via Guaman Poma, of which more will be said shortly.

So how did the *capac khipu*—royal *khipu*—work? To a string were attached some cardinal symbols corresponding to a specific Quechua word. From each symbol hung one, two, or more knots that indicated which syllable of the word was to be read. One knot indicated the first syllable, two the second, three the third, etc. The sequential reading of the syllables of the various threads that held the symbols spelled the message of the royal *khipu*. The cardinal symbols or words were called *ticcisimi* (foundation words). Valera knew of sixty-five symbols but was told that there were a total of two hundred.

One of the Miccinelli manuscripts, *Exsul Immeritus*, was found together with some of the cardinal symbols in metal and in wool and a little *khipu* in gold. In fact many cardinal symbols also appear depicted in the manuscript. Juan Antonio Cumis independently confirms the notion of the royal *khipus* that he has received, not from Valera, but from the *curaca* Mayachac Azuay. He gives a list of fifty-six such cardinal symbols.[16]

Another confirmation about Inca writing appears in the *Nueva Coronica* of Guaman Poma, subtly embedded in the chronicle itself, and mostly in the drawings. However, even in the text appears a reference to the value of the *khipus*. At one point the author states that "the Indians did not know of letters or writing, this is why everything that appears in this opus has been taken from *khipus*," and later, "The writers placed everything in the *khipu* with such skill that the recording made with the strings was equivalent to what is written in a letter."[17] A figure from *Nueva Coronica* suggests a parallelism between books and *khipus*; in it is represented an Inca official holding in one hand a *khipu* and in the other a book. In another a *chasqui* (messenger) is holding in his hand a *khipu* while he appears to be running; on the same hand is a little sign that says "letter," as if to specify the purpose of the *khipu*. Valera also gives a complex explanation—not given in the published Miccinelli text, and not accessible to the author—of how to transform a literary *khipu* into a numeric one and vice-versa.[18]

William Burns Glynn intuited that the *Nueva Coronica* conceals more than it wants to deliberately let out, before the appearance of, and independently from, the revelations of the Miccinelli documents.[19] He has arrived at this conclusion by looking at the symbols portrayed in the so-called *uncus*, the tunics of important Inca officials. In the *uncus* appear some vertical or horizontal bands called tucapo. The same symbols of the *uncus* also appear on vases and ancient clothes. It is interesting to note that the *tucapos* were prohibited by the Spanish viceroy, Toledo, because they were known to convey messages.[20] Burns Glynn found that the key for deciphering the characters lies in reading the signs that are used in the *tucapos* of all the Inca emperors. This is possible since the drawings are accompanied by the names, which are most often very short. A first observation will confirm the rightness of this approach. The same glyph characters appear as the last syllable of the names Sinchi Roca and Inca Roca in their respective *tucapos*. Burns Glynn observes that this kind of writing was done from right to left and vice-versa, from top to bottom and reverse. A word could also be written in zigzag or other broken forms. He further finds confirmation of his findings in the fact that in textiles we find the written symbols together with a graphic (drawing) confirmation of the sentence written, e.g., the youth with the smiling face, both in writing and in drawing.

How then did this second kind of literary *khipu* differ from the royal *khipus*? The chronicles tell us that the *khipu* used a decimal system. In order to use the decimal system for writing, the Inca had to use a system of conversion of sounds into letters, and obviously this is hardly possible with a decimal system. However, it becomes possible if only the consonants are used. The absence of vowels would only be a problem in reading an isolated word. In a sentence the context defines the word. Added to this would be the fact that those who read or wrote would obviously need a lengthy training.

Using consonantal writing has been done before by the Phoenicians with the so-called Ogham Consaine. Others who used similar systems (no vowels written) were the Egyptians and Hebrews. Ogham Consaine used a system of base 10. It is probably the extension of finger-signing and possibly derived from it. In Ogham Consaine it is as if the hand symbols (with up to five signs) were used on either side of a line—one hand above it, the other below. Ogham Consaine was also written indifferently from the right or the left, the top or the bottom.

To verify his hypothesis, Burns Glynn proceeded to reduce the sixteen Quechua consonants into their sounds. He finds that although there are sixteen of them, they can be reduced to ten sounds without any resulting loss of meaning in a message. The key for translating a letter into a number lies in one of the predominant sounds of each numeral: *Juk* = 1 ("one" is said *"Juk"* in Quechua) in which the letter J stands for 1; *iskay* = 2 ("two" is said *"Iskay"* in Quechua) in which the semi-vowel ay stands for 2; *kimsa* = 3, in which m stands for 3, etc. The final result of the conversion is the following: 1=j; 2=w(y); 3=m; 4=t; 5=r; 6=s; 7=q(k); 8=p; 9=n; 10=ch.[21] The interest of the hypothesis lies in its simplicity and directness. Ultimately it lies in the fact that it seems to work first of all in deciphering the names of all the emperors based on the symbols that are visible in the *tucapos* of their *uncus*. Much longer messages also convey coherent meanings.

Burns Glynn goes a step further in adding another hypothesis of how Quechua was used as a sort of mathematical language. He was moved to explore in this direction by the enigmatic drawing of the Inca accountant officer and treasurer in the *Nueva Coronica*. There we see a presumed accountant holding an outstretched *khipu* between extended arms (figure 4.3). Below, in the right corner appears a *yupana* (*yupai* means "to count")—the Andean abacus—with a precise numerical configuration.

Joseph de Acosta indicates that the Indians used maize grains to make complex calculations with great skill. The *yupana* was a system of 5 rows and 4 columns (see bottom of figure 4.3). The first column could be filled with 5 grains, the second with 3 grains, the third with 2 grains, and the last one served as a memory. The bottom row indicated the units, the next one up the multiples of 10, the third row the 100s, the 4th the 1,000s, the last the multiples of 10,000. When one row was full the memory next to it was used. Later it could be transferred as a unit to the next row above. The progression of prime numbers 2, 3, and 5 was used like a support table.

In looking at the drawing of the *yupana* of the *Nueva Coronica*, Burns Glynn simply applied the previous hypothesis of the letter to number conversion to the use of the abacus, since it is also keyed on a decimal basis. Converting the numbers of each row, starting from the top of the abacus, he reads RMSMS. In interpolating vowels he spells this further into: *rimai simasi*, which means "that which helps to speak." As if to congratulate those who would decode the meaning of his book Guaman Poma ends his treaty with the figure entitled "the author asks." It is the figure of Guaman Poma himself in which the symbols spell: KRCHTYCHR. Interpolating the vowels, Burns Glynn reads: *Qari Chiti Yacharii*. This means: "Diligent Man, Verify." It seems that the *Nueva Coronica* was a coded book, and that Guaman Poma wants to congratulate those who find the hidden meanings everywhere encoded in its pages.

What would be the advantage of this other type of *khipu* over the royal *khipus*? A first response lies in the ease it provides, since no symbols are needed; therefore, all the labor needed to produce them was eliminated, and there was no need to carry them around. The price to pay for this convenience is a loss of precision or a higher skill required, since consonantal writing is obviously less precise and more subject to misunderstanding than the syllabic spelling of the royal *khipus*. In essence this second kind of writing could have been an earlier form of writing, preserved for its usefulness as a sort of shorthand writing, and for its use while traveling.

Of added interest for our analysis is the hypothesis that the symbols visible in the *tucapos* far preceded Inca civilization. Glynn Burns recognizes them even in a Pukara stela in the first centuries AD: two characters on a stela spell w-k, a word that could easily refer to *waka*.[22] He is not the only one to think this! Valera knew of the tradition that attributed the *khipus* to Manco Capac.

Inca Esoteric Knowledge 243

Figure 4.3: Accountant holding a khipu (*Nueva Coronica*)

Writing: Innovation or Rediscovery?

In light of the continuity between Inca and previous traditions, it is not surprising to find at least some evidence that writing also accompanied the revolution of the Dawning. Such is the case for the earliest *khipu* found in Caral on Peru's north coast, going back to possibly two millennia before the turn of our era.

A tentative but solid response to the puzzle of writing comes from a very famous Peruvian archaeologist—Rafael Larco Hoyle—that was already stated as early as 1944.[23] Larco Hoyle finds evidence for his claims among Nazca, Paracas, Tiwanaku, and Moche! All of these are civilizations that arose at the turn of our era.

The archaeologist found Nazca vases adorned with beans of the type *pallar* that combined with others in order to form polychromatic ideograms. The same motifs appear in both Nazca and Paracas textiles. In some textiles the gods appear with vestments decorated with *pallares*; in others the *pallares* emanate from the mouth in order to graphically represent the beings' voices. The author finds parallels to these phenomena among the Maya at the same historical epoch (figure 4.4).

Comparing what appears to be Moche writing with the contents of the Mexican Troano Codex, Larco Hoyle has found that in both cultures, individuals hold similar signs (glyphs or *pallares*). In the same codex Larco Hoyle sees that scribes use the same stamps as the Moche scribes, that they hold in their hands a sign in the form of a kidney-shaped bean and in other instances they are shown in the act of painting these beans. Larco Hoyle has found that the Moche made incisions on their beans, whereas the Nazca people painted them.

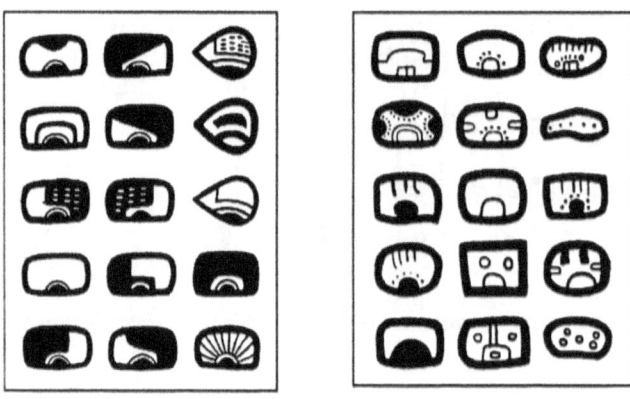

Figure 4.4: Nazca/Paracas (left) and Maya (right) ideograms

Finally, the archaeologist compares what he sees as Peruvian writing with its Maya counterpart. The Maya ordered their writing with either horizontal or vertical lines; at times they would write around the figures portrayed. Much the same can be said of Nazca and Paracas writing. The Moche wrote in horizontal lines or else next to the figures or the deities.

In almost all Maya glyphs, in the place where the sprout would emerge from the bean, there is a drawing of a circle, a square, parallel lines, or a wide rectangular line. These seem to be the symbols for the sprout.

The same motifs appear in Peruvian culture as among the Maya. Similar parallels are visible even in the more stylized forms originating from both cultures. Moreover, many elements constituting the glyphs appear both in Maya and Peruvian glyphs, e.g., dots of diverse dimensions and number, circles, straight lines both simple or parallel, curved lines and curved parallel lines, semicircles, broken lines, etc. However, Maya signs are more complicated and indicate a further evolution of writing.

There is little doubt that the Inca had achieved historical consciousness, which is only possible when acquiring a solar calendar. That they may have brought it back to the surface after a long interlude remains to be proved. The author believes that they had achieved restoration of the heritage of the time and legacy of Thunupa, which already included writing. Many of the gifts of Pachacuti's initiation were rediscoveries, carrying Thunupa's legacy to a new level in the changed conditions of the times. The reader will not be surprised therefore that together with writing, the Inca had full knowledge of the solar calendar. These two inventions go often hand in hand. Here too, there is indication from the work of Posnanski, Milla Villena, Makowski, Luizaga, and others that the solar calendar had already existed in Tiwanaku at the time of Christ. In fact the priesthood was probably already aware of the solar calendar in the centuries leading to our era, as we know now on the basis of the Chankillo site that dates back to the fourth century AD.

All of the above, both in North and South America, indicates that during and after a time of "Twilight of the Gods," the Mysteries lost their strength. The new consciousness at the time of Christ could no longer entrust to memory the body of knowledge of the Mysteries. Writing and calendar the world over have their origin from this cardinal necessity. It is not surprising to find confirmation in South America's central Andes of what we know from Mesoamerica. The turning point of time introduced the new possibility of gaining historical consciousness.

The Order of the Heavens and the Ordering of Time

Andean cosmology resembles in many aspects what is known of the Mesoamerican worldview, particularly in its Atlantean connotations. Thus, in the view that has prevailed in the Andes, the Earth can be compared to a round fruit or ball swimming in a bowl of water—in effect, the idea of turtle island of North America. The expanses of heavens and ocean completely encompass the globe.

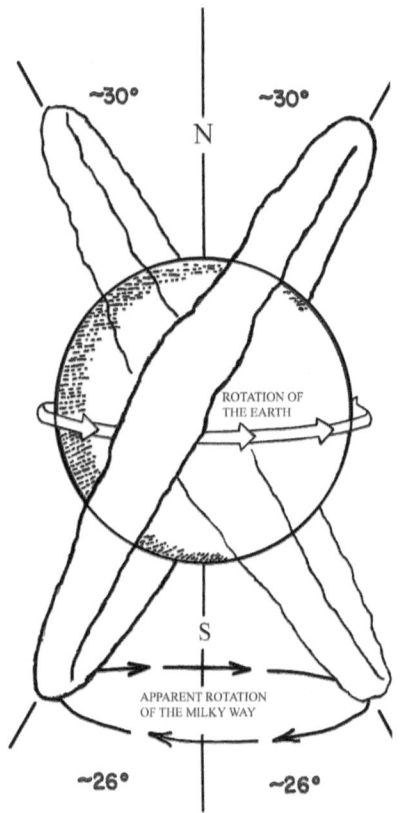

Figure 4.5: Yearly rotation of the Milky Way

What unites the Earth with the cosmic bowl of water is the Milky Way, which is seen as a two-headed serpent that encompasses the earth and connects the terrestrial waters with the cosmic waters. The Milky Way, more than the ecliptic, is the central astronomical axis of reference of Andean cosmology. The Milky Way enables a cosmic cycle of water. Its submerged part—the one not visible at any given time—acts in the recycling of water between cosmos and Earth. The waters of the ocean are absorbed and brought back into circulation by the hidden part of the Milky Way. The two-headed serpent originates from the north (Gemini, the thinnest part of the Milky Way) and their heads meet in the south near Sagittarius, close to Southern Cross, at the most expanded part of the Milky Way, the so-called "womb of creation." It is in the direction of the womb of creation that, we may say, we look from the Earth into the center of the galaxy.

The axis of the Milky Way forms an angle of 26–30 degrees with the Earth's rotational axis (figure 4.5). During the dry season (April to September) the Milky Way runs from northeast to southwest across the heavens. During the rainy season it can be seen in the direction southeast to northwest. The latter corresponds to the direction of the Sacred Valley and its sacred river! There is an added correspondence between the sunset position of the Milky Way and the solstitial sunrise positions of the Sun. The solstices are the only times of the year when the Sun rises at the same place in which the Milky Way rises at sunset. The Cruz Calvario—defined as the stars of Orion's belt plus other perpendicular stars—is the central place where the Milky Way stands stationary (at the intersection with the ecliptic).

These basic concepts help to frame a concept unique to Andean cosmology. It is expressed in the idea of *pacha* or space/time. This basic notion has already helped us to express the concept of *paqarina*. The *paqarinas* characterize the tribes' link with the time and space of origin at the time of the Dawning. *Paqar*, meaning "to be born" or "to dawn," defines both the period of time and the part of the heavens or of the earth illuminated by the morning twilight sun at the time of the Dawning. The *paqarina* can also be the star that rose on the horizon at the time. The tribes scattered across the spine of the Andes were each anchored to a unique place of the Andes. They had both a connection with the earth and with the particular moment of the Dawning. The spine of the Andes can somehow be compared with an earthly reflection of the Milky Way; each tribe in its own right forms a star or constellation on earth, reflection of another constellation in the heavens. In turn the *paqarinas* are connected to the place of the Sun's emergence—the Island of the Sun—through the waters of the underworld in which the lineage ancestors emerged at the time of the Dawning. Not only is there a connection in time, there is a further connection in space. The *paqarinas* hearken back to a point in time and a place in the Andes, a particular expression of the notion of *pacha*, space-time. Another place in which the notion of space-time was clearly expressed is in the ritual use of space, most of all in the use of the *ceques*, but also in the numerous astronomical clocks dispersed through Inca territory.

Astronomical Clocks

The notion of *pacha* was rooted in the calendar, and this could form a first bone of contention, at least for what academic science recognizes of Inca culture. Following our discoveries in relation to the Maya, it is no coincidence that writing, a solar cosmology, and a calendar appear at the turn of our era in Andean civilization. Once again, this confirms the findings of spiritual science. When the faculties of clairvoyance were dimming, initiation knowledge could not be preserved by memory alone. This is why recording of time and transmission of knowledge were entrusted to the calendar and writing very close in time, if not simultaneously. In light of the fact that Andean civilization had an earlier origin than Mesoamerica's counterpart, the legitimate question arises whether we will find an Andean form of calendar parallel to Olmec and Maya calendars.

Guaman Poma and Jose de Acosta state positively that there was a precise Inca calendar. Jose de Acosta refers to it in relation to the *ceque* system of Cuzco. That this is likely a correct assertion is what we want to turn to from the wealth of observations of Inca "astronomical clocks."

Through the observation of the stars, it appears that the Inca had acquired a correct interpretation of the solar calendar. This is most visible of all in Cuzco, Kenko, and Macchu Picchu, but also in a host of other places. Let us look first at a particular astronomical feature that has been dubbed the "eyes of Wirakocha." This device can be found, built in similar fashion, in the observatory of Kenko and in Macchu Picchu.

Kenko is an observatory carved in the rock, situated at a short distance to the northeast of Cuzco. It was called the Waka of Patallaqta and the house of the Inca Pachacuti.[24] The carved rock has a form reminiscent of a gigantic serpent, or rather dragon, oriented north to south. It ends on a serpent head with an erect tongue in form of a monolith. Around the head is built an elliptic structure that had a precise astrological function. We will return to it. In what corresponds to the spine of the dragon, there is a cut in the rock that lets light into an astronomical instrument, basically constituted of two cylinders. These are what Sanchez Macedo calls the "eyes of Wirakocha." The cylinders are admirably constructed. The tangent going from the lower right eye to the upper left eye points to the magnetic north.

At the June solstice, the first morning rays illuminate the center of the left eye. Later, during the day, both eyes are completely illuminated and the shadow around them forms what looks like the figure of a puma head. At the equinoxes only one eye is fully illuminated, while the other is completely obscured. While these are the most spectacular effects, another series of properties accompanies the observations that were possible within the period of time going from March 21 to September 21, roughly corresponding to the dry season. This is an astronomical geometrical progression that can be defined by the lines of light formed from month to month, thus expressed by Sanchez Macedo:

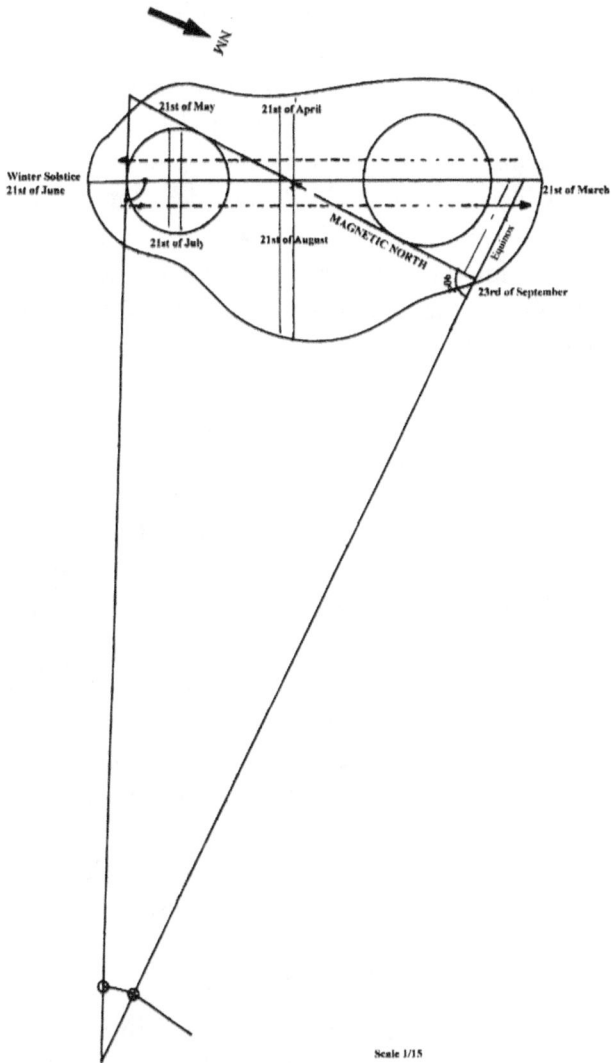

Figure 4.6: Yearly movement of the sun around the "eyes of Wirakocha"

- from May 21 to June 21 and from June 21 to July 21, the distance marked by the progression of the ray of light serves as the baseline: X

- from April 21 to May 21 and from July 21 to August 21, the distance is double the baseline: 2X

- from March 21 to April 21 and from August 21 to September 23, the distance is quadruple the baseline: 4X. (figure 4.6)

A similar observatory to the one in Kenko was present in Macchu Picchu. This one is situated in the so-called Hall of the Mortars. Here, the two cylinders had a cavity carved on the top that allowed them to be filled with water, like the "mortars" of Salinas del Chao we saw in chapter 2, "The First and Seconds Ages." As in Kenko, a slit in the rock above them lets a shaft of light into the astronomic instrument. The same progression X–2X–4X is present at the exact equivalent dates of the Kenko observatory.[25] Another solar observatory in Macchu Picchu allowed the observation of the solar year in the structure known as Temple of the Sun. It is a stone tower with two trapezoidal windows, a trapezoidal door-window, and six niches.[26] The two trapezoidal windows let the light perpendicularly through on the dates of the June solstice, the date of the Inti Raymi, and on the December solstice, the date of Capac Raymi. The six niches disposed in 3–2–1 sequence around the two trapezoidal windows allowed the recording of the six months one way and six months the other.

A structure that functioned in a similar way to the above is also present in the observatory of Kenko. In the low-wall elliptic form disposed around the head of the snake, there are eighteen niches. Each of them represents a ten-day interval and three niches form a month. The total adds to 180 days from solstice to solstice one way, 180 days the other. The five remaining days are represented by an extra niche at the northeast. The above findings confirm what we know from the chronicle of Guaman Poma that describes two half years going from solstice to solstice.[27]

A Calendrical Khipu

A possible confirmation of all the above is also given by the Miccinelli manuscripts. In the conclusive pages of *Exsul Immeritus* we find a drawing of a royal *khipu* entitled *pachakhipu*, or time *khipu*. It furnishes complete astronomical observations and annotations of a single calendar year.[28]

The *khipu* is formed of 13 strings. The 12 first strings represent 12 lunar months of 29 or 30 months for a total of 355 days. Each one of them has a month and a symbol of the most important event of the month. The last string contains the remaining 10 days. Each month lists waxing and waning moons, full and new moons, eclipses of sun and moon, equinoxes, solstices, and the sun at the zenith. Red and green colors form groups of 15 knots, whereas the spacing between knots divides the strings in 3 groups of 10 knots. The following is the order of the strings with some of the astronomical observations that accompany them:

String 1: June, time of the festival of the sun, Inti raymi. This is also the time of first visibility of the Pleiades.
String 2: July, time of the hundred red llamas. They were sacrificed in request for good weather for the new crops sowed.
String 3: August, time to plow.
String 4: September, time of the festival of the queen, the Qoya Raymi.
String 5: October, time to request the rain. In this period the sun transits at the zenith.
String 6: November, time to take the dead in procession.
String 7: December, solstice and Capac Raymi.
String 8: January, Waka Pacha or time to honor the wakas.
String 9: February, time to give the males the first breech cloth. The sun passes through the zenith.
String 10: March, time for rain.
String 11: April, time to have the ears pierced. End of the time of visibility of the Pleiades.
String 12: May, time of the maize harvest.
String 13: time of what needs to be added for the solar year. The yellow symbol affixed to the cord obviously represents the sun, all the more so since the string has ten knots that complete the solar year.

This *pachakhipu* indicates very precise events for a given year. Comparing recorded data, it appears that this was the year in between 1532 and 1533. All the events for the year coincide. A black ball (misfortune) appears for the day of November 16, the date of the battle of Cajamarca.

To fully understand the Inca calendar, we need to integrate the astronomical component with its earthly counterpart. Everything that the stars described in the heavens had a counterpart on earth. It was lived through and integrated in the ritual and ceremonial life of the Inca and their subjects. It was further incorporated in the dimension of daily life, in the way the cities themselves were built. An exploration of this sacred geography or what some authors have called "fields of power" will further allow us to complete the understanding of the Inca solar calendar attempted thus far.

The Order of Earth and the Ordering of Space

The Inca not only had a remarkable understanding of the course of time; they ordered all of space according to this understanding. This was not novel in and of itself. It actually corresponded to a tradition possibly going back to the time of Chavin. This tradition received a new impulse during the Early Intermediate Period, through the deeds and teachings of Thunupa.

The Fields of Power of Ollantaytanpu

Extensive evidence of Inca astronomical knowledge has been uncovered in the Sacred Valley. We have already seen that its central section—in Ollantaytanpu—contains some of the most significant sacred landscapes of all Inca civilization. There, not far from each other, we have already seen the monumental sacred pyramid and the colossal sculpture of Thunupa. As the brothers Elorrieta Salazar have found, the representation of the Sacred Tree encloses the pyramid in its canopy and borders the carved image of Thunupa and the Waka of the Condor that commemorates the first brother, Ayar Cachi. To build these forms, as many others that stand on irregular topography, it was necessary to have observatories on the nearby hills in order to draw the lines of construction. In many instances, traces of these observatories still exist, as is the case for the great pyramid of Ollantaytanpu.

The sacred pyramid of Ollantaytanpu is an elaborate time-clock. We have already mentioned the light effect on the date of the June solstice, when the first rays of the sun illuminate the middle window, the one corresponding to the Capac-toco. This is only the first of other truly remarkable phenomena. Later during the day, the light first illuminates the edge between two sides of the pyramid and the last rays exit at the top of the truncated pyramid. During the December solstice, the rays of the rising sun illuminate the middle of the western façade of the pyramid. At the September equinox a special light effect allows for the illumination of the southern façade while the western one remains in the shade. These light and shadow effects are too numerous to be mentioned in this brief overview. Other, similar ones are abundantly referred to in the work of Sanchez Macedo, Elorrieta Salazar, and Merejildo Chaski quoted in the bibliography.

The pyramid and its associated sacred landscape offer a first indication of the message that the Inca priesthood carved across the Sacred Valley. Other large imprints are present in the Sacred Valley, all the way from Pisaq in the south to Macchu Picchu in the north.

Dark Cloud Constellations and Crosses

Before turning to further aspects of the sacred geography of the Sacred Valley, we need to add another important aspect of Andean astronomy—knowledge of the so-called "dark cloud constellations" of the Milky Way.

The Inca, like present indigenous people, oriented themselves primarily through the Milky Way, rather than the ecliptic. Here is where are found the dark cloud constellations, defined by the shapes formed by clusters of stars within the Milky Way around them. The Inca and the indigenous at present consider the dark cloud constellations earthly, and call them *pachatierra* or *pachatira* (combining the Quechua word *pacha* and the Spanish *tierra* meaning earth). The contrast between the regular kind of constellations and the dark cloud constellations is reinforced in the names given to them. Star to star constellations, except for the celestial puma, have the names of geometrical figures or inanimate objects. Most of the ones frequently observed and mentioned lie along the path of the Milky Way and are especially numerous in the area of Taurus and Orion. All these constellations are given the names of animals.

Based on the knowledge presently preserved in the Andes, Gary Urton recognizes four major crosses among the star to star constellations.[29] Although they are called "crosses" in popular parlance, they have rather the form of a T or Y. These are the following: Hatun Cruz (Northern Cross, roughly located in Gemini); Huchuy Cruz (Southern Cross): Alpha and Epsilon Centauri and Rho and Sigma Lupi; Calvario Cruz, (Cross of the West, comprising the belt of Orion); and Linun Cruz (Cross of the East, formed by the head of Scorpio). The four crosses are closely associated with the Milky Way and two of them (Hatun Cruz and Calvario Cruz) with the ecliptic. These four crosses stand opposite in the heavens two by two. They are associated in time and space with the solstices.

The Southern Cross reaches its highest declination on May 2. This is the time of the zenith sun, celebrated as the Christian festival of the Holy Cross. Another cluster of stars that plays an important role in Andean astrology are the Pleiades, called Collca—whose meaning also stands for warehouse, place for storage. Cobo called them the most important stars of the Inca. The Pleiades announce the beginning of the agricultural cycle. They rise heliacally in June and are used to determine when the planting should begin. Another group of stars, also known as Collca, form part of the five tail stars of Scorpio. They are better known as Choquechinchay, the Celestial Puma. The observation of one Collca is closely linked to the other Collca.

According to Garcilaso, the Inca believed that for every animal on earth, there was a constellation in the heavens that acted like a "group soul" for them. The dark cloud constellations all appear in the southern portion of the Milky Way. They rise in the heavens during the rainy season. The accentuation of the dark clouds occurs in the absence of rain. When they become obscured this means that the rain is approaching. Let us now look at the sequence of the dark clouds. They follow each other in the following order: Yutu (*tinamou* partridge), A'toq (fox), Catachillay (llama) and Uñallamacha (the baby llama), a second Yutu (*tinamou* partridge), Hanp'atu, (toad), and Mach'acuay, (serpent). Each dark cloud constellation is associated with its animal counterparts in ways that relate to their behavior. Thus, the celestial toad rises in the early morning sky just after the toads have come out of hibernation. The celestial serpent appears at the beginning of the rainy season, at which time the serpents emerge from hibernation. At the upper and lower culmination of the Celestial Llama, the Inca offered sacrifices of llamas.

The Fields of Power of the Sacred Valley

Let us now return to the Sacred Valley with the knowledge gleaned around important Andean stars and dark cloud constellations. Probably the oldest of the sacred animal forms found in the valley is, according to the Elorrieta Salazars, the Temple of Urcuchillay, found in Pallata, close to the hill Huanacauri, three miles northeast of Ollantaytanpu.[30] The

Urcuchillay is most likely a single star located close to the Sacred Llama, Catachillay, a dark cloud constellation. The outer form of the llama of Pallata appears in the same way it does in the *illas*—stylized figures of alpacas sculpted on hard, fine-grained stones. To the back of the carved animal *illa* was added a hole called cocha (sea), where was placed the grease of the animal. The *illa* stands for the group soul of the alpacas. If the animals are given to humanity by the gods, then it was the Incas' duty to give them access to the forces coming from the universe that sustain them.

The sacred form of the animal shape found in Pallata is divided into a Hanan sector, comprising the front and head, and a Hurin sector with the internal organs. The Hanan sector included a ceremonial corral, called Aricancha. It served for the selection and reproduction of the herds. In the Hanan sector is found the place that corresponds to the hole in the back, the *cocha*. It has an enormous rock with a carved altar in it—an element still presently known with the name of Khuya Rumi. This was the place for offerings and llama sacrifices. The Hurin sector was mostly devoted to the cult. Next to the sacred precincts of the Urcuchillay there is the wetland of Napacocha. *Napa* stands for the spirit of the herd, a synonym of *illa*.

Not far from the Temple of Urcuchillay, on the side of the mountain Tamboqhasa—close to Ollantaytanpu and on the other side of the valley from the carved image of Thunupa—stands the "field of power" of the Sidereal Llama, Catachillay. The four observatories that helped in the construction of the sacred llama are still visible. Once again, in the head and front are found the sacred corrals and the Solar Temple; the eye can be recognized by the shape of a square building. The snout is where is found the famous Temple of the Six Monoliths.[31] The genitals serve for storage of food (*collcas*): from this area proceeds the irrigation of the terraces that form the body of the animal. In the place of the heart is built an astronomic observatory.

On the day of the December solstice, an inverted triangle of light positions itself on the heart of the sacred animal where the astronomic observatory is situated. On the solstice of June, it is first the genitals, then the eye that are illuminated. The *Catachillay* had a special importance for the Inca. The zenithal position of the *Catachillay*, on May 2, announces the June solstice. From June onward the llama sinks on the horizon, until on October 29, Alpha and Beta Centauri (eyes of the llama) disappear under the horizon. The myth says that the llama drinks the waters of the ocean. Through this drinking, the waters of the ocean reach the heavens and return to earth when the llama urinates.

Adjacent to the previous temple but only visible from another angle is the Temple of *Choquechinchay*, the sidereal puma.[32] The puma, as we have seen in relation to Cuzco, was the symbol of political power. It was also the animal deity associated with the phenomena of rain and hail. The puma therefore plays the role of guardian, and this is made graphically visible from its position in respect to the sacred llama.

To the south of the Sacred Valley, close to Pisaq, are found the forms of the Condor and the Partridge. The partridge, called *yutu*, was another dark cloud constellation. The condor too may have been another constellation of the Milky Way, according to Avila.[33] Little knowledge of it seems to have survived. The condor was the messenger of the gods and the one who carried the souls of the dead. This is the most likely reason for its placement above the necropolis of Tanta-namarca, in the proximity of Pisaq. It is thus possible that all of the animal forms of the dark cloud constellations may have been originally present in the Sacred Valley.

Finally, let us return to Ollantaytampu itself. The original city was called Tanpuquiro, which meant "palace in form of teeth [of maize]." The town is laid out in the form of a maize cob with ten parallel rows of houses crossing the length of the cob.[34] A plaza is present in the middle. The top part corresponds to Hanan, the bottom to Hurin. The city, corresponding to the cob, lies not far under the Thunupa sculpture and is adjacent to the trunk of the sacred tree. The stalk of the sacred maize extends to the top of the tree's canopy, not far from the two windows of the sacred pyramid. The third window, Maras-toco, is located at the very base of the stalk.

The lower and middle part of the Sacred Valley formed a prelude for the culmination of the sacred architecture that was reached in Macchu Picchu. The brothers Elorrieta Salazar have recognized the use of many animal forms in its landscape. Practically all of Macchu Picchu is imbued with sacred landscape representations.[35] We will only look at the main part of the city and the classical division of the Hurin and Hanan moieties. The space of Hurin is the space of the lizard. The animal is represented in such a way that it fits the description of the Amaru Tupac of some myths (e.g., myth of the birth of the son of Pachacuti).[36] On the back of the lizard is found the Acllahuasi, or House of the Chosen Women. The stomach corresponds to the warehouses and in the tail is found the Temple of the

Dead. Next to the Hurin complex is the Hanan half of the city, configured as a puma. On the head of the puma is placed an observatory. On the shoulder one can see the Temple of the Three Windows, evoking the myth of emergence of the Inca. In the Hanan part is also included the Qoricancha or Temple of the Sun.

What we have called the "fields of power" represent the Inca attempt to harmonize and strengthen the forces of the cosmos in human activities, particularly (but not only) agriculture and animal husbandry. This basic principle is present from the very first of Pachacuti's practical reforms. We see it at work in Cuzco's garden of gold of the Qoricancha. This was in effect a duplicate of the natural world. Through it the Inca felt they could exert an influence upon the natural world. Under this view, the animals are entrusted by the spiritual world to human beings, who must not only care for their physical well-being but also for the renewal of the spiritual forces that come from the cosmos, helping to perform this same mission. This also has practical applications, since it no doubt played a part in the selection and amelioration of the animal and plant species according to processes that are lost to our knowledge. This was the case for the sacred pyramid of Ollantaytanpu. It not only stood for the sacred place of emergence, but was also a space for the cultivation and improvement of the strains of maize and quinoa. Part of this can be understood by the fact that the pyramid was built to make use of the special phenomena occurring at the solstices and equinoxes. There is another confirmation of Inca cosmic agronomy not far from the Sacred Valley.

Inca Agronomy Stations?

John Earls is one of the few researchers who has turned his attention to Inca agriculture from a scientific perspective.[37] He draws our attention to the feats of the Inca thus: "At every stage in Andean history the size of the maize kernel grows suddenly, not gradually. With random hybridization, it would grow more gradually." This observation seems to show that a whole part of Andean and Inca Mystery knowledge was devoted to the improvement of animal and plant species.

The site of Moray is situated in the Pampa of Maras, south of the Urubamba River, at an altitude of 11,500 feet (3,500 m), not far, as the crow flies, from Ollantaytanpu. The site, which had little urban presence, is most remarkable for its four perfectly circular terraced depressions (*muyus*). The largest one is 230' (70 m) deep and 600' (183 m) wide and comprises twelve regularly-spaced terraces. The depressions, known scientifically as dolinas, are due to a natural phenomenon whereby the alkaline soil is eroded from underneath, and the ground collapses above subterranean caverns. The water resurges nearby in places where salt naturally accumulates.

Two of the *muyus* were left unfinished, suggesting that they may have been under construction when the Spaniards arrived. However, most of the researchers and Earls himself attribute the site to early Inca occupation. The Inca had to apply a lot of manpower to move the soil in order to achieve the perfectly circular shape. At present there is a significant temperature drop from the top to the bottom of the bowls. However, that is no longer true when the terraces are irrigated, and evidence shows that all four *muyus* were irrigated, in fact, in a very sophisticated way! The water came from the melting of nearby glaciers.

Some terraces receive much more light than others, and obviously the position around the circle greatly modifies solar exposure. Elements of variability upon which the *amautas* could have played are: upper, middle, and lower terraces; and orientation within the same terrace. Analysis of the site showed that the main crop in Inca times was maize used mainly for making *chicha*, the fermented drink used for ritual purposes.

John Earls, and others who agree with him, believe that Moray had the function of a laboratory. Many also believe that it had a ritual function; indeed ritual is everywhere present in Inca life, and it is not difficult to surmise that this was so in Moray, too. However, the notion of a laboratory conjures up very modern ideas of how maize gets modified, and our previous analysis seems to point to a wholly different way to improve plants and animal strains, based upon cosmic laws that the Inca seem to have known and exploited with uncanny ability. Note in passing that the depressions could have worked as a polar condition to the action of the pyramid of Ollantaytanpu, in whose terraces maize and quinoa were cultivated. There too, the *amauta* could play on a combination of cosmic influences (through the different exposures around the pyramid) in conjunction with the effects of different altitudes (lower and higher terraces) and types of soil.

All of the architecture of the sacred landscapes forms a striking contrast with the orthogonal architecture of Wari of the preceding Epoch of the Warriors. Wari presents us with an architecture of alienation. No consideration is given to the functional needs of the inhabitants, to aesthetics, to topography or surrounding landscape, much less to cosmic factors. Through this contrast, we can measure the magnitude of the Inca revolution. Thus, to the theory that the Incas adopted Wari's earlier form of empire, we can counter that they acted from a completely different and new cosmology.

It is not just the Milky Way that is reflected in the Sacred Valley. The whole of Inca mythology and cosmology is present. The Incas' desire to reconnect with the time of the Dawning is made graphic in the positioning of the Thunupa sculpture close to the Sacred Pyramid, and of the Sacred Tree of the village of Ollantaytanpu. The second creation is thus closely associated with the founding of the Inca genealogy hearkening back to Manco Capac. This titanic undertaking shows to what length the Inca would go to build an earth that would be a reflection of the order of the heavens. Everything that has been expressed in the result of this work makes manifest the intentions of Pachacuti. Only the highest initiate could have inaugurated such encompassing reforms that interconnected all realms of knowledge with the arts and a new way to look at the political realm. Maybe this is the depth of Inca thinking that—as Gary Urton says—presently eludes us.

The impressive nature of Inca innovations is a further testimony to the importance of the knowledge of the Inca priests. Theirs was a very comprehensive intervention into all processes of alignment of earthly reality with the ordering of the cosmos. Without this paramount enterprise, Inca politics is hardly understandable. That this had immediate results is also reflected in the remarks of John Earls, that the Inca had astonishing knowledge in matters of plant selection; the same is likely true in terms of animal breeding. There is a last place to visit in which all of this knowledge is integrated: the *ceques* present in Andean cities and villages, and most of all in the imperial capital, Cuzco.

LINKING HEAVEN AND EARTH: THE *CEQUES* OF CUZCO

To further understand what some authors have called the "sacred landscape" of Inca cities, let us turn to its simpler manifestation, visible in the villages. Consider Misminay, just south of the Sacred Valley, a village that has been studied by Gary Urton.[38]

Misminay is situated at an elevation of between 10,500 and 12,000 feet (3200 and 3600 m), close to the Sacred Valley, southeast of present day Urubamba. The well-known intersolstitial cross (rising and setting positions of the sun at the solstices) is associated with corresponding topographical features, and with the heliacal rise or setting of the stars of the Milky Way. In this way a time of the year is associated with both a topographic feature and an astrological point of reference. Heaven and earth are tied by the course of the sun.

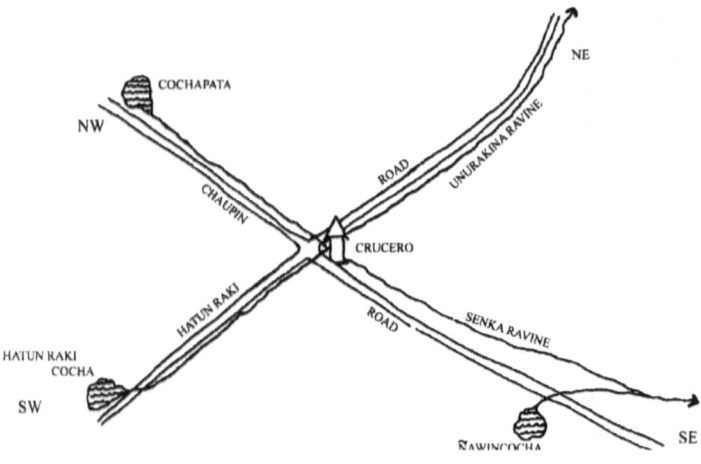

Figure 4.7: Quadripartition of Misminay

The main arteries of Misminay are modeled after the cosmological axis of the Milky Way in its solstitial positions. At the center of Misminay lay a chapel called Crucero (meaning cross and crossroads). It is the point where the two main footpaths and irrigation channels intersect. The main street, Chaupin Calle, cuts Misminay in a southeast to northwest direction (parallel to the Sacred River), dividing the village into the higher grounds of Hanan and the lower ground of the Hurin moieties. Another path forms a cross with the first one and is called Hatun Raki Calle (Street of Great Division), also going through the Crucero. Thus the village is divided into quarters through the inter-solstitial axis (figures 4.7 and 4.8). To each quarter corresponds a mountain. The main irrigation channels replicate the scheme of things; one goes from northwest to southeast, the other from southwest to northeast. Three reservoirs are situated to the southwest, to the northwest, and to the southeast.

The rather simple space organization of Misminay finds its fullest and more elaborate expression in the imperial capital of Cuzco. Various levels of symbolic meaning interpenetrated each other. From a wider perspective, the city was designed after the idea of the puma. Betanzos indicates that Pachacuti named the entire town "lion's body." This is confirmed by the general outline of the old Cuzco with the head situated in the fortress of Sacsayhuaman and the tail in the location called Puma Chupan (tail of the puma), formed by the junction of two rivers. Between the two lay the long artery called Pumaurco (trunk of the puma). This layout of the city was subservient to a larger view of things, particularly visible at the winter solstice, leading to a phenomenon that Merejildo Chaski calls the "awakening of the puma." On the dawn of June 21, the rays of the sunrise first reached the head of the puma in the fortress of Sacsayhuaman.[39] Immediately after, the light reached the tail and later progressed from the tail to the head. Various streets along the median section of the puma's spine were exactly aligned with the direction of the Sun. These and other phenomena gave to the puma an important symbolism in the city.

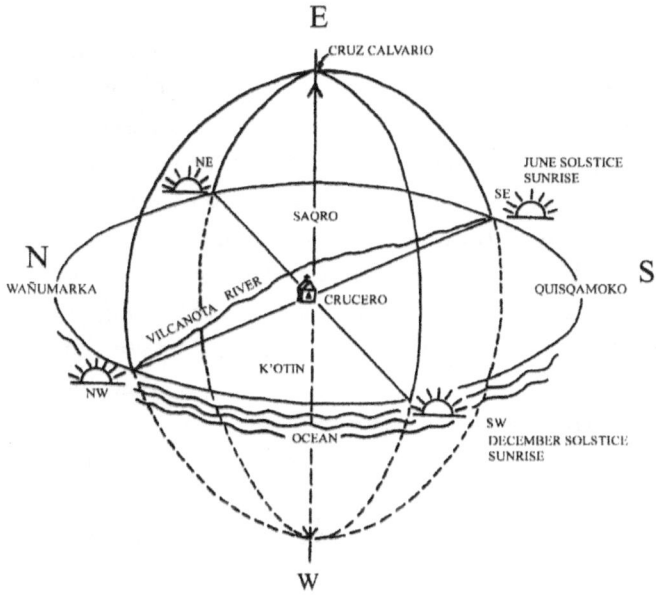

Figure 4.8: Cosmology of Misminay

Like Misminay, Cuzco was divided in an Upper Cuzco, Hanan Cuzco, this time to the north; and a lower Cuzco, Hurin Cuzco to the south. Like

Misminay, Cuzco was divided into four quadrants. The four roads led to the four directions of the empire here again, oriented toward the intersolstitial cross rather than to the cardinal directions, dividing the space into four *suyus* (see figure 3.1, page 228). To the north-east lay the Antisuyu, to the northwest the Chinchaysuyu, to the southwest the Cuntisuyu, and to the southeast the Collasuyu. Around Cuzco there were four mountains corresponding to the four suyus and two others along the line dividing Hurin from Hanan Cuzco. In the capital too the water system was divided in two: Hananchacan and Hurinchacan. The waters were directed to the fountains and basins of Cuzco, all of which had their *waka* placed in a system of *ceques* that radiated out from Cuzco's center.

Ceque's closest meaning is "line." We have seen that a *ceque* is walked as a straight line in the examples quoted in the chapter about Nazca and the EIP. It is walked as a straight line regardless of the topography. Contrary to what we saw in Nazca, the *ceques* were not absolutely straight lines in Cuzco; however, they generally did not intersect. The *ceque* system was another of the reforms introduced—or rather reintroduced and further elaborated—by Pachacuti, together with the new ceremonies and the reform of the calendar. The system served as a tool for rehabilitation of water use through knowledge of water resources, astrology, and the ancestors who had a hold on the land. It also served social purposes. Thus, for example, the lower classes were the first ones to use the water. In the *ceque* system, the Inca worldview reaches full integration.

Molina and Polo de Ondegardo state that the *ceque* system worked as a calendar with each *waka* standing for a day of the year. It also worked as a system for the recognition of astronomical events on the horizon through the use of pillar markers called *suqanqas* that marked the solstices and other important astronomical dates.

There seems to be a contradiction in the fact that there were only 328 *wakas*, recorded in a *khipu*, as Polo de Ondegardo transmitted them to us. Blas de Valera describes the *ceques* as a spread-out *khipu*, or as the "lines that knotted the *wakas* to the heart of the Inca." [40]

The *wakas* themselves have been recognized in many instances. According to B. Bauer, 29 percent of them were springs or sources of water; 29 percent standing stones (some of which are said to be the famous *pururaucas* remaining from the Chanca invasion); 10 percent were hills and mountain passes (the place from where Cuzco could be first sighted on a path sometimes acquired the status of *waka*); 9 percent were palaces or temples of the royal Inca; and 3 percent were tombs. Finally, others were represented by ravines, caves, quarries, stone seats, sunset markers, trees, roads, etc.[41]

It is interesting to refer to scattered information that we can collect from the many different chronicles about the Inca month. Betanzos, Avila, and Guaman Poma inform us of months of thirty days, divided into half-months of fifteen; and three periods (weeks) of ten days. Blas Valera records that Cuzco was divided into twelve parts and that the king had given each one of them the name of a month. Cobo enumerates the names of the twelve groups, adding that each of them was associated with a group of three *ceques*. Three *ceques* formed a month, nine of them a season.

Four chroniclers (Polo, Cobo, Betanzos, Sarmiento) mention groups of three pillars used for specific observations of sunrises and sunsets. Polo and Acosta indicate that the Inca calendar had a duration similar to ours. The tripartition of the gods that has become familiar throughout the previous chapters is reaffirmed in yet another way. The four months around the solstices were dedicated to the Sun, the main festivals being Capac Raymi and Inti Raymi. The four months around the equinoxes were dedicated to the Creator God Wirakocha, the cult of water, and to the Moon; Situa, at the September equinox, was one of them. There is an inherent logic here too, since the months of the equinoxes marked both the beginning and end of the dry season. Finally, the four remaining months were consecrated to agriculture, to Illapa and Venus.[42]

This division of the year was echoed on a more seasonal basis in the fact that three succeeding clusters—in effect a month—within a *suyu*, were dedicated to the three main deities: Wirakocha, the Sun, and Illapa. From the chronicles we can also gather the nature of the precise solar observations: the June solstice, observed from a temple north of Cuzco; the December solstice from a temple south of Cuzco; the dates of October 30 and February 13 of the zenith passages; the six-month-opposite dates to the previous (April 25 and August 18) that R. T. Zuidema calls "antizenith." Note in passing that February 13 and October 30 are important dates observed in the Mesoamerican calendar of the Maya!

In his detailed study of the pillars of Cuzco (*suqanqas*), R. T. Zuidema has reached the conclusion, in agreement with Blas de Valera, that these structures probably served to indicate the time for agricultural operations, particularly sowing.[43] Confirmation of this hypothesis comes from modern-day observations in the village of Misminay. There, the location of the setting and rising sun against set topographic markers on the horizon define an area of what is called the "planting sun," indicating when it is safe to start planting after the last danger of frost. The planting sun is defined as the sun that rises between 80° and 105° azimuth east. Below 80° the sun is called "harvest sun." What finds a definition in space is commemorated in the course of the year. This is what gives the special character to Christian celebrations, otherwise seemingly random. The four saints that have a special importance in the village are St. Anna (July 26), Mamacha Asunta (Assumption on August 15), Mamacha de las Mercedes (September 23), and Saint Francis (October 4).[44]

Evidence pointing to the existence of *suqanqas* comes from the site of Muyucmarca in Sacsayhuaman. *Muyu* means round; *marka* means site, place, position, sign. The tower of Muyucmarca is located in the summit of Sacsayhuaman (figure 4.9). Everything indicates that it was a solar calendric device. The ruins consist of three concentric walls connected between them by radial walls. Three water channels probably filled a reservoir at the center, according to information provided by professor Erwin Salazar Garces.[45]

Garcilaso wrote that there were three towers at the top of the walls, built equidistant from each other, and forming a triangle.[46] The main tower, placed at the center and shaped as a cylinder, was called *Muyuqmarka;* the other two *Paucarmarka* and *Sallaqmarka,* and they were rectangular in shape. It is quite remarkable that the chroniclers do not refer to this place. The site was demolished and buried three or four years after the arrival of the Spaniards. However there is one reference in archival material. This comes from a legal contention between the Dominican Order and the last *Qillawata khipucamayoc* of Cuzco, Juan Iñaca Sawaraura, regarding the use of subterranean waters going from Sacsayhuaman to the Qoricancha.[47] Here it is said that twice a year at the time of the solstices, the Inca, the representatives of the four *suyus,* and the Qillawata khipucamayuoc of Cuzco met together at the site. The khipucamayoc was the one who diligently recorded the date and events.

We are coming closer to identifying the function of the *ceque* system. It can be defined as the unifying thread that brought together Inca worldviews about astronomy, religion, social organization, and mythology. It also served very practical purposes for agriculture. Thus, for example, the order of the *ceques* indicated the rules for the maintenance and servicing of the irrigation canals, and Cobo mentions four *wakas* that played a special role in relation to the beginning and ending of the use of the irrigation system.[48]

As it was mentioned before, the *ceque* system was passed down in the mnemonic threads of a *khipu*. What is interesting indeed is the fact that if one spreads out the strings of this *khipu*, one can obtain the same radial configuration of a *ceque* system—yet another admirable link between the various realms of Inca knowledge and proof that nothing other than initiation knowledge could be the source of it. And there was yet another remarkable way in which the *ceque* system was a reminder of all Andean cosmology. The *ceques* unified the frame of reference of the *wakas* with the *panaqas* (royal *ayllus*) and other *ayllus*. Let us now look at this system more in detail.

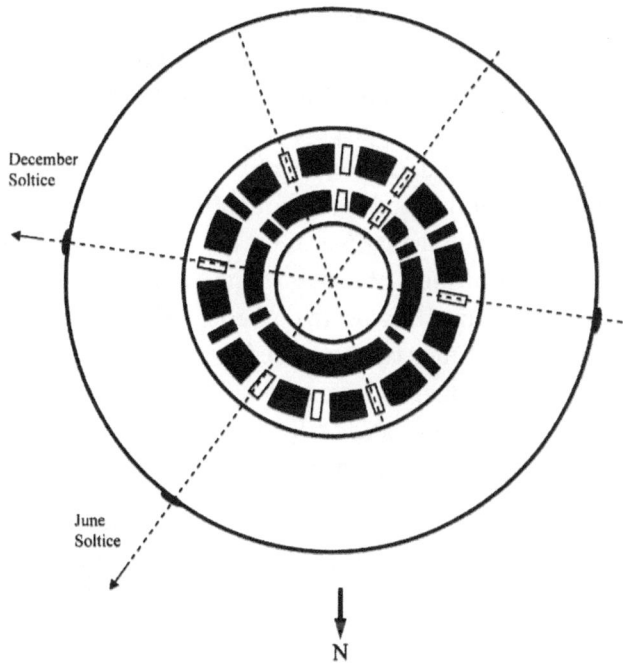

Figure 4.9: Tower of Muyuqmarca

The *wakas* were irregularly distributed along the *ceques*, which were not homogeneous for number of *wakas*, nor for length. Some had as little as three *wakas*, others as many as fifteen. The first shrine or *waka* of the *ceque* was generally within Cuzco, and often near to the Qoricancha; the last ones often near or just beyond the border of the Cuzco Valley.

Each geographical *suyu* or quarter had a group of nine *ceques*, which would sum up to the three months (of three *ceques* each), or one season. In the division of the month in three *ceques*, we find the configuration of the tripartition that we have discussed in political matters. The first of each three *ceques*, named *qollana*, ("excellent" or "principal thing") was attached to an *ayllu* of Inca descent, most often a royal *ayllu* or *panaqa*. The second, named *payan* (close relation) was the offspring of the Inca, presumably including mixed blood; the last one, *kayaw*, was assigned to non-Inca groups. However, there was a total of 41 or 42 *ceques*, not 36 as one would expect from the above. The reason for the discrepancy lay in the anomaly of the Cuntisuyu, the southern *suyu*. In this direction was found the sacred hill of Huanacauri and the *wakas* of the Capac Raymi. Here were 14 or 15 *ceques*, according to different chronicles. The one we called *suyu* 4, meaning the least of political importance, was the first one from a religious/astronomical perspective.

The Cuntisuyu was divided into two parts: one with 37 *wakas*, the other with 43. Zuidema hypothesizes that through the division of this *suyu* in two parts were made the calculations of the solar year. Thus by adding the 37 *wakas* of one half of the Cuntisuyu to the total of 328, we obtain the solar year of 365.[49] As much as his hypothesis could be pleasing, we may not know for sure yet if they corresponded to the reality of the use of the *ceques*. However, it seems now beyond doubt that the *ceque* system was indeed a recorded geographic solar calendar that tied the solar year to the whole social organization of Cuzco and the empire.

An Appraisal of Pachacuti's Reforms

It now appears that Pachacuti's reforms had been more than a patchwork of separate initiatives. They seemed, rather, to come from the concerted homogeneous worldview that could have been attained only by a high initiate. His reforms pointed both to the past, by clarifying notions that had become confused over the centuries; and to the future, by rendering possible a new integration of political and spiritual powers. Pachacuti had in effect brought back with clarity the events of the time of the Dawning, the reality of the teachings of the initiate Thunupa and of the Christ-Sun that inspired his actions. As we know in a fragmentary way from Tiwanaku and Nazca, the time-spatial organization of society with the reference to the lineage *wakas* had also been inaugurated at the time of the Dawning or Second Creation. This isn't the sole extent of Pachacuti's vision and message.

The Inca had devised a way to harmonize the competing, centrifugal forces of the *wakas*, the local cults. Their diversity and the cults devoted to them were a source of perpetual disharmony, unless they could be harmonized by the force that can reconcile diversity and unity, the Sun-Christ. We have seen how the cult of Pachacamac worked in the Age of the Warriors, by instilling fear of the earthquakes, and calling on tribute as a form of appeasement. The cult of the Sun, in contrast, was a highly organized cult of a completely different nature, as can be seen mostly by the esoteric applications spread out in the Andes. It was a highly organized knowledge calling on an informed collaboration with the deity, one not based on fear but on acts of co-creation. This is the fruit of the transition to the Fifth Age—a restoration of the fruits of the Fourth Age. The largest body of Inca religion comes from initiatic knowledge carefully cultivated within the precincts of the priesthood of the Sun. Shamanic cults of the Third Age played only a peripheral role.

The cult of the Sun was meant to bring order in the local cults. Whereas in the Age of the Warriors, each *waka* had been competing against its neighbors for ascendancy, Pachacuti was superseding their cult through the deity that could remind each *ayllu* that their lineage *wakas* had the same origin in time. Their cults, practiced in separation, is what Santa Cruz Pachacuti called idolatry; in effect it was an invitation for demonic powers and for politics of continual warfare.

It was a huge task that was thus entrusted to the central Inca religious authority. It is generally underestimated how important its role was. This role can now be placed in perspective through all that has been brought to light in the investment of time and resources used to order the earth as a reflection of the heavens; to use cosmic influences for plant and animal selection; and to build towns according to cosmological, sacred patterns. However, no matter how crucial the role of the Sun God and the legacy of Thunupa, none of these goals could have been attained in the age of the Fifth Sun without the aid of a new political system, and that was the novelty of the Inca Fifth Age. Inca political power is what made possible the renewal of the message that had been eclipsed by the end of the Third Age and throughout the second part of the Fourth Age.

All of the above conclusions were already contained in the vision of Pachacuti and the legacy he instituted in the spiritual arena. Remember that the sovereign saw himself as the "son of the Sun" and the "brother of Illapa-Thunupa." These two terms are synonymous. As the son he was the initiate of the Sun; as the brother, the equal to Thunupa, and entrusted with the role of civilizing hero. He was a servant in the first instance, a ruler in the second. The path he devised to rulership included the whole of the initiation that the Inca had to undergo, the long process of schooling that most likely covered Quechua language and writing, astronomy, understanding of natural phenomena, Sun spirituality, arts, martial arts, political schooling, and more. This initiation is what the Inca extended to the sons of all the *curacas*. In light of the leading role of the new spirituality it is understandable why Pachacuti elevated the Sun high priest to the second highest position in the empire and that he chose him from a different *panaqa* than his own.

Political and spiritual powers formed a closely interwoven fabric, as we have seen from the worldview embodied in the landscape of the imperial capital, particularly in the layout of the *suyus* and the *ceques*. The political power was sanctioned through spiritual authority, i.e., initiation. This is clearly signified in the complementarity between Capac Raymi and Inti Raymi. In the vision of Pachacuti, the king was invested with the authority of initiation, and that was certainly his own lot as first emperor. Whether this was maintained by his successors is a matter to which we will return. The priesthood of the Fifth Age could no longer survive on the power of the ideas that had sustained the change brought in by Thunupa. His legacy could not survive without a newly devised political power that would hold it in place.

Political and spiritual-cultural power together brought to fruition the central tenet of Andean spirituality: reciprocity, especially in the economic arena. The economy of reciprocity rested on the premises of the Sun religion and a political power subordinated to its goals. The geography of the Andes is a reality of precariousness: the rugged environment of the high mountains, the unpredictable climate of droughts and floods, frosts and earthquakes, makes economic integration and interdependence a must. The tragedy of the Age of the Warriors was the fact that all local cultures were merely surviving because no community could trust its neighbors. Fertile valley land could not be farmed; villages had to be built on high places and fortified; the marginal land around them could only be devoted to pastures, scarcely to intensive farming, since terracing and irrigation could not be maintained.

Economic integration was thus the end result of Inca renewal. However, economy for the Inca was much more than the production of goods. We have already seen how the sacred pyramid, the *muyus* of Moray, and the fields of power of the Sacred Valley were much more than laboratories. The same is true of the whole idea of reciprocity that underlies Inca "economic policy." Reciprocity means living in harmony with all the forces of the cosmos: human and divine, the living and the deceased, higher and local deities, Sun and *wakas*, etc. This was the high, and often precarious, distant goal for which the Inca were striving, at least in the ideal.

To the Western mind the amount of sacrifices that the Inca devoted to the cult is astounding, not one that would speak to modern economists! And yet in a higher sense it was highly economical. Here more than anywhere else appears the true dimension of reciprocity. The populations of llamas and other domesticated animals, and the cultivated plants lived in balance and harmony with their group souls radiating from their respective constellations. The fields of power, the rituals, and the sacrifices served to cement that relationship between the earthly and its cosmic counterpart. This was the true foundation of Inca and Andean economy. Moreover, Inca reciprocity did not just address the plant and animal, and their heavenly archetypes. It was supremely practical in the dimension of the "policy of generosity." The *mitimaes* served to support the flow of goods between regions and grant the local *curacas* the access to those environments and goods that were not locally accessible.

In more than one way the *mit'a* can be envisioned as ritual participation, and all of work as an exchange with the gods. This obliterates the differences between sacred and profane. Ritual is a participation in an act of co-creation that affects all of life. It is not a separate moment from what has a practical purpose. When one sees this in the background of the fields of power, it becomes all the more true that the final Inca ideal would have been a sacred economy.

The two main aspects of Inca worldview—its political and religious aspects—nourished thus the economy itself. The cult of the Sun established the first part of the equation: balance between the earth and the cosmos. Its influence was far from negligible, if we refer once more to the remarks of John Earls. Inca amelioration of cultivated species and domestic animals yielded truly remarkable results. State policies favored the production and redistribution of goods in such a way that local communities could have access to the farthest and most prized products and the effects of natural catastrophes could be mitigated.

We could say the Inca were struggling to embody a far ideal of humanity, and justifiably they fell short of it in more than one way. But their short-lived empire did something else. It brought into place the ideals that could have built a bridge between the Old and New Worlds. The Sun of the Inca and the Christ of the Spaniards are one and the same, as was well intuited by Santa Cruz Pachacuti, Blas de Valera, and others. This is what lived in the legends of Saint Thomas, Saint Bartholomew, or Saint James supposedly conducting their ministries in South America at the time of Christ, or soon after. Had the Spaniards come to the Andes before the advent of Inca Pachacuti, this historical possibility would have been absent or very limited. Even if to outer history this encounter was a failure, much went on in the undercurrents of history that facilitated an understanding between cultures, and at least made more things possible. Many seeds were sown for the future of the Americas.

Conclusions:
A Perspective on North and South American Spirituality

WE CAN NOW GATHER THE RESULTS of our studies and characterize the uniqueness and singularity of the South American Mysteries. While we do this we will carry in mind what we have learned from the Northern continent, particularly Mesoamerica.

Let us start by characterizing the origins and contrasts between North and South America. Crucial to the development of Mesoamerican and South American civilizations were the developments of the Mysteries of Southern Atlantis before and after the mid-point of the Atlantean era. The first Mysteries were Saturn Mysteries, which pervade all of the Americas. They were succeeded by the establishment of Venus and Mercury Mysteries. This movement from outer to inner planets meant a shift from revelation from above to development of thoughts and ideas within the soul.

After the fourth period of Atlantean development, two closely related groups emigrated toward the Americas. Among the first were the forerunners of the Maya and Toltecs. Their legends speak of the original water paradise in the terms of Tlalocan or Aztlan. This is the stream that concerned us in the North American studies. Another stream directed itself toward South America. The Aymara of the high plateau of Bolivia and Peru were most likely the descendants of this primeval group in South America. They preserved a very complex social differentiation and flourished most around the Lake Titicaca basin, where the famous Tiwanaku civilization developed.

The beings who influenced American cultures were great hierarchical beings from Venus and Mercury who sacrificed themselves by remaining closer to the Earth rather than working from the Sun sphere.[1] It was particularly the Venus mysteries that flowed into the Ancient Toltec civilization. This was manifested most strongly in the adoption of the Venus calendar. To the north we have identified the prevailing spirit in the name of Quetzalcoatl, which the Popol Vuh identifies as a Venus spirit, confirming what Steiner brings from direct spiritual research. This spirit ceased to have an evolutionary function some time before the Mystery of Golgotha. After the time of Golgotha, the decadent Venus impulses resurfaced first in Teotihuacan, and later in Chichen Itza where the first human sacrifices of a certain large scale were reintroduced. This movement was finally amplified in Aztec civilization.

The Nature of the South American Mysteries

From the Second to the Fourth Age

The Second Age in the Andes, especially along the north coast, anticipated and surpassed its counterpart in Mesoamerica. At this stage emerged a momentous cultural revolution accompanied by the building of imposing ceremonial centers, and the definition of a worldview centered around the Southern Cross. This translated into the cult of the Andean Cross, the worship of the mountains and water deities, basically all that represented the worship of Great Spirit, the Atlantean Tao, and the deities of the night.

At this point there were regional cultures that interacted with each other and formed extensive networks of cooperation in the building of what is known as the "vertical archipelago." The cult of the Andean Cross introduced the sunken courts, in which one cannot fail to see an equivalent to the ball courts of Mesoamerica. Both are structures buried in the ground. In both continents they form the third ladder to the cosmological division of space into upper world (the pyramids), middle world (the platforms), and lower world (sunken courts and ball courts). This movement of differentiation was only reached in the Third Age in Mesoamerica.

Knowledge of the underworld is the watershed in time in which different cultures experience the condition known as the "Twilight of the Gods." This is accompanied by the progressive weakening of natural clairvoyance of old, ushering in the possibility of human freedom. Signs that accompany this are counting, writing, and the calendar, as well as the introduction of human sacrifice on the negative side of the scale. Evidence of counting, and possibly writing, has emerged of late in the retrieval of the oldest *khipus* in Caral. We can surmise that a first agricultural calendar was very likely in use, though no archaeological proof of it has been brought to light. Human sacrifice constitutes a decadent way to acquire spiritual knowledge, and finding its evidence is another corroboration of the change of consciousness ushered in from the time of the Second Age in some parts of the Andes.

The transition to the Third Age marked the new role of the cosmopolitan Chavin center. Here an impulse flowed out of a center toward the periphery. The Chavin cult flourished far and wide from its own center and was adopted by the receiving cultures each in their own time. Chavin brought order in the cult of the *wakas*; it maintained their harmonious collaboration until a few centuries before the turn of our era. It also prepared the message for the new deity of the Fourth Age, prefigured in the Staff God of the Stela Raimondi. There is ample evidence pointing to the oracular-shamanistic nature of the Chavin cult, in keeping with the general characteristics of the Third Age and of matriarchy that accompanied it.

The Fourth Age marks a more definite change of cosmology. Here is introduced the solar calendar, and with it historical consciousness. The Second Creation makes of the Sun the supreme *waka* to which all *ayllus*, tribes, and nations look back. The Dawning marks their common origin in time. It is the reason for unity in diversity, the foundation of peaceful collaboration, and the base of an economy of reciprocity. At the same time the cult seems to be going hand in hand with the reordering of society around the new form of the matrilineal-patrilineal social unit of the *ayllu*. Where the nature of the cult appears with most clarity from the archaeological record—as it does in Nazca—the *ayllu* itself plays a major part in the sacred ordering of time and space. That is not to say that there was no priesthood, but very likely a new solar priesthood, and the role of the shaman decreased. Another difference from the previous Age is the formation of regional pilgrimage centers, such as Tiwanaku and Cahuachi, rather than a central Mystery center radiating its impulses throughout the land, such as Chavin was in the previous epoch.

Pacha: Time-Space

Central to the Mysteries of the South is the notion of *pacha*, the time-space dimension that dominates all use of sacred space and ceremonialism, as it was made clearest of all in Inca times in the use of the *ceque* lines that gathered in themselves both the ordering of time and the calendar, and the ordering of space for ceremonial and practical uses. In fact, the year and its festivals and the use of space were intimately tied together through the *ceques* as they appear most clearly of all in Cuzco.

C. Milla Villena and M. Scholten d'Ebneth have illustrated in a striking way how all religious symbolism, elements of design, and spatial organization were subjected to the Andean measuring operational system. This is why Thunupa, the initiate par excellence, is represented with the two measuring staves. The unity of measurement in the Andean system is the functional counterpart to the dated stela in South America. Everything from the building of the temples to their relationships and the ordering and placement of cities in the territory was subjugated to this ordering principle. The *ceques'* organization in the south is contrasted with the Long Count of Mesoamerica; the landscape of the fields of power in the south with the *codices* of the north.

Even writing acquires mathematical qualities as appears most clearly in the conversion of Inca letters to numbers in the use of the *khipus*. And of the Quechua language, Valera asserts that it presented a great advantage over all other languages in the way it could be used in commerce and spiritual and temporal affairs. It was a vehicular language, very easy to learn because of rational grammatical principles. It may be considered the special language of the Mysteries.

A comparison with the Mesoamerican Mysteries of the north highlights a greater role played in the north by the Venus Mysteries and in the south by the Mercury Mysteries, the Mysteries of measure and of number.

The Sun Orientation of the Early Intermediate Period and Inca Cultures

The southern Mysteries of the Andes appear most clearly revealed in two times in history: during the Early Intermediate Period (EIP) and in Inca civilization. Let us look at some of the characteristics of the changes introduced by the EIP. This Fourth Age is a period of cultural renaissance, framed on either end by periods of strife. Most striking of all is the pattern of settlements—from the rise of *pukaras* and fortified settlements in the time immediately preceding the Fourth Age (first century AD) to the return of similar conditions in the "Age of the Warriors." In between appears a new monumental architecture, settling the plains.

Civilizations at war with each other carried the need for safety in the settlement patterns, hence the abandonment of fertile lands and the location of cities and villages on mountain ridges and places that afforded more defensibility. In times of peace, expansion occurred in the fertile valleys and ecosystems like the altiplano, where different ethnicities and *ayllus* could coexist peacefully and introduce the revolution of technical and artistic innovations of great dimension that could only be carried out through large coordination of manpower, knowledge, and resources. Since this had already been possible during the Second Age, it is necessary to explore the similarities and the differences.

During the EIP the achievements of the preceding Second Age were restored. Such was the exploitation of the environment through what has been called the vertical archipelago, basically allowing different ethnic groups the access to ecosystems other than their own, through colonies distant from the motherland, and through routes of commerce open to all. As a result of this atmosphere of peaceful coexistence, grand architectural undertakings were possible, such as the construction of imposing pyramids and large canals of water tied to complex systems of irrigation and terracing, making it possible to extend the use of resources to fragile or marginal ecosystems.

What happened in the north coast during the Second Age was brought a step forward through the Gallinazo culture, after the Salinar interlude. The same was true most noticeably in Tiwanaku and Nazca, and all of this at the turn of our era. What appeared that was new to the EIP was the solar reference frame of the Mysteries and their special brand of ceremonialism. We can follow this in a number of steps.

The first cultural revolution introduced the cult of the Great Spirit—Wirakocha—or cult of the *ahpus*, carried out by the whole of the Second Age, most clearly and earlier than elsewhere along the north coast. Here, as few authors have proved conclusively, the cosmology of the Southern Cross and the resulting Andean Cross was developed in great depths. The gods worshipped were deities of the night. From this time originates the impulse leading to the building of the pyramids and of the sunken courts. As Milla Villena conclusively demonstrates, the pattern of the Andean unit acquired increasing importance and permeated the whole of ceremonialism.

Toward the end of this period appeared the cosmopolitan impulse of Chavin—the Andean Third Age—continuing the trends of the Second Age and preparing the ground for the fourth. In a fashion similar to the Olmec civilization, Chavin laid the grounds for the revelation of the future. In South America we have no such revelation as that of the Maya *tzolkin* or sacred calendar—at least no such recorded one. There are, however, two important indications of what gets carried in the time of the EIP; the first is the announcement of the new solar deity of the Staff God, most clearly visible in the Stela Raimond; and the second is that of the new solar orientation of the most important civilizations of the EIP. The first, very isolated instance is that of Chankillo, appearing side by side with the more decadent late examples of the Chavin civilization (that is, Sechin) where human sacrifice resurfaced. The solar revolution appeared with the inauguration of a solar calendar, indications of which are most clearly visible in Tiwanaku's Sun Gateway. The calendar must have been previously present in other, simpler forms, and so, most likely, writing.

The Sun referential played an important role in subordinating the *wakas*. The Second Creation, at the turning point of the Fourth Age, meant that all tribes were united to a common point in time, to the Dawning of the time of Thunupa, and that, although they all had their own *paqarinas* and honored their own *wakas*, they all did so in reference to a higher reality of the Sun deity and to the time of the Dawning from which they all issued. This is the thread of all the myths concerning the Second Creation. Until this impulse maintained ascendancy, equality among tribes and *ayllus* was an established matter of fact. The Sun worship had an equalizing effect upon Andean civilization.

The Fourth Age ended in what was called the "Age of the Warriors" in which once again the *wakas* were variously subordinated to regional *wakas*, and those in turn most likely subjugated to an "empire *waka*." Wari marked a return to the conditions prevailing at the end of Chavin's Third Age, a state of continued struggle for ascendancy among the *wakas*.

After the Age of the Warriors, the Incas reestablished the preeminence of the harmonizing cult of Inti, the Sun. This could no longer be done as it had been in the EIP because of the consciousness of the time. The Inca themselves battled against their own centrifugal tendencies embodied in the conflicting interests of the royal *panaqas* and regional groups. Inca Pachacuti established subtle balances of power in the political and spiritual realms to bring a civilizing impulse and a unifying impetus among the people of the empire. This cannot be understood from a European perspective.

Central to Pachacuti's reforms was the importance of the new cult of the Sun and the establishment of its priesthood throughout the empire. All local cults survived in the harmony of the Sun impulse, avoiding thus the centrifugal tendencies leading to continuous sustained warfare among the *wakas*. Inca culture played the same role. It aimed at creating and spreading the common language of the Mysteries of the Sun. In the instruction of the Inca nobility and of the regional *curacas* was the effort to spread a common culture, and loosening the ethnic ties in various ways. The first was the spreading of Inca blood through the gift of Inca women to the local *curacas*, or conversely the marriage of the Incas with foreign noble women. To this loosening of ethnic ties followed the adoption of Quechua language, and the unifying culture deriving from the common initiation of the nobles, whether Inca or foreign born.

Central to the Inca revolution was the establishment of a state structure that could spread the teachings of the Sun religion, and those are considerable. All of the architecture of the fields of power is the result of the Mystery knowledge preserved within the precincts of the Sun temples that the Inca introduced after each territorial conquest. We could argue that what survives about Inca culture at present is but a pale version of what existed prior to the Spanish Conquest. None of the deeper knowledge of the Sun Mysteries could be preserved without the social form of the empire that sustained them.

Inca civilization played another important role in creating the grounds for a possible rapprochement between the Christianity of the Spaniards and the Sun religion of the Andes. Through the memory of the deeds of Thunupa and his teachings, the possibility existed for the religion of the Gospels to meet with the Inca revelations of the Sun God. This was intuited by the indigenist Jesuits and individuals such as Santa Cruz Pachacuti. What was possible in Peru and the Andes had not been even remotely imaginable in Mexico given the complete cultural rift between Aztec and Spanish cultures. Historically this possibility was left mostly unfulfilled in the Andes, where Spanish greed for gold played a great hindering role. But perhaps Pachacuti's dream had been vitiated even prior to the Inca defeat. We should remember that a civil war was raging when Pizarro arrived in the Tawantinsuyu, and the empire was already greatly debilitated.

The Dream and the Reality

It could be argued that Inca cosmovision was a generous gift to the world that came too early for the human capacities of the time. Already at his succession, the ideal that Pachacuti established was soon vitiated by power struggles and political infighting that cost a great deal to the credibility of the Inca mission. In times of political succession, the spirits of the Age of the Warriors reared their heads through intrigues and plots. Later on, the path to initiation cast its shadow reflection when the Inca asserted spiritual powers he did not have, leaving room for manias of grandeur. Let us review this in some detail.

Topa Inca, Pachacuti's successor, forged alliances with local ethnic groups and their *wakas*. This was a strategy to loosen the bonds with his collateral kin (other *panaqas*) and reduce his dependence on them in times of difficult relationships. In doing so, however, Topa Inca was offering power and autonomy to local rulers who had no interest in carrying further the old ideas of reciprocity or the message of Pachacuti. In particular he created a strong alliance with the *waka* of Pachacamac. That meant giving prominence to gods other than the Sun and weakening the harmonizing and equalizing effect the cult had among competing *wakas*.

The story of what the oracle exacted from Topa Inca is quite indicative. First it asked that the temple be enlarged and therefore be given more importance. Then it asked for "sons," meaning branch oracles. The first two were built in Mala and Chincha; the third in Andahuaylas and at Andahuaylillas.[2] Pachacamac had other offshoots too: "wives" in Chincha and Mamaq, further "sons" in Huarochiri, and a house near Chan Chan, in the heart of a restive old Chimú kingdom and a dangerous potential rival. Investigations at the site of Mamaq show an absence of Inca pottery vessels and indicate what degree of independence Pachacamac acquired from the Cult of the Sun. The same is true in the core of Pachacamac's temples, even though Inca artifacts are found in the immediate environment.[3] The oracle had a vast local following on the northern coast, and pilgrims visited it from great distances. The rise of Pachacamac served to foment local political ambition and the return to the rivalry of the *wakas*. This gives an idea of the oracle's ambition and of the price that Topa Inca paid for political expedience.

Wayna Capac was born in Tumibamba, Ecuador, and inherited the title of emperor while still an infant. During his childhood his throne and his life had been threatened by plots. He was later forced to assume the rule because of a time of high inner political turmoil, and he transformed the throne into a remote place of intrigues and luxury. He established a second center of gravity of the empire in the north, by building important cities in Ecuador—Tumibamba, Carangui, Quito—and was thus long absent from Cuzco. One of his first early moves was to degrade the office of high priest by creating above it the post of Shepherd of the Sun and filling it himself. With that he could claim closer proximity to the divine than had all the earlier Incas. The immediate result of it was the severance of the functional relationship and balance of power between political and spiritual functions at the head of the state. Santa Cruz Pachacuti also reproaches the emperor for having made recourse to the oracle of Pachacamac.

Wayna Capac created confusion in his succession. He first named Washkar his heir, and then reversed his decision in favor of his other son Ninan Cuyochi. However, there was a clause in his will that specified that Washkar would be invested of the highest charge if the omens revealed that Ninan Cuyochi was not favored by the gods. What happened later was that Ninan himself contracted the plague. His brother, unaware of it, had already moved forward to oppose the legal heir.

Washkar had an unbalanced personality, at least in his later days. He was disdainful and combined weakness with sadistic traits. In his effort to wrest power from the *panaqas*, he broke off from Hanan Cuzco and even from his own kin, and reaffiliated with Hurin Cuzco. He established a residence fortress away from Cuzco's center in Collcampata to the north of it. This had been a sacred place—Manco Capac's first *chacra* (cultivated ground)—and the choice constituted a sort of desecration. The emperor also incited the marriage of his mother with his father's mummy. He claimed that this was the wish of the mummy as expressed by its medium. He died prematurely from the effect of a plague that ravaged Ecuador. In all of the above one cannot fail to see the result of failed initiations!

The Apocalyptic Dimension of South American Spirituality

The geography and climate of the Andes point to modern and future times. Exceptional geographic conditions place Andean humanity at the mercy of turns of fate, such as droughts, floods, or earthquakes. Collaboration and integration are a sine qua non of survival and cultural expansion. When that possibility was realized, natural catastrophes could better be dealt with; when civilization cyclically sank to its depths, a stark struggle for survival ensued. It is even legitimate to ask oneself if climatic changes to some extent followed human disharmony, as the tenets of Andean reciprocity hold to be true. All of this seems to point to the challenges of the present time and prefigure them—a time of ecological upheavals, in which civilization as a whole depends on planetary collaboration. In a sense Andean civilizations have known far ahead of the rest of humanity what we experience at present with global warming and ecological crises. Andean geography and ecology themselves are a microcosm of the world at large; suffice to think that 85% of world ecosystems are present in the Andes.

To a higher extent than any other contemporary civilization, Andean culture played a role of co-creator with its natural environment. It collaborated with the elemental world and cosmic influences to fashion its environment in a way that modern man can only rediscover if science turns again from the exclusive focus on earthly influences that offer us such questionable innovations as genetically modified organisms, to the interplay of earthly and cosmic factors. The interplay between the human and spiritual worlds is the foundation upon which is based Andean reciprocity in times of cultural renewal and expansion. The fields of power, the sacred pyramid of Ollantaytanpu, the *muyus* of Moray point to an incredible wealth of knowledge of the religion of Inti in mastering the use of cosmic influences for the advantage of human beings.

Reciprocity is the central nexus of all Andean ethics, and the support of its economic life; it is a principle of cosmic justice. This worldview goes beyond the individual and the present generation. Natural disasters are considered the result of lack of reciprocity; the same is true of human-made calamities. Communities may have to shoulder the guilt of an individual; indeed, even posterity may have to do the same. God inflicts a chastisement in order to allow the correction of the cosmic imbalance, which is not seen as a gratuitous punishment.

The apocalyptic nature of Andean spirituality is most present of all in the notion of Pachacuti or change of time. There were larger and smaller periods of time. The way of defining the smaller ages is more explicitly stated in Montesinos' *Memorias Antiguas Historiales*. The one-thousand-year interval was called *Capac-huata* or *Intip-huata*, the "great year of the Sun." Each millennium was subdivided into two five-hundred-year periods known as *pachacuti*. The emperor of that name came to power close to the year 1500. We know that Inca division of time corresponds to a deeper esoteric reality. Every thousand years, Lucifer and Ahriman can join forces and make a particularly strong attack on human culture. This is the root idea that is outwardly reflected in millennialism.[4] The Inca believed great epochal changes occurred every 500 and 1,000 years.

The apocalyptic theme also appears in the contrast between cultures that attained an almost complete secularization, such as Wari and Chimú, and the future-oriented impulses of the Inca. What occurred in the Age of the Warriors prefigured by many centuries the movement toward secularization that became visible in Aztec society. This reflects the fact that the Twilight of the Gods saw its onset earlier in South America, at least on the north coast of Peru where human sacrifices were already recorded in the third millennium before our era.

The Inca lived in a very high ideal of earthly and cosmic collaboration that humanity can only start to develop at present. This is the overarching impulse to shape the whole of the earth as a refection of the heavens, as best exemplified in the Sacred Valley. To what extent the Inca went in order to reshape the landscape cannot be understood from a utilitarian perspective. The massive undertaking of the sacred pyramid of Ollantaytanpu is a point in case, and so is the rest of the sacred landscape around the city. Through this undertaking the Inca could have recourse to the use of the cosmic forces in the selection and amelioration of plants and animals—an example of what humanity can hope to achieve in the far future.

The Incas included in their planning of the landscape a balanced integration of artistic, functional, and environmental concerns. Theirs was a complete reshaping of the natural world, a sanctification of the environment through the integration of earthly and cosmic concerns. This extended to the alignment of cities and ceremonial sites with the ordering of the heavens, e.g., the path of Wirakocha. Wari or Chimú offered the complete mirror image, one of the earliest indigenous examples of an architecture turned completely utilitarian, estranged from cosmic influences and even from its environment.

North and South America: Parallels and Contrasts

Three initiates—and perhaps others—played a central role in ushering in the fifth post-Atlantean epoch in the New World, which some sources to the north and to the south have called the Fifth Age. The first was the Peacemaker, Deganawidah, introducing a modern social spirituality in the form of the Iroquois League of the northeastern United States, some time between the twelfth and fifteenth centuries. The second was the emperor Pachacuti, introducing a sociopolitical system that points to a further future combining the principles of conscious initiation and earthly-cosmic reciprocity, challenging ideas that the Inca nation could only embody in its first rudiments before the arrival of the Spaniards. Against these two tendencies stood the centralizing, freedom-denying impulse of the Aztecs impelled by the black magician Tlaclael.

Aztec spirituality had a counter-evolutionary tenor. Through state ideology, the human soul was prevented from perceiving the difference between good and evil, and thus estranged from its own cosmic destiny. The earth would have been rendered sterile and mechanized had Aztec spirituality extended to the whole of the Americas, and human beings would have relinquished the desire to incarnate.

The decadent impulse of the Aztecs in Mesoamerica was countered in the north by the Iroquois, in the south by the Incas. The Iroquois speak the modern language of the social forms that will evolve in the near future. Central to Iroquois cultural revolution was a social sacramentalism that renders sacred all dimensions of human relationships. The Iroquois Ritual of Condolence was the counterpart of the Aztec heart sacrifice from a live victim. Through the Ritual of Condolence the Iroquois knew that individual and group destinies are intimately bound to each other. Healing of grief at the individual level assures the preservation and continuation of healthy social relationships. In modern spiritual terms, upholding a social compact—representing the collective karma—is intimately bound to and conditioned by the healing of karmic imbalances at whatever level they appear.

It is no wonder that Iroquois ideas formed a spiritual launching pad for the form of government of the United States. In essence the Iroquois sowed the first seeds for the modern idea of the separation and healthy interrelation of the spiritual-cultural and political realms. This attempt was continued in American federalism where the economic sector posed and still poses a formidable challenge to its integration with the realms of government and culture. The antithesis to this evolutionary process persists in the form of the centralized authoritarian government, an heir to the Aztec spiritual blueprint.

The Incas reversed the entrenched tendency toward decadence of the Age of the Warriors, and all of that was carried single-handedly through the civilizing impulse of the emperor Pachacuti and his Christ-Solar revolution. Culture flourished anew where it had been lingering and order was brought among the *wakas*. This could only be achieved through a restoration of the message of Thunupa within the new social form of the empire. Pachacuti's reforms aimed at a vast integration of social and cosmic needs, all of them captured in the idea of reciprocity and the subordination of the *wakas* to the Christ Sun. The emperor's goals point further into the future than what was achieved by Deganawidah, the Peacemaker of the Iroquois. In essence, Inca culture announces the future transformation and sanctification of the earth, the complete integration of earthly and cosmic influences into a new culture.

Conditions prevailing before the forming of the Longhouse and of Tawantinsuyu speak of a dark Age of the Warriors both among the Iroquois and in the Peruvian-Bolivian Andes. The power that the Popol Vuh and Steiner recognized as Quetzalcoatl was rearing its head both north and south. We have recognized a decadent Venus spirit to the north and its Mercury counterpart to the south. Arguably, these two impulses unchecked would have led at the time of the fifth post-Atlantean epoch to the return of the most decadent Taotl impulses both to the north and to the south, and their culmination in widespread human sacrifices with organ removal from live victims. While that was the case within the Aztec state, the same danger was prevented by Deganawidah and Pachacuti, thus blunting the overall effect of a new Ahrimanic attack against the Americas and the world. At the time of the Conquest, the Spaniards, quite unwittingly and for unrelated motivations, inflicted a mortal blow to the Aztec Empire, bringing to a halt that Ahrimanic thrust in the Americas.

In essence we could conclude that the civilizing impulses of Deganawidah and Pachacuti point one to the immediate, the other to the distant future. They offer us an image at a pre-individual level of what form the social impulses will take over the next cultural epochs in the service of the Christ/Solar being. Neither Iroquois nor Inca impulses can be continued nor resurrected without transformation, but they have sown precious seeds for what can be transformed in the new consciousness of the time.

NOTES AND REFERENCES
LIST OF ILLUSTRATIONS
BIBLIOGRAPHY

NOTES AND REFERENCES

PART I: SOUTH AMERICAN PREHISTORY

CHAPTER 2: FIRST AND SECOND AGES

1) Alfonso Klauer, *El Mundo Pre-Inka: Los Abismos del Condor*, tomo 1, chapter "El Territorio Andino," p. 26, PDF found at <www.nuevahistoria.org>
2) Ibid., p. 44.
3) Ibid., p. 45.
4) Ibid., p. 45.
5) Michael E. Moseley, *The Incas and Their Ancestors: The Archaeology of Peru* (London: Thames and Hudson, 2001), p. 223.
6) Ruth Shady, "La neolitizacion en los Andes Centrales y los origenes del sedentarismo, la domesticacion y la distincion social," in Ruth Shady and Carlos Leyva, eds., in Shady, *La ciudad sagrada de Caral-Supe: las origenes de la civilizacion andina y la formacion del Estado pristino en el antiguo Perú*, (Lima: Instituto Nacional de Cultura, Proyecto Especial Arqueologico Caral-Supe, 2003), p. 39.
7) Quinn, *Registros del Fenómeno El Niño en el Perú*, Ifea, pp. 17–18, quoted in Klauer, *El Mundo Pre-Inka: Los Abismos del Condor*, tomo 1, p. 38.
8) Ibid., p. 39.
9) Ibid., p. 49.
10) Ruth Shady, "Del Arcaico al Formativo en los Andes Centrales", pp. 17–35, and "La neolitizacion en los Andes Centrales y los origenes del sedentarismo, la domesticacion y la distincion social," pp. 35–49, in Shady, *La ciudad sagrada de Caral-Supe.*
11) Ibid., p. 45.
12) Andrew Whalen, "Ancient Ceremonial Plaza Found in Peru," February 26, 2008, <http://www.freerepublic.com/focus/f-news/1976727/posts>.
13) James Q. Jacobs, *Early Monumental Architecture on the Peruvian Coast: Evidence of Socio-Political Organization and the Variation in Its Interpretation*, 2000, <http://www.jqjacobs.net/andes/coast. html>.
14) Carlos Williams Leon, "Inicios de la tradicion arquitectonica andina," in Victor Rangel Flores, ed., *Symposium: Arquitectura y arqueologia: pasado y futuro de la construccion en el Perú* (Chiclayo, Peru: Universidad de Chiclayo, 1988).
15) In 2007 a 4,000-year-old temple was unearthed in Ventarron, Lambayeque, on Peru's northern desert coast. The sophisticated design and colorful artwork found there suggest that early Andean civilization was more complex than

originally thought, archaeologists said. Ventarron is a 7,000-square-foot site—just a bit larger than a basketball court. Fragments of paint found on the walls and an almost completely intact white and red inner mural portraying a deer hunt are the earliest of their kind to be documented. The structure's design is typical of later temples and demonstrates remarkable precision. In fact, many early temples probably were painted and had murals, but most were not preserved. (Leslie Josephs, <http://dsc.discovery.com/news/2007 /11/13/peru-temple-mural.html?dcitc=w19–502-ak-0000>).

16) Ibid.
17) Jacobs, *Early Monumental Architecture on the Peruvian Coast.*
18) Ruth Shady and Sonia Lopez, "Ritual de enterramiento de un recinto en el Sector Residencial A en Caral-Supe," in Shady, *La ciudad sagrada de Caral-Supe*, p. 187.
19) Ruth Shady, "Caral-Supe y la costa norcentral del Perú: la cuna de la civilizacion y la formacion del Estado pristino," in Shady, *La ciudad sagrada de Caral-Supe*, pp. 139–45.
20) Ruth Shady, "Las Flautas de Caral-Supe: aproximaciones al estudio acustico-arqueologico del conjunto de flautas mas antiguo de America," in *La ciudad sagrada de Caral-Supe*, pp. 293–300.
21) Ruth Shady, Carlos Leyva,. Marhta Prado, Carlos Jimenez and Celso Llimpe, "Una tumba circular profanada de la Ciudad Sagrada de Caral-Supe," in Shady, *La ciudad sagrada de Caral-Supe*, p. 229.
22) Ruth Shady, "Practica mortuaria de la sociedad de Carla-Supe durante el Arcaico Tardio, in Shady, *La ciudad sagrada de Caral-Supe*, pp. 267–75.
23) Ruth Shady, "Practica mortuaria de la sociedad de Carla-Supe durante el Arcaico Tardio, in Shady, *La ciudad sagrada de Caral-Supe*, pp. 267–75.
24) <http://agutie.homestead.com/files/Quipu_B.htm>. See also <http://archaeology.about.com/od/ancientwriting/a/caralquipu.htm> and <http://terraeantiqvae.blogia.com/2005/071602-peru.descubren-quipu-con-mas-de-4500-anos-de-antiguedad-en-caral.php>.
25) Ruth Shady, "Caral-Supe: la civilizacion mas antigua de America," in Shady *La ciudad sagrada de Caral-Supe*, p. 331.
26) Marion Popenoe Hatch, "An Hypothesis on Olmec Astronomy, with Special Reference to the La Venta Site," in *Contributions of the University of California Archaeological Research Facility: Papers on Olmec and Maya Archaeology,* (Berkeley: University of California Press, June 1971). Popenoe Hatch's ideas are further elaborated in J. M. Jenkins, *Maya Cosmogenesis 2012: The True Meaning of the Maya Calendar End-Date,* (Santa Fe, NM: Bear & Co., 1998). See more about this in Luigi Morelli, *Spiritual Turning Points of North American History*, chapter 4.
27) Carlos Milla Villena, *Genesis de la Cultura Andina*, Colegio de Arquitectos del Peru, (Lima, Peru, Fondo Editorial C. A. P., Coleccion Bienal, 1983), pp. 60–61.

28) Ibid., pp. 17, 60.
29) Guillermo Illescas Cook, *El candelabro de Paracas y la Cruz del Sur*, (Lima, Perú, self-published, 1981), p. 49.
30) These were some of the operations possible through the Operating System of Measurement:
    - multiplication by 2, $\sqrt{2}$, $2\sqrt{2}$, 4, etc.
    - division by 2, $\sqrt{2}$, $2\sqrt{2}$, 4, etc.
    - multiplication by π, π^2, π^3, π^4, etc.
    - division by π, π^2, π^3, π^4, etc.
    - multiplication by 2π, $\sqrt{2\pi}$, $2\sqrt{2\pi}$, etc.
    - division by 2π, $\sqrt{2\pi}$, $2\sqrt{2\pi}$, etc.
    - multiply and divide by 3, 3π, etc.
    - multiply by $\sqrt{3}$, $\sqrt{5}$, $\sqrt{6}$, $\sqrt{7}$, etc.
    - divide the circumference in 2, 4, 8, 16, 32, 64 equal parts
    - divide the circumference in 12, 24, 48 equal parts
    - divide the circumference in 5, 10, 20, 40 equal parts
31) Maria Scholten d'Ebneth, *La Ruta de Wirakocha, (conferencia dictada en la ANEA con occasion del homenaje al Dr. Luis E. Valcarcel al serle concedido el premio de la cultura)*, (Lima, Peru: Editorial J. Mejia Baca, 1977), p. 16.
32) *Genesis de la Cultura Andina*, opus quoted, p. 155.
33) Ruth Shady, Marco Machacuay and Rocio Aramburú, "La Plaza Circular del Templo Mayor de Caral: su presencia en Supe y en el area norcentral del Perú," in Shady, *La ciudad sagrada de Caral-Supe: las origenes de la civilizacion andina y la formacion del Estado pristino en el antiguo Perú*, pp. 150–154.
34) *Genesis de la Cultura Andina*, p. 155.
35) See Rudolf Steiner, *Egyptian Myths and Mysteries*, lectures of Sept 10 and 11, 1908, (Hudson, NY: Anthroposophic Press, 1997); and Steiner, *Wonders of the World, Ordeals of the Soul, Revelations of the Spirit*, lectures of August 25 and 26, 1911, (London: Rudolf Steiner Press).
36) Rudolf Steiner, *The Apocalypse of Saint John*, lecture of June 23, 1908, (Hudson, NY: Anthroposophic Press, 1993).
37) Guenther Wachsmuth, *The Evolution of Mankind: Cosmic Evolution, Incarnations on the Earth, The Great Migrations, and Spiritual History*, (Dornach, Switzerland: Philosophic-Anthroposophic Press, 1961), 85-90.
38) Steiner, *Wonders of the World, Ordeals of the Soul, Revelations of the Spirit*, lecture of August 26, 1911, (Rudolf Steiner Press, London, 1983).
39) Rudolf Steiner, *From the History and Content of the First Class of the Esoteric School, 1904-1914*, lecture of January 6, 1907, (Great Barrington, MA: SteinerBooks, 2010).
40) Rafael Girard, *Los Chortis ante el problema Maya*, volume 3, (Mexico, D. F.: Antigua Libreria Robledo, 1949), 865-867.
41) Rudolf Steiner, *The Mission of Folk Souls in Relation to Teutonic Mythology*, lecture of June 14, 1910, (Forest Row, UK: Rudolf Steiner Press, 2005).

42) Rudolf Steiner, "The Guardian of the Threshold," 1912, in *Four Mystery Dramas*, (Great Barrington, MA: SteinerBooks, 2007). See Scene One, the speech of the Grand Master Hilary. In reference to Teachers of Wisdom.
43) Grace Cooke, *The Illumined Ones*, (New Lands, U. K.: The White Eagle Publishing Trust, 1966).
44) Ibid., pp. 51-53.

CHAPTER 3: THIRD AGE: CHAVIN

1) Thomas C. Patterson, "Chavin, an Interpretation of Its Spread and Influence," in Elizabeth P. Benson, ed., Dumbarton Oaks Conference on Chavin, October 26–27, (Washington DC: Dumbarton Oaks Research Library and Collection, 1968), p. 29.
2) Richard L. Burger, *Chavin and the Origins of Andean Civilization*, (London: Thames and Hudson, 1992), pp. 204–6.
3) Richard L. Burger, "The Sacred Center of Chavin de Huantar" in Richard Townsend, ed., *Ancient Americas: Art from Sacred Landscapes*, (Munich: Prestel Verlag, 1992), p. 265.
4) Burger, *Chavin and the Origins of Andean Civilization*, p. 266.
5) Ibid., pp. 195–96.
6) Luis Lumbreras, Chacho Gonnzalez, and Berbard Lietaer, *Acerca de la función del sistema hidráulico de Chavín*, Publicaciones del Museo Nacional de Antropología y Arqueología, serie investigaciones de campo #2, Junio 1976, (Lima, Peru: Museo Nacional de Antropología y Arqueología, 1976).
7) Federico Kauffman Doig, *Historia y Arte del Perú Antiguo, vol. 2*, (Lima, Peru: Peisa, 2002), p. 180.
8) Burger, *Chavin and the Origins of Andean Civilization*, pp. 144–58.
9) Chiaki Kano, *The Origins of the Chavin Culture*, Studies in Pre-Columbian Art and Archaeology, #22, (Washington DC: Dumbarton Oaks, 1979).
10) Peter G. Roe, *A Further Exploration of the Rowe Chavin Seriation and Its Implications for North Central Coast Chronology*, (Washington DC: Dumbarton Oaks, 1979).
11) Rafael Girard, *Historia de las civilizaciones antiguas de America*, (Madrid: Ediciones Istmo, 1976), p. 1804.
12) Jorge Miranda-Luizaga, *La Puerta del Sol: Cosmologia y Simbolismo Andino*, (La Paz, Bolivia: Artes Graficas Editorial "Garza Azul," 1991), p. 51.
13) Burger, *Chavin, an Interpretation of Its Spread and Influence*, p. 44.
14) Lorenzo Samaniego, Mercedes Cardenas, Henning Bischof, Peter Kaulicke, Erman Guzman, Wilder Leon, *Arqueología de Cerro Sechin; Tomo II: escultura*, (Lima: Pontificia Universidad Catolica del Perú, 1995), p. 103.
15) Ibid, pp. 100–101.
16) In Lambayeque (north coast) we see some elements of Phase EF on a turquoise vase, such as in the motif of a warrior carrying a trophy head, which

is thematically akin to the Cerro Sechin's monoliths. It has a typical EF mouth configuration and many other EF traits. It holds a trophy head portrayed as a feline, which in turn holds a smaller human trophy head upside down with its hair flowing down, rather than the blood streams as in Sechin.

The site of Moxeke shares elements of the end Chavin sequence (EF), such as the pleated kilt. Here we find other correspondences with the figures of Cerro Sechin, such as the eyes in form of half-moon with a band descending from the eye down the cheek (called lagrimon or big tear). The eye-line appears only on the warriors. It seems that this represents a body painting, a custom carried further by the Moche after the beginning of our era. They have been called by some "hawk markings."

Two art pieces from Huaylas town display stylistic closeness to Sechin's art style. However, the Huaylas pieces have been taken out of context. They resemble Sechin style much more than Chavin. In them we can recognize the scalloped line indicating decapitation. Ear and mouth treatment are very similar to Sechin motifs, and so are the eye and looped hair.

In the site of Punkurí (Nepeña Valley) there is a painted bas-relief displaying a feline that links the gap in the traditions going from late Chavin to Moche. Punkurí presents stylistic closeness with Cerro Sechin. There are similarities between the warriors attire (e.g., girdles with extension of plumes falling down and clubs) depicted in Sechin. From Roe, *A Further Exploration of the Rowe Chavin Seriation,* pp. 29–37.

17) Carlos G. Elera, "El complejo cultural Cupisnique: antecedents y desarrollo de su ideologia religiosa," in Luis Millones and Yoshio Onuki, eds., *El Mundo Ceremonial Andino,* (Lima, Peru: Editorial Horizonte, 1994), pp. 225–49.

18) Federico Kauffman Doig, *Historia y Arte del Perú Antiguo,* vol. 2, (Lima, Peru: Peisa, 2002), p. 242.

19) *Paracas, Art and Architecture: Object and context in South Coastal Peru,* edited by Anne Paul, (University of Iowa Press, 1991), p. 259.

20) Victor M. Paredes Ruiz, Sechin, *Possible centro de conocimientos anatómicos y de disección en el antiguo Perú,* (Cuzco, Peru: El Sol, 1975), p. 15.

21) C. C. Mann, "Mystery Towers in Peru are Ancient Solar Calendar," *Science* 315 (2007): 1206–7, and I. Ghezzi and C. Ruggers, "Chankillo: A 2300 Year-Old Observatory in Coastal Peru," *Science* 315 (2007): 1239–43.

22) Rudolf Steiner, The*Gospel of Saint John and Its Relation to the Other Gospels,* lecture of July 2, 1909, (Spring Valley, NY: Anthroposophic Press, 1982).

CHAPTER 4: THE MYTHS OF CREATION OF THE TITICACA: THE SECOND CREATION

1) Juan de Betanzos, *Narrative of the Incas,* (1551), translated and edited by Roland Hamilton and Dana Buchanan, (Austin: University of Texas Press, 1996 [1551]).

2) Veronica Salles-Reese, *From Viracocha to the Virgin of Copacabana: Representation of the Sacred at Lake Titicaca,* (Austin: University of Texas Press, 1997).
3) Among the myths are the following: Bartolome de las Casas (1550), Juan de Betanzos (1551), Pedro Cieza de Leon (1553), Pedro Sarmiento de Gamboa's two versions (1572), Cristobal de Molina (1575), Pedro Gutierrez de Santa Clara (end of the sixteenth century), Jose de Acosta's two versions (1590), Juan de Santa Cruz Pachacuti Yamqui (1613), Antonio de la Calancha (1637), and Bernabe Cobo's five versions (1653).
4) Such are the Catiquilla myth of the region of Hamachuco, close to the Callejon de Huaylas; Pariacaca's myth from the area between Jauja and the coast; and the myth of Coniraya that comes from the great mountain chain between Jauja and the coastal shrine of Pachacamac, in effect very close to the preceding one. In Burr Cartwright Brundage, *Empire of the Inca* (Norman: University of Oklahoma Press, 1963), pp. 63–67, 335.
5) See Salles-Reese, *From Viracocha to the Virgin of Copacabana,* p. 56.
6) F. E. Elorrieta Salazar and E. Elorrieta Salazar, *La gran piramide de Pacaritanpu: entes y campos de poder en los Andes,* (Cusco, Peru: Sociedad Pacaritanpu Hatha, 1992), p. 106.
7) Don Juan de Santa Cruz Pachacuti-Yamqui Salcamayhua, *Narratives of the Rites and Laws of the Incas,* translated by Clemens R. Markham, (New York: Burt Franklin Publisher, 1873 [1613]).
8) Carlos Ponce Sangines, *Tunupa y Ekako: estudio arqueologici acerca de las efigies precolombinas de dorso aduncо,* 1969, Academia Nacional de las Ciencias de Bolivia, publicacion No 19.
9) Santacruz Pachacuti, "An Account of the Fables and Rites of the Incas by Cristobal de Molina," *Narratives of the Rites and Laws of the Incas,* p. 5.

CHAPTER 5: THE FOURTH AGE: THE AGE OF THUNUPA

1) Edward P. Lanning, *Peru Before the Incas,* (Englewood Cliffs, NJ: Prentice-Hall, 1967), p. 121.
2) Alfonso Klauer, *El mundo pre-Inka: los abismos del condor,* volume II, 2000, pp. 192–93. <www.nuevahistoria.org>.
3) William Sullivan, *The Secret of the Incas: Myth, Astronomy and the War Against Time,* (New York: Three Rivers Press, 1996), see chapters 2, 6, and 7.
4) Gordon R. Willey, *An Introduction to American Archaeology,* volume 2: *South America,* (Englewood Cliffs, NJ: Prentice Hall, 1971), p. 156.
5) Quoted in Garth Bawden, *The Moche,* (Cambridge, MA: Blackwell Publishers, 1996), p. 179.
6) Carlos G. Elera, "El complejo cultural Cupisnique: antecedents y desarrollo de su ideologia religiosa," in *El Mundo Ceremonial Andino,* ed. Luis Millones and Yoshio Onuki, (Lima, Peru: Editorial Horizonte, 1994), p. 237.
7) Elorrieta Salazar and Elorrieta Salazar, *La gran piramide de Pacaritanpu: entes y campos de poder en los Andes,* pp. 38–39.

8) Ibid, pp. 37–39.
9) Ibid., p. 44.
10) Michael E. Moseley, *The Incas and Their Ancestors: The Archaeology of Peru*, (London: Thames & Hudson, 2001), p. 229.
11) Alan Kolata, *The Tiwanaku: Portrait of an Andean Civilization*, (Cambridge, MA: Blackwell Publishers, 1993), p. 86.
12) William H. Isbell, "City and State in Middle Horizon Wari," in *Peruvian Prehistory: An Overview of Pre-Inca and Inca Society*, ed. Richard W. Keatinge, (Cambridge: Cambridge University Press, 1988), p. 174.
13) Ibid, pp. 174–75.
14) Alan Kolata and Carlos Ponce Sangines, "Tiwanaku: The City at the Center," in Townsend, ed., *Ancient Americas: Art from Sacred Landscapes*, p. 329.
15) Jorge Miranda-Luizaga, *La Puerta del Sol: Cosmologia y Simbolismo Andino*, (La Paz, Bolivia: Artes Graficas Editorial Garza Azul, 1991), p. 330.
16) Ibid, pp. 156–57.
17) Kolata and Sagines, "Tiwanaku: The City at the Center," p. 327.
18) Krzysztof Makowski Hanula, "El panteon Tiahuanaco y las deidades con baculos," *Los dioses del antiguo Peru*, volume 2, (Lima, Peru: Banco de Credito de Peru, 2002).
19) Ibid, p. 88.
20) Miranda-Luizaga, *La Puerta del Sol*, chapter 5: Gateway of the Sun, and chapter 6: Andean Calendar.
21) Katharina Schreiber and Josué Lancho Rojas, *Irrigation and Society in the Peruvian Desert: The Puquios of Nazca*, (Lanham, MD: Lexington Books, 2003), p. 55.
22) Anthony F. Aveni, *Between the Lines: the Mystery of the Giant Ground Drawings of Ancient Nazca, Peru*, (Austin: University of Texas Press, 2000), p. 50.
23) Krzysztof Makowski, "Los seres sobrenaturales en la iconografia Paracas y Nasca," *Los dioses del antiguo Peru*, volume 1, (Lima, Peru: Banco de Credito de Peru, 2002), p. 278.
24) Helaine Silverman, "Nazca: geografia sagrada, ancestors y agua," *Los dioses del antiguo Peru*, volume 1, (Lima, Peru: Banco de Credito de Peru, 2002), p. 242.
25) Helaine Silverman, "The Identification of Cahuachi as a Ceremonial Center," in *Cahuachi in the Ancient Nasca World*, (Iowa City: University of Iowa Press, 1993), chapter 22.
26) Ibid.
27) Makowski, "Los seres sobrenaturales," p. 245.
28) Schreiber and Lancho Rojas, *Irrigation and Society in the Peruvian Desert*, pp. 155–58.
29) M. Scholten d'Ebneth indicates dates of 100 BC to 100 AD, corresponding to Nazca 3 and 4 of the Nazca series of Menzel and Rowe. *Nazca, testimonio de una alta cultura : descubrimiento del más grande libro de geometría del mundo*, (Lima, Peru: Editorial J. Mejia Baca, 1984), p. 7.
30) Aveni, *Between the Lines*, p. 6.

31) Rafael Girard, *Historia de las civilizaciones antiguas de America,* (Madrid: Ediciones Istmo, 1976), pp. 1898–99.
32) Scholten d'Ebneth, *Nazca, testimonio de una alta cultura,* p. 62.
33) Ibid., p.6.
34) Girard, *Historia,* pp. 1903–4.
35) Johan Reinhard, *The Nazca Lines: A New Perspective on their Origin and Meaning,* (Lima, Peru: Editorial Los Pinos, 1988), pp. 25–28.
36) Aveni, *Between the Lines,* p. 203.
37) Johan Reinhard, "Interpreting the Nazca Lines," in Townsend, ed., *Ancient Americas: Art from Sacred Landscapes,* p. 292.
38) Helaine Silverman, *Cahuachi in the Ancient Nasca World,* opus quoted, chapter 22.
39) Silverman, "The Identification of Cahuachi as a Ceremonial Center."
40) Aveni, *Between the Lines,* p. 170, 173.
41) Quoted in Carlos Ponce Sangines, *Tunupa y Ekako: estudio arqueologico acerca de las efigies precolombinas de dorso adunco,* Publicacion N° 19, (La Paz: Academia Nacional de las Ciencias de Bolivia, 1969), p. 181.
42) *Relation of Juan de Santa Cruz Pachacuti-Yamqui Salcamayhua: An Account of the Antiquities of Peru,* quoted in C. Burland, I. Nicholson, H. Osborne, *Mythology of the Americas,* (London: Hamlyn Publishing Group, 1970), p. 338.
43) See chapter 2 of the creation myth's version of Betanzos in chapter 4 of this book.
44) Anita G. Cook, *Wari y Tiwanaku: entre el estilo y la imagen,* (Lima: Pontificia Universidad Catolica del Peru, Fondo Editorial, 1994).
45) Rudolf Steiner, *Supersensible Influences in the History of Mankind, with Special Reference to Cult in Ancient Egypt and in Later Times,* (London: Rudolf Steiner Publishing Co., 1956), lecture of September 22, 1922.
46) Ibid., lecture of September 24, 1922.
47) Ibid., lecture of September 29, 1922.
48) Cristobal de Molina, *Narratives of the Rites and Laws of the Incas,* trans. Clemens R. Markham, (New York: Burt Franklin Publisher, 1873 [1575]).
49) Pedro Sarmiento Gamboa, *History of the Incas,* trans. and ed. Clemens Markham, (Nendeln, Liechtenstein: Hakluyt Society, Klaus Reprint Limited, 1967 [1752]).
50) Scholten d'Ebneth, *Nazca, testimonio de una alta cultura,* pp. 14–15.
51) Ibid, p. 14.
52) Maria Scholten d'Ebneth, *La Vara Magica,* (Lima, Peru: Grafica Morsom, 1985), p. 7.
53) Pukara is exactly midway between Tiwanaku and Cuzco. This is true of the old Pukara, not the new one. The same is true for Cuzco. It is the Huanacaure hill (sacred to the Incas) that is situated exactly on the line, not the city itself. This is why Cuzco was in reality founded on Huanacaure. Maria Scholten d'Ebneth, *La Ruta de Wirakocha,* (conferencia dictada en la ANEA con occasion del

homenaje al Dr. Luis E. Valcarcel al serle concedido el premio de la cultura), (Lima, Peru: Editorial J. Mejia Baca, 1977) p. 11.
54) See Luigi Morelli, *Spiritual Turning Points of North American History*, 1: "Prophet Legends Across the Americas," (Great Barrington, MA: SteinerBooks 2010).
55) See ibid., chapter 7: "Ixbalamqué, the Initiate of the Americas."
56) Rudolf Steiner, *Inner Impulses of Evolution: the Mexican Mysteries and the Knights Templar*, (Spring Valley, NY: Anthroposophic Press, 1984). See particularly lecture 3 of September 18, 1916.
57) *Popol Vuh*, Part II, Chapter 1, English version by Goetz, Delia and Morley, Sylvanus G., translation of the Spanish version by Adrian Recinos, (Norman, OK: University of Oklahoma Press, 1950).
58) Rudolf Steiner, *Inner Impulses of Evolution*, lecture 5 of September 24, 1916.
59) Ibid.
60) Rudolf Steiner, *Karmic Relationships*, vol. 5, (London: Rudolf Steiner Press, 1977), lecture 7 of May 25, 1924.
61) Rudolf Steiner, *Inner Impulses of Evolution*, lecture 3.
62) Marko Pogacnik, *Turned Upside Down: A Workbook on Earth Changes and Personal Transformation*, (Great Barrington, MA: Lindisfarne Books, 2004), p. 207.
63) Rudolf Steiner, *Inner Impulses of Evolution*, lecture 5.
64) Ibid.

PART II: CULTURAL DECLINE AND THE INCA SPIRITUAL REVOLUTION

CHAPTER 1: AGE OF THE WARRIORS AND CULTURAL DECLINE

1) Quoted in Garth Bawden, *The Moche*, (Malden, MA: Blackwell Publishers, 1996), pp. 193–94.
2) Ibid., p. 196.
3) Ibid., p. 203.
4) Ibid., p. 207.
5) Ibid., p. 242.
6) Ibid., p. 245.
7) Walter Alva and Christopher B. Donnan, *Royal Tombs of Sipan*, (Los Angeles: Fowler Museum of Cultural History, University of California, 1993) p. 298.
8) Quoted in *The Moche*, p. 158.
9) Ibid., p. 162.
10) Ibid., p. 285.
11) Ibid., p. 301.
12) Sullivan, *The Secret of the Incas: Myth, Astronomy and the War Against Time*, p. 207.
13) Michael E. Moseley, *The Incas and Their Ancestors: The Archaeology of Peru*, (London: Thames and Hudson, 2001), p. 221.

14) Jonathan Haas, Sheila Pozorski, and Thomas Pozorski, eds., *The Origins and Development of the Andean State*, chapter 8: "State Origins in the Ayacucho Valley, Central Highlands of Peru," (Cambridge: Cambridge University Press, 1987), p. 85.
15) Richard W. Keatinge, ed., *Peruvian Prehistory, an Overview of Pre-Inca and Inca Society*, (Cambridge: Cambridge University Press, 1988), pp. 177, 187–88.
16) Klauer, *El mundo pre-Inka: los abismos del condor*, vol. 2, p. 204.
17) Ibid., pp. 167, 172–73.
18) Moseley, *The Incas*, p. 223.
19) William H. Isbell, "Conclusions: Huari Administration and the Orthogonal Cellular Architecture Horizon," in William H. Isbell and Gordon F. Mc Ewan, eds., *Huari Administrative Structure: Prehistoric Monumental Architecture and State Government*, (Washington DC: Dumbarton Oaks Research Library and Collection, 1991).
20) William H. Isbell, "City and State in Middle Horizon Huari," in Keatinge, ed., *Peruvian Prehistory*, p. 169.
21) Ibid., p. 182.
22) Moseley, *The Incas*, pp. 219–20.
23) Katharina J. Schreiber, *Wari Imperialism in Middle Horizon Peru*, Anthropological Papers Museum of Anthropology, no. 87, (Ann Arbor: University of Michigan, 1992), pp. 78–79.
24) William H. Isbell, "City and State in Middle Horizon Huari," in Keatinge, ed., *Peruvian Prehistory*, p. 180.
25) Isbell and Mc Ewan, eds., *Huari Administrative Structure*, p. 88.
26) Cook, *Wari y Tiwanaku: entre el estilo y la imagen*, pp. 193–97.
27) Sullivan, *The Secret of the Incas*, pp. 158, 252–53.
28) Maria Rostworowski, "La Religiosidad Andina," in *Los dioses del antiguo Peru*, vol. 1, (Lima, Peru: Banco de Credito de Peru, 2002), p. 199.
29) Ibid., p. 194.
30) Ibid., p. 197.
31) Ibid.
32) Moseley, *The Incas*, p. 244.
33) Roger Ravines, *Chan Chan, Metropoli Chimú*, (Lima, Peru: Instituto de Estudios Peruanos, Instituto de Investigacion Tecnologica Industrial y de Normas Tecnicas, 1980), pp. 65–81.
34) R. M., Czwarno, F. M. Meddens, and A. Morgan have inquired on the extent of Wari influence on Chimú civilization. From *The Nature of Wari: A Reappraisal of the Middle Horizon Period in Peru*, (Oxford: B.A.R., 19890). See the article "Spatial Patterning and the Investigation of Political Control: The Case from the Moche/Chimú area," pp. 115–42. This is a study of the spatial relations between boundary walls and the spaces they enclose to discover whether there is a cultural continuity between Chimú and Wari, or whether the latter borrowed from the previous culture. The studies are based on the following assumptions:

- spatial patterning in the elite places reflected the society's cosmography
- variations in spatial patterning are still consistent with an overall cosmographic theme, particular to a given society
- change of patterning in elite places of cult would have been gradual, unless there was submission to a new external authority
- a new pattern may emerge from societies creating a new common structure

In short, through an analysis of spatial patterns in sacred architecture we can follow where new cultural developments arise.

In this study the authors look at the *ciudadelas* of Chan Chan and compare them to the patterns of Wari on the north coast during the Middle Horizon. They use as a reference point the spatial patterning of Moraduchayoq (in Chimor), which are similar to the patterns occurring in places of the Ayacucho Basin that best represent the Wari spatial pattern.

The authors conclude, "The Chan Chan patterns, as those from Cajamarquilla, demonstrate a complete absence of the Wari pattern, and a high degree of internal homogeneity." The analysis of spatial patterning shows internal homogeneity between 900 and 1470. In any case the author rules out any significant influence from Wari. This seems to suggest that the area was not conquered by Wari in the Middle Horizon and that the area continued to develop its local patterns. This is also suggested in the apparent developmental sequence between Pampa Grande and Chan Chan.

35) Moseley, *The Incas*, p. 248.
36) Moseley Michael E. and Cordy-Collins Alana, *The Northern Dynasties: Kingship and Statecraft in Chimor*, a Symposium at Dumbarton Oaks, article "The Urban Concept of Chan Chan" Alan Kolata, (Dumbarton Oaks Research Library and Collection, Washington D.C., October 12 and 13, 1985), p. 138.
37) Federico Kauffman Doig, *Historia y Arte del Perú Antiguo*, vol. 2, (Lima, Peru: Peisa, 2002), p. 432.
38) Ravines, *Chan Chan*, p. 229.
39) Moseley, *The Incas*, p. 256.
40) Ibid., p. 226.
41) Alan Kolata, "The Urban Concept of Chan Chan," in Moseley and Cordy-Collins, eds., *The Northern Dynasties: Kingship and Statecraft in Chimor*, p. 141.
42) Christopher Donnan, "The Huaca 1 Complex," in Donnan and Cock, eds., *The Pacatnamu Papers*, vol. 1, p. 78.
43) Kauffman Doig, *Historia y Arte del Perú Antiguo*, p. 434.
44) Ravines, *Chan Chan*, pp. 77–78.
45) John W. Verano, "A Mass Burial of Mutilated Individuals at Pacatnamu," in Donnan and Cock, eds., *The Pacatnamu Papers*, p. 117.
46) Ibid., p. 135.
47) M. Rea, "Black Vultures and Human Victims: Archaeological Evidence from Pacatnamu," in Donnan and Cock, eds., *The Pacatnamu Papers*, p. 143.
48) Maria Rostworowski, *Pachacutec y la leyenda de los Chancas*, (Lima, Peru: Instituto de Estudios Peruanos Ediciones, 1997), p. 17.

49) Klauer, *El mundo pre-Inka*, see chapter on Wari, pp. 189–210.
50) Ibid., p. 39.
51) Ibid., pp. 47, 49.
52) Enrique Gonzalez Carré, *Los Señorios Chancas*, (Lima, Peru: Universidad Nacional de San Cristobal de Huamanga, Instituto Andino de Estudios Arqueologicos, 1992), p. 81.

CHAPTER 2: Inca Foundation Myths

1) Pedro Sarmiento Gamboa, *History of the Incas*, translated and edited by Clemens Markham, (Nendeln, Liechtenstein: Hakluyt Society, Klaus Reprint Limited, 1967).
2) Ibid, 44.
3) F. E. Elorrieta Salazar and E. Elorrieta Salazar, *El Valle Sagrado de los Incas: mitos y simbolos*, (Cusco, Peru: Sociedad Pacaritanpu Hatha, 1996) 169, 189-190.
4) Ibid, 136-139.
5) Ibid, 178.
6) Ibid, 191-3, 216 -218.
7) Ibid, 27, 156.
8) Ibid, 60-62, 153-156
9) Ibid, 20-28.
10) Maria Rostworowski, *Pachacutec Inca Yupanqui*, (Lima, Peru: Instituto de Estudios Peruanos, 1953) 9.
11) F. E. Elorrieta Salazar and E. Elorrieta Salazar, *El Valle Sagrado de los Incas*, 198-9.
12) Joan de Santa Cruz Pachacuti Yamqui Salamanca, *Narrative of the Rites and Laws of the Incas*, Clemens R. Markham translator and editor, (New York: Burt Franklin Publisher, 1873 [1613]) 75.
13) Quoted in *La Vara Magica....*, Maria Scholten d'Ebneth, (Lima, Peru: Grafica Morsom, 1985) 16.
14) Ibid.
15) Ibid, 18.
16) Elizabeth della Santa, *La celebre Huaca del Ticci Viracocha en Urcos (Calca) y su flavo gigante*, (1969; edition of the author, Arequipa, 1968).
17) Ibid, 3. See also Walid Barham Ode, *El retorno del Inka: descubrimiento del origen del mito Unu-Urco*, (Peru: Editorial Colmillo Blanco, 1998).
18) Barham Ode, *El retorno del Inka*, 72.
19) Quoted in E della Santa, *La Celebre Huaca del Ticci Viracocha en Urcos*, 7
20) Ibid, 9.
21) F. E. Elorrieta Salazar and E. Elorrieta Salazar, *La gran piramide de Pacaritanpu: entes y campos de poder en los Andes*, (Cusco, Peru: Sociedad Pacaritanpu Hatha, 1992).
22) Ibid, 183.
23) Fernando Montesinos, *Memorias Antiguas Historiales del Peru (1591)*, translated and edited by Philip Ainsworth Means, introduction by Sir Clemens Markham,

(Nendeln/Liechstenstein: Hakluyt Society 1920, reprinted Klaus Reprint Limited, 1967) 7.

CHAPTER 3: INCA EMPIRE AND THE FIFTH AGE

1) Elizabeth della Santa, *Wiracocha, l' empereur–dieu des Incas, d'apres les principales chroniques du temps,* (Brussels: self-published, 1963), p. 161.
2) Alain Gheerbrant, ed., *The Incas: The Royal Commentaries of the Inca,* Garcilaso de la Vega, (1539–1616), (New York: Discus Books, 1961), Book 4, p. 147.
3) Della Santa, *Wiracocha,* p. 163.
4) Ibid., pp, 68–69 and 81.
5) Betanzos, *Narrative of the Incas,* chapter 8.
6) Rostworowski, *Pachacutec y la leyenda de los chancas,* pp. 25–26.
7) De Molina, *Narratives of the Rites and Laws of the Incas,* trans. and ed. Markham. The original text reads: "Veni aca hijo, no tengas temor, que yo soy el Sol, vuestro padre, y se que habeis de sujetar muchas naciones."
8) Quoted in Sullivan, *The Secret of the Incas: Myth, Astronomy and the War Against Time,* p. 27, p. 293. Both Martin de Murua and Guaman Poma speak of the Ages of Andean civilization and refer to the time of the Incas as the Fifth Sun.
9) Arthur A. Demarest, *Wiracocha: The Nature and Antiquity of the Andean High God,* (Cambridge, MA: Harvard University Press, Peabody Museum Monographs, number 6, 1981) pp. 13–14.
10) Krzysztof Makowski Hanula, "El panteon Tiahuanaco y las deidades con baculos," in Kauffman Doig, *Los dioses del antiguo Peru,* volume 2, pp. 92–93.
11) Betanzos, chapter 14, quoted in Della Santa, *Wiracocha,* p. 126, p. 172.
12) Cartwright Brundage, *Empire of the Inca,* p. 131.
13) Makowski Hanula, "El panteon Tiahuanaco…" in Kauffman Doig, *Los dioses del antiguo Peru,* volume 2, p. 103.
14) Ibid, p. 100.
15) Brian S. Bauer and Charles Standish, *Ritual and Pilgrimage in the Ancient Andes: The Islands of the Sun and the Moon,* (Austin: Univeristy of Texas, 2001), pp. 224–30.
16) Susan A. Niles, "Inca Architecture and the Sacred Landscape," in Townsend, ed., *Ancient Americas: Art from Sacred Landscapes,* p. 352.
17) Ibid., p. 350.
18) Julio Palomino Diaz, *Intiwatanas y numeros: ciencia del pasado Andino,* (Cuzco: Municipalidad del Qosqo, 1994), p. 41.
19) A central festival celebrating the whole empire was the Capac Hucha. The ritual, according to Cristobal de Molina, was devised by Pachacuti. (Brian S. Bauer, *The Sacred Landscape of the Inca: The Cusco Ceque System,* [Austin: The University of Texas Press, 1998], p. 360.) Its most likely etymological origin is Capac Hucha, meaning the "plea of the Inca" or "royal obligation." Murua reveals one such plea addressed during the festival: "May the Sun remain a young man and the Moon a young maiden; may the world not be turned over;

let there be peace." This celebration occurred during the summer solstice. On the basis of its nature and due to the fact that this was the time of the Capac Raymi, some believe that it was only held on very special occasions, as in the rise to power of a new Inca. It was a ritual of inclusiveness of all the parts of the empire. The Capac Hucha began with the caravans that brought tribute from the many parts of the empire. In the Aucaypata, the main square of Cuzco, the priests surrounded the assembled crowd with an enormous chain of gold set to rest over pillars of silver the size of a man. The procession circled slowly around the statues of Wirakocha, Sun, Moon, and Illapa. Later, the priests redistributed the tribute in four portions for the four *suyus* of the empire. Some young children, coming from all parts of the empire, were then sacrificed and their remains buried on the Chuquicancha hill, which was used in the observations of the December and June solstice suns. More children were sacrificed at the Huanacauri hill, one of the major *wakas* of Cuzco. Legations were sent back in all the directions of the empire. They did this by following a *ceque* and giving offerings at *wakas* placed along the way. The priests went on the system of *ceques*, lines that radiated from the center of Cuzco. (according to Molina in Bauer, *The Sacred Landscape of the Inca*, p. 10.) Along the way the priest would give offerings to the *wakas*. Once past the boundaries of Cuzco, they would proceed to the farthest boundaries of the empire, where the Incas had placed boundary markers.

During this sacred and exceptional ceremony, young children would be sacrificed to their lineage *wakas* by the priests of the respective nations. The children to be sacrificed had to be age six to ten and be of unblemished beauty. Boy and girl were symbolically married before being sacrificed. The children were sons and daughters of lords (*caciques*). The Inca emperor played the role of matchmaker, marrying the daughter of one chief with the son of another. Thus it was a strengthening of kinship. A name for the sacrifice was *cachawakas*, which meant "messenger to the *wakas*," according to Molina.

In the Capac Hucha the children traveled to the farthest confines of the empire—there to be sacrificed—replicating the path taken by the emperor in his travels and conquests and sanctifying his earthly journey. It was as if the circle of the ecliptic that was held within the expanse of the Aucaypata in Cuzco—during the initial ceremonies—was to extend to the edges of the empire of which Cuzco was the Sun, radiating out through the *ceques*.

In essence, the Capac Hucha had a rhythm of contraction from the periphery of the empire toward Cuzco, and from the center to the boundaries of the empire. Central to the unfolding of the festival was the radial organization of space in the system of straight lines called *ceques*. The Incas were mainly reintroducing and further elaborating the system whose evidence survives in the desert pampas around Nazca.

20) Marti Pärssinen, *Tawantinsuyu: el estado inca y su organizacion politica*, (Helsinki: Finnish Historical Society, 1992), chapter 5, p. 161.

21) Mariusz S. Ziolokowski, "Los wakakuna de los cuzqueños," in Kauffman Doig, *Los dioses del antiguo Peru*, volume 2, (Lima: Banco de Credito de Peru, 2002), pp. 299–300.
22) Maria Scholten d'Ebneth, *La Ruta de Wirakocha*, conferencia dictada en la ANEA con occasion del homenaje al Dr. Luis E. Valcarcel al serle concedido el premio de la cultura, (Lima, Peru: Editorial J. Mejia Baca, 1977).
23) Below is the placement of the most important *wakas* of Cuzco.

   Sun
   The Sun was venerated in the Qoricancha and in two temples in the Antisuyu and one in Cuntisuyu:
   Chuquimarca (An-3: fourth *waka*) and Chuquicancha (An 6: third *waka*)
   Puquicancha at the foot of the hill Viracchaurco (Cun 10: second *waka*). Zuidema thinks that here was celebrated the solstice day at Inti Raymi.

   Wirakocha
   A symbol of the oval (same form in which it supposedly was displayed in the Qoricancha) appears in the Antisuyu (An 1: second *waka*); it was called Turuca, and was "an almost round stone."

   Illapa
   The most important aspect, Inti-Illapa had a *waka* in the second *ceque* of the Cuntisuyu.
   An exception to the above is Chuqui Illa (*"huaoqui"* that Pachacuti and following emperors carried with them in battle) had its temple in Pucamarca in Chinchaysuyu (Chin 5, second *waka*)

   Huanacauri
   Huanacauri was a *waka* of the Cuntisuyu (Cun 6:7) (From Ziolokowski, "Los wakakuna").

   Additionally the Cuntisuyu is the *suyu* that has the largest number of *pururaucas*—the *wakas* of the lineage spirits that had assisted Pachacuti in his struggle against the Chancas. Seven were found in the north quarter (Chinchasuyu), four in the south quarter (Collasuyu), and fifteen to the west (Cuntisuyu), as mentioned earlier in the chapter.
24) Terence N. D'Altroy, *The Incas*, (Oxford: Blackwell Publishers, 2002), p. 95.
25) Maria Rostworoswski, *Estructuras Andinas del poder : ideologia religiosa y politica*, (Lima, Perú: Instituto de Estudios Peruanos, 1983) pp. 156–59.
26) D'Altroy, *The Incas*, 100.
27) Pärssinen, *Tawantinsuyu*, p. 231.
28) Ibid., chapter 5, heading 4.1, pp. 181–87.
29) Ibid., p. 198.
30) Santa Cruz Pachacuti Yamqui, quoted in Pärssinen, *Tawantinsuyu*, p. 191.
31) Ibid., p. 192.
32) There are no *khipu* records referring to the political situation during the reign of Wayna Capac. However, it is possible to form an idea of who were the second and third persons. After the death of Wayna Capac, two candidates had claims

for the throne: Capac Guari and Tito Cusi Hualpa. Two other names given independently by Betanzos and Sarmiento were Apo Hilaquita and Auqui Topa Inca. Auqui Topa was a brother of Wayna Capac, whereas Apo Hilaquita was a son of Pachacuti, or uncle of Huayna Capac. That Auqui Topa Inca was the "second person" is confirmed by the texts of "Señores" and by Santillan. They say that important texts had to be seen by the secretary before being brought to the Inca's attention. Betanzos, Sarmiento, Cobo, and Murua call Auqui Topa Inca this secretary. Quoted in Pärssinen, *Tawantinsuyu*, p. 201.

33) Patricia J. Netherly, "Out of Many, One: The Organization of Rule in the North Coast Politics," in Moseley and Cordy-Collins, eds., *The Northern Dynasties: Kingship and Statecraft in Chimor*, pp. 461–84.

34) At a first level were the *hatun apogazcos*. These were political units larger than the provinces and smaller than the *suyus*. Collao (Bolivian altiplano) seems to have belonged to this category of political entity. The same seems to have been true of the Lupacas, Charcas, or the Pacasa in the same altiplano area. Guaman Poma calls these entities "muchos Cuzcos" (many Cuzcos) which gives an idea of their level of importance. Some of these were: Quito, Tomebamba, Huanuco, Hatuncolla, and Charcas, as confirmed by other sources.

Immediately under those that could have been called *hatun apogazcos* were the provinces. In many cases, the political division was based on quadripartition, through which the first halves are divided further into halves. In some other places the division followed other patterns. Cajamarca province was subdivided into seven *guarangas* (unities of 1000) and subsequent *pachacas* (unities of 100). The province of Lupaca was subdivided in seven districts in a way similar to Cajamarca; six of these were further subdivided in two according to ethnic lines (Aymaras and Urus). In Huayla four sectors were subdivided in three *guarangas* and these into various *pachacas*. The community had two supreme chiefs: one in Hanan Huayla, the other in Hurin Huayla. This was a rather exceptional situation, since the two lords had equal rights. Each chief had a second person who was present in cases of political relationships between the halves.

In some communities the ternary principle prevailed: it is the principle based upon "double opposition." One half of a pair is opposed to its complement and the two together oppose the third one. These oppositions could be organized along ethnic lines; the two first of one ethnicity, the third of a second ethnicity. An example of this was in the province of Collagua, where a majority of Aymara lived close to the Quechua (third group). Each of the subprovinces was organized according to the dual principle of halves and these were subdivided in three (*qollana, payan, kayaw*).

In fact, overall, the internal organization of the province was as often ternary as quaternary. It is interesting to note that the majority of provinces organized on ternary principles were situated close to Cuzco, and many of these were conquered by Pachacuti and his "brother" Capac Yupanqui. In conclusion, the organization of the provinces followed previous historic precedent rather than Inca political choices. The Inca left the local administration quite unchanged.

In summarizing, Inca political power was much more complex than has been surmised heretofore and has not been completely elucidated yet. That both tripartition and quadripartition played a role in the political administration is further made clear by the fact that in the provinces there were different political formats that reflected most of one or the other form of division. In addition, conciliar politics may have been based on a system granting power at the local level. History bears out that the Incas left intact local administrative forms to quite a degree. From Pärssinen, *Tawantinsuyu*, chapters 7 and 8.

35) Ibid., chapter 9. 1. "La teoria y sus problemas."
36) Ibid., see chapter 7, heading 3.1.1.

CHAPTER 4: INCA ESOTERIC KNOWLEDGE

1) Davide Domenici and Viviano Domenici, *I nodi segreti degli Inca: gli antichi manoscritti Miccinelli riscrivono la tragica storia della conquista del Perú*, (Milan: Sperling and Kupfer Editori, 2003).
2) Sabine Hyland, *The Jesuit and the Inca: The Extraordinary Life of Padre Blas Valera, S. J.*, (Ann Arbor: The University of Michigan Press, 2001), p. 225.
3) Ibid.
4) Hyland mentions the examples of some of Valera's contemporaries reprimanded for sexual transgressions. Father Miguel de Fuentes, who had seduced most of the younger nuns at the convent of La Concepcion in Lima, continued to serve as a priest but could not confess women for ten years. Father Luis Lopez, who had raped various young women, received two years of house arrest and was barred from ever giving confession to women. Both of them remained Jesuit members. *The Jesuit and the Inca*, pp. 187–88.
5) Ibid., p. 186.
6) See Domenici and Domenici, *I nodi segreti delgi Inca*, pp. 30–33.
7) Hyland, *The Jesuit and the Inca*, pp. 145–46.
8) Ibid, pp. 149–50.
9) Roger Atwood, "Mystery Circles of the Andes," in *Archaeology* (September–October 2007): 55–61.
10) Garcilaso de la Vega, Royal Commentaries of the Inca, Book 9, quoted in Domenici and Domenici, *I nodi segreti degli Inca*, p. 80.
11) William Burns Glynn, *Legado de los Amautas* (Lima, Peru: CONCYTEC, 1990), p. 33.
12) Domenici and Domenici, *I nodi segreti degli Inca*, p. 187.
13) Ibid., pp. 82, 88.
14) Hyland, *The Jesuit and the Inca*, pp. 137–39.
15) Domenici and Domenici, *I nodi segreti degli Inca*, p. 98.
16) Ibid., p. 52.
17) Quoted in Glynn, *Legado de los Amautas*, p. 32.

18) Domenici and Domenici, *I nodi segreti degli Inca*, pp. 90–92.
19) Glynn, *Legado de los Amautas*.
20) Domenici and Domenici, *I nodi segreti degli Inca*, note p. 192.
21) Glynn, *Legado de los Amautas*, p. 42.
22) Ibid., pp. 89–90.
23) Rafael Larco Hoyle, "La escritura peruana sobre pallares," in *De las relaciones de la sociedad argentina de antropologia IV*, (Lima, Peru: 1944): 57–77.
24) Marino Orlando Sanchez Macedo, *Enigmas, misterios y secretos de la sagrada astronomia Inca*, (Cuzco, Peru: MSM editor, 2000), p. 36.
25) Ibid., chapter "El observatorio astronomico de los ojos solares del sagrado Kon Titi Wiraqocha," pp. 100–104.
26) Ibid., chapter "El templo del sol, el culto a los intersolsticios y al choquechinchay," pp. 89–95.
27) R. T. Zuidema, "The Inca Calendar," in Anthony F. Aveni, ed., *Native American Astronomy*, (Austin: University of Texas Press, 1975), p. 229. See also Elorrieta Salazar and Elorrieta Salazar, *La gran piramide de Pacaritanpu: entes y campos de poder en los Andes*, pp. 219 and 223.
28) Domenici and Domenici, *I nodi segreti degli Inca*, pp. 91, 188–91.
29) Gary Urton, *At the Crossroads of the Earth and the Sky, an Andean Cosmology*, (Austin: University of Texas Press, 1981), pp. 131-145.
30) Elorrieta Salazar and Elorrieta Salazar, *La gran piramide de Pacaritanpu*, pp. 65–75.
31) Ibid., pp. 81–95.
32) Ibid., pp. 96–100.
33) F. E. Elorrieta Salazar and E. Elorrieta Salazar, *El Valle Sagrado de los Incas: mitos y simbolo*, p. 54.
34) Ibid., pp. 73–77.
35) Ibid., pp. 82–106.
36) Ibid., pp. 96–99.
37) Atwood, "Mystery Circles of the Andes," pp. 55–61, and John Earls, *Planificacion agricola andina: bases para un manejo cibernetico de sistema de andenes*, (Lima, Peru: Ediciones COFIDE, 1989).
38) Urton, *At the Crossroads*.
39) James Arevalo Merejildo Chaski, *El Despertar del Puma: camino iniciatico*, (Cuzco, Peru: self-published, 1997), pp. 82–86. See also Diaz, *Intiwatanas y numeros: ciencia del pasado Andino*.
40) In *Exsul Immeritus*, Blas de Valera shows the drawing of a *khipu* extended centrifugally like a *ceque*. He agrees between the similarity of the two. "Questi fasci di linee sono come le corde di una cetra che armonizzava quei pagani." (These sheaths of lines are like the strings of a lyre that harmonized these pagans) (*author's translation*) (Domenici and Domenici, *I nodi segreti degli Inca*, p. 44) After these words follows a drawing of the Qoricancha represented as a yellow square from whose center emanate strings with knots, each ending with an eye (representative of a *waka*). Below to the right is a *yupana*, where the first row of slots is surmounted by the letter chin (Chinchasuyu), the second by

Co (Collasuyu), the third by Ant (Antisuyu), the fourth by Cun (Cuntisuyu), and the last one by an eye. In every *suyu* the three strings of a different color could correspond to the so-called *kayaw, payan,* and *qollana ayllus* (of which more below), reflecting the threefold social division of the Inca empire. The Cuntisuyu shows a supplemental string, part green, part red (which seems to point to a mixed fourth group) and an extra green string for a fifth group. Adding the grains in the *yupana* and the knots on the strings we obtain 328, a number that corresponds to the number of *wakas* identified by Cobo in *Historia del Nuevo Mundo*. (Domenici and Domenici, *I nodi segreti degli Inca*, pp. 181–82).

41) Bauer, *The Sacred Landscape of the Inca: The Cusco Ceque System,* p. 23.
42) Zuidema "The Inca Calendar," p. 236.
43) R. Tom Zuidema, "The Pillars of Cuzco: Which Two Dates of Sunset Did They Define?" in Anthony F. Aveni, ed., *New Directions in American Archaeoastronomy, Proceedings of 46th International Congress of Americanists,* BAR International Series, 454, (Oxford: British Archaeological Reports, 1988), p. 145.
44) Urton, *At the Crossroads,* p. 29.
45) 45) This is why the last Qillawata Quipucamayoc of Cuzco, Juan Iñaca Sawaraura, calls the place "espejo de agua sagrada" (sacred water mirror), quoted in <http://qoyllur.blogspot.com/2008/04/muyuqmarka-un-enigma-resuelto.html>. See also Alfonso Klauer, "Sacsahuaman: el reloj mas costoso del planeta" in *Tahuantinsuyo: El condor herido de muerte,* p. 137, PDF found at <http://www.nuevahistoria.org>.
46) <http://qoyllur.blogspot.com/2008/04/muyuqmarka-un-enigma-resuelto.html>
47) Ibid. Erwin Salazar Garces does not have access to the original but to the one given by Luis Enrique Tord in his novel *Espejo de constelaciones.*
48) Zuidema, "The Inca Calendar," p. 242.
49) Ibid., p. 244.

CONCLUSIONS

1) *The Influence of Spiritual Beings upon Man,* Steiner, Lecture of February 15, 1908, (Spring Valley, NY: Anthroposophic Press, 1982).
2) *The Inca Empire: The Formation of a Pre-Capitalist State,* Thomas C. Patterson, (New York: Berg Publishers, 1991), p. 89.
3) Ibid., p. 90.
4) *Das Geheimnis des Todes: Wesen und Bedeutung Mitteleuropas und die Europaischen Volksgeister,* Rudolf Steiner, lecture of February 21, 1915, quoted in Richard Seddon, *Europa, a Spiritual Biography* (London: Temple Lodge, 1995), pp. 55–56.

BIBLIOGRAPHY

BOOKS AND JOURNALS

Alva, Walter and Donnan, Christopher B. – *Royal Tombs of Sipan* (Los Angeles: Fowler Museum of Cultural History, University of California, 1993).

Atwood, Roger – "Mystery Circles of the Andes," in *Archaeology* (September–October 2007).

Aveni, Anthony F., editor –
New Directions in American Archaeoastronomy, Proceedings of 46th International Congress of Americanists (Oxford: British Archaeological Reports International Series, 454, 1988).

—— *Native American Astronomy* (Austin: University of Texas Press, 1975).

Aveni, Anthony F. – *Between the Lines: the Mystery of the Giant Ground Drawings of Ancient Nazca, Peru* (Austin: University of Texas Press, 2000).

Barham Ode, Walid – *El Retorno del Inca: Descubrimiento del origen del mito Unu-Urco* (Lima, Peru: Editorial Colmillo Blanco, 1998).

Bauer, Brian S. – *The Sacred Landscape of the Inca: The Cusco Ceque System* (Austin: The University of Texas Press, 1998).

Bauer, Brian S. and Standish, Charles – *Ritual and Pilgrimage in the Ancient Andes: The Islands of the Sun and the Moon* (Austin: Univeristy of Texas, 2001).

Bawden, Garth – *The Moche* (Cambridge, MA: Blackwell Publishers, 1996).

Benson, Elizabeth P., editor – *Dumbarton Oaks Conference on Chavin*, October 26–27, (Washington DC: Dumbarton Oaks Research Library and Collection, 1968).

Betanzos, Juan de – *Narrative of the Incas*, trans. and ed. Roland Hamilton and Dana Buchanan from the Palma de Mallorca manuscript (Austin: University of Texas Press, 1996 [1576]).

Burger, Richard L. – *Chavin and the Origins of Andean Civilization* (London: Thames and Hudson, 1992).

Burland, Cottie; Nicholson, Irene and Osborne, Harold – *Mythology of the Americas* (London: Hamlyn Publishing Group, 1970).

Burns Glynn, William – *Legado de los Amautas* (Lima, Peru: CONCYTEC, 1990), p. 33.

Cartwright Brundage, Burr – *Empire of the Inca* (Norman: University of Oklahoma Press, 1963).

Cook, Anita G. – *Wari y Tiwanaku: entre el estilo y la imagen* (Lima: Pontificia Universidad Catolica del Peru, Fondo Editorial, 1994).

Cooke, Grace – *The Illumined Ones* (New Lands, U. K.: The White Eagle Publishing Trust, 1966).

Czwarno, R. M.; Meddens F. M. and A. Morgan, editors – *The Nature of Wari: A Reappraisal of the Middle Horizon Period in Peru* (Oxford: B.A.R., 1989).

Della Santa, Elizabeth – *La celebre huaca del Ticci Wiracocha en Urcos (Calca) y su flavo gigante* (Arequipa, Peru: self published, 1963).
Demarest, Arthur A. – *Wiracocha: The Nature and Antiquity of the Andean High God* (Cambridge, MA: Harvard University Press, Peabody Museum Monographs, number 6, 1981).
Domenici, Davide and Domenici, Viviano – *I nodi segreti degli Inca: gli antichi manoscritti Miccinelli riscrivono la tragica storia della conquista del Perú* (Milano: Sperling and Kupfer Editori, 2003).
Donnan, Christopher B. and Cock, Guillermo A. editors – *The Pacatnamu Papers*, vol. 1 (Los Angeles: Museum of Cultural History, University of California, 1986).
Earls, John – *Planificacion agricola andina: bases para un manejo cibernetico de sistema de andenes* (Lima, Peru: Ediciones COFIDE, 1989).
Elorrieta Salazar, F. E. and Elorrieta Salazar, E. –
  La gran piramide de Pacaritanpu: entes y campos de poder en los Andes, (Cusco, Peru: Sociedad Pacaritanpu Hatha, 1992).
—— *El Valle Sagrado de los Incas: mitos y simbolos* (Cusco, Peru: Sociedad Pacaritanpu Hatha, 1996).
Gheerbrant, Alain editor – *The Incas: The Royal Commentaries of the Inca*, Garcilaso de la Vega, (1539–1616) (New York: Discus Books, 1961).
Ghezzi, I. and Ruggers, C. – "Chankillo: A 2300 Year-Old Observatory in Coastal Peru," *Science* 315 (2007).
Girard, Rafael –
  Historia de las civilizaciones antiguas de America (Madrid: Ediciones Istmo, 1976).
—— *Los Chortis ante el problema Maya*, volume 3, (Mexico, D. F.: Antigua Libreria Robledo, 1949).
Goetz, Delia and Morley, Sylvanus G. translators – *Popol Vuh: The Sacred Book of the Ancient Quiché Maya* (Norman OK: University of Oklahoma Press, 1950)
Gonzalez Carré, Enrique – *Los Señorios Chancas* (Lima, Peru: Universidad Nacional de San Cristobal de Huamanga, Instituto Andino de Estudios Arqueologicos, 1992).
Haas, Jonathan; Pozorski, Sheila, and Thomas Pozorski, editors – *The Origins and Development of the Andean State* (Cambridge: Cambridge University Press, 1987).
Hyland, Sabine – *The Jesuit and the Inca: The Extraordinary Life of Padre Blas Valera, S. J.* (Ann Arbor: The University of Michigan Press, 2001).
Illescas Cook, Guillermo – *El candelabro de Paracas y la Cruz del Sur* (Lima, Perú, self-published, 1981).
Isbell, William H. and Mc Ewan, Gordon F. editors – *Huari Administrative Structure: Prehistoric Monumental Architecture and State Government* (Washington DC: Dumbarton Oaks Research Library and Collection, 1991).
Jenkins, John Major – *Maya Cosmogenesis 2012: The True Meaning of the Maya Calendar End-Date* (Santa Fe, NM: Bear & Co., 1998).

Kano, Chiaki – *The Origins of the Chavin Culture*, Studies in Pre-Columbian Art and Archaeology, #22 (Washington DC: Dumbarton Oaks, 1979).

Kauffman Doig, Federico – *Historia y Arte del Perú Antiguo* (Lima, Peru: Peisa, 2002).

Keatinge, Richard W., editor – *Peruvian Prehistory: An Overview of Pre-Inca and Inca Society* (Cambridge: Cambridge University Press, 1988).

Klauer, Alfonso –
 El Mundo Pre-Inka: Los Abismos del Condor, volumes 1 and 2, PDF found at <www.nuevahistoria.org>.
—— *Tahuantinsuyo: El condor herido de muerte*, PDF found at <http://www.nueva-historia.org>.

Kolata, Alan – *The Tiwanaku: Portrait of an Andean Civilization* (Cambridge, MA: Blackwell Publishers, 1993).

Lanning, Edward P. – *Peru Before the Incas* (Englewood Cliffs, NJ: Prentice-Hall, 1967).

Larco Hoyle, Rafael – "La escritura peruana sobre pallares," *De las relaciones de la sociedad argentina de antropologia IV*, (Buenos Aires, Argentina: Sociedad argentina de antropologia, 1944).

Lumbreras, Luis; Gonzalez, Chacho and Lietaer, Bernard – *Acerca de la función del sistema hidráulico de Chavín*, Publicaciones del Museo Nacional de Antropología y Arqueología, serie investigaciones de campo #2, Junio 1976 (Lima, Peru: Museo Nacional de Antropología y Arqueología, 1976).

Mann, C. C. – "Mystery Towers in Peru are Ancient Solar Calendar," *Science* 315 (2007): 1206–7,

Merejildo Chaski, James Arevalo – *El Despertar del Puma: camino iniciatico* (Cuzco, Peru: self-published, 1997)

Milla Villena, Carlos – *Genesis de la Cultura Andina*, 1983, (Lima, Peru: Colegio de Arquitectos del Peru, Fondo Editorial C. A. P. , Coleccion Bienal).

Miranda-Luizaga, Jorge – *La Puerta del Sol: Cosmologia y Simbolismo Andino* (La Paz, Bolivia: Artes Graficas Editorial "Garza Azul," 1991), p. 51.

Millones, Luis and Onuki, Yoshio editors – *El Mundo Ceremonial Andino* (Lima, Peru: Editorial Horizonte, 1994).

Molina, Cristobal de – *Narratives of the Rites and Laws of the Incas*, trans. Clemens R. Markham (New York: Burt Franklin Publisher, 1873 [1575]).

Morelli, Luigi – *Spiritual Turning Points of North American History* (Bloomington, IN: Trafford Publishing, 2008).

Moseley Michael E. and Cordy-Collins Alana – *The Northern Dynasties Kingship and Statecraft in Chimor*, a Symposium at Dumbarton Oaks, October 12 and 13, 1985, (Dumbarton Oaks Research Library and Collection, Washington D.C., 1985)

Moseley, Michael E. – *The Incas and Their Ancestors: The Archaeology of Peru* (London: Thames and Hudson, 2001).

Palomino Diaz, Julio – *Intiwatanas y numeros: ciencia del pasado Andino* (Cuzco: Municipalidad del Qosqo, 1994).

Paredes Ruiz, Victor M. – *Sechin, possible centro de conocimientos anatómicos y de disección en el antiguo Perú*, (Cuzco, Peru: El Sol, 1975).

Pärssinen, Marti – *Tawantinsuyu: el estado inca y su organizacion politica* (Helsinki: Finnish Historical Society, 1992).
Patterson, Thomas C. – *The Inca Empire: The Formation of a Pre-Capitalist State* (New York: Berg Publishing, 1991)
Pogacnik, Marko – *Turned Upside Down: A Workbook on Earth Changes and Personal Transformation* (Great Barrington, MA: Lindisfarne Books, 2004).
Ponce Sangines, Carlos – *Tunupa y Ekako: estudio arqueologico acerca de las efigies precolombinas de dorso adunco*, Publicacion N0 19 (La Paz: Academia Nacional de las Ciencias de Bolivia, 1969).
Popenoe Hatch, Marion – "An Hypothesis on Olmec Astronomy, with Special Reference to the La Venta Site," in *Contributions of the University of California Archaeological Research Facility: Papers on Olmec and Maya Archaeology* (Berkeley: University of California, June 1971).
Rangel Flores, Victor, editor – *Symposium: Arquitectura y arqueologia: pasado y futuro de la construccion en el Perú* (Chiclayo, Peru: Universidad de Chiclayo, 1988).
Ravines, Roger – *Chan Chan, Metropoli Chimú* (Lima: Instituto de Estudios Peruanos, Instituto de Investigacion Tecnologica Industrial y de Normas Tecnicas, 1980).
Reinhard, Johan – *The Nazca Lines: A New Perspective on their Origin and Meaning* (Lima, Peru: Editorial Los Pinos, 1988).
Roe, Peter G. – *A Further Exploration of the Rowe Chavin Seriation and Its Implications for North Central Coast Chronology* (Washington DC: Dumbarton Oaks, 1979).
Rostworowski, Maria –
—— *Pachacutec Inca Yupanqui* (Lima, Peru: Instituto de Estudios Peruanos, 1953).
—— *Estructuras Andinas del poder:ideologia religiosa y politica* (Lima, Perú: Instituto de Estudios Peruanos, 1983).
—— *Pachacutec y la leyenda de los Chancas* (Lima, Peru: Instituto de Estudios Peruanos Ediciones, 1997).
Salles-Reese, Veronica – *From Viracocha to the Virgin of Copacabana: Representation of the Sacred at Lake Titicaca* (Austin: University of Texas Press, 1997).
Samaniego, Lorenzo; Cardenas, Mercedes; Bischof, Henning; Kaulicke, Peter; Guzman, Erman and Wilder Leon, *Arqueología de Cerro Sechin; Tomo II: escultura* (Lima: Pontificia Universidad Catolica del Perú, 1995).
Sanchez Macedo, Marino, Orlando – *Enigmas, misterios y secretos de la sagrada astronomia Inca* (Cuzco, Peru: MSM editor, 2000).
Sarmiento Gamboa, Pedro – *History of the Incas*, trans. and ed. Clemens Markham (Nendeln, Liechtenstein: Hakluyt Society, Klaus Reprint Limited, 1967 [1752]).
Santa Cruz Pachacuti-Yamqui Salcamayhua, Don Juan de – *Narratives of the Rites and Laws of the Incas*, translated by Clemens R. Markham (New York: Burt Franklin Publisher, 1873 [1613]).
Sarmiento Gamboa, Pedro – *History of the Incas*, trans. and ed. Clemens Markham (Nendeln, Liechtenstein: Hakluyt Society, Klaus Reprint Limited, 1967).
Scholten d'Ebneth, Maria –
La Ruta de Wirakocha, (conferencia dictada en la ANEA con occasion del homenaje

al Dr. Luis E. Valcarcel al serle concedido el premio de la cultura), (Lima, Peru: Editorial J. Mejia Baca, 1977).
—— *Nazca, testimonio de una alta cultura : descubrimiento del más grande libro de geometría del mundo* (Lima, Peru: Editorial J. Mejia Baca, 1984).
—— *La Vara Magica* (Lima, Peru: Grafica Morsom, 1985).
Schreiber, Katharina – *Wari Imperialism in Middle Horizon Peru*, Anthropological Papers Museum of Anthropology, no. 87 (Ann Arbor: University of Michigan, 1992).
Schreiber Katharina, and Lancho Rojas, Josué – *Irrigation and Society in the Peruvian Desert: The Puquios of Nazca* (Lanham, MD: Lexington Books, 2003).
Seddon, Richard – *Europa, a Spiritual Biography* (London: Temple Lodge, 1995).
Shady, Ruth, and Leyva, Carlos editors – *La ciudad sagrada de Caral-Supe: las origenes de la civilizacion andina y la formacion del Estado pristino en el antiguo Perú* (Lima: Instituto Nacional de Cultura, Proyecto Especial Arqueologico Caral-Supe, 2003).
Silverman, Helaine, – *Cahuachi in the Ancient Nasca World* (Iowa City: University of Iowa Press, 1993).
Steiner, Rudolf –
—— *Supersensible Influences in the History of Mankind, with Special Reference to Cult in Ancient Egypt and in Later Times* (London: Rudolf Steiner Publishing Co., 1956).
—— *From the History and Content of the First Class of the Esoteric School, 1904-1914* (Great Barrington, MA: SteinerBooks, 2010).
—— *The Apocalypse of Saint John* (Great Barrington, MA: SteinerBooks/Anthroposophic Press, 1993).
—— *Egyptian Myths and Mysteries* (Hudson, NY: Anthroposophic Press, 1997).
—— *The Influence of Spiritual Beings upon Man*, (Spring Valley, NY: Anthroposophic Press, 1982).
—— *The Mission of Folk Souls in Relation to Teutonic Mythology* (Forest Row, UK: Rudolf Steiner Press, 2005).
—— *Wonders of the World, Ordeals of the Soul, Revelations of the Spirit* (London: Rudolf Steiner Press, 1983).
—— *Inner Impulses of Evolution: The Mexican Mysteries and the Knights Templar* (Spring Valley, NY: Anthroposophic Press, 1916).
—— *Karmic Relationships*, vol. 5 (London: Rudolf Steiner Press, 1924).
Sullivan, William – *The Secret of the Incas: Myth, Astronomy and the War Against Time* (New York: Three Rivers Press, 1996).
Townsend, Richard, editor – *Ancient Americas: Art from Sacred Landscapes* (Munich: Prestel Verlag, 1992).
Urton, Gary – *At the Crossroads of the Earth and the Sky, an Andean Cosmology* (Austin: University of Texas Press, 1981).
Wachsmuth, Guenther – *The Evolution of Mankind: Cosmic Evolution, Incarnations on the Earth, The Great Migrations, and Spiritual History* (Dornach, Switzerland: Philosophic-Anthroposophic Press, 1961).
Willey, Gordon R. – *An Introduction to American Archaeology*, volume 2: *South America* (Englewood Cliffs, NJ: Prentice Hall, 1971).

INTERNET AND NEWS SOURCES

Jacobs, James Q. – *Early Monumental Architecture on the Peruvian Coast: Evidence of Socio-Political Organization and the Variation in Its Interpretation*, 2000, – <http://www.jqjacobs.net/andes/coast.html>.

Josephs, Leslie – Ventarron temple on Peru's north coast: <http://dsc.discovery.com/news/2007/11/13/peru-temple-mural.html?dcitc=w19–502-ak-0000>).

Whalen, Andrew – "Ancient Ceremonial Plaza Found in Peru," February 26, 2008, <http://www.freerepublic.com/focus/f-news/1976727/posts>

About early khipus in the North Coast of Peru see:
<http://agutie.homestead.com/files/Quipu_B.htm>
<http://archaeology.about.com/od/ancientwriting/a/caralquipu.htm>
<http://terraeantiqvae.blogia.com/2005/071602-peru.-descubren-quipu-con-mas-de-4500-anos-de-antiguedad-en-caral.php>.

About Muyuqmarka towers in Sacsayhuaman see:
<http://qoyllur.blogspot.com/2008/04/muyuqmarka-un-enigma-resuelto.html>.

LIST OF ILLUSTRATIONS

PART I

CHAPTER 2

Figure 2.1   map by the author
Figure 2.2   Leon Williams, *Complejos pirámides con plaza en U*
Figure 2.3   Ruth Shady and Carlos Leyva, *La ciudad sagrada de Caral-Supe*
Figure 2.4   Gary Urton, *At the Crossroads of the Earth and the Sky*
Figure 2.5   Carlos Milla Villena, *Genesis de la Cultura Andina*
Figure 2.6   Guillermo Illescas Cook, *El candelabro de Paracas*
Figure 2.7   Carlos Milla Villena, *Genesis de la Cultura Andina*

CHAPTER 3

Figure 3.1   Federico Kauffman Doig, *Historia y Arte del Perú Antiguo*
Figure 3.2   Peter G. Roe, *A Further Exploration of the Rowe Chavin Seriation*
Figure 3.3   Peter G. Roe, *A Further Exploration of the Rowe Chavin Seriation*
Figure 3.4   Federico Kauffman Doig, *Historia y Arte del Perú Antiguo*
Figure 3.5   Lorenzo Samaniego et alia, *Arqueología de Cerro Sechin*
Figure 3.6   Peter G. Roe, *A Further Exploration of the Rowe Chavin Seriation*

CHAPTER 5

Figure 5.1   Juan V. Albarracin-Jordan, *The Archaeology of Tiwanaku*
Figure 5.2   Jorge Miranda-Luizaga, *La Puerta del Sol*
Figure 5.3   Jorge Miranda-Luizaga, *La Puerta del Sol*
Figure 5.4   Maria Scholten d'Ebneth, *Nazca, testimonio de una alta cultura*
Figure 5.5   Maria Scholten d'Ebneth, *La Ruta de Wirakocha*
Figure 5.5   Anthony F. Aveni, *Between the Lines*

PART 2

CHAPTER 1

Figure 1.1   Federico Kauffman Doig, *Historia y Arte del Perú Antiguo*
Figure 1.2   Roger Ravines, *Chan Chan, Metropoli Chimu*

CHAPTER 2

Figure 2.1   F. E. Elorrieta Salazar & E. Elorrieta Salazar, *La gran piramide de Pacaritanpu*

List of Illustrations   313

CHAPTER 3

Figure 3.1   Cartwright Brundage Burr, *Empire of the Inca*

CHAPTER 4

Figure 4.1   Gary Urton, *At the Crossroads of the Earth and the Sky*
Figure 4.2   Domenici Davide and Domenici Viviano, *I nodi segreti degli Inca*
Figure 4.3   Guaman Poma, *Nueva Coronica*
Figure 4.4   Larco Hoyle Rafael, *La escritura peruana sobre pallares*
Figure 4.5   Gary Urton, *At the Crossroads of the Earth and the Sky*
Figure 4.6   Sanchez Macedo, Marino, Orlando — *Enigmas, misterios y secretos de la sagrada astronomia*
Figure 4.7   Gary Urton, *At the Crossroads of the Earth and the Sky*
Figure 4.8   Gary Urton, *At the Crossroads of the Earth and the Sky*
Figure 4.9   Erwin Salazar Garces, http://qoyllur.blogspot.com/2008/04/muyuqmarka-un-enigma-resuelto.html

www.ingramcontent.com/pod-product-compliance
Lightning Source LLC
Chambersburg PA
CBHW022051160426
43198CB00008B/187